OLIVER

CLINICAL MICROSCOPY
AND CHEMISTRY

BY

F. A. McJUNKIN, M.A., M.D.

Professor of Pathology in the Marquette University School of
Medicine; formerly an Assistant in the Pathological Laboratory
of the Boston City Hospital

ILLUSTRATED

PHILADELPHIA AND LONDON

W. B. SAUNDERS COMPANY

1919

PRINTED IN AMERICA

PRESS OF
W. B. SAUNDERS COMPANY
PHILADELPHIA

PREFACE

In medical curricula there is little uniformity in regard to the place and scope of the subject comprising the common laboratory methods employed by the physician in the practice of medicine. That such a course of study is desirable in order to bring to the attention of the student the clinical application of chemical and biologic methods seems certain; and, since the question is largely one of selecting and applying methods from a clinical standpoint, the subject is usually placed under the direction of an instructor with training in clinical medicine. There appears to be a definite indication for the presentation of this subject from the laboratory point of view, for the instructor usually wishes to supply the clinical interpretations and discussions. This is attempted in this volume; and special emphasis is given the chemical, bacteriologic, serologic and pathologic methods, while lengthy clinical descriptions which are readily accessible in text-books on clinical medicine are omitted.

In the preparation of a course of study for students in Clinical Microscopy and Chemistry free use has been made of Emerson's "Clinical Diagnosis," Simon's "Clinical Diagnosis," Mallory and Wright's "Pathological Technique," Mallory's "Principles of Pathologic Histology," Wells' "Chemical Pathology," MacCallum's "Text-book of Pathology," Hiss and Zinsser's "Text-book of Bacteriology," Kendall's "Text-book of Bacteriology," and certain original publications. It is on this course of study that the present volume is based. In all cases in which the determination of the author of a method has been possible, credit has been given in the text. Minor variations in a few methods have been introduced when the tests have proved to be of greater value when so modified. Only those methods are included which have a definite and practical use, and no attempt has been made to offer an encyclopedic tabulation of a great number of technical procedures.

13

Throughout the book emphasis is placed on the relationship between the materials commonly examined by the clinician and the body tissues. Examples of this connection are seen in the relationship between the blood cells and the tissues from which they arise, viz.: the bone-marrow, lymphoid tissue and vascular endothelium; between the sputum and the pulmonary mucosa; between exudates and inflammatory processes; between urine sediment and the lesions of the kidney and lower genito-urinary tract, and so on. Aside from the close association of clinical medicine and postmortem examinations, the introduction of the chapter on histologic and autopsy technic seems advisable in order to correlate the normal and pathologic tissues with the materials commonly made the subject of clinical laboratory examination.

The writer is indebted to Prof. Chester J. Farmer for valuable suggestions in regard to the chemical methods applicable to the blood, to Prof. Henry C. Tracy for suggestions on nervous tissue stains, and to Mr. L. Massopust for most of the illustrations.

F. A. McJunkin.

MILWAUKEE, WISCONSIN,
January, 1919.

CONTENTS

16 CONTENTS

CLINICAL MICROSCOPY AND CHEMISTRY

BLOOD

INTRODUCTION

Although hematologists generally speak of the blood as a tissue, this conception has not been consistently followed; for the specificity of cells, which is the one factor characterizing a tissue, is often entirely lost sight of in the study and interpretation of blood cells. That differentiated cells of a tissue have a particular embryologic origin and that in the adult body they pass from the stage of mitosis to the stage of senile disintegration with constant uniform changes in morphology are facts that here possess a significance even greater than in the study ·of the cells of other tissues. While, too, most tissues are more or less stationary and have resistance, the blood is carried rapidly from one part of the body to another by the circulatory apparatus and is a fluid. Its characteristic feature is that the corpuscles and white cells, suspended in its liquid or unformed portion known as plasma, are swept away from those which undergo mitosis to form them. This makes it impossible to determine directly the origin of the cells by their position and relationship to one another.

In the early hematologic studies it was noted that in addition to the non-nucleated corpuscles the blood contained nucleated cells; and, since these formed elements do not normally arise by mitosis in the general blood stream, the question of their origin was not readily solved. With improved technical methods two varieties of white blood cells were recognized, and it was shown that the lymph ducts continuously discharge into the great veins a liquid that contains a moderate number of cells identical in morphology with one of these varieties and with the cells that make up the lymph nodules, and further that the same cells gain entrances to the lymph sinuses and flow away in the lymph stream and so finally reach the large lymphatic vessels. These cells (*lymphocytes*) are in the blood and, since their nuclei are round rather than broken masses of nuclear material, two varieties of cells (mononuclear and polymorphonuclear) may be distinguished microscopically in fresh unstained preparations.

Tracing the origin of the polymorphonuclear cells was attended by more difficulties than the establishment of a connection between the lymphocytes of the blood and of the lymphoid tissue. In certain conditions characterized by the appearance in the blood of greatly increased numbers of polymorphonuclear white cells, red bone-marrow was found where white marrow is normally present and microscopic examination of such red marrow revealed numerous islands of cells of the polymorphonuclear type. This suggested the bone-marrow origin of the polymorphonuclear leukocytes and this is now quite generally agreed upon. As the polymorphonuclear cells which arise in the bone-marrow become older they acquire, before gaining entrance to the blood stream, tinctorial granules that are so characteristic that there is no hesitancy in speaking of them as *neutrophiles*, *eosinophiles*, and *basophiles*.

The demonstration of these characteristic granules by the improved stains of comparatively recent date makes it easy to trace the connection between the myeloblastic bone-marrow islands and the three varieties of polymorphonuclear leukocytes of the blood. At present there is little question that the white cells are partly lymphoblastic and partly myeloblastic in origin. The latter, as they are found in the normal peripheral blood, have differentiated sufficiently to be called neutrophiles, eosinophiles and basophiles. Although the lymphoblastic cells differ from one another in size and shape, these differences are not marked enough to prevent all being grouped under the term "lymphocyte."

Besides these four cells (lymphocytes, neutrophiles, eosinophiles, and basophiles) there are definite indications that a cell of endothelial origin (*endothelial leukocyte*) is present in normal and pathologic conditions. This cell which is mononuclear is discussed later.

In addition to the five white blood cells there is present the red blood corpuscle or *erythrocyte*. The erythrocyte differentiates from the erythroblast of the bone-marrow, the cytoplasm of the latter acquiring hemoglobin and losing its nucleus.

The other formed element of the blood of importance is the *platelet* which takes its origin from the pseudopodia of the megakaryocyte of the bone-marrow. In this work the formed elements of the blood are considered first, and later the best known normal and pathologic constituents of the plasma are discussed.

The formed elements of the blood vary within limits normally and pathologically but the variations of substances in solution in the plasma or unformed portion are much greater. The *plasma* forms about 60 per cent. of the total weight of the blood, the remaining part being largely corpuscles since the weight of the other formed elements is insignificant. It carries food to the cells and receives waste products from them. The great variations of normal and abnormal constituents that may exist in the plasma depend on this passage of substances to and from the cells and since the pathologic changes are secondary to a deviation from normal in the activity of the tissue cells, they cannot be regarded as primary blood diseases. The true *blood diseases* have to do with the formed elements and especially with the tissues from which these elements arise. The plasma is not living protoplasm and is not the seat of a primary disease. Since pathologic conditions of organs and tissues are dependent on their cellular components, and since the metabolic products of an abnormal cell that pass into the plasma are different from those of a normal one, a study of the plasma is of great importance in the study of disease; and at present significant advances in clinical medicine are being made by thoses studying the substances in solution in the plasma.

HEMOGLOBIN AND RED BLOOD CORPUSCLES

Of the dry red blood corpuscles about 85 per cent. is *hemoglobin*, the remainder being nucleoproteins (so called), lecithin, and cholesterin. Its function is to transport oxygen from the lungs to the tissue cells. Its ability to do this rests on the adsorption of oxygen by hemoglobin to form *oxyhemoglobin*. A reduced oxygen tension, such as is found in the capillaries of the general circulation, leads to the separation of the oxygen from the oxyhemoglobin with the formation of *reduced hemoglobin*. Oxyhemoglobin gives the bright red color to arterial blood, while the color of venous blood is due to the presence of the reduced hemoglobin in the veins. The combination, which is a loose one, is readily affected by variations in oxygen tension.

Gases other than oxygen unite with hemoglobin, and to the stability of some of these combinations substances such as carbon monoxid owe their poisonous properties. After inhalation of large amounts of coal-gas the blood in the veins as well as in the arteries takes on a cherry-red color (carbonmonoxid hemoglobin). Hydrocyanic acid forms a stable red compound (cyan-hemoglobin) with hemoglobin, destroying its oxygen-carrying properties. Hydrogen sulphid is said to cause a dark appearing blood with a greenish tinge, dependent on the formation of a compound (sulphur-methemoglobin) that is different from *methemoglobin* but readily changed into it even by carbon dioxide. This compound must be distinguished from the sulphids formed by the action of hydrogen sulphid produced by bacteria in putrefactive processes on loosely combined iron in the tissues. This black discoloration is known as *pseudomelanosis*. These are all additive compounds, and in their formation the general structure of the molecule appears to be changed little or not at all.

Methemoglobin is a dark brownish compound that forms when blood is allowed to stand exposed to air for a long time. Without doubt the hemoglobin molecule undergoes fundamental change when methemoglobin is formed. Poisoning with potassium chlorate, nitrites, acetanilid, aniline, nitro-benzol, and other organic compounds, produces this change in the hemoglobin of the circulating blood, and the new compound manifests itself in the changed color of the skin and mucous membrane surfaces. Toxins of infectious origin (small-pox, scarlatina, tropical malaria, and infections with pneumococcus, hemolytic streptococcus and gas bacillus) may lead to solution of the corpuscles (hemoglobinemia) and a transformation of the dissolved hemoglobin into methemoglobin (methemoglobinemia). Severe and extensive superficial burns, cobra venom and other hemolytic poisons may have the same effect.

Although hemoglobin may become crystalline and appears to be one of the simplest of the proteins, its constitution is unknown and considerable confusion exists in regard to its derivatives. Carbon monoxid, hydrogen sulphid, and hydrocyanic acid combinations with hemoglobin, as well as methemoglobin, are best detected (Fig. 67) by means of a suitable spectroscope. They probably do not represent radical changes in the hemoglobin. In the following paragraphs are given some of the terms applied to hemoglobin derivatives that represent more extensive changes in this substance than those of methemoglobin or of the combinations with the gaseous compounds previously mentioned.

Hematin.—If an aqueous solution of hemoglobin is heated to 70°C. it turns brownish, due to the formation of an iron-containing substance known as hematin. When hematin is formed, a protein (globin) that does not contain iron is split off. Although this is the coloring-matter of the hemoglobin and is readily separated from globin *in vitro*, it is not commonly found in pathologic processes in the tissues. The spectroscopic appearance of acid and alkaline solutions of hematin is characteristic.

Hemin crystals (Teichmann), Fig. 16, are formed by the combination of hematin with hydrochloric acid to form hemin. These crystals do not occur in the living tissue and the exact hydrolytic action exerted by the acid on the hematin or hemoglobin is not known. To form the characteristic crystals, evaporate a drop of normal saline to dryness on a slide and place on the dry salt a very minute amount of the dried blood. Add 2 drops of glacial acetic acid, and evaporate very carefully high above a Bunsen flame until a brownish tint appears. Now hold the preparation above the flame where it is scarcely warm, drive off the last of the glacial acetic acid, add a drop of glycerine apply a cover-glass, and examine with high-dry lens for the characteristic brownish crystals. Teichmann's crystals are formed from any hemoglobin, and the hemoglobin of lower animals reacts to this test in the same way as that of man.

Hematoidin.—When blood escapes into a body cavity or becomes mixed with the feces, the urine, or the sputum, the reddish rhombic crystals of hematoidin may result. The crystals are iron-free, are formed from hemoglobin, and are probably identical in composition with bilirubin. There is some proof that hematoidin is hematein from which the iron has been removed but it is doubtful if hematin is an intermediate step in its formation from hemoglobin.

Hemosiderin (Fig. 103, *l*) is an iron-containing yellowish or brownish pigment and is formed from hemoglobin by the action of living tissue cells. It appears in the cells as granules and this formation of granules indicates that the color is not simply due to a staining of the protoplasm with inorganic iron compounds but that it may be foreign protein substance stained by iron salts. In what way it is related to hematin has not yet been fully determined.

Hematoporphyrin is an iron-free substance of hemic origin and is said by some to be isomeric with hematoidin. It apparently occurs in normal urine in minute traces, and may occasionally occur in quantities sufficient to give the urine a somewhat darkened or Burgundy red color. When present in large quantities, direct spectroscopic examination of the urine is sufficient for identification; but an alcoholic extract is preferable for this examination and may be obtained by precipitating 100 c.c. urine with 20 c.c. 10 per cent. caustic soda, washing the precipitate so obtained with absolute alcohol, and dissolving it in 20 c.c. Czaplewsky's solution. There is doubt in regard to its significance. In many acute infections and after the administration of sulphonal, trional or veronal the amount in the urine may be greatly increased but the greatest increases have been noted in men exhibiting skin lesions and other changes that appear to be inherited. Such individuals are very sensitive to light waves and to ultraviolet waves.

ESTIMATION OF HEMOGLOBIN

The hemoglobin has a normal variation between 70 and 120 per cent. (11 to 17 gm. per 100 c.c. blood), with the smaller percentage in children. The number of corpuscles varies between 4,000,000 and 6,500,000. Apparatus for collecting blood for the estimation of hemoglobin, for a determination of the number of red blood corpuscles and white blood cells, and for making smears of blood is carried to the bedside of the patient. For the examination of patients in their homes this apparatus may be conveniently placed in a hemocytometer case by providing the pipets with tips made from small soft rubber corks and, after filling, transporting the pipets in a horizontal position. For puncturing the ear or finger, place in the case a Hagedorn needle attached to a cork inserted in a small vial containing 80 per cent. alcohol in which there is an excess of sodium carbonate. One of the automatic blood lancets (Fig. 1) is convenient for making the puncture and may be kept in a suitable bottle containing 80 per cent. alcohol saturated with sodium carbonate. A small vial containing Hayem's solution and another containing one-half per cent. acetic acid may be carried in the case in the grooves provided for the pipets. Cover-glasses and a Tallquist scale complete the equipment.

FIG. 1.—Automatic lance for obtaining blood from the ear or finger. Keep in small bottle in 80 per cent. alcohol saturated with sodium carbonate. To secure 2 c.c. or more of blood puncture deeply 5–7 mm. from thumb angle of nail of middle or index finger (palmar surface), allow arm to hang down and alternately compress and release the patient's finger by grasping with thumb and index finger of right hand.

The Sahli method for the estimation of hemoglobin is practical and quite accurate and is, perhaps, the best method for routine work. For a close determination of the percentage of hemoglobin the Miescher method is highly recommended in text-books, but it is not much used in practice outside a few laboratories and its superiority is questionable. The Dare instrument is reliable, makes possible the direct comparison of blood with a standard scale, and is well adapted for routine work. The Tallquist scale answers for rough estimations above 70 per cent. and is useful in determining whether anemia exists.

Tallquist Scale Method.—At the bedside of the patient a small surface on the lobe of his ear or the tip of his finger is painted with iodin, wiped with cotton moistened with alcohol, then wiped dry with dry cotton and pricked. A Hagedorn needle or an automatic lancet is used. The blood must flow freely. If 1 c.c. of blood, or more, should be required, the patient's ring or middle finger is pricked rather deeply with the automatic lancet on the palmar surface, one-fourth inch from the corner of the nail that lies toward the thumb. A large drop of blood is pressed out, and the pressure released, allowing the capillaries to fill. The first blood is wiped away with a small sheet of filter paper or a dry cloth, and the second small drop is allowed to touch the filter paper provided with the Tallquist scale. As soon as the blood has been absorbed by the paper and before it dries the stained area thus made is slipped beneath the Tallquist scale and carefully matched with the scale colors. If the hemoglobin is below 70 per cent., a more careful examination by another method is made. The scale should be new, and protected from light when not in use. Whenever possible, daylight is employed in making the readings.

Sahli Hemometer Method (Fig. 2).—In this method the solution to be tested is compared with a standard solution containing 1 per cent. of the same substance which is a solution of acid hematin representing 1 per cent. of normal blood by volume. A standard hemoglobin solution cannot be used in the same way because it is not stable. Fill the tube—which is graduated from o to 140—to 10 with decinormal hydrochloric acid, and to this acid add 20 c.mm. of blood obtained by filling the pipet to that mark. Rinse the pipet by drawing the blood-acid solution into it and blowing it back into the graduated tube. Shake; and at the end of one minute add water to the dark brown blood-acid solution until the yellow color of the diluted solution matches that in the standard tube when the two tubes are placed side by side. Shake; allow a few seconds for the liquid to run down the side of the tube, and at once make the reading. The number that corresponds to the upper surface of the liquid in the graduated tube is the percentage of hemoglobin. Shake the standard solution before making the readings.

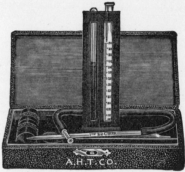

Fig. 2.—Sahli hemometer.

The standard tube contains 1 per cent. of normal blood and is readily prepared by mixing 1 c.c. of blood with a corpuscle count of 5,000,000, 10 c.c. decinormal hydrochloric acid, 39 c.c. distilled water, and 50 c.c. glycerin. The hemoglobin derivative, acid hematin, is the same in both tubes, and for that reason either daylight or artificial light may be used in making the readings. The solution in the standard tube is protected from the light as much as possible, carefully stoppered with a cork covered with paraffin, and renewed at the end of each year.

The standard solution that comes with the imported instruments is too strong and, as a result, low readings are obtained with normal blood. To rectify this error some instrument dealers and makers have put out scales for correcting the percentage readings. The use of such scales has given rise to some confusion. If the new instrument is found to give too low a percentage of hemoglobin with normal blood, a new standard solution is prepared according to the formula given above. Again, standard tubes that originally contained too strong a solution may, after standing a number of years, contain a solution that is too weak.

To cleanse the pipet, draw through it one-half per cent. acetic acid and then one after the other, 95 per cent. alcohol, ether, and air. This may be done by attaching the pipet to a suction pump; by filling and expelling the solution by means of a thick rubber valveless bulb; or by suction from the mouth through a rubber tube. Hair from the tail of a horse may be employed to remove any accidental dirt, but a wire should not be used. Such hairs may be kept for this purpose in a bottle of 95 per cent. alcohol. Occasionally, in order to remove albumin from its lumen, it may be necessary to fill the pipet with nitric acid and set it aside for a number of hours.

Miescher Hemoglobinometer Method.—Draw the blood into the pipet to the two-thirds mark, and fill with 0.1 per cent. sodium carbonate to the mark above the bulb. By shaking, mix the diluted blood; blow it out into the half of the cell which is 15 mm. deep, and fill the other half with water. Place above the scale the half that has been filled with the water. Seal the cell with the glass cover and then with the metal cap. Place the slit of the metal cap at right angles to the partition dividing the cell. Transfer the instrument to a dark room before a candle, move the red scale until the two colors match, and record the reading on the scale. Make five such readings; add them together, and divide by 5. Now, by means of the pipet transfer the diluted blood to one-half of the 12-mm. deep chamber, which is similar to the 15-mm. deep one, and proceed to make five more readings. Add these five readings together, take the average and multiply by fifteen-twelfths. Add the two averages together and divide by 2. The result represents the number of grams of hemoglobin per 100 c.c. of blood according to the key which comes with the instrument. In cases of anemia, draw the blood in the pipet up to 1 instead of to two-thirds, thus obtaining a 1–200 dilution instead of a 1–300. In this case divide the final average by 1.5. To get the percentage of hemoglobin, follow the directions for the scale that come with each instrument. Clean the pipet as indicated under the Sahli method. The color-scale of the imported instrument is too high, and it is advisable to multiply the final result by ten-ninths. For accurate work this method is usually stated to be the best.

Dare Hemoglobinometer Method (Fig. 3).—The determination of hemoglobin by Dare's hemoglobinometer rests on the comparison of a film of undiluted blood of definite thickness with a standardized colored glass disk. The finger or ear is pricked, and the slit of the blood chamber of the instrument is brought into contact with a rather large drop of blood, which immediately fills it by capillarity. The excess of blood is re-moved and the blood chamber replaced in its slot or carrier with the white glass facing out. If undiluted oxalated or citrated blood of the pa-tient is at hand this is pre-ferable, since coagulation does not then take place. Light the candle, and looking through the eyepiece, rotate the milled rubber disk until the colors match. The hem-oglobin percentage is read directly from the scale. For the daily routine, many pre-fer to use this instrument in-

Fig. 3.—Dare hemoglobinometer; U, eyepiece; Y, candle; R, milled wheel for revolving the colored disk. After the slit, W, has been filled with blood it is placed in position at X.

stead of the Sahli. It is required that the readings be taken at once, before the blood in the slit clots.

Coagulation Time of the Blood (Bogg's Coagulometer).—Coagulation period is determined at this point because the test is conveniently made at the time the hemoglobin is estimated and the diluting pipets filled. The second or third small drop of blood escaping from a fresh puncture is placed on the lower surface of the conical glass disk and the disk inverted in the moist chamber. The disk is then placed under the low-power of the microscope and the drop brought into focus.

When clotting has taken place, gentle pressure on the rubber tube, after the end of the tubing has been pinched off, moves large bodies of the corpuscles which spring back as an elastic mass, while just before coagulation took place the individual corpuscles could be moved about separately and with perfect freedom. The time is taken from the moment the glass cone is touched to the drop of blood to the jellying of the corpuscles to form a clotted mass. The normal coagulation time is from three to eight minutes and any time above nine minutes may be looked upon as delayed coagulation. This determination is of value in detecting hemorrhagic conditions, such as hemophilia and acquired purpuric affections, in which coagulation is retarded (ten minutes to one hour); and is of interest in infections such as pneumonia and rheumatic fever in which the coagulability of the blood is increased. In long continued jaundice the time required for coagulation which may be increased to a considerable extent is shortened by the administration of calcium chlorid. The time of coagulation is about parallel to the number of platelets in the peripheral blood.

ENUMERATION OF THE RED BLOOD CORPUSCLES

The pipet marked 101 at a point above the bulb is used in making the dilution for counting the red blood corpuscles, and the one bearing the mark 11 is used for the leukocytes. Some of the older diluting pipets for the leukocytes have a mark 21 instead of 11. These two pipets are filled at the same time that the blood is taken for the hemoglobin estimation. Domestic diluting pipets on the market are accurate and should be accompanied by the Bureau of Standards certificate.

The red corpuscle pipet (small bore) is placed in a small drop of blood that has freely escaped upon the skin surface immediately before the pipet is touched to it, and gentle suction is made from the mouth by means of a rubber tube. A small space, for making the suction and for stopping the column of blood in the capillary at the desired point, is shut off with the tongue in the front part of the mouth. The blood is drawn into the pipet which is held in as nearly a horizontal position as possible, until it reaches the 0.5 mark, when the suction is stopped and the pipet quickly withdrawn from the drop of blood. If the column of blood reaches more than 1 mm. above the 0.5 mark, the column of blood is drawn to the 0.6 mark for the dilution. If the column of blood reaches 1 mm. or less above the 0.5 mark, the excess may be expelled by touching the tip of the pipet very lightly to the adjacent dry skin surface. Filling the pipet must be practised until it can always be done accurately. As soon as the blood has been drawn to the 0.5 mark, the tip of the pipet is inserted into a vial of *Hayem's solution* (mercuric chlorid 0.5 gm., sodium chlorid 1.0 gm., sodium sulphate 5.0 gm., and distilled water 200 c.c.), and this diluting fluid drawn up to 101. The index finger and the thumb are placed over the ends of the pipet which is shaken for one-half minute. In case the pipets are to be transported to the laboratory some distance away, rubber caps (page 23) are applied; but if the laboratory is at hand this is not necessary.

To make the preparation, the pipet is again shaken for one-half minute, one or two drops forced out of it, and then a small drop permitted to escape upon the center of the counting-chamber island (Fig. 4) by touching the glass surface of the ruled part of the island with the tip of the pipet. The special cover-glass, which is thick, flat, and carefully ground, is applied to the drop from one side by holding the cover against the raised portion of the slide with the thumb and slowly lowering it. The diluted blood just covers the island if the size of the drop is correct and it is free from bubbles of air. No liquid or moisture from the fingers is permissible between the cover and the part of the slide on which it rests; and when viewed tangentially Newton's rings should appear here.

Counting the Corpuscles (Fig. 4).—The ruled part of the island is 3 mm. square, while the central, finely ruled area is 1 mm. square. The distance between the under surface of the cover and the upper surface of the island is 0.1 mm. Each side of the central, finely ruled 1-mm. square is divided into 20 equal parts, so that 20 strips $\frac{1}{20}$ mm. wide and 1 mm. long run horizontally across the slide, and 20 similar strips run at right angles to these. One of these strips, measuring $\frac{1}{20}$ by 1 mm., may be used as a basis for the count. Such a strip is made up of 20 small squares. At least 10 such strips are counted, and it is better to count 5 in the first preparation, and 5 in a second one made by wiping the diluted blood from the island and replacing it from the pipet. It is desirable to move these strips by means of a mechanical stage as the corpuscles are counted. One of these strips has a volume of $\frac{1}{10}$ by $\frac{1}{20}$ by 1, equaling $\frac{1}{200}$ c.mm., and the dilution of the blood in the pipet is $\frac{1}{200}$ because the one-half volume of blood originally placed in the pipet is made up to 200 halves in the

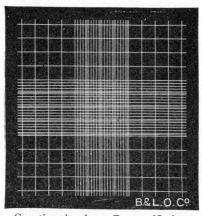

Fig. 4.—Counting-chamber. Zappert-Neubauer Ruling.
A mechanical stage is very desirable for blood work. Counting by strips faciliates the enumeration of the corpuscles. The entire ruled area 3 mm. square is divided into nine equal squares of 1 sq. mm. each.

bulb, the one volume of diluting fluid left in the pipet not entering into the dilution. Therefore, multiply the average number of red blood corpuscles in one strip by 200 times 200, equaling 40,000, to get the number of corpuscles in 1 c.mm.

To facilitate the enumeration, count all corpuscles touching left hand and upper borders although they may lie entirely without the strip except for this contact. No corpuscle that touches the lower or right hand border must be enumerated although it may lie entirely within the area being counted.

Other methods of enumerating the corpuscles are in use.

Many of the different rulings of the counting-chamber agree in having a central finely ruled area 1mm. square consisting of 400 small squares that measure $\frac{1}{20}$ mm. In a method extensively employed and one that does nor require the use of a mechanical stage (Fig. 5), the small square ($\frac{1}{20}$ times $\frac{1}{20}$ mm.) is used as the basis for the count. The area of small squares to be counted (usually 16 squares) is placed under the high-dry objective (Fig. 6), having the diaphragm well closed. Artificial light is better than daylight. The depth of the blood between the island and the under surface of the cover is $\frac{1}{10}$

FIG. 5.—Mechanical stage. The instrument attaches to square stage of microscope.

mm.; therefore the volume of blood above each small square is $\frac{1}{20}$ by $\frac{1}{20}$ by $\frac{1}{10}$, or $\frac{1}{4000}$ c.mm. The dilution is 1–200. The corpuscles in 80 small squares (that is, all corpuscles in five of the areas indicated) are counted and the average number in each square computed. This average is multiplied by 800,000 (contents times dilution) to get the number of corpuscles in 1 c.mm. of undiluted blood. Example: 480 corpuscles in 80 squares equals 6 cells as an average; 6 times 800,000 equals 4,800,000 corpuscles in 1 c.mm. Since we divided by 80 and again multiply by 800,000 the number of corpuscles in 80 squares may be counted and four ciphers annexed to this number.

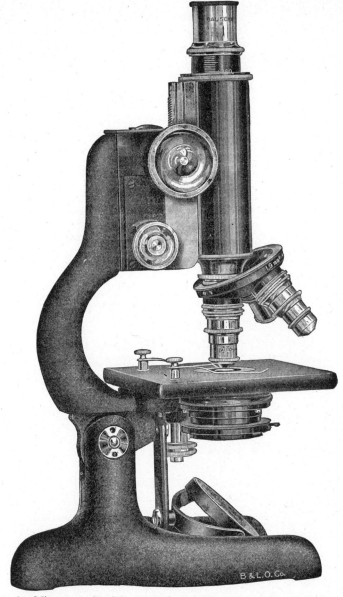

FIG. 6.—Microscope (B. & L. O. Co.) with No. 7.5 and No. 10 oculars and 16 mm., 4 mm. and oil-immersion objectives.

The Levy counting-chamber (A. H. Thomas Co., Phila.) is of domestic make and reliable. It may be obtained with two counting-chamber islands (rectangular and not circular) so that preparations for both red and white counts may be made at one time. In using this chamber the cover-glass is first applied and the diluted blood allowed to cover the island by touching the tip of the pipet to the open margin.

To cleanse the counting-chamber all parts are thoroughly wiped off with a soft, dry, starch-free cloth. The pipet is cleansed as in the case of the Sahli pipet (page 26).

Color-index.—In normal blood there are 4,000,000 to 6,500,-000 red blood corpuscles per cubic millimeter. The color-index is obtained by dividing the percentage of hemoglobin by the percentage of corpuscles (5,000,000 corpuscles equals 100 per cent.). If the index is below about 1 (0.82 to 0.9 [Emerson]), the individual corpuscle is poor in hemoglobin. A high index is found in primary pernicious anemia (as high as 1.75 with 1,000,000 corpuscles and 35 per cent. hgbl.; case of Cabot) and in a few varieties of secondary anemia, such as bothriocephalus infection; while it is low in the usual secondary anemia (as low as 0.5), and in the primary anemia of chlorosis (as low as 0.3). In the differentiation between gastric carcinoma (secondary anemia) and pernicious anemia the color-index may be of value, but to be of value the deviation from the normal ratio should be considerable.

Examination of Corpuscles in Fresh Blood.—The chief value of this examination is to determine the exact size and shape of the corpuscles and cells, since these cannot be determined accurately in stained preparations. Since the number of corpusles in undiluted blood is too great for the study of individual ones, and since clotting takes place readily, 1 part of blood measured in a small capillary, made by drawing out a piece of glass tubing, is mixed with 5 parts of Locke-citrate solution in the well of a concave slide. The next step is to place a 5-mm. piece of a cover-glass upon the center of a No. 1 cover-glass, 22 by 40 mm., and to permit a minute amount of the diluted blood from the pipet to be drawn between the two

3

covers by capillarity. The slide about the well of a clean concave slide is covered with cedar oil and the large cover-glass
inverted and applied to it, so that the small piece of cover-
glass with the blood beneath it is entirely within the well. The
cover-glasses are dust- and fat-free. The use of a large cover-
glass prevents its being lifted when the preparation is examined
with the oil-immersion lens.

The *Locke-citrate solution* is prepared by dissolving 10 gm.
sodium citrate in one liter of Locke's solution. Locke's solution is prepared by dissolving 9.2 gm. sodium chlorid,
0.15 gm. sodium bicarbonate, 0.5 gm. potassium chlorid, and
0.1 gm. calcium chlorid (dry), and 1.0 gm. glucose in 1000 c.c.
distilled water. Preparations made with this solution are very
satisfactory for examinations for malarial parasites; but less so
for relapsing fever organisms and other parasites, where it may
be desirable to examine larger volumes of blood. The nuclei of
cells and eosinophilic granules especially may be distinguished
with considerable accuracy. If the slide is kept warm the
ameboid activity of the leukocytes may be observed. In such
a preparation an increased number of ultramicroscopic particles
may be seen by dark-field illumination if the blood is taken from
the subject a short time after he has had a full meal. The
chemical nature of such ultramicroscopic particles has not been
determined but in their physical behavior (active Brownian
motion) they are colloids.

PATHOLOGIC CHANGES IN THE RED BLOOD CORPUSCLES

It is preferable to speak of blood changes rather than of
blood diseases, because of the fact that most conditions of the
blood result from a primary change in the cells of some extravascular tissue. In such cases the blood findings are signs of
the disease, but they should not be looked upon as the disease
itself.

Abnormalities in the Size and Shape of Corpuscles.—In
anemic conditions many small corpuscles (microcytes or corpuscles under 6 microns) together with large forms (macrocytes) make their appearance in the peripheral blood. This

variation in size from the normal corpuscle (normocyte) which in the adult does not vary more than 1.5 microns from the average (7.5 microns) is spoken of as *anisocytosis* (Fig. 9 [11, 12]). There is no uniformity in regard to the terms applied to corpuscles measuring more than 9 microns (megalocytes or gigantocytes). In the peripheral blood of normal adults the corpuscles are non-nucleated, but, if a great excess is withdrawn from the bone-marrow, the loss of nuclei is incomplete and nucleated red cells (Fig. 9 [15, 16, 17]) of normal size (normoblasts), small nucleated cells (microblasts) and large forms (megaloblasts) make their appearance in the peripheral blood. The corpuscles may show clear spaces (endoglobular degeneration). The hemoglobin content of the individual corpuscle is frequently below normal and appears pale. In anemia there is usually not only a variation in size of the corpuscles but also an irregularity in shape (poikilocytosis [14, Fig. 9]). Irregularities in both size and shape are more accurately observed in fresh preparations, and care must be exercised in distinguishing an endoglobular degeneration from artefacts brought out in staining.

Abnormal Staining of Corpuscles.—A remnant of the nuclear membrane which stains red (Cabot's ring) is sometimes seen. *Polychromatophilia* is a term applied to the mixed basic and acid staining of erythrocytes in anemia. The basic color is the unusual reaction; and, since the cytoplasm of nucleated corpuscles (erythroblasts) stains a greenish blue with eosin-methylene blue stains, it seems quite certain that often the corpuscles showing polychromatophilia are immature. This property is also called *basophilia*. The peculiar greenish tinge of the cytoplasm and the small spherical nuclei make the recognition of nucleated red cells very easy.

"Stippling" is a term applied to a basophilic granulation of erythrocytes. It frequently is found to run parallel in degree to the polychromatophilia in cases of anemia; and the more or less definite basophilic granules are often found in the corpuscles and cytoplasm of erythroblasts that show diffuse basophilic staining. In this case the granulation is evidence of im-

maturity of the corpuscle or cell. That much of the basophilic granulation of lead poisoning (Fig. 9 [13]) is not of this
character, but that it is a cytoplasmic change due to the immediate presence of lead in the corpuscle, has been conclusively
shown by the writer (Jour. of Med. Research, xxxii, 1915,
p. 271). In the peripheral blood of experimental animals
after large doses of lead salts have been given, corpuscles with
basophilic granules giving a positive reaction for lead appear,
before nucleated red cells and polychromatophilia are found.
In the later stages of experimental lead poisoning the granulation is present in polychromatophilic and in non-polychroma-
tophilic corpuscles as well.

In a severe acute anemia following a hemorrhage many
nucleated red cells and basophilic corpuscles may be present
with no granulation of the type seen in lead poisoning. The
"strippled" corpuscles in plumbism present discrete and
for the most part spherical granules of a rather uniform size,
in distinction to the coarse and frequently irregular granules
seen in basophilic corpuscles of severe anemias (pernicious
anemia; also cancer of stomach, leukemia and other conditions
with severe secondary anemia) not due to lead. Spherules
which are found in corpuscles and which stain more or less of a
plum color with polychrome stains are known under the name
of *Howell's bodies*. The coarse basophilic granules, Howell's
bodies, and Cabot's ring body all may be nuclear remnants so
far as any tinctorial reactions are concerned.

ANEMIA

This term is applied to a reduction below normal of the
percentage of hemoglobin or of the number of red blood corpuscles, or of both. If it is desired to indicate a deficiency
in the quantity of blood *oligemia* is a preferable term. Since
the purpose of the hemoglobin is to carry oxygen to the tissue
cells, the morphologic and functional results of the loss of hemoglobin, aside from those caused by disintegration products
of the corpuscles themselves, are dependent upon insufficient
oxygen. They vary according to the duration of the anemia

and its degree of severity. Associated with a deficiency of hemoglobin there is usually a diminished amount of blood protein and this must be considered in the production of cell injury, since deficient food reaches the tissues.

Acute Anemia.—This is the simplest type and is seen in a typical form after large hemorrhages (acute post-hemorrhagic anemia). If there is a sudden loss of more than about one-half or a somewhat slower loss of about two-thirds of the blood the individual dies from *asphyxia* resulting from paralysis of the respiratory and cardiac centers, since the nerve cells of these centers do not have enough oxygen to perform their functions. Estimations of the total volume of blood by the administration of a given amount of carbon monoxid and the subsequent determination of the concentration of this gas in a sample of blood indicate that the total volume is from 5 to 5.3 per cent. of the body weight.

If the hemorrhage is less severe, within a comparatively short time (two days) the loss in volume of blood is made up with fluid from the tissue lymph which results in a dilution of all the constituents of the blood. If the pre-hemorrhagic percentage of hemoglobin is known, the volume of blood lost may be calculated from the percentage of hemoglobin found within a short time after the hemorrhage. The blood proteins return to the normal amount more slowly than the total volume, and more slowly yet (one month after a very severe hemorrhage) the red blood corpuscles are brought back to the normal number by an increased rate of proliferation of the red blood cells (erythroblasts) in the bone-marrow. Many small corpuscles, poor in hemoglobin, and a few nucleated red cells appear in the peripheral blood during the period of return to normal. The number of corpusles reaches normal more rapidly than the hemoglobin so that during the period of regeneration the color-index is low. Pulmonary tuberculosis, gastric ulcer, traumatic injury, hemorrhoids, typhoid ulcers, abortion, child birth, tubal pregnancy, cancer, fibroids of the uterus and hemophilia are common causes of hemorrhage. Type case: male, forty-two years old. Internal hemorrhoids.

Hemoglobin (Sahli) 37 per cent.; red corpuscles 2,072,000;
leukocytes 6,100. Many microcytes, few microblasts and polychromatophilia in the stained film.

Chronic Anemias.—These are more complex than acute anemias, and several types that are frequently not well defined etio-
logically are considered. At present, if the causative factor is
known a chronic anemia is said to be secondary; while if it
is not known the condition is spoken of as *primary anemia.*
Subsequent to a hemorrhage, if the corpuscles are regener-
ated at or below the normal rate, a chronic secondary anemia
follows. This is seen especially in cachectic individuals. A
chronic anemia may also result in cases where, although regeneration is increased above normal, an abnormal destruction of corpuscles is taking place. Hemolytic poisons such as
potassium chlorate, aniline derivatives and certain bacterial
toxins (streptococcus) are examples of factors that produce
a chronic anemia in spite of the fact that the rate of regeneration is much increased. It appears also that there may be an
abnormal acceleration of the physiologic process of blood
destruction through the phagocytosis of corpuscles by the endothelial cells and leukocytes in the spleen, liver, lungs and
bone-marrow. In cases other than hemorrhage, an increased
destruction of red blood corpuscles is indicated by hemosiderin deposits in the liver, spleen, kidneys, and bone-marrow,
as well as by an increased elimination of bilirubin and urobilin. In cases of chronic anemia it is often difficult to determine whether a diminished rate of erythroblastic proliferation
exists. With the present knowledge it is not possible to
ascribe to each of the factors—regeneration and destruction
—the exact part that they play in many of the anemic conditions.

Chlorosis.—Acute anemias are very similar and do not vary
to any extent, but clinical types of the chronic anemias may
be very dissimilar in character and etiology. Chlorosis is a
type or clinical variety of chronic anemia of unknown etiology
(a primary anemia). It occurs in females at puberty. If
typical, the skin shows a marked pallor with a greenish tinge,

but the face in some cases is red. In mild or early cases the blood may be unchanged and in all cases the clinical findings are required for a diagnosis. No extrinsic cause has been established; the condition is not inherited. There appears to be a diminished rate of corpuscle and hemoglobin production, with a normal rate of destruction. The number of red blood corpuscles is usually somewhat decreased, but not in proportion to the great decrease in hemoglobin and there is no condition in which the color-index is so low as in a typical case of chlorosis. The variation in size is not great and the number of poikilocytes is small, but the individual corpuscle is poor in hemoglobin. This is shown at the height of the disease by the great narrowing of the staining peripheral margin; an increase in the width of this margin is observed during convalescence. In certain cases at least, the platelets are increased in number and the blood coagulates rapidly. Iron in any form benefits these cases, and appears to do so by stimulating hemoglobin formation. Autopsies on well-defined cases are few. Type case: girl, twenty-four years old. Severe chlorosis. Hemoglobin 36 per cent.; corpuscles 4,200,000; leukocytes 4,500. Many microcytes. No nucleated red cells.

Secondary Anemias.—As it has already been pointed out, the chronic anemias are secondary or primary depending on whether the etiology is known or not. Anemias that were formerly regarded as primary are now placed with the secondary. The anemia associated with dibothriocephalus infection is an example. Chronic infections (tuberculosis, malaria, syphilis, suppuration, ankylostomiasis), chronic intoxications (lead, mercury, arsenic, retained poisons in individuals with sclerotic kidneys), malignant tumors, conditions accompanied by constant loss of blood, and malnutrition (intrinsic and extrinsic) are common causes of a secondary anemia. The cause is often difficult to determine, and this makes the classification into primary and secondary anemias types of less value. Often there is increased bone-marrow activity but this may be lacking. Usually there is evidence of increased blood destruction. The anemia of chronic lead poisoning is like the other secondary anemias except that the "stippling" is more marked. It has not been shown whether the alkaline sulphid reaction for lead in the corpuscles is of value in the usual human case.

Polychromatophilia, variations in size, and poikilocytosis, with a diminished red blood corpuscle count and low hemoglobin, are the common findings. Nucleated red cells appear in the severer cases. The fewer the immature forms in a given grade of anemia, the less the activity of the erythroblastic function of the bone-marrow. In general, the individual corpuscle is poor in hemoglobin (low color-index). The number of leukocytes is normal or decreased unless increased by the cause of the anemia. If an anemia is found, a search for the cause is indicated. Whether the cause is found or not, it is established that the body is receiving insufficient oxygen, and this should be remedied if possible. Type case: man, sixty-two years old. Carcinoma of the stomach. Hemoglobin 42 per cent.; corpuscles 2,653,000; leukocytes 9,200. Microcytes, a few macrocytes, and a few normoblasts.

Splenic Anemia (Banti's disease).—The two terms here used have been applied to clinical conditions and by many are used synonymously. In Osler's series of cases there was a rather severe secondary anemia (average of 3,000,000 corpuscles) without leukocytosis. Hemorrhage from the stomach ,and esophageal veins is the rule. At autopsy cirrhosis of the liver is present in some cases and absent in others; many cases in which there was found at autopsy a thrombosis of the splenic vein have now been recorded. In general chronic passive congestion of cardiac origin the spleen is involved but the enlargement is not extreme (under 1 kilo), perhaps, owing to the interposition of the liver in the venous circuit. If there exists a high-grade cirrhosis of the liver or, if the splenic or portal vein is obstructed by thrombus formation, the damming back of the blood on the spleen becomes much more severe and the cyanotic spleen in these cases may reach a weight of 3 kilograms. These anatomic findings appear to explain perfectly many of the clinical cases diagnosed as splenic anemia.

Pernicious Anemia.—This is a clinical term used to designate a certain type of anemia of the primary variety. That the cause of an anemia is unknown does not, however, place it in the pernicious class, since chlorosis, both pathologically and clinically, is very different from this disease. The term pernicious, then, is applied to an anemia of unknown etiology characterized by symptoms and signs including the blood picture that characterize it. A diagnosis is important, for on it rests the prognosis. While it may be said that a diagnosis is usually possible, it must not be forgotten that some cases cannot be differentiated from secondary anemias, and that an early diagnosis is often difficult.

In this disease the blood is usually characteristic and of the isolated findings the presence of megaloblasts (16 microns in diameter) and the high color-index are the most important, but the blood picture taken as a whole is of the greatest value. Although many corpuscles show a much narrowed rim, others have the normal amount of hemoglobin, and numerous macrocytes are present. That is, the individual corpuscle is large and rather well supplied with hemoglobin and to these facts is due the high color-index so often present. When there is 20 per cent. of hemoglobin for each 1,000,000 of corpuscles in the cubic millimeter of blood, the index is 1; while if there is more than 20 per cent. the index is high, or greater than 1. The *oligocythemia* is usually marked (below 1,000,000 corpuscles).

The second striking feature of the blood picture is the presence of megaloblasts and macrocytes, and this apparently is partly responsible for the high color-index. In the differentiation of cells a shrinkage takes place as the cells grow older unless their size is increased by the collection of some substance such as fat in their cytoplasm. This normal skrinkage is well illustrated by the *erythroblastic islands* of the bone-marrow (best seen in rabbits after benzol injections) in which the largest red cells are at the center. These large cells that correspond to the megaloblasts, undergo mitosis, and are pushed more and more toward the periphery of the groups as mitosis goes on near the center until nuclei are lost and they shrink to about one-half their original size, in which form they enter the blood as erythrocytes. In this variety of anemia, regeneration is so rapid that entire islands are made up of the large forms and in about one-half of the cases some of these enter the blood as megaloblasts. If about 5 per cent. of corpuscles consists of nucleated red cells, a "blood crisis" or "erythroblastic shower" is said to exist and often this is followed by an improvement in the blood picture. If the nuclei of the large nucleated forms are lost they become macrocytes. Polychromatophilia is of course present, and in such basophilic corpuscles a rather coarse granulation is frequently very conspicuous. There is no such pronounced evidence of regeneration of the blood in the usual case of secondary anemia or chlorosis. Marked poikilocytosis is present only in the last stages. Along with the large forms, numerous microcytes are found.

The duration of the disease is variable, but the prognosis is always bad. A severe leukopenia is a bad sign; a leukocytosis usually indicates infection. Type case: woman, fifty-one years old. Pernicious anemia. Hemoglobin 29 per cent.; corpuscles 892,000; leukocytes 4,200. Normoblasts and megaloblasts present; marked variation in size of corpuscles, polychromatophilia and "stippling." A few myelocytes are present. No platelets demonstrable.

That there is a great increase in the destruction of blood is shown by the marked accumulation of hemosiderin in the internal organs (liver, kidney, spleen, heart muscle), by jaundice, by the increase of urobilin in the urine, and by hemoglobinemia. Red marrow replaces the yellow, and erythroblasts divide in the spleen, liver, and peripheral blood.

Aplastic Anemia.—This is a term which will serve a useful purpose until more is known of the etiology of the anemias. So far as the appearance of the patient and the prognosis are concerned, the aplastic type is like pernicious anemia; but there is no increased bone-marrow activity, and evidence of hyperplastic bone-marrow is lacking in the blood.

The prognosis is bad in these cases of progressive anemia of the aplastic type. Since the bone-marrow shows less than the normal activity, and nucleated red blood cells are not present in the peripheral blood, regeneration seems to be at fault.

Hemoglobinemia.—Hemoglobin is practically synonymous with the hemoglobin content of the red blood corpuscles. Occasionally, hemoglobin may be free in the blood plasma (hemoglobinemia). Hemoglobin in solution in the plasma may be detected by carefully drawing the blood into a paraffined centrifuge tube and centrifuging. When it becomes free, it is rapidly taken up by the liver, where the iron is split off and retained and the iron-free part (bilirubin) eliminated in the bile. If the free hemoglobin content becomes more than about 2 per cent. of the total hemoglobin, this coloring matter is eliminated in the urine (hemoglobinuria).

An increase or decrease in the osmotic pressure may render the corpuscles unable to retain their hemoglobin, but the setting free of hemoglobin (hemolysis) is more often brought about by some primary change in the lipoidal envelope or in the stroma of the corpuscle, and by hemolytic poisons acting on the corpuscle.

Paroxysmal hemoglobinuria occurs at intervals in certain individuals from some slight extrinsic cause such as muscular exertion or a cold bath. It is said that an abnormal hemolytic amboceptor is present in the blood of these individuals, and that this amboceptor under certain conditions attaches itself to the erythrocytes causing their solution. That this is due to an abnormal amboceptor has been urged because many of these cases are syphilitic, and there is some indication that this foreign amboceptor may in some cases be the same as that concerned in the Wassermann reaction.

The pathologic effects of extensive hemolysis are due to the loss of oxygen-carrying hemoglobin and to toxic substances liberated from the dissolved corpuscles. Such substances cause capillary thrombosis and injury to the kidney epithelium, shown by casts and often by large amounts of albumin in addition to the protein present as hemoglobin.

Polycythemia.—As used, the term practically means an increase above normal of the number of red blood corpuscles in the skin capillaries and veins. At present, a certain number of cases with a corpuscle count above 10,000,000 that progressed to a fatal ending have been described. In such cases nucleated red cells appear in the peripheral blood, and at autopsy the bone-marrow is hyperplastic. The terms *erythremia* and *polycythemia rubra* have been used to distinguish this condition from non-fatal forms of polycythemia. It has been suggested that the condition is a malignant tumor arising from the erythroblast (erythroblastoma).

Certain conditions (severe diarrhea, profuse sweating) decrease the fluid content of the blood in the skin capillaries and veins, and thereby produce a relative increase in the number of corpuscles in the vessels. Such a relative increase in corpuscles is transient since the deficiency in fluid is rapidly made up. The best example of such a polycythemia is seen in cases of venous stasis. In stasis resulting from both cardiac and pulmonary causes, there is a deficiency in oxygen reaching the tissue cells, and some observations point to a compensatory increase in the total number of corpuscles rather than to a relative decrease in fluid. In man and animals at high altitudes there is a polycythemia; and since there is a diminished oxygen content of the air in the lungs and in the plasma, it appears that a compensatory increase in the number of the erythrocytes takes place. Nucleated corpuscles are not present. In such polycythemias the count is almost always below 10 million (6,000,000 to 8,000,000), and the cases must be differentiated from those that progress to a fatal termination (polycythemia rubra).

ENUMERATION OF THE WHITE BLOOD CELLS

The blood is drawn into a white pipet (large bore) to 0.5, and the pipet filled to the 11 mark with one-half per cent. acetic acid to which a minute amount of dry methyl violet sufficient to color it (20 mgm. to 100 c.c. of the dilute acetic) has been added. A stock bottle of the colored acetic acid, containing a small amount of thymol to prevent the growth of moulds, is kept on hand. The counting-chamber is filled as in the enumeration of the red blood corpuscles, and all the leukocytes in the 9 square millimeters of surface are counted with the high-dry lens, with the aid of a mechanical stage. All cells touching the left and upper lines of divisions, but none touching the right and lower lines, are enumerated. Some prefer to dispense with the mechanical stage and use the low-power lens. To obtain the number of leukocytes in 1 c.mm., multiply the number in 1 square by 200 (contents times dilution).

Enumeration of Corpuscles and White Cells from a Single Pipet.—Draw blood to 1.0 in the red blood corpuscle pipet and fill to the 101 mark with *Toisson's solution*, which is sodium sulphate 8 gm., sodium chlorid 1 gm., glycerin 30 c.c., distilled water 160 c.c., and methyl violet 0.025 gm. (crystal of thymol in stock bottle). Make a preparation as above, and count the red blood corpuscles in the same way. All the white cells in the 9 square millimeters of surface are counted. The number of white blood cells counted by this method is too small to give results as accurate as those obtained by dilution in the large bore pipet.

Interpretation of the Number of White Cells.—The enumeration of the white cells just described gives no information as to the variety of the leukocytes; but, since an increase is most often due to the presence of a greater number of neutrophiles (neutrophilic leukocytosis), any moderate increase, may, until disproved, be looked upon as due to the neutrophiles. The normal variation in the number of leukocytes lies approximately between 5,000 and 10,000 per cubic millimeter. They are increased above this number in certain normal conditions as in the newborn (about 25,000), in women during pregnancy (about 12,000), and in all persons after meals or exercise (about 10,000). Such increases are spoken of as *physiologic leukocytoses;* and, unlike the pathologic ones the mononuclear-polymorphonuclear ratio is usually maintained to a greater extent than in the pathologic leukocytoses. In some of these conditions there is an increase in the total number of cells in the blood, while in others there appears to be an increase in the peripheral blood only.

A *pathologic leukocytosis* is seen chiefly in infections. Like a normal leukocytosis, the pathologic increase is often preceded by a decrease in number (leukopenia or hypoleukocytosis). In chronic intoxications, in cachexias, and in malnutrition in general, in which there is not a specific substance producing an increase in one or another variety of leukocyte, there is a leukopenia, and the different leukocytes appear to be decreased in about the same proportion. Typhoid fever and malaria are two infections in which a leukopenia is frequently noted; but here the decrease is in the neutrophiles, and it is generally stated that there is not only a relative increase in lymphocytes but an absolute increase as well. In the light of recent work (Archives of Internal Medicine, Vol. xxi, 1918, p. 59; American Journal of Anatomy, In Press), it appears that the increase in mononuclear cells may be due not to lymphocytes but to endothelial leukocytes. Unlike the physiologic varieties in which the lymphoblastic and myeloblastic cells are increased in proportion, a pathologic increase is, as already shown, usually due to neutrophiles. In some infections, such as pertussis, there is an increase of lymphocytes (lymphocytosis); while in others, such as trichiniasis, the increase is due to eosinophiles (eosinophilic leukocytosis). Since the variety of leukocyte producing the total increase in number can be determined only by a differential count of the leukocytes in a stained film, the various leukocytoses are taken up in detail under that heading (page 56). Leaving lymphatic leukemia out of account, there are few conditions in which there is a great increase above 10,000 except those in which there is a neutrophilia.

Among the causes of leukocytosis (neutrophilic), infections with *pyogenic organisms* hold first place. Thus in the surgical wards of hospitals a leukocyte count is a frequent examination. Since the increase is in the neutrophiles, there is a relative increase of these cells in the stained film shown by percentages from 80 upward. The initial leukopenia, often seen in infections, is probably due to a rapid withdrawal of leukocytes from the blood into the infected area, through the agency of chemotactic disintegration products coming primarily from the bacteria and perhaps secondarily from the solution of the leukocytes themselves. Later when these chemotactic substances pass into the blood stream, increased numbers of the leukocytes are called out from the tissues, and especially from the the bone-marrow provided sufficient time (twenty-four hours) has elapsed to permit an acceleration of myeloblastic proliferation. They must be transported through the blood stream, and the chemotactic substances there present may hold them in the circulating blood, giving the increases observed. That the bone-marrow is the source of these leukocytes is indicated by its hyperplasia in cases of prolonged and marked leukocytosis. It is well known that there may be a leukopenia in pyogenic infections in which the body is overwhelmed with toxins, but the mechanism of such increases and decreases in the peripheral blood is not entirely understood. Besides the infections with staphylococcus, streptococcus, pneumococcus, gonococcus, and colon bacillus, a leukocytosis is seen in acute tubercular processes, diphtheria, scarlet fever, meningococcus meningitis and several less common infections.

In *malignant disease* there may or may not be a moderate leukocytosis. It is perhaps most often observed in rapidly growing connective-tissue tumors. In cancer, an increase in leukocytes frequently accompanies secondary infection of the cancerous tissue, but is seen when no infection is present. A careful study of the blood cells by methods that clearly differentiate endothelial leukocytes has not been made in these cases. Following a severe *hemorrhage*, the leukocytes may be greatly increased (18,000 one hour postoperative). Later as the volume of blood is made up by fluid from the tissues there is a leukopenia. There are many *drugs* that cause a transitory rise to about 10,000.

The myelogenous and lymphatic *leukemias* are the conditions in which the greatest numbers of white cells are found in the peripheral blood. If more than 30,000 leukocytes per cubic millimeter are present, a careful examination of stained preparations is made, since this number is not often exceeded in leukocytoses; but counts as high as 70,000 have occasionally been recorded in infections.

PREPARATION OF BLOOD FILMS (Fig. 7)

Blood films are required for the study of the morphologic elements of the blood. Cover-glasses (No. 1, 22 mm. square) are placed overnight in an *acid cleaning solution* consisting of 50 per cent. sulphuric acid containing 5 per cent. sodium or

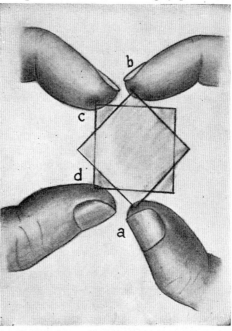

FIG. 7.—Blood film by the cover-glass method. With thumb and forefinger of the right hand firmly grasp the upper cover-glass (22 mm. square No. 1) at the diagonal corners, *a* and *b* and the lower one at the adjacent corners, *c* and *d* and quickly pull apart keeping the two parallel.

potassium bichromate. After removing all acid by washing each cover separately in running water, they are covered with 95 per cent. alcohol and finally transferred to chloroform. With forceps the covers are removed from the chloroform, wiped dry between two small boards covered with laundered unstarched muslin, and by means of forceps placed in a box

or glass dish. The removal of all fat is an absolute require-
ment if satisfactory films are to be obtained. Cover-glasses
smaller than 22 mm. square cannot be recommended; No. 2
cover-glasses are entirely unsatisfactory because they do not
yield as the droplet of blood spreads out between them. With
forceps, new cover-glasses may be placed directly in distilled
water; wiped dry with laundered cloth free of starch, dust or
lint; transferred to 95 per cent. alcohol, and again wiped dry.
In handling the covers, the fingers may be used if they are
washed with soap and water followed by alcohol, and only the
edges of the covers grasped. Just before use, the surface of the
covers is dusted with a camel's hair brush.

One fat-free cover is brought into contact near its center with
a small drop of blood that has just escaped from the ear or finger,
so as to pick up a drop twice the size of a pin-head; and a second
cover is applied to it at once, so that the diagonal corners of
the uppermost one may be grasped with the thumb and finger
of the right hand while the two adjacent corners of the under
cover-glass are held with the thumb and fingers of the left
hand.

Before thus taking up the covers, it is desirable to wipe the
fingers with cotton moistened with alcohol and to let them dry.
As soon as the blood has spread out between the covers, pull
them rapidly apart, being careful to keep the two parallel. The
size of the drop must be such that the film does not thicken at
the sides when one cover-glass is pulled away from the other.
The drop must be sufficiently small that some force is required
in pulling the covers apart. Cover-glass forceps may be used
for pulling the covers apart but are much less satisfactory than
the fingers. The two preparations made in this way are stained
and mounted on a single slide, with their edges in contact.
It is not possible to secure an even preparation on a slide, and
the leukocytes are very apt to be drawn off to the edges. A
further disadvantage in the use of slides is that a precipitate
is almost certain to be present on some part of the slide, provided
a good polychrome stain is used. The nearer these stains
approach the correct reaction, the greater is the tendency for a

4

precipitate to form on the preparation. Good films must be secured; and fat- and dust-free cover-glasses and dry fingers, reasonably fat-free, are pre-requisites in making them.

To label towels such as are used for cleaning cover-glasses, and other cloth that must be laundered often, it is usually desirable to use a *permanent laundry mark*. This may be prepared by dissolving 2 gm. silver nitrate and 5 gm. tartaric acid in 50 c.c. distilled water, and adding concentrated ammonia drop by drop until the abundant white precipitate goes into solution. Add 5 gm. gum tragacanth (powdered) and keep in a bottle of colored glass. In lettering, use a brass stencil and apply with a camel's hair brush.

STAINING OF BLOOD FILMS (Fig. 8)

In the earlier work on blood a single stain was used, or if more than one was employed they were applied to the preparation successively. Later, a *neutral stain* was made by combining a dye in which the staining radicle is basic with another whose staining group is acid, in such a way that leukocytic granules invisible with other stains were brought out. This important advance in staining technic made possible the certain differentiation of the myeloblastic cells. Ehrlich's triacid stain which is of this variety has now been largely superseded by combinations of methylene blue and eosin. In eosin the red staining radicle is united with sodium or ammonium, while in methylene blue the blue staining radicle is present in combination as a hydrochlorid or double zinc salt. If these two dyes are brought together in aqueous solution, a precipitate forms. This precipitate in which the exact chemical linkage is not known is a combination of the two dyes. Such a precipitate dissolved in methyl alcohol gives staining properties not obtainable with the eosin and methylene blue when applied independently. Jenner first obtained results by this method.

In 1891 Romanowsky, working with malaria, found that an old methylene blue solution combined with eosin gave a red tinge to certain nuclear material (chrom tin) of the parasites. Following this observation, many stains involving the principle of this method were devised and published. The change, which was first detected in the methylene blue solution that has stood at room temperature, was found to take place much more rapidly if the solution is made alkaline and a certain amount of heat applied. It is now generally agreed that the formation of the red chromatin-staining constituent results from a hydrolytic splitting off of methyl groups from the methylene blue. These red chromatin-staining derivatives are di- and tri-methyl compounds, while methylene blue has four methyl groups. These derivatives are frequently referred to under the Grübler trade name of methylene azur, but they are mixtures of dyes. The stains are commonly spoken of as *Romanowsky* or *polychrome stains*.

The combination of eosin with the demethylated methylene blue is the best for the staining of protozoa and the differential staining of blood films. Giemsa's stain, which requires a preparatory fixation in methyl alcohol, or equal parts of absolute ethyl alcohol and ether, has been extensively used as a protozoon stain and is quite satisfactory. Giemsa has described at length the results obtained by his stain, but has not published the method of preparation. The stain is obtained from Grübler & Co., and is used in the same way as the writer's protozoon stain described below.

There are about twelve well known eosin-demethylated methylene blue stains for blood (Romanowsky or polychrome blood stains). In none of these is the reaction adjusted by an accurate volumetric titration; and herein lies the chief fault of these stains. In the preparation of many of them, the precipitate formed by the combination of demethylated methylene blue with eosin is collected and later dissolved in methyl alcohol. A varying amount of alkali is carried down with the precipitate from the alkaline solution, and more or less of this may be removed by washing. In all of them the change produced in the methylene blue is satisfactory, but many purchased from dealers give no red chromatin staining whatever, and the neutrophilic granulation is brought out poorly or not at all. The writer's blood stain differs from a Wright, Hasting, Leishman, Wilson or Goldhorn stain in having a constant and definite reaction that insures good chromatin staining.

McJunkin's Protozoon Stain.—(Journal of American Medical Association, 1915, Vol. lxv, p. 2164; obtained from B. & L. Opt. Co., Rochester, N. Y.). The purpose of this stain is to color intensely the chromatin of tissue cells, protozoa, and bacteria. Common applications are met with in the staining of treponema pallidum, malaria, Leishman-Donovan bodies, trypanosomes, and Negri bodies. To prepare the stain, 1 gm. methylene blue (Grübler's B.X.), 50 c.c. decinormal (no factor) sodium carbonate, 35 c.c. distilled water, and 15 c.c. glycerin (Merck U.S.P.) are placed in a 500-c.c. beaker, and heated on asbestos gauze, over a low Bunsen flame for one hour at 87° to 89°C., the ingredients, meanwhile, being constantly stirred with a mechanical stirrer. The heating and stirring must be carefully carried out to secure correct polychroming. A mechanical stirrer may be improvised by unscrewing the top from a small electric centrifuge, replacing it with a small wooden drive-wheel and running a small shaft from the wheel. At the end of the 15 min., 30 min., and 45 min., respectively, 15 c.c. distilled water are added.

The carbonate solution that has been made decinormal by titration against decinormal hydrochloric acid, using methyl orange as an indicator, is run in accurately from a buret. Some experience and care are required to determine the correct end-point in the titration of carbonate solutions with methyl orange.

At the end of the hour the beaker is removed from the flame, 5 c.c. normal hydrochloric acid added accurately from a buret and the stirring continued for five minutes or longer. The polychrome solution is poured from the beaker while hot into a 100-c.c. graduated cylinder and methyl alcohol (Merck Reagent or Kahlbaum acetone-free) added to make 100 c.c. A portion of the alcohol is used for removing the last traces of dye from the beaker and stirrer before it is added to the graduate. The contents of the graduated cylinder are then emptied into a 4-ounce bottle, and 0.25 gm. eosin (Grübler's yellowish, water-soluble), and 0.75 gm. methylene blue (Grübler's B.X.) added. Place the tightly stoppered bottle in the paraffin oven at 52°C. for one hour or more, and shake vigorously until solution is complete. Granules of some salt may precipitate on standing but no dye.

To use, 1 or 2 drops of the stain are added to each cubic centimeter of 0.003 normal sodium carbonate, and the cover-glass preparations that have been previously fixed are floated on the surface of the diluted stain for sixty minutes or longer. A small uncovered Stender dish, in which about 10 c.c. of the dilute carbonate solution have been placed, is convenient for staining cover-glasses. Slides are stained in the oblong dishes. In the winter, unless the room is warm and dry, it is better to carry out the staining in the incubator. The stained preparation is washed with distilled water, differentiated for one minute in one-fiftieth per cent. eosin, washed, dried in the air, and mounted in colophonium-xylol. The differentiation in eosin may be omitted and the preparation washed for five minutes under the tap. To fix the preparations, the smears whether on cover-glasses or slides are placed for from ten minutes to a week or more in methyl alcohol, or in equal parts of absolute ethyl alcohol and ether. The 0.003 normal sodium carbonate is prepared by placing exactly 15.0 c.c. decinormal sodium carbonate in a 500-c.c. volumetric flask and making up to volume.

A sample of Grübler's yellowish, water-soluble eosin that cannot be used is occasionally encountered. If the stain is made with such an eosin, red blood corpuscles stain a blue that cannot be washed out. When once an eosin that is satisfactory is found, it should be kept for this purpose. In no case can one grade of dye be substituted for another unless it is found to react in exactly the same way.

McJunkin's Blood Stain (Journal of the American Medical Association, 1915, Vol. lxv, p. 2164; obtained from B. & L. Opt. Co.).—This stain is used to color blood films for the differential counting of leukocytes and malarial organisms and other protozoa. It differs from the other polychrome blood stains in being uniform, due to an accurately adjusted reaction. To prepare the stain, add 150 c.c. methyl alcohol (Merck Reagent or Kahlbaum acetone-free) and 0.25 gm. eosin (Grübler's yellowish water-soluble) to 50 c.c. of the Mc-Junkin's Protozoon Stain.

In the titration to a definite alkalinity of the carbonate solution used in the preparation of the protozoon stain, and in the other volumetric manipulations, accuracy is required;

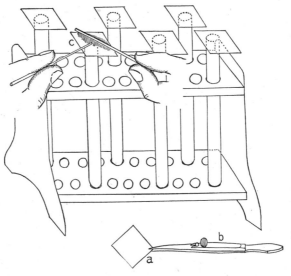

FIG. 8.—Staining of cover-glass preparations. *a*, 22 mm. square, number 1, fat-free cover-glass; *b*, Novy cover-glass forceps (B. & L. O. Co.); *c*, cover-glasses supported on the tops of small test-tubes (5 mm. diameter). This method saves time if a number of preparations are to be stained. The alcoholic stain is spread with a 1-mm. glass rod while the center of the cover is pressed upon by a second rod.

and this can be secured only by careful technic in weighing and measuring.

To apply the blood stain (Fig. 8) to unfixed blood films, use 22-mm. cover-glasses, and place 2 drops of the stain on a cover-glass held in suitable forceps for one-half minute. Add 4 drops of 0.0015 normal sodium carbonate, and allow the stain so diluted to act for from three to five minutes. Wash with distilled water until the film turns uniformly pink. On making or purchasing a new bottle of stain, trial stains should be made. If the nuclei stain faintly and bluish and the corpuscles are a deep red the stain has an insufficient alkalinity as the result of a faulty technic in the preparation of the volumetric solutions. If the corpuscles retain a deep blue color that does not wash out the stain is too alkaline. Such defective stains may possibly be used by altering the diluting carbonate solution, but it is better to discard the stain and to prepare it correctly.

As originally prepared the alkali in the protozoon stain was not neutralized at the completion of the polychroming process, but it has been found that after many months the stain deteriorates just as the other polychrome stains do unless the alkali is exactly neutralized. This necessitates the use of an alkaline diluting fluid but it is required for uniform results in staining.

Wright's stain which is widely used is applied in the same way as the writer's blood stain except that distilled water is used for diluting the stain instead of 0.0015 normal sodium carbonate.

Leukocytic Granule Stain (McJunkin; Archives of Internal Medicine, 1918, Vol. 22). The stain is based on an observation made by Graham (Jour. of Med. Res., 1916, Vol. xxx, New Series) that granules made prominent by solutions of alphanaphthol (oxydase or indophenol reaction) stain heavily with certain anilin dyes. The chief use of the stain is for the identification of endothelial leukocytes (page 72). The granules in the cytoplasm of endothelial leukocytes and cells and neutrophilic and eosinophilic granules are blue; nuclei are red.

The stain is made by treating the unfixed cover-glass film with 5 drops of the alphanaphthol-methyl-violet solution for thirty seconds, diluting with 5 drops of distilled water and staining five minutes. The stain is washed off, the preparation dried with filter paper, and counterstained for about two minutes with 0.01 per cent. basic fuchsin (Grübler). A 0.02 per cent. basic fuchsin solution may be used instead of distilled water for diluting the alphanaphthol-methyl-violet solution and the counterstaining with 0.01 per cent. fuchsin omitted but this does not give as clear a differentiation of structures.

The alphanaphthol-methyl-violet solution is made by dissolving 15 mg. methyl-violet 5 B (Grübler) and 0.2 gm. alphanaphthol (Merck Reagent) in 100 c.c. warm 80 per cent. alcohol (made from absolute ethyl alcohol Merck Reagent) and adding to this 0.2 c.c. commercial hydrogen peroxid. The hydrogen peroxid should be titrated with a standard solution of potassium permanganate to determine whether it contains approximately 3 per cent. of the gas.

In making differential counts, the cedar oil almost unavoidably spreads over the margin of the usual white label placed on the left end of the slide. It is preferable, therefore, to write the data on this end with a *glass marking fluid* that is not affected by alcohol, xylol, etc. This fluid is prepared by adding from 1 to 2 c.c. of a thick solution of sodium silicate (Merck) or commercial liquid glass to 30 c.c. black india ink (Dr. H. V. Ogden).

DIFFERENTIAL COUNTING OF LEUKOCYTES

The difficulties underlying the identification of cells in the peripheral blood stream cannot be emphasized too much. In the tissue, the grouping and functional activity of cells may be studied, and the morphologic characters of the different cells as brought out by stains may be compared with other known cells in the same tissue. Such comparisons are of first importance and cannot be practised on cells floating free in the blood plasma. The great advantage that exists is that more perfect stains may be made of cells from the blood than from any other tissue.

The prominence of neutrophilic, eosinophilic, and basophilic granules in leukocytes already characterized by polymorphous nuclei, the finding of identical cells in the bone-marrow, and the ability to trace the development of such cells from non-granular cells leaves little question in regard to the polymorphonuclear or myeloblastic leukocytes. Much more difficulty has been encountered in identifying cells in the mononuclear group. That the majority of the mononuclear cells are lymphocytes seems certain, owing to their morphologic and functional identity with the cells of lymphoid tissue and the presence of some of these cells in the large lymph-vessels. There are a certain number of mononuclear cells present, however, that have not been looked upon as lymphocytes; "transitional leukocytes" and large "mononuclear leukocytes" are two common terms that have been applied to the non-lymphoblastic cells of the mononuclear group.

"*Transitional leukocyte*" is a term commonly given to leukocytes that have a nucleus more or less horseshoe or saddleback in shape. The views of the origin and identification of this cell are almost as numerous as the publications on the subject. Most of the recent workers agree that this cell has granules with polychrome stains that cannot be readily differentiated from neutrophilic granules, that it has neutrophilic granules with Ehrlich's triacid stain, and that it gives the indophenol reaction.

The chief reason that this cell has not been considered an immature or young neutrophile (metamyelocyte so called) is that the neutrophilic myelocyte, which is the youngest granular form in the myeloblastic series, has a granulation in its cytoplasm more distinct than that present in the transitional leukocyte. If it were a transition or intermediate form between myelocyte and polymorphonuclear neutrophile, the granules in it would be more distinct and the cytoplasm more acidophilic than that of the myelocyte, which is younger and less mature. Another point frequently urged against the classification of this cell as one of the usual myeloblastic cells is that it is increased in diseases such as typhoid fever, in which a neutrophilic leukocytosis is not present. These cells are somewhat larger than neutrophiles, with a more or less deeply indented nucleus and cytoplasm that shows a neutrophilic granulation (Fig. 9 [34]).

Another common term in blood work is "*large mononuclear leukocyte.*" As in the case of the transitional cell, this term, in regard to the use of which there is little uniformity, is not a histologic one and gives no indication of the origin of the cell.

It differs from the transitional type especially in not having a horseshoe-shaped nucleus. As noted below (page 72), there is now proof at hand that most of the cells classified under these two terms (transitional and large mononuclear) arise from the endothelium of certain blood- and lymph-vessels. In the usual differential count the cells of the blood may, by employing special methods, be grouped as lymphocytes, endothelial leukocytes, neutrophiles, eosinophiles, and basophiles, rather than as lymphocytes, neutrophiles, eosinophiles, basophiles, transitionals, large mononuclears, immature neutrophiles, irritation forms, etc.

In the identification of cells for the differential classification there are a number of practical considerations. The drop of blood used for the smears is allowed to flow freely from the puncture so that it represents the blood in the capillaries. It is of such a size that the entire drop is spread out evenly on the two covers when they are separated, without any undue thickening of the film at the edges. The two covers are mounted on the same slide and both moved by means of a mechanical stage beneath the oil-immersion lens from right to left and left to right as the cells are identified. The endothelial leukocytes may be registered as seen by shifting with the left hand small objects such as pennies; the eosinophiles and basophiles are marked on the paper as encountered; and the number of lymphocytes and neutrophiles kept in mind until about fifty of the latter have been enumerated, when all are recorded on the paper. It is not advisable to keep a mental record of more than two kinds of cells. Certainly no less than 200 leukocytes should be counted, and for accuracy it is advisable to count 500 from three pairs of cover-glasses.

At the present time it is necessary to use the leukocytic granule stain (page 55) in order to identify the endothelial leukocytes. No cell is enumerated that is so crushed that it cannot be accurately identified. Such cells are especially noticeable in smears of leukemic blood, on account of the large number present, and are frequently spoken of erroneously as "degeneration forms." A slight error may be introduced in this way if one form of cell is more subject to crushing than another. This can be overcome only by making the smears so that as few cells are crushed as possible.

Lymphoblastic Cells (Fig. 9 [21 to 25]). These cells arise in the germinal centers of lymph nodules by mitosis, become differentiated as they are pushed toward the periphery of the nodules, and finally gain entrance to the blood stream by way of the large lymphatic trunks, or by migration through the vessel walls. Under certain conditions (lymphatic leukemia) the larger and younger form of cell (lymphoblast) may be found in the peripheral circulation, since time has not elapsed for complete differentiation of the cells in the lymphoid tissue; or mitosis may even take place in the blood stream in such cases. The cytoplasm of these young cells—which are spoken of as lymphoblasts in distinction to the older ones or *lymphocytes*—is is more reticular than the lymphocytes, and it forms a wider rim about the nucleus (Fig. 9 [24]); but the entire cell is larger. The cells are otherwise like the lymphocytes. *Plasma cells* (Fig. 9 [22]) are but rarely found in the peripheral blood. The only unquestioned example coming under personal observation in which plasma cells were present in the blood films in considerable number was a case of chronic appendicitis. In sections, the recognition of plasma cells is easy; but in smears, artefacts due to the spreading of the films must be ruled out. The presence of lymphoblasts indicates a very active proliferation of lymphoid tissue.

The identification of the lymphocyte, which is the usual form of lymphoblastic cell found in the blood, depends largely on negative properties. The nucleus, as in the identification of all cells, is of less importance than the cytoplasm. It is round, usually lies in the center of the cell, and the chromatin tends to be arranged in small pyramidal masses just within the nuclear membrane. The cytoplasm of the lymphocyte is a robin's-egg blue if spread out somewhat, or a sky blue if the rim of cytoplasm about the nucleus is narrow (Fig. 9 [23]). Near the nucleus in lymphoblastic cells, a minute acidophilic area that contains two granules (centrosomes) may be seen.

The cytoplasm is usually entirely homogeneous; but, if the preparation is overstained with a polychrome stain, minute granules thickly peppered in may be seen. With proper fixation and staining with acid fuchsin paranuclear granules (Schridde) are in evidence. In the lymphocytes with the more abundant cytoplasm, and especially in those in which the nucleus is eccentric, azur granules staining purple with the usual polychrome blood stain may be present. The lymphocyte has some ameboid activity. It has no phagocytic properties.

In the usual cover-glass smears stained with a good polychrome stain, as many as 30 per cent. of the lymphocytes may show discrete and rather coarse reddish granules (azur granules), usually under twelve in number. They stain like the nucleus, and it is possible that they are particles of nuclear material. It is stated that the lymphocytes of lymph-nodes do not show these granules; but smears from lymph-nodes, made so thin that the lymphocytes are the same size as those of the blood films, have lymphocytes with the azur granules. Much of the rather abundant light staining cytoplasm of the larger forms, which are most likely to have azur granules, is due to the pressing out of the cells on the glass; and the size of the lymphocytes (Fig. 9 [24 and 25]) in smears may vary from that of a neutrophile to that of a red blood corpuscle.

The relative percentage of lymphocytes in the adult may vary normally between 20 and 30 per cent. with an average of about 25 per cent. In children under five years of age there are usually more lymphocytes than there are myeloblastic cells, and in infants (a few months old) the ratio of polymorphonuclears to mononuclears may be 3 to 7, instead of the usual 7 to 3 ratio seen in adults. The diseases in which there is said to be an absolute increase in the number of leukocytes are mostly in children. There is need for more investigation in regard to such increases. The one condition in which there is no question about a great increase in the total number of lymphocytes in the blood is lymphatic leukemia. Typhoid fever, malaria, tuberculosis, measles, pertussis, influenza, syphilis, diphtheria, intestinal diseases of children, and rickets

Fig. 9.—Cells drawn to same scale with camera lucida, making the comparative size of the cells and structures exact. All preparations stained with a polychrome blood stain except the two cells at the right in group 34.

Erythrocytes. 11, Normocytes; 12, a group of corpuscles from a case of secondary anemia containing normocyte, microcyte and macrocyte; 13, group from a case of lead poisoning showing one "stippled" corpuscle and one with basophilia; 14, group of poikilocytes from secondary anemia; 15, 16 and 17, normoblast microblast and megaloblast respectively from a case of pernicious anemia.

Lymphoblastic Cells from Smears of Normal and Leukemic Blood. 21, Two lymphocytes (normal blood). The larger one has "azur" granules; 22, a lymphocyte with slightly indented nucleus (normal blood) and a plasma cell. The latter drawn from the blood of a case of chronic appendicitis; 23, two rather large lymphocytes (normal blood); 24, a group of four lymphoblastic cells from a case of lymphatic leukemia. The two lower ones are of a type not often seen in normal blood and correspond to the large lymphoblasts seen in the germinal centers of lymph nodules; 25, a group from a different part of the well-spread cover-glass preparation from which 24 is drawn. Note the great difference in size resulting from the smearing-out process. This serves to illustrate the necessity of comparing cells with others in the immediate vicinity rather than on a distant portion of the preparation and the absurdity of adopting absolute measurements for cells in any sort of smear.

Myeloblastic Cells and Endothelial Leukocytes from Smears of Normal Blood. 31, Two neutrophiles and one of the so-called irritation cells of Türk. The last named cell from blood from a case of typhoid fever during the second week of the disease. This cell does not appear to be of myeloblastic origin because no myelocytes are present in the peripheral blood. It is held by some to be a young lymphoblastic cell but it is not certain that some of these are not endothelial leukocytes. 32, Eosinophile, basophile and a blood platelet pseudopodium; 33, a group from myelogeneous leukemia with one myeloblast (no granules), two neutrophilic myelocytes and one neutrophile; 34, two endothelial leukocytes on the left stained with polychrome blood stain and on the right one neutrophile and one endothelial leukocyte stained with leukocytic granule stain. Note the large dark granules in the neutrophile. The morphology of the endothelial leukocyte is shown in Fig. 11.

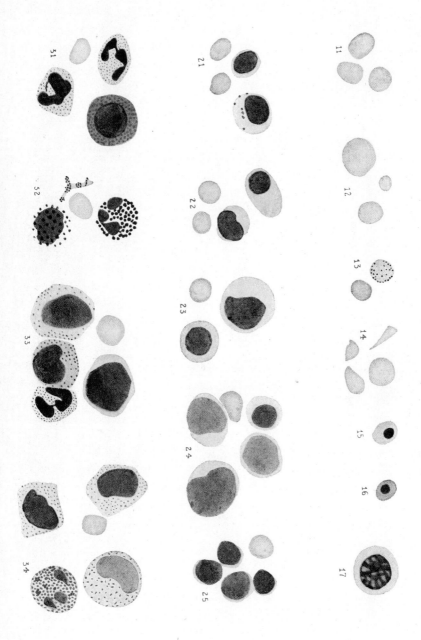

are common diseases in which there is said to be a relative lymphocytosis. Type case: female child, four years old. Summer diarrhea. Leukocytes 13,500 of which 52 per cent. are lymphocytes. Type case: man, thirty-two years old. Typhoid fever. Leukocytes 6,400; lymphocytes 36.6; transitionals (probably endothelial leukocytes) 11 per cent.; neutrophiles 48.6 per cent.; eosinophiles 2.1 per cent.; basophiles 0.4 and irritation forms 1.3 per cent. It seems certain that the older counts are of value only in so far as they show a relative and frequently an absolute increase in the number of mononuclear cells. To determine in which of these diseases the lymphocytes are increased will require investigation by a method (page 55) that will separate the mononuclear cells into the two classes of lymphocytes and endothelial leukocytes. At present, one can only speak of an increase in the mononuclear cells in the above-mentioned diseases.

A division into *large and small lymphocytes* is often made, but such a classification appears to have little value. That cells become smaller as they grow older, due to a shrinkage of both nucleus and cytoplasm, is a well recognized change. Exceptions to this are seen when cells swell up under pathologic conditions, and when they accumulate substances such as fat or hyaline material, or ingest by phagocytosis foreign material like fat or other cells. In fresh preparations, the smaller ones are the older ones; but in films, and especially in very thin films, any lymphocyte may be smeared out so that it is a large cell; but when the large size is produced in this way the entire cell is likely to be lightly stained and the cytoplasm frequently becomes polygonal in shape, and shows depressions produced by contact with corpuscles or leukocytes.

Leukemia.—Peripheral blood may be easily obtained for examination and the early blood workers noted conditions in which 100,000 or more leukocytes per cubic millimeter were present. The term leukemia was applied. Later, with improved technic, lymphoblastic cells were found to predominate in some cases; while in others those of myeloblastic origin were found to dominate the blood picture. The second important feature of the condition is that immature cells not normally present in the peripheral blood appear there.

It was not until extensive studies were made on the organs and tissues of leukemic cases that many observers came to regard the leukemias as malignant neoplasms. The study of cases of malignant disease (lymphoblastoma), before and after the entrance of tumor cells in large numbers into the peripheral blood, aided in this conception. Whatever the ultimate solution of tumor etiology may be, it is likely that the leukemias shall remain as typical examples of true tumors.

Lymphoblastoma.—This is a malignant tumor of the lymphoblast, and it may arise in any tissue or organ in which there is lymphoid tissue. It most commonly arises from the cervical, axillary, mediastinal, inguinal or retroperitoneal lymph-nodes. When the tumor cells gain entrance to the blood and proliferate there in large numbers a *lymphatic leukemia* is said to exist. This tumor, unlike the myeloblastoma (*myelogenous leukemia*), may never form metastases in the blood stream, and develop there to give great absolute increases of lymphocytes per cubic millimeter of blood; that is, there is an *aleukemic lymphoblastoma* to which such terms as lymphosarcoma, lymphoma, lymphocytoma, and pseudoleukemia have been applied. Recently two cases of marked glandular enlargement in neck, axilla, and groin, and with leukocyte counts below 10,000 came under personal observation. Within approximately six months both patients presented a typical lymphatic leukemia, with a leukocyte count above 100,000 of which 96 per cent. were lymphocytes.

This tumor metastasizes in the same organs as the myeloblastoma, but the bone-marrow changes which are not due to proliferation of myeloblastic cells but to the proliferation of lymphoblasts are usually not so marked in the lymphatic type. The anemia in the lymphatic type may be very severe with the appearance in the blood of numerous nucleated red cells. The lymph-gland involvement is likely to be more pronounced in the lymphatic type, while the spleen reaches its greatest size in the myelogenous variety. In the more chronic cases of both tumors, there is no difficulty in diagnosis; either type, however, may run an acute course, and in such cases the diagnosis may be difficult or even impossible. It is better to speak of such conditions as an *acute leukemia*, and to defer a diagnosis until the condition becomes less acute and the cells older and more differentiated. The young myeloblast averages somewhat larger than the young lymphoblast. The indophenol reaction in such cases may aid, but the youngest myeloblastic cells do not color typically. Most of such cases rapidly progress to a fatal termination and a positive diagnosis is not made. Type case: male, seventeen years old. Rapid onset with high temperature, nosebleed, enlargement of the cervical glands, ulceration about the gums and a marked anemia with a fatal termination in four and a half weeks. Hemoglobin 32 per cent.; corpuscles 1,268,000, leukocytes 41,000 of which only 4.8 per cent. of the cells (neutrophiles) are identified, the others being young cells that correspond to lymphoblasts or myeloblasts. An occasional definite neutrophilic myelocyte is present. Mitoses are present in the tumor cells. Of course in such a case if practically no cells give the indophenol reaction and a considerable number appear to be unquestionable lymphocytes a diagnosis of *acute lymphatic leukemia* may be returned.

The clinical picture and the blood in *chronic lymphatic leukemia* are quite characteristic. Type case: male, fifty-two years old. Swellings in neck and axilla for two and one-half years, which have become much larger during the past year; spleen is enlarged; only moderate cachexia. Hemoglobin 110 per cent.; corpuscles 5,208,000; leukocytes 73,000 with 5.3 per cent. neutrophiles; 0.4 "transitionals" and eosinophiles, and the remainder lymphocytes. A few myelocytes are seen. The platelets are moderately increased in number. Although numerous typical small lymphocytes are present, the great majority of cells correspond to lymphoblasts. Very thin smears are required to bring out the characters of the cells (Fig. 9 [24]). Owing to the great number of the cells and also, perhaps, as a result of their being more fragile than normal, the nucleus and cytoplasm often cannot be distinguished; with the result that the cell appears as a diffuse, irregular, and lightly staining nuclear mass. These crushed cells are not present in carefully prepared fresh preparations, and it is incorrect to speak of them as degeneration forms of leukocytes.

Hodgkin's Disease.—This is a clinical term that was originally applied to chronic glandular enlargements conforming to those described in the original clinical description. As the result of subsequent histologic and experimental research, certain forms of tuberculosis were excluded. As used clinically today, the tendency is to apply the term to malignant (terminating fatally) chronic glandular enlargements of unknown etiology. Tuberculosis must be ruled out in each case, if necessary by guinea-pig inoculation. Occasionally, malignant enargments and tuberculosis may be present in the same case. The most important single feature of these cases is that all presenting the typical histologic picture end fatally within a few years. Mitoses of cells are more numerous than they are in any inflammatory conditions of like chronicity, which indicates that the condition is a malignant tumor. Identification of the type of cell has not been conclusive. Many cells that appear to be of the lymphoblastic series are in mitosis. A large multinucleated cell commonly present is not clearly of this series of cells; but morphologically resembles large cells found in the germinal centers of lymph-nodes. In many ways the cells in mitosis resemble endothelial cells and endothelial leukocytes.

A recurring leukocytosis is common, and the non-lymphoblastic mononuclear cells of the blood appear to be greatly increased in number, but the identification of these cells has been very unsatisfactory. An examination to determine the phagocytic properties of mononuclear cells is indicated; and a stain (page 55) must be used that differentiates endothelial leukocytes from other forms.

Myeloblastic Cells (Fig. 9 [31 to 34]).—The young cells (myeloblasts) of this series which are found normally only in the bone-marrow are microscopically much like the young lymphoblasts found normally in the germinal centers of lymph nodules. They average somewhat larger in size, may give the indophenol reaction, and do not show the paranuclear acid-fuchsin granules (page 60) that lymphoblasts may show. However, the only certain means of identification rests on the further differentiation of the young cells which in the case of the myeloblasts consists of the appearance of one of three varieties of granules in the cytoplasm. The youngest mononuclear cells containing granules are known as *myelocytes*. The transition form between the parent myeloblast of the bone-marrow and the *neutrophile, eosinophile*, and *basophile* of the blood is the myelocyte of the bone-marrow, which is neutrophilic, eosinophilic, or basophilic according to the variety of granules in the cytoplasm. The myeloblastic cells normally remain in the bone-marrow until they have become fully developed into mature polymorphonuclear leukocytes. The recognition of the eosinophilic and] basophilic myelocyte offers no difficulties on account of the large and conspicuously colored granules. In fact the cytoplasm of all the mature myeloblastic cells possesses so typical an appearance, due to the presence of cytoplasmic granules, that there is no difficulty in classifying them. The development of these mature cells from non-granular young forms may be followed so conclusively in bone-marrow smears and sections that there is little question about their origin.

There is scarcely any other cell in which so perfect a differentiation may be traced. The observations may be made on smears of bone-marrow, but smears of the blood of cases of myelogenous leukemia, in which condition the young forms of the cell enter the peripheral blood, are even better. The non-granular myeloblast has a diameter one-third greater than the neutrophile, and the size of the myelocyte is about the same, but the size may be greatly increased by the smearing out process when the cover-glasses are pulled apart. The first granules that appear in a myeloblast may be few in number and present an indefinite staining reaction. Such cells have been spoken of as *promyelocytes;* and later, when the coloring of the granules becomes typical, they are then one or another of the three varieties of myelocytes according to the kind of granules. As the myelocytes grow older to become neutrophiles, eosinophiles

5

and basophiles, the cytoplasm becomes less basophilic and more acidophilic with some shrinkage of the granules, which are placed more closely as the result of the smaller amount of cytoplasm. The nucleus also shrinks and becomes more pyknotic. The contracting nucleus does not remain spherical, as the nuclei of lymphoblastic cells do as they become older, but at one or more points an indentation takes place, and quite rapidly the nucleus shrinks to the true form of a horseshoe and becomes constricted into lobules disconnected or connected by filaments of nuclear material. The form with the dense horseshoe nucleus that has not separated into masses connected by filaments has been called a *metamyelocyte*. If the so-called metamyelocytes were frequently present in pathologic blood, it would not be possible to estimate by the polychrome staining methods even the approximate number of endothelial leukocytes, because the two cells when compared side by side in the blood of cases of myelogenous leukemia cosely resemble each other, although the less pyknotic nucleus of the endothelial leukocyte has a kidney shape and the cytoplasm is less acidophilic. However, the leukocytic granule stain (page 55) makes the differentiation certain.

Some workers (Arneth) attach diagnostic and prognostic importance to the number of lobules in the polymorphonuclear neutrophile. The view that the number of nuclear parts increases with the age of the cell is not entirely correct, and proof of this may be obtained by the incubation from one to four days, of the leukocytic layer obtained by adding under aseptic conditions 3 c.c. of blood to 2 c.c. of 3.8 per cent. sodium citrate and centrifuging. The number of nuclear masses increases during incubation under such optimum conditions until five to eight appear, after which some of them dissolve and the oldest cells may contain single spherical masses. It is therefore doubtful if a classification of the neutrophiles according to the number of nuclear masses in them is of use.

Neutrophiles (Polymorphonuclear Neutrophiles).—Neutrophilic granules appear in the cytoplasm of at least 95 per cent. of the myeloblasts in the way indicated above, so that the neutrophiles constitute 60 to 75 per cent. of the total number of white cells in normal blood (4,500 to 6,000 per cubic millimeter). These cells are twice the size of erythrocytes, and the pyknotic masses of nuclear material are usually connected by filaments. This leukocyte is an end product of differentiation, and mitosis does not take place. It is ameboid and especially phagocytic for bacteria.

A *neutrophilic leukocytosis* (neutrophilic hyperleukocytosis) is due most commonly to infection with pyogenic organisms and has been discussed in connection with white cell counts. The absolute number of white cells may be increased even to 50,000 per cubic millimeter with above 90 per cent. neutrophiles. Counts that show more than 8,000 neutrophiles per cubic millimeter making 80 per cent. of the total number of leukocytes usually indicate a pathologic increase. This percentage places the number of leukocytes above 10,000 with a relative and absolute increase in the number of neutrophiles. In infections with very virulent organisms such as hemolytic streptococcus the total number of white cells may be diminished with 90 per cent. neutrophiles. In this case there is a marked *relative increase in neutrophiles* while the total or absolute number may be even decreased. Such a count taken in connection with the clinical condition of the patient may give an indication of a very severe toxemia. A relative *neutrophilic leukopenia* is present in those cases in which there is a relative lymphocytosis. In a neutrophilic leukocytosis the relative and often the absolute numbers of lymphocytes, eosinophiles, and basophiles are decreased. Type case: male, twenty-four years old. Resolving pneumococcic lobar pneumonia, pleuritis and pericarditis. Leukocytes, 38,000 with 91 per cent. neutrophiles. Blood platelets are greatly increased. The neutrophilic granules are larger and more prominent than normal which may indicate that the cells are comparatively young. Type case: child, two years old. Otitis media (streptococcus). Leukocytes 15,500 with 54 per cent. neutrophiles. While there is an absolute increase in the number of neutrophiles in the case, there is also a great increase in the number of mononuclear cells. Whether the increase in mononuclear cells is due to lymphocytes or to endothelial leukocytes was not determined. Type case: male, sixty-four years old. Carcinoma of the prostate with metastases in all the bones examined. Hemoglobin 46 per cent.; corpuscles 2,480,000; leukocytes 16,200 of which 83 per cent. are neutrophiles and 2.6 per cent. myelocytes.

Eosinophiles.—The differentiation of the myeloblasts into eosinophilic myelocytes and finally into eosinophiles is much like the differentiation of neutrophiles from neutrophilic myelocytes, except that the granules are entirely different (large, bright red with eosin; blue with leukocytic granule stain with center light and refractive) and the nucleus of the end-stage cell more often consists of one or more separate spherical masses rather than of the polymorphous nucleus connected by filaments seen in neutrophiles. The eosinophiles which average somewhat larger than the neutrophiles are ameboid, do not ingest foreign material by phagocytosis, and do not undergo mitosis. The percentage in the blood varies normally between 0.5 and 6 per cent. An increase above 6 per cent. may be looked upon as an eosinophilia. Eosinophilia as usually understood refers to the relative number of these cells as determined by the differential count.

An *eosinophilia* is seen in bronchial asthma, various skin diseases, and in helminthiasis. The absolute number of eosinophiles is greatly increased in myelogenous leukemia. In malignant growths such as lymphoblastoma involving the bone-marrow the eosinophiles are usually increased. They may be increased in osteomyelitis. After a positive tuberculin test the number of eosinophiles may be increased. During the recovery from infectious diseases increases in the eosinophilic counts have been recorded. In a number of conditions such as Hodgkin's disease, epidermoid cancer of the lip, epidermoid cancer of the cervix uteri, or healing appendicitis in which local accumulations of eosinophiles in the pathologic tissue take place there is no eosinophilia. Type case: male, twenty-nine years old. Trichiniasis. Leukocytes 16,000 with 43 per cent. eosinophiles.

Basophiles.—(Fig. 9 [32]).—The number of myeloblasts that become basophiles is small, the percentage usually being below 0.5. Occasionally an apparently normal blood may show 1.5 per cent. of basophiles. The cells are the size of the neutrophiles and in their cytoplasm there are large discrete basophilic granules, staining purple with the polychrome blood stains and a red with the leukocytic granule stain. The nucleus is much like that of the eosinophile, but more frequently consists of a single mass which may be in the form of a rosette. The development through the myelocytic stage is much like that of the eosinophile except in the character of the granules. Owing to the large size of the granules and their staining reaction they are seen to overlie the nucleus where the cytoplasm has been flattened out on the top of this structure.

A *basophilia* may be present in Asiatic cholera in the sense that the absolute number per cubic millimeter is increased but this is due to the concentration of all the cellular elements of the blood. The total number of basophiles is greatly increased in myelogenous leukemia. There are several local conditions, such as leiomyoma of the uterus, in which there is an infiltration of the tissue with mast-cells. There is no material increase of basophiles in the blood in these cases, and it is uncertain whether mast-cells and the basophiles of the blood stream and bone-marrow are identical.

Myeloblastoma or Myelogenous Leukemia.—These two terms are practically synonymous because a myeloblastoma— tumor arising from the myeloblast or parent cell of the granular leukocytes—always forms a metastasis in the blood stream where the tumor cells proliferate extensively. That is, this cell finds conditions in the blood stream suitable for its growth, while the great excess of these cells formed in the bone-marrow and other tissues find their way into the blood just as they do when produced in the bone-marrow in normal numbers. The metastasis in the blood (leukemia) is delayed somewhat in the form of myeloblastoma known as *chloroma*. The number of white cells in the blood (100,000 to 1,500,000) is often greater than in lymphatic leukemia. They consist not only of the mature cells (neutrophiles, eosinophiles, and basophiles) but of the earlier forms of these leukocytes, namely, myeloblasts, promyelocytes and neutrophilic, eosinophilic and basophilic myelocytes and metamyelocytes. Although the number of platelets is enormously increased, the coagulation time of the blood may be prolonged. Frequently the relative percentage of eosinophiles or basophiles is greater than in normal blood, and cases may be met with in which the granules are very irregular in size and staining reaction and no typical neutrophilic myelocytes are present. In the average case there is a moderate *secondary anemia* (low color-index), but the number of nucleated red cells present is large and all stages of dissolution of these cells with formation of corpuscles may be seen. The duration of the disease may be a number of years, and the relative number of the different cells varies in different cases. Since the blood cell formed is subject to much greater variation in children than in adults more care must be used in interpreting the blood findings in early life. The count is reduced by treatment with x-ray, benzol, or arsenic, and by sepsis. Cases may come under observation when the count is normal or even when there is a leukopenia and at this time the diagnosis must be made by identifying the immature myeloblastic cells present.

Type case: ill for three years; enlargement of spleen noted two years ago, at which time diagnosis of myelogenous leukemia was made by examination of blood smears. Hemoglobin 75 per cent.; corpuscles 3,700,000; leukocytes 285,000; neutrophiles 4.1 per cent.; myelocytes 39.3 per cent.; lymphocytes 2.3 per cent.; eosinophiles 3.8 per cent.; basophiles 10.8 per cent.; endothelial leukocytes 2.7 per cent. The number of platelets is greatly increased. Many normoblasts are present.

The tumor cells infiltrate all organs, but tumor nodules consisting of myeloblastic cells are found especially in the marrow of the long bones, and in the spleen, liver, lymph-nodes, and intestine. As a result of the proliferation of the tumor cells in the vessels and extravascular tissue of the spleen

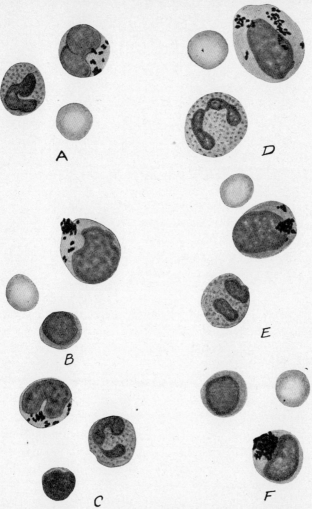

FIG. 11.—Endothelial Leukocytes. Reproduced with permission from Archives of Internal Medicine. Cells from normal human blood after incubation with a carbon suspension. *A*, Group consisting of neutrophile, erythrocyte and endothelial leukocyte with ingested carbon; outline of the phagocytic cell is a broken curve; *B*, lymphocyte, erythrocyte and endothelial leukocyte with irregular nucleus; *C*, lymphocyte, neutrophile and endothelial leukocyte with saddleback nucleus; *D*, neutrophile, erythrocyte and endothelial leukocyte. Note that all elements in this part of the smear are large. The nucleus of the carbon-containing cell is oval; *E*, erythrocyte, neutrophile and endothelial leukocyte with oval nucleus; *F*, erythrocyte, lymphocyte and endothelial leukocyte. The phagocytic cell resembles the lymphocyte morphologically.

this organ becomes enormously enlarged which has led to introduction of the term *splenomyelogenous leukemia.*

Endothelial Leukocytes (Fig. 9 [34] and Fig. 11).—The average number of these cells found in thirty-four counts of normal
blood is 5 per cent. (Archives of Internal Medicine, 1918, Vol.
22, 1918).

The cells lining blood- and lymph-vessels are spoken of as
endothelial cells, while those cells that separate from the vessel
wall and become extravascular, or float free in the blood or
lymph stream, are known as *endothelial leukocytes.* It appears
that few, if any, of these leukocytes arise from the flattened
and highly differentiated cells that line the heart and large
and medium sized blood-vessels. In pathologic processes in
human tissue (lesions of the skin in measles [Mallory], typhoid
lesions) two or more mitoses of the endothelial cells lining a
small arteriole and the migration of a similar cell through the
wall of the vessel may be brought into a single oil-immersion
field. Such vessels do not lengthen, and the cells formed in
this way become free. Conclusive proof of the origin of endothelial leukocytes is furnished by the injection of experimental animals with a suspension of carbon (American Journal of Anatomy, in Press). No cells, except those lining
small blood-vessels and those of similar morphology in the blood
stream, ingest the carbon in quantity. In organs (liver,
spleen and lung), mitoses of endothelial cells containing the carbon are present and there is no extravascular lesion that might
permit a lengthening of the vessel. That is, the cells arising
in this way enter the blood stream.

Identification of the myeloblastic (polymorphonuclear) leukocytes, as pointed out above, is not difficult; but the separation
of the mononuclear leukocytes into groups has been unsatisfactory. With the usual polychrome blood stains no accurate
separation of the mononuclear cells can be made, but after incubation of the whole blood with carbon suspensions a differentiation into lymphocytes (non-phagocytic) and endothelial leukocytes (phagocytic) is possible. By the leukocytic granule
stain (page 55) these cells may be identified. There is no

evidence of the existence of a variety of cells in the peripheral human blood besides the lymphocyte, endothelial leukocyte, and the three myeloblastic cells.

The endothelial leukocyte averages slightly larger than the neutrophile, but variations in size are marked. The nucleus is usually eccentric and the contour a broken curve but it may be centrally placed and round or oval. The slightly basophilic cytoplasm (bluish tinge with polychrome stain) usually contains granules identical with or closely resembling the neutrophilic granules (Fig. 9 [34]). Its phagocytic properties *in vitro* and *in vivo* characterize it (Fig. 11).

This leukocyte may be identified by the leukocytic granule stain. The nuclei of all the leukocytes are red; those of the endothelial leukocytes stain less heavily than the nuclei of other leukocytes. The eosinophilic granules are blue with an unstained center so that they appear ring-like. The basophilic granules are red. The neutrophilic granules are large, colored a dense blue and very thickly placed while the granules in the endothelial leukocytes are blue, less heavy and discretely placed. The presence of the distinct bluish granules in a mononuclear leukocyte makes its identification as an endothelial leukocyte certain. The cytoplasm of the lymphocytes is red and non-granular or has an indefinite reddish granulation. The platelets which are stained an even red are rather faint.

Phagocytic Method for the Enumeration of Endothelial Leukocytes in Blood (Archives of Internal Medicine, 1918, Vol. xxi, p. 59). This method is based on the ability of the leukocytes of endothelial origin to ingest carbon when placed in a suspension of carbon particles at the body temperature. A small test-tube, 45 mm. long, is prepared from glass tubing with a 6-mm. lumen; and four glass beads, 2 mm. in diameter, and 8 mg. of a citrate-lampblack powder are placed in it. One cubic centimeter of water is added, and the upper surface of the liquid is marked by a file scratch. The tube and beads are cleansed and dried, the beads together with 8 mg. of the lampblack-citrate powder that has been weighed accurately on analytic balances placed in it, and the blood dropped into the tube from the finger until the file scratch is reached. A wire in the shape of the inverted letter V is placed in the upper end of the tube, and the drops of blood as they are pressed out freely and rapidly from the finger after puncture with an automatic lance are brought into contact with the apex of this wire. The tube is stoppered with a rubber cork and vigorously shaken for one minute. After centrifugation at a moderate speed for fifteen minutes, the tube is placed in the incubator at 37.5°C. for thirty minutes, care being taken not to disturb the leukocytic layer. It is removed from the incubator, shaken vigorously for one minute, recentrifuged and re-incubated. Cover-glass films are made by placing a small drop of the blood on a cover-glass from a millimeter capillary pipet with nipple-bulb attached. The films are stained with polychrome blood stain or preferably with the leukocytic granule stain.

The lampblack-citrate powder is prepared by thoroughly mixing 7.6 gm. fine sodium citrate (Merck U. S. P.) with 0.4 gm. lampblack that has been ground in a mortar for thirty minutes. This concentration of citrate prevents most of the neutrophiles from ingesting the carbon. The disadvantage of the method is that even by a second centrifugation and incubation all of the leukocytes are not brought into contact with the carbon so that all of the endothelial leukocytes have not ingested the carbon.

In malaria, typhoid fever, measles, tuberculosis, and Hodgkin's disease increases in "transitional leukocytes" have been reported. As indicated (page 58) cells of this type are endothelial leukocytes.

Irritation Forms of Leukocytes (Türk).—During the active stage of typhoid fever cells are present in the peripheral blood that are not present in normal blood and that are unusual in pathologic conditions. These cells are larger than the neutrophiles and larger than any of the lymphocytes excepting the young lymphoblasts. The cytoplasm is a deep blue, and blue nodal points are apparent which give the cytoplasm a richly staining reticular appearance that is different from the homogeneous appearance of the lymphocytic cytoplasm (Fig. 9 [31]). The nucleus is usually round and centrally placed. The greatest number coming under personal observation was 2.4 per cent. in a case of typhoid fever during the second week of the disease. These cells cannot be of the myeloblastic series because the cytoplasm is non-granular and no myelocytes are present in the blood. Some of them may be young lymphoblasts, but they correspond more closely to endothelial leukocytes. These cells which are not found in normal blood and are given here as a class in a tentative way are said to be present in the blood after various severe inflammatory processes other than typhoid fever.

Platelets (Fig. 9 [32]).—These elements, about one-third the diameter of a red blood corpuscle but often with long processes, are detached portions of megakaryocyte pseudopodia. Frequently leaf-like structures are present. They occur singly, but more often in small groups, and when increased form large masses. When stained with a polychrome blood stain, they are bluish, with purplish granules toward the center. There are 250,000 to 500,000 per cubic millimeter. Perhaps the best method of estimating their number is by comparison with the corpuscles in properly stained smears on cover-glasses. The normal ratio between platelets and erythrocytes has an average of about 1 to 12. In order to prevent the collection or agglutination of the platelets to form large granular or hyaline masses in which they cannot be counted accurately it is necessary to place a drop of Hayem's fluid on the finger, puncture through this and make the smears from the blood diluted in this way. Another method is to wipe off a skin surface with 14 per cent. magnesium sulphate, express a drop of blood, draw the blood to the mark in the red hemocytometer pipet, and then dilute to the upper mark with the magnesium sulphate solution, when the platelets may be enumerated in the counting-chamber in the same way as erythrocytes.

In certain severe anemias where there is delayed clotting, these elements are diminished and in all cases in which an aplastic bone-marrow is present at autopsy they are below normal. In chronic myelogenous leukemia and in conditions (pneumonia, erysipelas, rheumatic fever, and other infections) in which the tendency to clot is augmented, the number of platelets is increased.

PROTOZOA IN BLOOD FILMS (Fig. 10)

Protozoa are frequently possessed of motility that is highly characteristic; and a fresh preparation (page 33) is examined whenever possible. Malarial parasites, trypanosomes, and the treponemata of relapsing fever are searched for with the high-dry or oil-immersion lens in a preparation made by dropping a cover-glass on a small drop of blood on a slide. The demonstration of malarial organisms in the blood is of considerable practical importance. A polychrome stain is best for the demonstration of these parasites in dry films, the chromatin of the parasites staining red in contrast to the blue of the cytoplasm. In order to stain the parasites heavily for the study of structure, a polychrome protozoon stain is used.

Malarial Parasites.—In general, protozoa in smears of blood, or in smears made up mostly of blood, are most successfully stained by a polychrome blood stain; but heavier chromatin staining is secured by using a polychrome protozoon stain. Parasites in fresh preparations, except those approaching the stage of segmentation, show ameboid movements. The pigment is in active motion. There is yet considerable discussion among protozoologists in regard to the classification and number of parasites concerned in the production of human malaria. Clinically, attacks of chills and fever occur every forty-eight hours (tertian fever), every seventy-two hours (quartan fever) or they occur at irregular intervals and are more or less continuous (estivo-autumnal fever). These attacks are produced by the simultaneous sporulation (schizogony) of great numbers of the plasmodia, which is due to the fact that development starts at the time the organisms were inoculated into the individual by the mosquito, and progresses to give crops of parasites of the same age. The general opinion is that the three clinical types are produced by three kinds of parasites.

FIG. 10.—*Parasites of Tertian Malaria (P. Vivax)*. Drawn from cover-glass preparations which were made from blood of the same individual. 11, Normocytes; 12 and 13, young (ring or hyaline) forms of the parasite in corpuscles somewhat larger than normal. Note the blood platelets on the right-hand blood corpuscle in 13. 14, 15 and 16 show the developing parasite while 17 and 18 show its segmentation. All the parasites except the youngest one (12) show dark pigment granules belonging to the parasite and contained within them. The corpuscle about the parasite frequently contains fine uniform granules which are brought out by staining and are known as Schüffner's granules.

Parasites of Estivo-Autumnal Malaria (P. Falciparum). Drawn from a single cover-glass preparation. 21, Two young forms of the parasite and a nucleated red cell. Note that the corpuscles containing the parasites are about the average size; 22, two young parasites in a single corpuscle (multiple infection) and a fully developed parasite (crescent). Group was drawn from two separate fields.

Parasites of Quartan Malaria (P. Malariæ). Drawn from a single cover-glass preparation. 23, Young form; 24, and 25, older forms; 26, segmenting form. In both estivo-autumnal and quartan the corpuscles containing parasites average smaller than those not infected while in tertian the infected ones are larger. The pigment granules of the quartan parasites are coarser than those in the tertian and estivo-autumnal.

Protozoa and Treponemata (Except 35). Drawn from five different smears with camera lucida. 31, Trypanosome gambiense from a cover-glass preparation made from the blood of a guinea-pig infected with the parasite recovered from a case of sleeping sickness; 32, leismania infantum from a cover-glass preparation made from a splenic smear from a dog infected with the parasite recovered from a case of infantile leismaniosis (Northern Africa). Leismania donovani (Kala-azar) and l. Tropicum (Delhi boil, etc.) morphologically are like this parasite; 33, treponema obermeirei from a rat infected with blood from a case of European relapsing fever; 34, treponema pallidum from a hard chancre; 35, Negri bodies from ganglion cell of the brain of a dog infected with "street rabies."

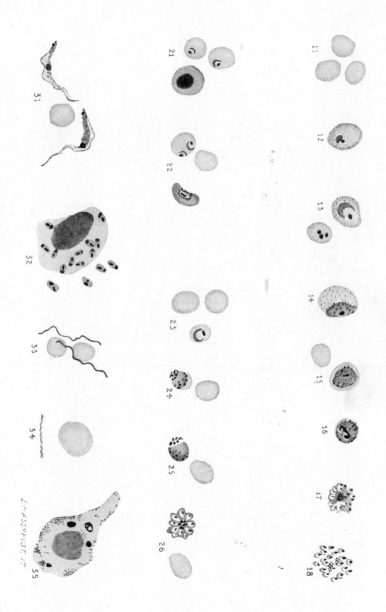

The period required for the formation of a sufficiently large number of parasites to produce symptoms (incubation period) is one to three weeks.

Plasmodium vivax (Fig. 10 [11 to 18 inclusive]) causes the common tertian malarial fever of tropical, subtropical and temperate climates. The young parasite (ring or hyaline form) occupies only a fractional part of the red blood corpuscle, and consists of a minute red nucleus of chromatin surrounded by blue cytoplasm. The signet-ring appearance is said by some to be a vacuole in the cytoplasm and by others to be due to the union of pseudopodia so as to include portions of the corpuscle. The young parasites produced after fertilization which are the forms introduced from the mosquito are called *sporozoites* in distinction to those resulting from asexual division (merozoites). Morphologically these two forms are indistinguishable. At this stage the parasite may, in imperfectly stained films, be mistaken for a blood platelet overlying the corpuscle. The red chromatin of malarial parasites appears as a compact red mass which forms a contrast to the fine granules of the plum-colored center of the blood platelet which may be mistaken for malaria parasites. Both nucleus and cytoplasm increase in size, and when the parasite (schizont or asexual parasite that divides to form the merozoites) fills the corpuscle its nucleus and cytoplasm divide by segmentation to form a dozen or more young parasites (merozoites) which enter corpuscles where this asexual cycle is repeated. This method of reproduction is quite different from that of tissue cells which divide with the formation of two cells. When the parasite has reached a considerable size its ameboid activity and the motion of the rather evenly distributed pigment is very active. The growth and segmentation of the young parasites require forty-eight hours. Just before segmentation the pigment is gathered into a mass at the center or at some point near the periphery, and ameboid motion ceases. The chill occurs during segmentation. A comparatively small number of parasites continue to increase in size, become free of the corpuscle, reach the size of a neutrophile, and fail to segment. These are the male and female sexual cells. If blood containing such cells is withdrawn from the vessels and enters the gut of an anopheles mosquito, the male sexual cell may throw off spiral forms (microgametes) that are actively motile and capable of penetrating the female cell to fertilize it. The mature male cell is a *microgametocyte*, while the female sexual cell is spoken of as *macrogamete* in distinction to schizont or mature asexual cell that segments to form the young parasites. Such fertilization takes place in the gastro-intestinal tract of the mosquito (anopheles) where the fertilized female (zygote) encysts to form an oöcyst; and, in this, segmentation takes place to form young parasites (sporozoites). Many terms other than the ones indicated have been applied by protozoologists to the various stages of the life cycle of the sporozoa. If an infected mosquito bites a human individual, these young parasites may be introduced through the puncture, and malaria follow. With the growth of the parasite changes take place in the infected corpuscle, and of these a solution of the corpuscular substance made evident by a lighter staining may usually be demonstrated. Reddish granules (Schüffner's granules) appear in the corpuscles as the parasites increase in size. These granules also appear in corpuscles infected with P. falciparum, but are said to be absent in quartan fever.

There has been much discussion as to whether the parasite lies within the corpuscle or rests on its surface. It seems quite certain that some at least of the forms of the parasite are on the surface of the corpuscle rather than within its substance.

Plasmodium falciparum (Fig. 10 [21 and 22]), seen in corpuscles as the young hyaline form, cannot be easily differentiated from the tertian parasite; but, as it develops, fewer and coarser pigment granules form and the corpuscles that contain it frequently become smaller than normal, while the corpuscle containing the tertian form is usually increased in size. After about one week, extracorpuscular and intracorpuscular crescentic sexual forms (so-called *crescents*) appear in the peripheral blood, and these are so characteristic that a certain diagnosis is possible from examination of the blood. The time of the cycle (growth of young parasites into adults and segmentation of the adults) is not definitely established, since the parasites do not segment to any extent in the peripheral blood. For the same reason most of the parasites reach only a comparatively small size in the peripheral blood. This organism causes the estivo-autumnal (malignant or pernicious tertian) malaria of the tropics and subtropics.

Plasmodium malariæ (Fig. 10 [23 to 26 inclusive]) causes the tropical quartan malaria. The pigment granules are few and coarse, and the number of segments into which the adult form divides is below twelve. The segmenting forms are numerous in the peripheral blood and are not as large as those of the tertian parasite. In the western continents, infection with this parasite appears to be common only in limited tropical districts. The character of the segmenting forms, the arrangement of the coarse pigment granules about the periphery of the corpuscle, and the sluggish movement of the parasite make the identification of the organism easy.

Trypanosoma Gambiense (Fig. 10 [31]).—For diagnosis, fresh preparations of the peripheral blood and especially of the centrifuged cerebrospinal fluid are examined with the high-dry lens. It is only when the organisms are present in very large numbers that they can be demonstrated in stained smears. In smears properly stained with a protozoon stain, the flagellum may be traced along the undulating membrane to the *blepharoplast* (micronucleus). This flagellate causes human trypanosomiasis (sleeping sickness). This disease occurs extensively in tropical Africa and is transmitted by a tsetse fly (glossinia palpalis). This biting fly probably acts as a passive carrier of the disease and there is a lack of evidence to show that this trypanosome passes through a life cycle in any invertebrate. The condition of lethargy and finally the coma appear to depend on the cellular reaction and the action of toxins in the meninges of the central nervous system. Other varieties of trypanosomes infect a number of domestic and wild animals.

Leishmania (Fig. 10 [32]).—The cultural form of these flagellates is much like the cultural form of trypanosomes. Calkins and others place these organisms under the genus *herpetomonas* but leishmania is more often used.   Three diseases are due to species of this genus that are morphologically alike.   *L. donovani* causes the generalized disease of adults known as kala-azar, while *L. infantum* is found in a disease of infants (infantile splenic anemia) prevalent in northern Africa. In both these diseases the organism is abundant in smears made from material obtained by splenic puncture.   The bodies are contained within certain cells (endothelial cells and leukocytes) and since endothelial leukocytes that have ingested foreign bodies disappear from the peripheral blood within a few hours the parasites are entirely absent or are present in very small numbers in the blood.   Due to the mechanical smearing out of the cells the parasites frequently appear extracellular in the preparations.   When cultures of the material containing these protozoa are made on blood agar and are kept at room temperature, the spherical or oval intracellular bodies develop into actively motile flagellated forms much like the cultural forms of trypanosomes.   The parasite has been obtained in cultures from the peripheral blood when it was not possible to demonstrate it there by direct microscopic examination.   *L. tropicum*, which is the third species, produces a local ulceration of exposed surfaces such as the wrists.   The lesions are known as oriental sore, Bagdad button, Delhi boil, etc.   It is thought to be transmitted by the common bedbug (cimex rotundátus).

Treponemata.—The protozoon character and the generic name of these flexible spiral organisms have not been fully agreed upon.   The spiral organisms producing relapsing fever are found in the peripheral blood on direct examination, but those producing syphilis and yaws are not examined for in the circulating blood.   *T. obermeieri* (Fig. 10 [33]) which is the cause of European relapsing fever, *T. novyi* (American relapsing fever), and *T. duttoni* (African relapsing fever) are found in the peripheral blood during the febrile stages of the disease.   The relapsing fever organisms are quite large and, owing to their very active motion, are identified by examining fresh preparations of blood with the oil-immersion or high-dry lens by means of artificial light.   *T. pallidum* (Fig. 10 [34]) is not identified microscopically in the peripheral blood; but in serum or scrapings from focal lesions it is present in large numbers; and by the aid of a strong artificial light it may be identified by examining fresh preparations with the oil-immersion lens and dark-field substage which replaces the Abbé condenser. In smears fixed in methyl alcohol and stained with polychrome protozoon stain the spirals are plainly visible. The *treponema pertenue* (yaws) is similar in morphology to the pallidum.

Dark-field illumination is the best and simplest method of demonstrating treponema pallidum in primary and secondary syphilitic lesions. A dark-field substage is required. The Abbé condenser of the microscope is removed from its supporting ring and the dark-field substage inserted in its place. If the make of microscope differs from that of the dark-field substage, the ring of the microscope into which the substage fits should be sent to the manufacturer so that the dark-field condenser may be properly fitted. A stop which is fitted into the upper end of the oil-immersion lens after it has been unscrewed is also desirable. The best way to secure material for examination from a chancre is thoroughly to cleanse the lesion with saline and to compress the lesion between thumb and index finger of the gloved hand until a drop of clear serum exudes, when a cover-glass is applied and at once inverted on a slide and examined. To examine by dark-field illumination, one drop of oil is placed between the slide and the condenser, and another between the cover-glass and the oil-immersion lens, and the strongest light possible is centered on the preparation with the convex lens. The light is important. A 500-watt incandescent bulb is more satisfactory than an arc light. A stop for the oil-immersion lens is desirable. A Welsbach burner may be used for illumination but is not satisfactory. For the investigation of unknown organisms or colloidal solution, the improved apparatus known as the ultramicroscope should be employed.

If the apparatus has been set up properly and the preparation correctly focused, the field appears quite black except for small particles in motion. The small treponemata with regular turns

6

are quite typical and usually offer no difficulty in diagnosis. If large numbers of *treponema refringens* are also present it may be desirable to clean the oil from slide and cover-glass, draw them apart, fix, and stain with a polychrome stain. The pallidum is not only a small spiral with about eleven regular turns but the ends are seen to come to delicate points in the stained preparations.

Filaria Nocturna.—This parasite is the larval or embryonic form of a large (1 to 2 inches in length) nematode worm (filaria bancrofti or filaria sanguinis hominis) that has its habitat in large veins or lymph-vessels. The embryos are found in the peripheral blood during the night, where they may be identified by examining fresh preparations with the low-power lens. They are actively motile and are about the diameter of a corpuscle and one hundred microns in length. The *culex fastigans* apparently becomes infected on sucking blood containing the parasites and acts as an active carrier of the disease. The adult worms may produce an elephantiasis by obstructing the lymphatics. A hemato-chyluria is usually present. Several species of filaria have been described in man. It is a tropical and subtropical disease.

Trichinella Spiralis.—The embryos of this worm have been demonstrated in the peripheral blood during the acute stage of the disease by adding 0.05 c.c. acetic acid to 10 c.c. of blood withdrawn from the arm vein with a syringe and placed in a 15-c.c. centrifuge tube, centrifuging the laked blood, and examining a fresh preparation of the sediment with the low-power and the high-dry lens. The embryos are sluggishly motile and measure 50 to 100 microns in length.

PLASMA

In the preceding paragraphs, the morphologic elements of the blood have been considered. Pathologic changes in the fluid part are both marked and important. Serologic methods such as the Widal test, the demonstration of opsonins, and the Wassermann reaction drew attention to the fluid portion of the blood, and, more recently, chemical methods have been applied to determine the various non-protein compounds present. Owing to the rapid coagulation that takes place in the plasma, the chemical tests are performed on the serum, which differs especially from the plasma in not containing fibrinogen; or they may be performed on the plasma that has been treated in such a way that coagulation is prevented. Oxalate and citrate solutions are usually employed to prevent coagulation. For certain chemical tests, exactly 1 c.c. of blood is drawn into 9 c.c. of a solution made by adding 20 grams of sodium citrate to a liter of normal saline.

Fibrin constitutes by weight 0.1 to 0.5 per cent. of the blood, the highest fibrin content being reached in such infections as pneumonia, acute rheumatic fever, and erysipelas. The substances concerned in the normal *coagulation of blood* are not sufficiently known to permit definite statements in regard to them, but it is certain that a protein (fibrinogen) is thrown out of solution and that lime is carried down with the precipitate which is the fibrin. In order to bring about this precipitation, it appears that *thrombokinase* must be liberated from some of the formed elements of the blood (platelets) or of the tissues, and that this liberated substance acts on the prothrombin at all times normally present in the blood to form thrombin. The thrombin which is not present in normal blood appears to be formed at the time of coagulation by the action of the thrombokinase. Calcium is required for this reaction.

Chemical Methods of Blood Examination.—By way of the blood and lymph channels, food substances pass from the gastro-intestinal canal to the tissues, while the waste products from the cells are carried to the organs (kidneys, lungs, liver, gastro-intestinal tract, skin) concerned with excretion. It is with these two varieties of substances that the purely chemical determinations have to do. Serology in distinction to these chemical procedures, includes a number of reactions in which chemical substances of the serum are investigated indirectly by microscopic or macroscopic observations. Lipoids of various types are present in blood at all times. During fat absorption, the blood contains the glycerides brought to it by the inflowing chyle. Only in the postabsorptive period (eighteen to sixteen hours after the last meal) is the blood free from the influence of digestion and suitable for a comparative study. In lipemia an increase occurs, and may be seen microscopically between the corpuscles. Blood sugar may be estimated quantitatively. The reaction and reserve alkali are important. Non-protein nitrogen-containing substances are of great importance. (In this book an attempt is made to give only those chemical tests that are of practical use; and, since many of the methods are new, further improvements and corrections in technic are likely to follow.)

New methods together with modifications and simplifications of older methods requiring the employment of newly devised apparatus are especially numerous among the chemical procedures that have a clinical significance. By trying out new methods advances are made; but a tendency, especially with beginners in this field of work, to employ methods and apparatus that yield results so inaccurate that they are not only useless but even misleading in their application should be avoided. It must be kept in mind that when difficult and painstaking chemical manipulations and expensive apparatus are employed it is because they are required for obtaining accurate results.

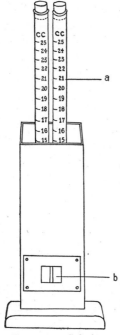

FIG. 12.—Colorimeter (devised by V. C. Myers). Two tubes, a, of equal bore graduated in cubic centimeters. The standard solution is placed in left tube and the unknown in the right tube is diluted until the two solutions have the same color when viewed against a white background through the opening, b, in the lower part of the box.

Lipemia.—The presence of microscopic fat in blood is not a common condition. It is seen most often in diabetes when an acidosis is present. The writer has observed a very marked lipemia in rabbits subjected to experimental lead poisoning (Journal of Medical Research, Vol. xxxii, p. 271). For its demonstration blood films are fixed in formalin vapor and stained by the scharlach R method as given under surgical specimens.

Chemical Fat (Bloor).—This test is a determination of turbidity. (The parts necessary for the conversion of a Duboscq colorimeter (Fig. 13) into a nephelometer required for the test may be obtained from the International Instrument Co., Brighton, Mass.)

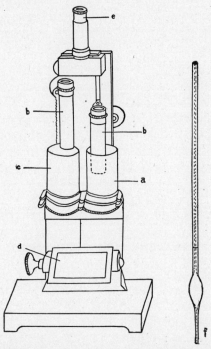

FIG. 13.—Duboscq colorimeter (Eimer and Amend). *a*, Left chamber in which standard solutions are placed. The unknown solution is placed in *c*, and the cylinder, *b*, lowered until the left side of the field in ocular at *e*, corresponds to the right side which represents the fluid in the left chamber; *d*, mirror; *f*, Ostwald 1-c.c. pipet.

Draw exactly 3 c.c. of blood from a vein into a 5-c.c. graduated syringe. Remove the needle, and immediately allow the blood to flow slowly into a 100-c.c. volumetric flask containing 80 c.c. of an alcohol-ether mixture (redistilled absolute alcohol 3 parts; redistilled ether 1 part). The flask should be gently revolved or agitated during the addition of the blood. Place the flask in a water-bath and heat with constant agitation until the boiling point of the alcohol-ether is just reached. Remove from the water-bath, cool rapidly under the cold water tap, and then add sufficient alcohol-ether mixture to make the volume exactly 100 c.c. Stopper, and mix the contents by inverting the flask a few times. Filter into another small flask and stopper. Measure 15 c.c. of the filtrate which contains about 2 mg. of fat into a small beaker containing 2 c.c. normal sodium ethylate and evaporate just to dryness on a water-bath. Dissolve the residue in 5 c.c. alcohol-ether mixture by gently warming until the flakes of alkali start to loosen. Add 50 c.c. water, and shake to make a suspension. To a second beaker add 5 c.c. of a standard solution of oleic acid in alcohol-ether (alcohol 1 part, ether 3 parts) of such a strength that the 5 c.c. contain 2 mg. oleic acid; add 50 c.c. water and shake. The standard solution of oleic acid must of course be made up accurately, but the amount of acid may vary somewhat. To each beaker add simultaneously 10 c.c. 10 per cent. hydrochloric acid; allow to stand five minutes and compare in the nephelometer. From the known standard solution calculate the number of milligrams in 100 c.c. of blood.

Nephelometer.—For the purpose of nephelometric comparison, the modification of the Duboscq colorimeter suggested by Bloor is extremely satisfactory. Having obtained the extra parts (supplied by the International Instrument Company) proceed as follows: Remove the glass prism from the colorimeter, and slide the grooved sleeves provided with the set-screw into place on the prism support. Fill one of the glass tubes (provided) with the standard fat suspension and another with the unknown and slip them into the long metallic tubes (jackets). Place the jacket containing the standard through the hole in the cup stage on the left side of the instrument, and the unknown similarly on the right. Lift the glass tubes until they enter the sleeves attached to prism supports, and are firmly held by the spring attached to the inside of the sleeve. By turning the milled head on the back of the instrument, the zero point of each tube may be taken, and any desired length of the column of suspension exposed to the light. The hinged cover should be removed from the colorimeter.

To make the reading, place the instrument in a box 48 cm. long, 32 cm. high, and 20 cm. wide. One end of the box is left out and a black curtain attached at the top only, substituted for it. A cover is provided which is grooved at one end to fit the telescope of the instrument. The instrument stands just in front of the black curtain. A 50-watt Mazda lamp supported on a bracket so that the center of the light is on a level with the tubes, is placed 30 cm. in front of the instrument. The apparatus is used in a dark room.

The reading is taken in the ordinary way, moving the jacket of the unknown up or down by means of the milled screw. The standard suspension is usually set at 30 mm. and the unknown adjusted until an evenly illuminated field is obtained. The unknown should read not less than 20 mm. or over 40 mm. to give dependable results. As the two solutions were made up to the same volume their values are inversely proportional to the instrument readings.

Carbohydrates.—The normal amount of sugar in the blood remains rather constant at 0.1 per cent., but may rise to 0.12 per cent. Although slight or moderate pathologic increases (0.14 to 0.35 per cent.) may be met with in a number of diseases, larger amounts are oftenest seen in diabetic conditions. An abnormal amount of sugar in the blood is spoken of as hyperglycemia. In severe diabetes the amount of sugar may reach one-half per cent., or even more. A slight hyperglycemia (rarely reaching 0.2 per cent.) may be met with in a number of acute infections, in some cases of syphilis, in kidney sclerosis, and in liver cirrhosis. The increase in hyperglycemia in diastatic activity by which reducing sugars are formed from starch is about in proportion to the increase in the sugar per cent.

Quantitative Determination of Sugar (Lewis and Benedict; Myers and Bailey).—Place 2 c.c. oxalated (page 91) blood in a 15-c.c. centrifuge tube, add 8 c.c. distilled water, shake, and let stand for five minutes. Add 0.5 gm. dry picric acid, stir with a very small glass rod, let stand for five minutes with occasional stirring, centrifuge, and filter the supernatant liquid into a dry test-tube. Place 3 c.c. of the filtrate into a tall test-tube graduated at 10 c.c. capacity and add 1 c.c. of a saturated sodium carbonate solution. Into a second test-tube graduated at 10 c.c. capacity place 3 c.c. of a 0.02 per cent. glucose solution in saturated picric acid, then add 1 c.c. saturated sodium carbonate. Place both tubes in a beaker of boiling water for fifteen minutes. Remove, allow to cool and dilute both the standard and unknown to 10 c.c. Compare in the usual way in the Duboscq colorimeter. The standard can be conveniently set at 20.

It will be seen that 3 c.c. of filtrate taken for the color development represents 0.6 c.c. of the original blood. The color produced by this is compared with that developed by 0.6 mg. of glucose. If both standard and unknown were diluted to the same volume (10 c.c.) the number of milligrams of dextrose per c.c. of blood is found by dividing the reading of the standard by the reading of the unknown. One-tenth of this figure represents the percentage of blood sugar. A colorimeter (Fig. 12), devised by Dr. V. C. Myers and made by E. Leitz, 30 East 18th St., New York City, is satisfactory for clinical use. When using this instrument the graduated tubes of the colorimeter are substituted for the two 10-c.c. graduated test-tubes spoken of above. The standard is made up to the 10-c.c. mark in the left-hand tube with water. The unknown is diluted with water with the diluting pipet, inverting after each addition, until identical in color with the standard. Since 0.6 c.c. of blood are employed and 0.6 mg. of glucose used as standard, the reading in the unknown tube gives the percentage of blood sugar directly.

Pure picric acid should be used in all analytical methods. To purify picric acid (Folin), place 600 gm. wet picric acid in a gallon enamelware saucepan, and add about three liters boiling water, and 200 c.c. 50 per cent. caustic soda. Stir, and if necessary heat until solution is complete. While stirring, add 200 gm. sodium chlorid to the hot solution, cool in running water to about 30°C., stirring occasionally, filter on a large Buchner funnel, and wash with 5 per cent. sodium chlorid. Transfer the wet precipitate (sodium picrate) to the vessel, dissolve in 3 liters boiling water, and add 50 c.c. 10 per cent. caustic soda, and 100 gm. sodium chlorid. Cool, filter and wash with sodium chlorid as before. Repeat the solution and precipitation of the sodium picrate twice more, washing the picrate, after the last precipitation with distilled water instead of the saline. Dissolve the purified picrate in the vessel in boiling water, filter and to the hot picrate add 300 c.c. 33⅓ per cent. sulphuric acid. Cool to 30°C. with running water, filter, and wash the filtrate with distilled water to remove sulphates. Preserve moist.

Salts.—The plasma contains about 8.2 per cent. of solids of which the proteins are approximately 84 per cent. and the inorganic constituent mainly chlorids, phosphates and bicarbonates (carbonates?) about 10 per cent. Sodium chlorid predominates as the chief inorganic constituent. The serum is marked by the absence of calcium phosphate. This salt is contained in the insoluble fibrin. Analytic determinations of the inorganic salts in health and disease have only been recently made to any great extent. In certain cardiac and renal diseases there is an unquestioned retention of sodium chlorid. Cases with salt retention usually show edema and are improved by a salt free diet.

Cryoscopy makes possible the determination of the general molecular concentration of the serum. The freezing-point of normal human serum is −0.55 to −0.57° C. The depression seen in the usual severe nephropathies is about −0.65, but −0.95 may be observed in severe cases of sclerosed kidneys with or without uremic symptoms. As a clinical test, a determination of the freezing-point of the blood serum at present has a doubtful value. For making the determination the Beckmann freezing-point apparatus is most suitable. Fill the battery jar with an ice and salt freezing mixture. About 10 c.c. of serum is placed in the small test-tube which is then inserted in the larger test-tube which serves as an air chamber. The assembled air-jacket and test-tubes are suspended in the freezing mixture. The tube containing the serum should be provided with a stopper carrying a Beckmann thermometer and a small platinum or glass stirrer. The zero point on the Beckmann thermometer must be determined in the usual way. The highest temperature recorded after the separation of ice from the serum should be taken as the correct freezing point. Care should be exercised to prevent excessive supercooling of the serum before the crystallization of the ice occurs.

The *specific gravity* of the blood is normally 1.050 to 1.065 with an average of 1.060 while that of serum is about 1.030. To determine the specific gravity, a small tube (10 cm. by 2 mm.) is cleaned, dried, and carefully weighed on the analytical balance. Fill the tube with distilled water, reweigh and subtract the weight of the empty tube. This gives the weight of a definite volume of water. Dry the tube, and then add about 10 mg. of powdered potassium oxalate and carefully weigh again. Fill the tube with blood, reweigh and subtract from this weight that of the tube plus oxalate. This difference gives the weight of a volume of blood equal to that of the water previously weighed. By dividing the weight of the blood by the weight of the water the specific gravity of the former is obtained.

A number of methods more or less complicated have been devised to determine the *viscosity* of the blood, but the test has a doubtful clinical application.

Proteins.—The proteins contained in blood serum are roughly thrown into two groups, the albumins and the globulins. The compounds contained in these two groups are so complex that little progress has been made in the study of these substances which represent the highest degrees of organic synthesis. However, the relative amount of protein may be significant.

Hydremia is a term applied to the condition of the blood in which the percentage protein content is decreased. Hemorrhages, anemias, malignant tumors, insufficient food, and emaciating infections are common couses of hydremia, and in these conditions it appears that there is not only a relative decrease in protein but an absolute one as well, since the total volume of blood seems to be decreased.

In certain cardiac and cardiorenal conditions the total volume of blood is increased, and the increase in volume is due to an excess of water (hydremic plethora) giving a relative decrease n the blood proteins, in distinction to the hydremic conditions, mentioned in the previous paragraph, in which there is an absolute decrease in the amount of proteins. Edema of the blood, like the edema of other tissues, appears to be due to the retention of water, dependent on an increased osmotic tension within the vessels. In chronic nephritis, and less commonly in cardiac incompetency, the specific gravity of the blood may reach 1.030, while normally it lies between 1.050 and 1.065. Such a decrease in specific gravity indicates that any rise in osmotic pressure in the blood stream due to an excess of crystalloids (sodium chlorid), is quickly equalized by a relative increase of water in the vessels.

In addition to the conditions indicated by hydremia and hydremic plethora, it appears that a certain type of individual has too great a volume of blood (true plethora). Such a person consumes excessive food and drink, has large muscles and much fat, a red face, an enlarged heart, and a full pulse. Experimental proof of this condition is lacking. Bleeding offers relief.

Non-protein Nitrogenous Substances.—Recent investigation shows that the amino acids, which are utilized in the synthesis of the proteins, are present in rather constant amounts in the blood; and the determination of these may throw light on the more complex substances (proteins) formed from them; but at the present time the methods employed for these determinations do not permit of easy application. Estimations of certain non-protein nitrogenous substances (creatinin, uric acid, urea, non-protein nitrogen, free ammonia) are practical, and have an importance indicated in the discussion of uremia.

Creatinin (Folin; Myers).—Draw blood from the arm vein into a syringe, and at once force it out into a wide-mouthed 2-oz. bottle that contains one-tenth gram potassium oxalate. Place 3 c.c. of the oxalated blood in a 15-cc. centrifuge tube, and add 12 c.c. water. After this stands for ten minutes, add one-half gram dry picric acid, and stir with a small glass rod for five

minutes.   Centrifuge, and filter.   To 5 c.c. of the filtrate
(corresponding to 1 c.c. of the original blood) in a test-tube add
0.25 c.c. 10 per cent. sodium hydrate.   Place this alkaline filtrate in the right-hand cup of a Duboscq colorimeter (Fig. 13)
and compare with a standard solution.   The standard stock
creatinin solution contains 0.2 mg. creatinin in 100 c.c. of a saturated picric acid solution.   To 5 c.c. of this solution (which contains 0.01 mg creatinin) add 0.25 c.c. 10 per cent. sodium
hydrate.   This solution is placed in the left-hand cup of the
colorimeter and set at 10 mm.   The alkali should be added to
the blood filtrate and the standard creatinin solution simultaneously.   They are then allowed to stand for ten minutes for
the development of color before being compared in the colorimeter.   From the colorimeter readings calculate the number of
milligrams per 100 c.c. of blood.   In most pathologic conditions without kidney involvement, the creatinin does not rise
appreciably above 2.5 mg. per 100 c.c. of blood, but it should be
remembered that such diagnoses as "slight chronic interstitial
nephritis," without albumin and casts in the urine and without
autopsy confirmation, are questionable; and, in these, creatinin
up to 3.5 mg. has been reported by several workers.   It is, however, in cases that are definitely nephritic that marked increases
are met with.   The early and mild cases of nephritis show up to
5 mg., with as high as 25 mg. in severe cases before their termination   An increase above 5 mg. warrants a grave prognosis.
Up to the present time there has been a complete failure to
correllate these findings as well as the others quantitative determinations of non-protein nitrogenous substances with the
exact kidney lesions present.   The test has a therapeutic value
since an increase in creatinin nitrogen (retention) is an indication for a low protein diet, just as chlorid retention indicates
a salt-free diet.

   Preparation of Pure Creatinin.—To 8 liters of a fresh urine
in a large precipitating jar are added with constant stirring 60
to 80 gm. of dry picric acid dissolved in 400 c.c. of hot alcohol.
Allow to settle overnight.   Siphon off the supernatant liquid,
filter on a large Buchner funnel and wash with cold water.

Allow the precipitate to dry. To 500 gm. of this dry precipitate add 100 gm. anhydrous potassium carbonate. Dissolve in 750 c.c. of hot water. Stir for ten minutes and allow to stand with occasional stirring for two hours. Filter through Buchner funnel, wash the sediment two or three times with small volumes of cold water and reject the residue. Transfer the filtrate to a large jar and add cautiously 100 c.c. glacial acetic acid to the foaming liquid without stirring. Avoid excessive foaming. To this solution add one-fourth of its volume of a saturated alcoholic zinc chlorid solution. Creatinin zinc chlorid should precipitate immediately. If it does not more alcoholic zinc chlorid should be added. When precipitation is complete filter the impure salt onto a Buchner funnel. To purify, the salt is dissolved in ten parts of boiling 25 per cent. acetic acid. Add to the hot solution one-tenth volume of saturated alcoholic zinc chlorid solution followed by one and one-half volumes of alcohol. Allow the mixture to stand overnight, filter and wash the precipitate with a little alcohol. Repeat the above solution and precipitate twice more. The salt is now about 100 per cent. pure and may be dried.

A convenient standard creatinin zinc chlorid solution is made by weighing out exactly 1.6106 gm. of the thoroughly dry salt and dissolving in sufficient tenth-normal hydrochloric acid to make 1 liter. Such a solution contains 1 mg. of creatinin per c.c. This solution keeps indefinitely.

Uric Acid (Folin and Denis; Myers).—To 5 c.c. oxalated (page 91) blood in a 200-c.c. casserole add about 25 c.c. hundredth-normal acetic acid (0.6 c.c. glacial acetic acid in 1 liter water), and while stirring, bring to a boil over a flame. Add 2 c.c. alumina cream, and stir. Wash down the sides of the dish with hot water, and filter through a hardened paper into a 200-c.c. cylinder. With about 75 c.c. of hot water wash the precipitate from the filter paper back into the casserole, and again boil the coagulated material. Through the same filter paper, filter the contents of the casserole into the 200-c.c. cylinder. (If the filtrate is alkaline, add about 2 c.c. 10 per cent. acetic acid.) Return the filtrates to the casserole after it has been thoroughly cleansed and evaporate to 1 or 2 c.c. volume. (The solution should be protein-free.) Pour into a 15-c.c. centrifuge tube and carefully wash the casserole into the centrifuge tube with a spray of hot water, keeping the total volume at or slightly below 5 c.c. Add 10 drops of ammoniacal silver-magnesium mixture to the 5 c.c. in the centrifuge tube, shake and place in cracked ice for fifteen minutes to precipitate the purin bodies. Centrifuge, decant carefully, and invert the tube to drain with the mouth resting on filter paper. After draining for five minutes, the ammonia is removed by suction through a capillary pipet inserted nearly to the bottom of the centrifuge tube. Add to the precipitate 1 to 2 drops of a 2.5 per cent. potassium cyanid solution, 0.5 c.c. of Folin-Denis reagent (Benedict modification), and 5 c.c. of saturated sodium carbonate solution. Transfer to a 20-c.c. volumetric flask, and after an interval of about one minute, dilute with water to the mark, using part of the water to remove traces from the tube. In case the color developed is too strong to be accurately read against the standard uric acid solution, the unknown should be diluted to 50 c.c. (or more) and 10 c.c. (or more) of saturated sodium carbonate used in the development of the color.

For a standard, pipet with an Oswald pipet 1 c.c. of uric acid standard (1 c.c. equals 0.2 mg. uric acid) into a 20-c.c. volumetric flask. Add 1 to 2 drops of 2.5 per cent. potassium cyanid (the same amount as added to the unknown), and 5 c.c. of saturated sodium carbonate solution. After standing for one minute, dilute with water to the 20-c.c. mark. The standard is placed in the left-hand cup of the Duboscq colorimeter, and the prism set for a depth of 20 mm. After placing the unknown in the right-hand cup, the reading is taken as usual. The amount of uric acid is calculated to milligrams per 100 c.c. of blood.

To make the Folin-Denis uric acid reagent, as modified by Benedict, boil 100 gm. sodium tungstate, 20 c.c. concentrated hydrochloric acid and 80 c.c. 85 per cent. phosphoric acid in 750 c.c. distilled water for two hours, using a reflux condenser. Make up to 1 liter.

To prepare the ammoniacal silver-magnesium solution, add to 100 c.c. concentrated ammonia, 70 c.c. of 3 per cent. silver nitrate solution and 30 c.c. magnesia mixture. Any turbidity which may develop may be filtered off. To prepare the magnesia mixture, dissolve 36 gm. magnesium sulphate and 70 gm. ammonium chlorid in 280 c.c. distilled water, and add 140 c.c. concentrated ammonia.

Aluminium cream is prepared by precipitating an 8 per cent. solution of aluminium acetate in 2 per cent. acetic acid with sodium bicarbonate. The precipitate should be washed with a large volume of distilled water and decanted a number of times and then filtered.

The standard uric acid solution (Myers and Fine) is prepared as follows: Dissolve 9 gm. pure crystalline hydrogen disodium phosphate and 1 gm. dihydrogen sodium phosphate in 200 to 300° c.c. hot water. Filter and make up to 500 c.c. with hot water. Pour this warm, clear solution on 200 mg. uric acid suspended in a few cubic centimeters of water in a liter volumetric flask. Agitate until completely dissolved. Add at once exactly 1.4 c.c. glacial acetic acid. Make up to 1 liter, mix and add 5 c.c. chloroform. Five cubic centimeters of this solution are equivalent to 1 mg. of uric acid. The solution should be freshly prepared every two months.

There are normally present 2 to 3 mg. of uric acid per 100 c.c. of blood, and amounts up to 10 mg. are not infrequently met with in various pathologic conditions in which there is no evidence of nephritis. Twenty milligrams may be present in a severe chronic nephritis. Uric acid appears to be eliminated with more difficulty than either urea or creatinin, and an increase of uric acid in the blood (9 mg. for example) may prove of value in the early diagnosis of nephritis.

Non-protein Nitrogen in Blood (Folin).—Measure 25 c.c. of acetone-free methyl alcohol into a 50-c.c. volumetric flask and add slowly from a pipet 5 c.c. of oxalated (page 91) blood. The flask should be gently agitated while the blood is flowing into the alcohol so as to form a very fine coagulum. Dilute to volume with methyl alcohol, stopper, shake, and allow to stand for two hours, then filter through a dry filter paper. To the filtrate add 2 or 3 drops of an ammonia-free saturated alcoholic solution of zinc chlorid. After the tube has stood for a few minutes, filter through a dry paper into a large test-tube. The fitrate should be water-clear and should be stoppered immediately to prevent evaporation. Pipet 10 c.c. of the filtrate into a large (200 by 22 mm.) Pyrex test-tube. To this add 1 drop of concentrated sulphuric acid, 1 drop kerosene and a glass bead. Place the tube in a beaker containing lukewarm water and gradually elevate the temperature of the water-bath until the alcohol evaporates freely but not violently. After the alcohol has been expelled add 1 c.c. of concentrated sulphuric acid, 1 gm. of potassium sulphate and 2 drops 10 per cent. copper sulphate solution. Proceed with the digestion as described under the determination of the total nitrogen of urine. The ammonia should be aspirated into a second Pyrex test-tube (instead of the usual flask) containing 1 c.c. decinormal hydrochloric acid and 3 c.c. of water (Fig. 64). As the amount of ammonia is extremely small, usually not over 0.3 mg. of nitrogen, the estimation is made colorimetrically using Nessler's reagent rather than by ordinary titration.

For accurate work a standard solution of ammonium sulphate and the unknown must be Nesslerized simultaneously. The standard solution is made by dissolving 4.7062 gm. of especially purified ammonium sulphate in water and making up to 1 liter. 1 c.c. of this solution contains 1 mg. of nitrogen. To proceed, pipet 1 c.c. of the standard ammonium sulphate solution into a 100-c.c. volumetric flask which contains 60 c.c. distilled water (using an Ostwald pipet [Fig. 13]). Next place 25 c.c. of distilled water in a 100-c.c. beaker. Add to this 5 c.c. of Nessler's reagent. Mix thoroughly and add it immediately to the volumetric flask containing the diluted ammonium sulphate solution. Care should be taken that only about 10 c.c. of diluted Nessler's reagent is added at a time and that the flask is rotated after each addition. This is to prevent the formation of turbidity. Make the final volume up to the 100-c.c. mark with distilled water. The color of the unknown is developed in the large test-tube (after washing down the absorption tube with 1. c.c. of water) at the same time as the standard. To do this measure 8 c.c. of distilled water in a 10-c.c. cylinder. Add 2 c.c. Nessler's reagent and then with the same caution as observed for the standard develop the color in the unknown using ordinarily 7 to 8 c.c. of the diluted Nessler's reagent. Transfer the solution to a 15-c.c. volumetric flask and dilute with water to the mark. As the color developed is extremely dark larger amounts of diluted Nessler's reagent may be required and the final solution must be diluted to a volume of 25 or 50 c.c. Invert each flask after stoppering to insure uniformity. Allow to stand for five minutes and then compare in the Duboscq colorimeter. The standard is placed in the left-hand cup and set at a depth of 20 mm. Four or five readings should be taken and 20 divided by the average. The nitrogen content is calculated to milligrams per 100 c.c. of blood.

Preparation of Nessler's Reagent.—Dissolve 200 gm. of potassium hydroxid (or sodium hydroxid) in 950 c.c. of distilled water in a flask, and cool under running water. Transfer 40 c.c. of distilled water, 55 gm. of potassium iodid, and 100 gm. of mercuric iodid to a large heavy beaker (capacity 1500 c.c.) or a glass jar. Immerse the lower part of the beaker in warm water (40°–50°C.), and shake gently until the last trace of the red iodid of mercury is dissolved. The solution occurs rapidly, and is usually finished in ten to fifteen minutes. Remove from the warm water, and pour the cooled hydroxid solution into the yellow iodid mixture in a slow but continuous stream and with vigorous stirring. The mixture should remain clear, or at the most slightly opalescent. If a moderate sediment has formed or should later form in the solution, the clear supernatant fluid is still good. Keep in well-stoppered bottles, preferably in the dark.

Determination of Urea in Blood (Marshall).—Pipet 5 c.c. of blood to which sodium citrate has been added in sufficient quantity to prevent coagulation (10 mg. per c.c.) into a 25-c.c. volumetric flask containing 15 c.c. of water. Shake gently and make up to the mark with distilled water. Any foam which may de-

7

velop is readily discharged by adding a drop or two of ether or caprylic alcohol. After the diluted blood has been thoroughly mixed pipet out 5 c.c. into a large test-tube. Add one drop of caprylic alcohol and either 0.1 gm. or 1 c.c. of a 10 per cent. suspension of Arlco-urease (procurable from the Arlington Chemical Co., Yonkers, N. Y.). Stopper the test-tube with the aeration apparatus (Fig. 64) used for the nitrogen determination and shake gently to insure thorough mixing of the urease with the blood. Place the tube in a beaker of warm water at 35° to 40°C. for one-half hour. Now attach the absorption apparatus used in the determination of non-protein nitrogen in blood, charged with 1 c.c. of decinormal hydrochloric acid and 2 c.c. water and aërate briskly for one-half minute. Stop the aëration and add 5 gm. of dry potassium carbonate to the blood-urease mixture. Stopper the tube again and continue the aëration for fifteen minutes. The receiving liquid is Nesslerized with from 3 to 5 c.c. diluted Nessler's reagent (1–5) and transferred to a 10-c.c. volumetric flask in case the color developed is too intense. The dilution and amount of Nessler's reagent should be increased and the determination completed according to the directions given under the determination of non-protein nitrogen. In making the calculation bear in mind that the blood has been diluted 1 in 5 so that the quantity actually taken is 1 c.c. of whole blood. Report the number of milligrams of urea in 100 c.c. of blood.

Free Ammonia in Blood.—The largest amount of free ammonia that is found in the blood amounts to only a few milligrams per 100 c.c. of blood. Again some of the nitrogenous substances of the blood decompose even at room temperature to form free ammonia. For these reasons an accurate determination of free ammonia in the blood is difficult.

Determination of Carbonate Content of Blood Plasma (Van Slyke).—A special apparatus is required but the determination is rather simple. Until uniform and accurate results are regularly obtained, the worker should on the blood plasma of normal individuals carry out the test with the particular apparatus to be used.

The apparatus (Emil Greiner Co., 55 Fulton St., N. Y. C.) consists of a 50-c.c. *bulb* above which there is a 3-way cock and below which there is a second 3-way cock. The 2 openings of the *upper cock* lead upward; one being a *capillary* for emptying the apparatus while the other connects with a small *reception funnel*. The 2 openings of the *lower cock* lead downward to form a U-tube, the right arm of which is a *cylinder*, the left a *tube*. The bottom of the U connects by a rubber tube with an open *cup*.

To make the test, fill the entire apparatus including the *capillary* with mercury by running it in from the *cup*. Place accurately 1 c.c. plasma in the *reception funnel*, holding the tip of the pipet against the very bottom of the funnel. Lower the *cup* so that the top of it is on a level with the 50–c.c. mark and turn the *upper cock* so that the solution is admitted to the 50-c c. *bulb*. Wash twice with 0.5 c.c. water and once with 0.5 c.c. 5 per cent. sulphuric acid, allowing the washings to escape into the bulb. Add one drop of caprylic alcohol and if the liquid does not reach exactly the 2.5-c.c. mark, add water until it does. Enough liquid is left in the reception funnel each time to make impossible any entrance of air into the bulb. Add a few drops of mercury and allow to flow in so as to seal the upper cock. The *upper cock* remains permanently sealed. Up to this time the *lower cock* has been turned so as to connect with the right arm. Now lower the mercury cup 80 cm. below its first level at the 50-c.c. mark so as to create a Torricellian vacuum in the bulb. When the mercury meniscus exactly reaches the 50-c.c. mark close the lower cock. Remove from clamp and turn bulb upside down fifteen or more times after turning lower cock so as to close off, replace in the clamp, open cock and allow liquid to flow into the right arm cylinder. Raise the *cup* and turn lower cock to connect with left *tube*. Raise the *cup* until the level of the mercury in it and that in the capillary stem of the 50-c.c. bulb is the same. There should be less than 10 mm. of water above the mercury in the 1-c.c. stem which is calibrated in 0.02-c.c. divisions. The carbon dioxid in the capillary between the upper cock and the upper meniscus of mercury is the amount in 1 c.c. of plasma. This must be corrected for the gas absorbed by the 2.5 c.c. liquid and must be reduced to 0°C. and 760 mm. pressure according to the appended table. For example, if the reading is 0.7 c.c., the room temperature 25°C. and the barometer at 740 mm., 0.7 less 0.043 equals 0.657 corrected for absorption by the 2.5 c.c. of liquid; $\frac{B}{760}$ is 974 ×

927 = 0.9; 0.657 times 0.9 = 0.59 c.c. or 59 c.c. carbon dioxid in 100 c.c. plasma. The normal lies between 53 and 77 while in severe acidosis the amount is below 30 c.c.

Before making the test eliminate any chance error from gas in the apparatus by lowering the *cup* until the right arm *cylinder* is half empty and then raising the cup when the mercury strikes the upper cock with a click if the pipet is air-free. Further the cup is washed out with 1 per cent. carbonate-free ammonia. To remove carbonates from ammonia add a small amount of saturated barium hydrate, an excess of ammonium sulphate and filter. A caprylic alcohol found reliable is Kahlbaum's Oktyl-alkohol, Secundär 1. After completion of the test the liquid is re-admitted to the *bulb* and forced out through the *capillary* together with a small amount of mercury; the apparatus now is ready for a second specimen. The blood is withdrawn by a syringe from an arm vein, forced into a 15-c.c. centrifuge tube containing 0.1 gm. potassium oxalate and immediately centrifuged at high speed. The plasma is added by means of a pipet not graduated to the very tip.

Room temperature	Gas in 2.5 c.c.	Factor
18°C.	0.048 c.c.	$\frac{B}{760}$ × 0.968
19	0.048	" 0.962
20	0.047	" 0.956
21	0.046	" 0.950
22	0.045	" 0.944
23	0.045	" 0.938
24	0.044	" 0.932
25	0.043	" 0.927
26	0.042	" 0.921
27	0.041	" 0.915

The value of $\dfrac{B}{760}$ is as follows:

Barometer reading	Factor	Barometer reading	Factor
736	0.967	754	0.992
738	0.971	756	0.995
740	0.974	758	0.997
742	0.976	760	1.000
744	0.979	762	1.003
746	0.981	764	1.006
748	0.984	766	1.008
750	0.987	768	1.011
752	0.989	770	1.013

Hydrogen-ion Concentration of the Blood (Henderson and Palmer; Marriott).—The hydrogen-ion concentration of blood is maintained at a remarakbly constant level due to the removal of volatile acidity (carbon dioxid) by the lungs and the salts of acid metabolites by the kidney. Owing to the reserve alkali of the blood the hydrogen-ion concentration shows little or no change except in the most severe types of acidosis.

A solution is alkaline when it contains more hydroxyl than hydrogen ions. A normal acid solution contains one gram of hydrogen ions per liter. Purest distilled water is considered as a standard of neutrality owing to the fact that its dissociation into hydrogen and hydroxyl ions is equal. This dissociation is extremely small—in fact one liter of water contains about one ten-millionth of a gram of hydrogenions. Its normality would then be $N \cdot 10^{-7}$. The reaction of the blood serum lies between 10^{-7} and $10^{-8}N$, that is, it is slightly more alkaline than distilled water. Phenolphthalein changes from colorless to pink between 10^{-8} and 10^{-10} N, and can be used, therefore, for determining ion concentrations between these points. Phenolsulphonephthalein shows variations in color between $10^{-6.4}$ and $10^{-8.4}N$, and is the indicator best adapted for use with dialysates from blood serum.

Preparation of the Standard Tubes.—Prepare a fifteenth-normal solution of acid potassium phosphate by placing 9.078 gm. pure primary (acid) potassium phosphate (KH_2PO_4) in a liter volumetric flask, dissolving, and making up to volume

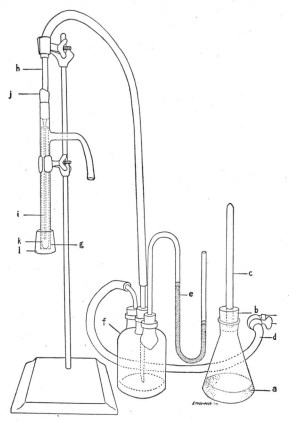

FIG. 14.—Apparatus for making collodion dialyzing thimbles of uniform thick, ness (drawn from apparatus devised by Prof. C. J. Farmer). The 350-c.c. flask-*a*, containing about 75 c.c. medium celloidin provided with rubber stopper, *b*, carrying a 10 by 130 mm. test-tube, *c*. The flask is inverted until the tube is filled when the flask is placed at an angle of 30 degrees and allowed to drain for exactly one minute after the test-tube has emptied itself. Note that the test-tube reaches only two-thirds way through the stopper. After draining for one minute the test-tube, *c*, takes the position, *k*, and is let dry for one minute in a current of air from the 1-mm. capillary *i*, of the tube, *h*, in which there is a negative-pressure represented by 50 mm. of Hg., *e*. Remove the tube, *k* (*c*), fill it with water, loosen the collodion about the mouth of the tube, run a 1-mm. glass rod with rounded ends to the bottom in order to detach the sac, pull out the sac with forceps and place it in distilled water. *l*, is a rubber stopper in which T-tube of glass, *g*, rests; *j*, connection of rubber tubing; *f*, Woulf bottle. Dialysis is complete in three minutes in thimbles prepared in this way. Suction is made through *d*.

with water. To prepare a fifteenth-normal solution of alkaline sodium phosphate ($Na_2HPO_4.12H_2O$), expose this salt to the air for two weeks to permit ten molecules of water to be driven off. Place 11.876 gm. of this partially dehydrated salt in a liter volumetric flask, dissolve, and make up to volume. Combine the two fifteenth-normal solutions as follows:

PH........	6.4	6.6	6.8	7.0	7.1	7.2	7.3	7.4	7.5	7.6	7.7	7.8	8.0	8.2	8.4
KH₂PO₄...	c.c. 73.0	c.c. 63.0	c.c. 51.0	c.c. 37.0	c.c. 32.0	c.c. 27.0	c.c. 23.0	c.c. 19.0	c.c. 15.8	c.c. 13.2	c.c. 11.0	c.c. 8.8	c.c. 5.6	c.c. 3.2	c.c. 2.0
Na₂HPO₄..	27.0	37.0	49.0	63.0	68.0	73.0	77.0	81.0	84.2	86.8	89.0	91.2	94.4	96.8	98.0

Place 3 c.c. of each of the fifteen combination in Jena or non-sol test-tubes of equal diameter (10 mm.); and to each tube, by means of a 1-c.c. pipet graduated in hundredths, add 0.3 c.c. of 0.01 per cent. phenolsulphonephthalein, and seal off the top. The 0.01 solution of the indicator is made by diluting 1.7 c.c. of 0.6 per cent. solution to 100 c.c.

To make the test, place 3 c.c. oxalated blood in a dialyzing sac (Fig. 14) which is lowered for ten minutes into 3 c.c. normal saline contained in a test-tube. Remove the sac, add 5 drops of phenolsulphonephthalein to the dialysate, and compare with the standard tubes against a white background. The normal lies almost between PH 7.6 and PH 7.8. The symbol PH is generally substituted for the negative logarithms such as those used in the second paragraph of this test.

The salt solution is prepared by dissolving 8.8 gm. sodium chlorid (Merck Reagent) in 1 liter of distilled water. To a few cubic centimeters of the saline in a test-tube add two drops 0.01 per cent. phenolsulphonephthalein. A yellow color should be obtained, which changes to a brownish tinge upon raising the temperature to the boiling point to expel carbon dioxid. If this change does not occur, the saline is unsuitable for use and another is made up.

To prepare the collodion for making the sacs, the procedure indicated under the preparation of medium celloidin is followed. It is important to use a good grade of celloidin and an alcohol that is 99.6 to 99.8 per cent. The preparation is allowed to stand for two weeks before using.

Carbon Dioxid Tension of Alveolar Air (Marriott).—Apparatus complete may be obtained from Hynson, Wescott and Co., Baltimore, Md.   The normal ratio of carbon dioxid to sodium bicarbonate in blood is about 1 to 20.   This is maintained chiefly by pulmonary ventilation, consequently the alveolar air being in diffusion relationship with the blood should have an equal carbon dioxid tension.   In case excessive amounts of non-volatile acids should be formed or accumulated in the body the amount of sodium bicarbonate in the plasma may be considerably reduced.   If this is the case the carbon dioxid tension in the blood is lowered and this lowering which is proportional to the reduction in reserve alkali may be detected by measuring the carbon dioxid tension of the alveolar air.   The determination is simpler than the estimation of the reserve alkali of blood plasma, and the tests may be performed daily without inconvenience to the patient.   A tension of 20 to 35 mm. is found in severe to mild acidosis (the normal tension is 40 to 45 mm.). The determination of reserve alkali in the blood may show a slight or moderate acidosis in which the hydrogen-ion concentration of the blood is normal.   This is due to the fact that such an amount of carbonic acid may be eliminated by increased pulmonary aëration that the increase in non-volatile acids— such as phosphoric or beta-oxybutyric—is compensated for and the hydrogen-ion concentration remains unchanged.

The air is collected by having the patient breathe four times in twenty seconds into a 1,500-c.c. rubber balloon half full of atmospheric air.

To make the analysis, place 3 c.c. standard carbonate solution in a test-tube and bubble air through it from the bag into which the patient has breathed.   For this purpose a fine capillary glass pipet is attached to the outlet of the bag, and this is inserted into the carbonate solution in the test-tube.   The air is bubbled through the liquid until there is no further change in color.   Compare immediately with the standard phosphate tubes.   The room temperature should be 20° to 25°C.   Make at least two determinations.

To prepare the standard carbonate solution, place exactly 100 c.c. tenth-normal sodium hydrate in a liter volumetric flask, and add 200 c.c. of 0.01 per cent. phenolsulphonephthalein; make up to volume, and blow air through the solution from the lungs until there is no further change in color.

Prepare fifteenth-normal acid potassium phosphate and alkaline sodium phosphate solutions as indicated under the hydrogen-ion concentration of the blood (page 101) and mix these two solutions as follows:

Corresponding tension in mm.....	10	15	20	25	30	35	40	45
Acid potassium phosphate c.c.....	17.8	25.2	31	35.7	40.5	45	47	50.2
Alkaline sodium phosphate c.c.....	82.2	74.8	69	64.3	59.5	55	53	49.8

Place 3 c.c. of each of these mixtures in tubes of equal diameter; seal, and use as the standard tubes for comparison.

SEROLOGY

Serology has become so complex and extensive with the introduction of the Wassermann and other tests that it assumes an importance in hospital laboratory work almost equal to pathology, and chemistry. Although innumerable reactions have been devised and used in experimental serologic work, the number employed in routine work is comparatively small. No attempt is made here to detail the many methods used in experimental work and in biologic laboratories in the preparation of vaccines and therapeutic sera.

WIDAL REACTION

A Wright pipet (Fig. 15) is filled with blood from the patient's ear or finger and the serum allowed to separate out; or the coagulated blood is stirred with a 1-mm. glass rod and the serum separated by centrifugation. To make the test, place 10 serum tubes in the front row of a rack and into the first tube measure with a pipet graduated in hundredths 0.1 c.c. serum and 0.9 c.c. saline; to each of the remaining 9 tubes add 0.5 c.c. saline. From tube 1 carry 0.5 c.c. into tube 2, 0.5 c.c.

from tube 2 to tube 3, and so on; finally discard 0.5 c.c. from tube 10. Each of the tubes now contain 0.5 c.c. and the dilutions range from 1–10 to 1–5120. Repeat this procedure in the second row of ten tubes in the rack and again in the third row.

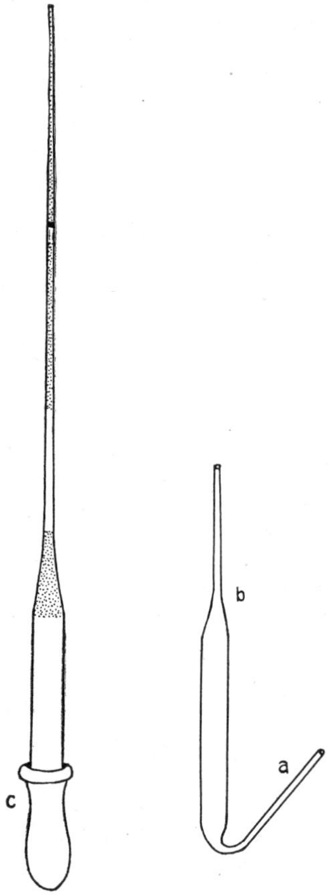

To each tube in the first row add 0.5 c.c. of a standard suspension of b. typhosus; to each tube in the second row b. paratyphosus A; to each tube in the third row 0.5 c.c. suspension of b. paratyphosus B. The dilutions now range from 1–20 to 1–10,240. Place in a water bath at 55°C. for two hours. The tube with visible agglutination but without sedimentation gives the reading. The dilution in this tube divided by the agglutinability factor gives a number representing the number of agglutinin units in 1 c.c. of serum.

A culture of b. typhosus is transplanted daily on broth and on the tenth day is planted in a flask of broth. After twenty-four hours 0.1 per cent. formalin is added, the flask placed on ice for five days, shaking repeatedly. Standardize for opacity by comparing dilutions with the same dilutions of known standard. Dilute the whole with 0.1 per cent. formalin according to the titration. The agglutinability factor is determined by comparing the suspension with the standard using a serum of known agglutinin

FIG. 15.—Wright pipets. Fill by touching the curved end, *a*, to large drops of blood. Seal at *a* in the flame. After clotting the tube may be scratched with a file at *b*, broken and the serum removed with a capillary pipet. *c*, Measuring capillary pipet.

content. This factor is written on the new suspension.

In isolating typhoid bacilli from the stools (page 192), the first rough slide agglutination should be made with a 1–100 polyvalent serum; while the suspension from the surface of the Russell-lead acetate tubes is agglutinated with monovalent typhoid, paratyphoid A and paratyphoid B sera in the proper dilutions. On this medium typhoid and paratyphoid B produce browning in upper part of the stab while paratyphoid A, dysentery bacilli and colon bacilli do not. The colon produces intense acid and gas throughout, the paratyphoids produce acid and gas in the bottom only, while typhoid and the dysentery bacilli produce only acid in the bottom. In typhoid fever positive cultures are obtained from the blood in 90 per cent. of the cases during the first week of the disease, 75 per cent. during the second week and 60 per cent. during the third week. It may be necessary to transplant the organism for several times on bouillon before they agglutinate typically.

During the first week of typhoid the Widal test is in more than three-fourths of the cases negative, and bacteriologic examination of the blood and of the feces is indicated. During convalescence agglutination is positive in about 90 per cent. of the cases. The increasing prevalence of vaccination also lessens the diagnostic usefulness of the reaction, since the serum of vaccinated individuals continues for a considerable period to give a positive agglutination. Dreyer has shown that in typhod fever the agglutinins rise quite rapidly and again fall during a period of about one month while the agglutinin content resulting from a vaccination a number of months previously remains rather constant. This curve may be drawn by doing five macroscopic tests as indicated above at five-day intervals.

AGGLUTINATING TEST OF BLOOD TO BE USED FOR TRANSFUSION

This test is of considerable practical importance. A serum that very strongly agglutinates the corpuscles of one individual may produce no agglutination of the corpuscles of another person. With a syringe draw blood from the subject who is to furnish it for transfusion (the donor) and expel it into two test-tubes, one of which contains one-tenth gram potassium oxalate. Allow the non-oxalated blood to clot. Repeat on the individual who is to be injected (the recipient). Centrifuge the oxalated blood from both, and wash the corpuscles three times as in the Wassermann test. With saline dilute the corpuscles to a light salmon pink. In small serum tubes (1 by 10 cm.) make the four possible combinations (RC plus RS, RC plus DS, RS plus DC, and DC plus DS) of sera and corpuscles, using equal amounts of each. (R and D represent recipient and donor; S and C, serum and corpuscles.) Allow fifteen minutes at 37.5°C. for agglutination. If agglutination takes place in any of the preparations the donor is not satisfactory. The tubes are again placed in the incubator for one hour and examined for both agglutination and hemolysis. The RC plus RS combination serves for a control.

PHAGOCYTOSIS IN VITRO (OPSONIC INDEX TEST)

To determine the influence of the serum on the ability of leukocytes to incorporate bacteria, it is necessary to prepare in a prescribed way the three ingredients employed in the reaction. Determination of the opsonic index in connection with vaccine therapy is not performed so much now as formerly, but the reaction appears to be in the line of important experimental developments. There has been an almost total lack of observation in regard to the relationship between neutrophiles and phagocytic mononuclear cells in the ingestion of bacteria, although the amount of routine and experimental work has been enormous.

Leukocytes.—First prepare the leukocytes by placing 2 c.c. of a 3.8 per cent. sodium citrate in a 15-c.c. graduated centrifuge tube, and adding three cubic centimeters of blood from a finger after puncturing deeply with an automatic lance. Shake; make up to 15 c.c. with normal saline; and centrifuge. Pipet off the supernatant fluid; again add normal saline to 15 c.c.; and centrifuge. Pipet off again; add saline to 3 c.c., and shake. This is the preparation of washed leukocytes.

Serum.—To enable leukocytes to take up actively foreign particles the presence of fresh unheated serum is required. The substances present in the serum that enable the leukocytes to act in this way have been named opsonins. These substances present in normal sera are increased during active immunization. At the time the 3 c.c. of blood is taken from the finger for the leukocytes, fill a small Wright pipet with blood and allow it to clot. Seal one end of the pipet, break off the other end, and with a minute glass thread stir the clot up. Place this tube in the centrifuge along with the preparation of leukocytes; and then centrifuge.

Suspension of the Bacteria.—Grow bacteria such as staphylococcus, streptococcus, or typhoid bacillus, for eighteen hours on an agar slant; fill the tube half full with normal saline and with a platinum loop rub off the growth into the saline. Pipet off the suspension into another cork-stoppered tube and shake for an hour in a mechanical shaker; or the suspension may be vigorously shaken by hand.

To make the test, equal parts of the leukocytes, serum, and bacterial suspension should, by means of a Wright pipet, be thoroughly mixed in the well of a concave slide. Draw the liquid in the mixing pipet into the middle portion, seal the tip in a flame and place it for fifteen minutes (colon and typhoid 10 min.) at 37.5°C. Break off the end of the capillary after scratching with a file and make smears on cover-glasses; stain with a polychrome blood stain, and count with the oil-immersion lens the bacteria in 100 leukocytes (neutrophiles and endothelial leukocytes) that have ingested the bacteria. The average number of bacteria per leukocyte is called the phagocytic index of the individual whose serum is used. The phagocytic index of a patient, divided by the phagocytic index of a normal (control) individual, is the so-called opsonic index. The control test is made in exactly the same way except fresh serum from several healthy individuals is placed together (pooled serum) and substituted for the patient's serum. The determination with tubercle bacilli is made in the same way except that the smears fixed in methyl alcohol are stained by placing 1 per cent. safranin on the preparation and steaming for a few minutes, and differentiating in 95 per cent. alcohol.

CYTOLYSIS IN VITRO

It has been observed that normal blood serum may have the property of dissolving a given variety of cancer cells, while the serum of the patient does not bring about solution of the cells. Again, it has been found that the blood serum of pregnant women contains a specific ferment that digests placental cells. Although these reactions have afforded valuable information in regard to the lytic properties of human serum, they do not at this time have any great diagnostic use. These ferments appear not to be exactly specific and their presence in the serum of a given condition is not constant.

To test the solution of cancer cells by a given serum, place 10 drops of the serum, 1 drop of 0.5 per cent. sodium fluorid, and 1 drop of a suspension of cancer cells in the well of a concave slide, and thoroughly mix. Make a preparation in a blood counting-chamber, count the cells in a given area, incubate for twenty-four hours, and again count the number of cells. To make the cell suspension, grind in a mortar 10 gm. fresh cancer tissue free of fat with 50 c.c. 1 per cent. sodium biphosphate, and squeeze through muslin. Centrifuge; wash with saline; pipet off the saline, and make up to 50 c.c. with 1 per cent. sodium fluorid to which normal alkali has been added until there is only a trace of violet with alizarin. This suspension keeps for one month on ice.

The manner of ascertaining the solution of placental cells (Abderhalden reaction) is different. To 1 gm. toluol-preserved placental tissue in a small dialyzing sac that permits the passage of peptones, add 3 c.c. blood serum from a pregnant woman, and a few drops of toluol. Immerse the sac in 15 c.c. water in a small beaker, and place in incubator overnight. To 10 c.c. of the dialysate in a test-tube add 0.2 c.c. of a 1 per cent. aqueous solution of triketohydrinden hydrate, and boil for one minute. A violet color is positive. The serum must show no hemolysis. The placental tissue is prepared by boiling in water which contains a few drops of glacial acetic acid small bits of a placenta that has been thoroughly washed. Pour off the water, and again boil until the washings react negatively with the triketohydrinden hydrate (ninhydrin) which reveals traces of albumin, peptone, polypeptids, and amino acids. The technic is difficult and contradictory findings have been the rule. Details in regard to testing the permeability of the celloidin thimbles are rather useless since the technician must familiarize himself with the technic employed by making extensive controls. The way in which the thimbles are made is described elsewhere (page 102).

FERMENTS AND ANTIFERMENTS IN BLOOD SERUM

Aside from the solution of cells by fermentative constituents of sera, much has been learned of their enzymic and anti-enzymic properties. Further work may attach diagnostic value to some of these reactions.

To test for *antitrypsin ferment*, add 1 drop of serum to 1, 2, 3, 4, 5, 6, 7, 8, 9, and 10 drops of 50 per cent. glycerin that contains 1 per cent. trypsin. Transfer a loopful of each of these mixtures to the surface of Loeffler's blood serum contained in a Petri dish. Incubate for five hours, and examine for a dimpling of the medium at the site of the serum-trypsin applications. The amount of antitrypsin in the blood of some cancer cases is large.

To test for the *diastatic activity* of blood (Myers and Killian), place in each of two graduated centrifuge tubes 2 c.c. oxalated blood. To the one that is to serve as a control add water to 10 c.c., and to the other add water to 9 c.c., and place both in a water-bath at 40°C. After ten minutes, add 1 c.c. 1 per cent. soluble starch to the second tube and continue the incubation for exactly fifteen minutes. Remove from the incubator, add 1 gm. picric acid to each tube, and estimate the sugar as indicated above (page 87). Calculate the amount of reducing sugar formed per 100 c.c. of blood during the period of incubation, which in normal individuals is about three-fourths milligram. In severe diabetes the diastatic activity may be increased five times. In general, the increase is in proportion to the increase of blood sugar. The action of the blood on glycogen is practically the same as on soluble starch.

PRECIPITIN REACTION FOR THE IDENTIFICATION OF HUMAN BLOOD STAINS

If a stain is found to be blood (hemin-crystal test, Fig. 16) the source of the blood may become a question of considerable importance. By the precipitin reaction human blood may be identified. This test requires painstaking controls. To 50 c.c. saline in a large test-tube, add pieces of cloth, wood, or other material on which the stain is present. A similar piece of the fabric or other material taken from near the stain, but macroscopically containing none of it, should be placed in a second tube and treated in the same way as the tube that contains the suspected blood.

After standing overnight, the tube is rotated gently in order

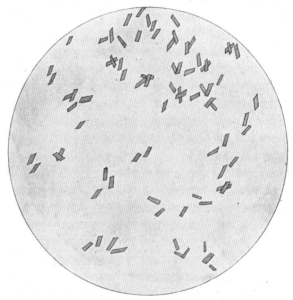

FIG. 16.—Hemin (Teichmann) crystals drawn with the high-dry lens.

to mix the contents. If red in color, the contents are diluted with saline until only a faint opalescence is produced by the heat-and-acetic-acid test, and until no color, or a very slight color, is apparent by transmitted light.

The immune serum is prepared as indicated under preparation of amboceptor (page 121). When immunized against whole human blood, 0.1 c.c. of the serum of a rabbit must produce a distinct cloudiness when added to 2 c.c. of a 1–1000 dilution of human serum. To perform the test, 0.1 c.c. of immune rabbit serum is added to 2 c.c. of a 1–1000 (approximate) of the extract of the suspected blood stain, to 2 c.c. 1–5000 (approximate) of the same extract contained in a second tube, and to 2 c.c. of extract of clothing or other material not included in the stain and contained in the third tube. Two cubic centimeters of the extract alone are used for a control. The number of controls varies according to the technic employed. If positive, the precipitate forms in twenty minutes. In important cases the kind of blood is determined, should it prove not to be human. The possibility of the blood being that of an ape may usually be ruled out by determining the existing circumstances. The blood of other animals does not precipitate with antihuman serum.

WASSERMANN TEST

Introduction.—In complement fixation reactions certain technical terms that are more or less common to all serologic work find a daily application. *Hemolysis* is the solution of red blood corpuscles, and it may be brought about by the action of complement and amboceptor on the erythrocytes. A given kind of erythrocyte laden with an amboceptor specific for that variety of corpuscle is known as a *sensitized corpuscle*. If such sensitized corpuscles are brought into contact with complement, hemolysis takes place. In the Wassermann technic, the *complement* is fresh guinea-pig serum, while the *amboceptor* is the serum of a rabbit that has been injected with the corpuscles of a sheep, and is known, therefore, as antisheep amboceptor.

Complement is destroyed by heating the serum for one-half hour at 55°C. This is known as *inactivation* of a serum. Amboceptor is not destroyed by this degree of heat, and in general is quite stabile. The *titre* of any ingredient is the smallest amount of the substance that will bring about a given reaction. The terms "one unit" and "titre" are usually employed interchangeably. In this sense, 1 unit of amboceptor together with 1 unit of complement brings about the solution of a given amount of corpuscles. If less than one unit of complement is combined with one unit of amboceptor or less, solution is not complete. However, if many units of amboceptor are used, a

8

deficiency in complement may be compensated for, and, with such an excess of amboceptor a small fraction of 1 unit of complement may bring about solution. Amboceptor for blood corpuscles is called hemolytic amboceptor, while that for bacteria is known as bacteriolytic amboceptor.

Sera containing amboceptor are produced by the introduction of foreign proteins into the animals from which the sera are taken (antibody is used in a somewhat less specific sense than amboceptor, and is applied to the substance [amboceptor] in a syphilitic serum that unites with the antigen and fixes the complement). Substances that produce antibodies when injected are known as *antigens*. As noted above, antigen (sheep's corpuscles), amboceptor (serum of a rabbit that has been injected with sheep's corpuscles), and complement (fresh guinea-pig serum) unite. This union destroys the complement, and the phenomenon characterized by disappearance of complement is known as *fixation of complement*.

Specificity of the Reaction.—The Wassermann test is based on the complement fixation reaction, but, since the antigen is not a specific one the reaction is not exactly specific in the same sense as those obtained with the bacterial antigens, and for syphilis the reaction is not absolutely specific. If the test is positive, the antibody of the syphilitic serum unites with the antigen and this amboceptor-antigen combination fixes the complement present, so that the sheep's corpuscles in the tube remain undissolved due to a lack of the complement required to sensitize the corpuscles. If the clinician is not familiar with the examiner's technic, it is advisable to offer interpretations along with results reported. Positive reactions not due to syphilis are often obtained in yaws and leprosy, not uncommonly in trypanosomiasis and relapsing fever, and occasionally some have observed complete or partial fixation in scarlet fever, malaria, lobar pneumonia, tuberculosis, malignant tumors, alcoholism, diabetes mellitus, pellagra, and immediately after ether or chloroform anesthesia. In the last group of conditions the reaction is not only of rare occurrence but the fixation is likely to be incomplete. A negative reaction in cases of syphilis may be obtained during treatment with arsenobenzol or mercury, and is said to occur rarely during acute alcoholism.

Occurrence of the Reaction in Luetic Cases.—Owing to the chronicity of syphilis and the tendency of the treponemata to persist in focal areas for long periods of time, activity of the syphilitic process and the amount of syphilitic amboceptor present in the serum are subject to extreme variation during the course of the disease, and only illustrative figures can be given in regard to the presence and strength of the reaction in luetic cases. Since the *primary* lesion must usually develop to a considerable extent before a positive reaction is secured, other methods should be resorted to for the diagnosis of this stage. The reaction is frequently obtained from the first to the third week after the appearance of the chancre, is almost always present after the sixth week, and persists strongly positive during the *secondary* stage. In general, the reaction is positive in *tertiary* syphilis if there is any demonstrable activity of the syphilitic process, and is frequently positive in so-called latent tertiary syphilis. Practically all *congenital* syphilitics develop a positive reaction a few months after birth. In general paresis, tabes dorsalis, and other *metasyphilitic* lesions of the central nervous system, the spinal fluid and blood serum are usually positive. One or many administrations of arsenobenzol may be required to render the Wassermann negative. If no arsenobenzol is given after the reaction first becomes negative with the smaller (see test) dose of antigen, it frequently becomes positive again after weeks or months. In cured cases of syphilis the reaction soon becomes negative. Luetic individuals without any signs or symptoms of the infection, who have not received treatment, or who have had insufficient treatment, are not looked upon as cured and the cases are spoken of as ones of *latent* syphilis. Of such cases, perhaps, one-fourth have a positive reaction. Some patients with a latent syphilis with a negative Wassermann are given mercurial inunctions for one week, and if a Wassermann test is made one week after the treatment is stopped, a positive reaction may be obtained. This method of obtaining a positive reaction has been spoken of as a *provocative treatment*.

Interpretation of Results.—In negative reactions, all the corpuscles are hemolyzed; while in perfect positive ones there is no hemolysis. Between these two extremes, all degrees of hemolysis occur. If there is only partial solution of corpuscles, the amount of inhibition is usually estimated by the degree of clouding; but all tubes may be placed in a refrigerator overnight and the amount of corpuscles noted and the reading of results made from these. Those that show only a slight clouding (less than one-fourth of the corpuscles undissolved) are marked "positive +." Such results have no diagnostic value except in cases of known syphilis under treatment. In such cases further active treatment is indicated. A greater clouding due to about one-half of the corpuscles remaining undissolved is recorded as "positive + +." If there is inhibition of the hemolysis of three-fourths of the corpuscles the result is recorded "positive + + +." In this case there is only a tinge of red in the liquid above the sedimenting corpuscles. "Positive + +" and "positive + + +" are considered as positive diagnoses of syphilis only in connection with strong clinical evidence. They call for further active medication in cases under treatment. If there is no tinge of red in the liquid above the sedimenting corpuscles, there is complete inhibition of hemolysis, and the result is recorded as "positive + + + +." If the conditions mentioned above are not present, such a result is considered a positive diagnosis of syphilis.

Choice of Methods.—In selecting one from the great number of methods described, the most important principle to follow is to introduce into the test no undesirable factor that might be eliminated. For this reason nucleated corpuscles such as those of the fowl should not be used since they do not hemolyze perfectly and give an undesirable clouding in the tube. For the same reason an antigen that is too cloudy should not be used. Test-tubes should be of such a size that the contents may be viewed to the best advantage. If such obvious disadvantages are eliminated the way in which the technic is executed is of greater importance than the method selected.

Care should be exercised in selecting glassware for the technic.

Test-tubes are washed, rinsed with several changes of water, placed upside down in wire baskets and dry-heat sterilized. Pipets after being washed are sterilized tip upwards.

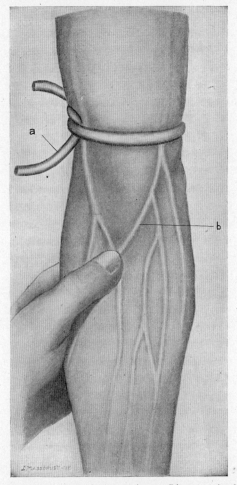

FIG. 17.—Drawing blood from the arm vein.   a, Ligature of soft black rubber tubing which is loosened before needle is removed from the vein.   Needle is inserted at b just in front of the left thumb which is firmly pressed down upon the vein to prevent its slipping from side to side and escaping the needle.   Frequently the vein may be distinctly felt in the position indicated when it cannot be seen.

Sera.—One-tenth c.c. is used in the actual test.   Before entering upon a consideration of the test it is desirable to describe in detail the six constituents entering into the reaction.   Blood is drawn from the vein at the bend of the elbow (Fig. 17) by means of a syringe (or sterile 25-gauge needle) and placed in a sterile cork-stoppered test-tube (serum tube 80 by 10 mm.).   The tube, with a brown slip wrapped about it, is placed in a refrigerator and a test of the serum made within forty-eight hours. Outfits such as those used by the N. Y. Board of Health containing both tube for blood and sterile needle are convenient.

Not less than 2 c.c. of blood are collected; and at times this amount may be obtained from the finger in the manner already indicated (page 23).   In children blood may be removed from the jugular vein or by scarifying the back and applying a wet cup.   When the test is to be made, the tube and the brown slip are numbered with a wax-pencil.   With a capillary pipet made from glass tubing and provided with a nipple for suction the serum is removed from the tube and placed in another of the same size that bears the same number.   A different capillary pipet is used for each serum.

If the serum is not clear—and this is usually the case—the clot in the original tube is thoroughly broken up by means of a small sterile glass rod.   It is then placed in a centrifuge and whirled for five minutes, when the clear serum may be pipeted off.   If the serum shows marked hemolysis, it is advisable to secure a fresh specimen; but if there is only a slight tinge of red it may be possible to perform the test. Heart blood collected at autopsy almost always shows marked hemolysis and the test should be performed with one-half the usual amount.   In all cases, a note of the hemolysis is entered in the record.   A milky color due to lipoids in the serum usually does not interfere with the test.   Serum colored with bile may give a false positive reaction and any suggestion of bile pigment in the serum should be noted on the slip.   Separate pipets and glass rods are used for each specimen.   After using the rods, pipets and tubes are placed in a wash-basin, washed with running water, drained, dried, and sterilized.

The tubes containing the clear sera are inactivated for thirty minutes in a water-bath at 55°C.   One-tenth c.c. from each of the tubes is used for each test, and 0.2 c.c. for an *anticomplementary control*. To meet with a serum giving a negative reaction with 0.1 c.c. and partial inhibition of hemo-ysis with 0.2 c.c. is a rare occurrence.

A 1-c.c. pipet, graduated in hundredths to the very tip, is used for measuring the patient's serum. It is washed four times with saline between each serum. By placing 0.1-c.c. drops of serum on paper and then letting them dry, a "positive + + + +" serum may be kept for three months. Five-tenths c.c. of non-inactivated cerebrospinal fluid is used for each test. Less commonly the test is performed on pleural exudate, pericardial fluid, ascitic fluid, etc.

Uncommonly a serum contains sufficient natural antisheep amboceptor to produce a negative reaction in the face of par-tial fixation of the complement. If only 0.1 c.c. of serum is used, this false result does not happen often enough to warrant an additional control for each test. In using 0.2 c.c. or more of serum the possibility of *natural antisheep amboceptor* present in the serum playing a part in the test should be kept in mind and it is better to dilute the inactivated serum 1-5 with 5 per cent. suspension of sheep's corpuscles, allowing them to remain together for one-half hour and removing the corpuscles by centrifugation. If an excessive amount of natural sheep amboceptor is suspected, the control is set up by placing 0.05 c.c. patient's serum, 1 unit complement, 0.5 c.c. corpuscles, and 2.5 c.c. saline in the tube and incubating for one hour.

Complement.—Two units contained in 0.5 c.c. are used in the actual test. If a dilution of more than about 1-10 is found on titration to be required the serum should be viewed with some suspicion. If the number of reactions to be done is above thirty, it is perhaps better to obtain the blood by cutting the throats of guinea-pigs with an amputating knife, after a numbing knock on the head of the animal in each case, when the blood is allowed to drip into a 10-cm. porcelain dish. A second person defibrinates the blood by stirring it with a heavy nickel-plated wire or a heavy platinum wire.

If there are fewer tests, the blood is removed from the heart of an etherized guinea-pig strapped to a holder. In this way, several cubic centimeters of blood may be removed from a large pig. A fine platinum-iridium needle is used for insertion through the intercostal space into the heart at the point where the greatest pulsation appears. If the needle does not enter the heart at once, reinsert without withdrawing from the thoracic wall. The blood is at once forced from the syringe into a sterile 30-c.c. Erlenmeyer flask containing six pieces (1 cm. square)

of bright, fine-mesh wire-gauze. The flask is shaken by hand, or in a mechanical defibrinator, until defibrination is complete. After the blood is obtained in either of these ways and defibrinated, it is placed in 15-c.c. sterile centrifuge tubes (Fig. 18) and whirled for fifteen minutes. The tubes are removed from the centrifuge and the serum which must be clear and free from corpuscles is pipeted off. A pipet like that employed for measuring the patient's serum is used for measuring the complement.

Some prefer to cut the throats of the guinea-pigs and allow them to bleed into sterile Petri dishes, which are placed in the refrigerator overnight after the clot has been loosened about the edges. The clear serum is removed with a pipet.

FIG. 18.—Graduated centrifuge tube. These tubes are plugged with cotton, dry-heat sterilized and kept on hand for centrifuging fluid aseptically.

In order to make accurate measurements possible, it is necessary to dilute the guinea-pig serum with 9 parts of saline to make a 10 per cent. strength. One-half cubic centimeter is diluted 1–10 and titrated as indicated under standardization of the hemolytic system (page 131). The remainder of the complement is so diluted according to this titration that 0.5 c.c. contains 2 units, which is the amount used in the test. If the complement is for a considerable number of tests, the serum may be measured with a pipet into a 100-c.c. graduate and the correct dilution (1–10) of the entire amount made. In the original Wassermann technic a constant 0.1 c.c. of undiluted guinea-pig serum was used, but the serum of normal guinea-pigs is subject to considerable variation in complement content and should be titrated. Poorly nourished or diseased animals usually have a diminished amount of complement. Not only does the amount of hemolysin vary but its power of being fixed by antigen also varies. The latter is best corrected by pooling the sera from a number of guinea-pigs. The serum of no other common laboratory animals is so suitable as that of the guinea-pig.

Amboceptor.—Two units contained in 0.5 c.c. are used in the actual test. At intervals of three or four days (Tuesday and Friday of each week), inject into the peritoneal cavity of a rabbit which weighs above 2000 gm., 5, 8, 12, 15, and 20 c.c. sterile, washed sheep's corpuscles. Five days after the last injection, 1 c.c. or more of blood is obtained by slitting the ear veins (or by inserting a needle into the marginal ear vein, withdrawing the needle and allowing the wound to bleed); and if it is not strong enough, a sixth injection of 25 c.c. is given. The animal is bled ten days after the last injection.

Another method is to give intravenously four injections of 1 to 3 c.c. of the sterile, washed corpuscles, and bleed ten days after the last injection.

To obtain the sterile, washed corpuscles, place 20 c.c. sterile defibrinated sheep's blood in a sterile 50-c.c. centrifuge tube, mark the upper surface of the blood with a blue pencil, fill the tube with sterile saline, and whirl for five minutes. Siphon off the supernatant fluid, add saline, and again centrifuge. Wash the corpuscles in this way four times. After decanting the saline the last time, add a sufficient amount of saline to bring the corpuscle suspension to the blue mark.

To bleed, fasten the animal in a rabbit holder (page 187), shave the neck, anesthetize with ether, and dissect out both carotids for at least one inch. Tie one carotid as high as possible, and place a soft spring artery clamp on the vessel half an inch below the ligature. Cut the vessel just below the ligature, secure a firm hold in the adventitia of the loose end of the artery, so as to guide the vessel into the mouth of the flask, and then remove the clamp. The blood collected in a sterile 250-c.c. Erlenmeyer flask is allowed to clot, the clot loosened about its periphery, and the flask placed in a refrigerator overnight for the clot to harden. The clear serum is removed, and inactivated by heating for one-half hour at 55°C. to destroy complement.

Bulk Amboceptor Titration.—To determine the strength of the entire bulk of hemolytic serum (amboceptor), dilute the inactivated serum 1–100, 1–200, 1–250, 1–300, 1–350, and 1–400; and place 0.25 c.c. of each of these dilutions in six test-tubes, together with one unit of complement and 0.5 c.c. 5 per cent. suspension of corpuscles. Add saline to 3 c.c., and incubate for one hour. One unit of complement is determined as indicated under standardization of the hemolytic system (page 131). The smallest amount of amboceptor that completely hemolyzes all the corpuscles is 1 *unit*. If 0.25 c.c. of the 1–200 dilution of the serum is not sufficient to hemolyze the corpuscles, it is better to immunize another animal. If the titration proves satisfactory, the serum after inactivation at 55°C. for one-half hour is sealed in the flame in small sterile tubes made from glass tubing, placing about 2 c.c. in each.

Amboceptor Titration for Actual Test.—If the bulk titration (titration of the entire volume of serum from a rabbit) shows that 0.25 of a 1–300 dilution contains 1 unit, the amount of amboceptor to be used for the tests that day is diluted 1–250 with saline for the trial titration described under standardization of the hemolytic system (page 131). According to this titration, enough saline is added to the 1–250 dilution so that 0.25 c.c. will contain 1 unit. In the test 0.5 c.c. are used. The dilute amboceptor may be kept in a refrigerator for two weeks with little deterioration, but must be retitrated before using.

To make the correct dilution of amboceptor, if the number of tests is above 30, the hemolytic or amboceptor serum (0.4 c.c.) is usually measured accurately with a pipet graduated in hundredths into a 100-c.c. graduate or volumetric flask and made up to a given volume which is less than that indicated by the primary titration. If there are only a few tests a 15-c.c. graduated centrifuge tube may be used. According to the titration add sufficient additional saline so that 0.25 c.c. contains one unit.

Antigen.—The antigens used in the Wassermann test are not specific, and more changes have been made in them since the test was first described than in any other part of the technic. The syphilitic antibody (amboceptor) has the property in the presence of lipoids of absorbing complement. The lipoidal substance has been called antigen but this term is not correct but may be retained for convenience. The tendency now is toward the use of a cholesterinized alcoholic extract of human or guinea-pig heart as antigen. By using a large and small dose this antigen appears to be as accurate as the acetone-insoluble antigen in the diagnosis of syphilis.

Cholesterin Antigen.—Five-tenths c.c. is used in the actual test. Place in a pint Mason jar 50 gm. human heart muscle which has been finely ground in a meat-chopper and freed from all visible particles of fat, and add 500 c.c. absolute alcohol. Guinea-pig heart muscle may be used but human heart is preferable. Cover tightly, and place in the incubator for two weeks, shaking daily. Filter; allow the filtrate to stand for two days at room temperature; and if a precipitate forms, filter again. The filtrate is the heart extract and keeps for one year. Once in four weeks, or more frequently as required, add 0.1 gm. cholesterin (previously found to be satisfactory) to 25 c.c. of the extract and place in the incubator overnight. The heart extract cholesterinized in this way is likely to become anticomplementary in one month.

Dilution of the Antigen.—The alcoholic cholesterinized extract is diluted with saline, and definite amounts of such dilutions used in the test. The amount of antigen used is of prime importance and is decided upon only after the titrations outlined below. The antigens prepared in this way are quite uniform and 0.5 c.c. of a 1–8 dilution (12.5 per cent. emulsion) usually proves to be one-fourth to one-third the anticomplementary dose, while 0.5 c.c. of a 1–10 dilution (10 per cent. emulsion) is about one-fourth the anticomplementary quantity. These are the amounts used in the test. The dilutions are made just before use, and may be made in 100-c.c. graduates by adding slowly from a pipet the alcoholic cholesterinized extract to the correct amount of saline. It has been shown that a slow mixing of the two gives a more opalescent liquid and that such a liquid has greater antigenic properties. This antigen of course must be titrated.

A large dose of antigen may give a positive test in a serum that with a smaller amount is negative, while all sera positive with a small dose of antigen are positive with large ones. The large dose (0.5 c.c. of a 1–8 dilution) is of value in cases under treatment indicating that the treatment should be continued; but in the diagnosis of new cases, results obtained with the larger doses should not alone be considered certain evidence of syphilis. In the diagnosis of new cases either two doses of cholesterin antigen or a large dose of cholesterin antigen and a dose of acetone-insoluble antigen should be used.

Acetone-insoluble Antigen.— One-tenth c.c. which contains twice the antigenic dose is used in the actual test. The older so-called lipoid or acetone-insoluble antigen has been replaced in most laboratories by cholesterin antigen. It is so variable in strength that two *antigenic units* as determined by titration are used instead of a definite volume. Sera positive with this antigen are strongly positive with the cholesterin antigen. In new cases some workers prefer to use this antigen instead of two different amounts of cholesterin antigen.

To prepare the antigen, place in a pint Mason jar 50 gm. fresh beef heart, or fresh human heart, that has been ground in a sausage-grinder, and add 450 c.c. absolute alcohol. Place in the incubator at 37.5°C., shaking daily. Filter through paper; place the filtrate in a flat dish 12 inches across, and evaporate with an electric fan. Take up the residue in a dish with 200 c.c. of ether. Place the milky ether overnight in a Mason jar with cover clamped to prevent evaporation. The following morning decant the ether—which is now clear—into a beaker, and evaporate to about 50 c.c. Add 450 c.c. of acetone

(C.P.) to the 50 c.c. remaining, thoroughly mix, and decant the supernatant solution from the insoluble residue. By means of an electric fan, it is usually necessary after decanting, to evaporate the acetone-insoluble extract to the desired sticky mass, which contains the antigenic lipoids. To 0.3 gm. of this mass add 1 c.c. ether and 9 c.c. methyl alcohol. The entire mass is made up in this way into the ether-methyl-alcohol solution, which is permanent.

To 1 c.c of this ether-alcohol solution add 9 c.c. saline, and make the test titrations as outlined below. If the titration is satisfactory, seal the ether-methyl-alcohol solution in tubes, placing about 2 c.c. of the ether-alcohol solution in each tube. Each time before beginning to make Wassermann tests, such a dilution is made with saline that 0.5 c.c. of the resulting emulsion contains twice the antigenic dose. If the dilution required is less than about 1 in 10, it is usually too cloudy and should be discarded. The stock antigen in the 2-c.c. tubes keeps for several years.

Gonococcus Antigen.—Five-tenths c.c. which contains twice the antigenic dose is used for the actual test. Grow the gonococci for twenty-four hours on hydrocele or ascitic agar slants. By means of bulb pipet, take up the growth from each tube with 2 c.c. of distilled water, and place the suspension of gonococci in a 500-c.c. glass-stoppered bottle. Shake the bottle in a mechanical shaker overnight. Heat for two hours at 55°C. Filter through a Berkfeld filter, and add 0.9 per cent. sodium chlorid and 0.5 per cent. phenol. Make such a dilution of this solution that 0.5 c.c. contains twice the antigenic dose. Most serologists prefer to make gonococcus antigen from a number of different strains of the organisms (polyvalent antigen). Bacterial antigens other than gonococcus are prepared in the same way. Such a dilution of the stock antigen is made that 0.5 c.c. contains *twice the antigenic dose.* Double this amount should not be anticomplementary.

Echinococcus Antigen.—Five-tenths c.c. which contains twice the antigenic dose is used for the actual test. The great majority of cases of echinococcus infection gives a positive complement fixation reaction with echinococcus antigen, and most observers find that a positive reaction with such an antigen is not obtained in other conditions. A few have reported positive tests in individuals infected with tenia saginata and tenia solium. The antigen is prepared by adding as a preservative 0.5 per cent. phenol to the cyst fluid from a human or sheep case of the disease. It must be determined before each test that twice the antigenic dose is not anticomplementary. Such a dilution is made that 0.5 c.c. contains twice the antigenic dose.

Testing the Antigens.—All antigens are titrated before using. To make these initial tests, 9 c.c. saline are added to 1 c.c. of the stock (alcoholic) antigen. In the case of all antigens except the cholesterin antigen, variations from this 10 per cent. emulsion are later made according to the results of these titrations, in order that 0.5 c.c. of the dilution used in each test may contain two antigenic units.

Hemolytic Property.—All antigens contain lipoids which are hemolytic. The hemolytic action of lipoids is inhibited by the presence of serum (complement). If the antigen is hemolytic in about five times the antigenic dose, it is not used. An antigen that is hemolytic in somewhat less than five times the antigenic dose may work satisfactorily, but this empirical standard is adhered to as closely as possible. To test, place in each of the four tubes 0.5, 1, 3, and 5 c.c. of a 1 in 8 emulsion of antigen, add 0.5 c.c. of 5 per cent. suspension of corpuscles, make up to 6 c.c. with saline, and incubate for one hour at $37.5°C$. No protective serum is added in this titration. The smallest amount that completely hemolyzes all the corpuscles is known as the hemolytic dose. The liquid above the sedimenting corpuscles is not tinged with red unless the antigen added has produced hemolysis. The tubes containing the most antigen are milky owing to the opalescence of the antigen emulsion.

Anticomplementary Property.—All antigens contain substances which render complement inactive and, if used in large enough quantities, completely prevent hemolysis. Therefore, this titration is of first importance. Eight times one antigenic unit which is about four times the amount used in the actual test should not be anticomplementary (*i.e.*, it should not contain an excessive amount of a substance that absorbs complement to render it inactive). It is desirable to determine the exact amount of antigen that is anticomplementary. To do this, place ten tubes in a rack and add an increasing amount of the antigen to each: 0.2, 0.3, 0.4, 0.5, 0.6, 0.8, 1.0, 1.5, 2 and 3 c.c. of the 12.5 per cent. emulsion. To each of the tubes add 0.5 c.c. amboceptor (two units as determined under the standardization of the hemolytic system), 0.5 c.c. diluted complement (two units as determined under standardization of the hemolytic system), 0.5 c.c. 5 per cent. suspension of corpuscles, and 1 c.c. saline. Incubate for one hour. One-tenth c.c. of normal serum may be added to each tube but in this case an extra tube without antigen must be set up. Even perfectly fresh normal serum contains some anticomplementary substance. The first tube in which there is incomplete hemolysis contains an anticomplementary dose. The tube containing about eight times the antigenic dose as determined below should be completely hemolyzed.

Antigenic Property.—An antigenic dose is the smallest amount of antigen that gives a complete inhibition of hemolysis with pooled "positive + + + +" sera. To determine the antigenic property of a new antigen, place in ten tubes decreasing amounts of the 12.5 per cent. emulsion: 0.8, 0.7, 0.6, 0.5, 0.4, 0.3, 0.2, 0.1, 0.05 and 0.02 c.c. Add to each tube 0.1 c.c. of a known "positive + + + +" serum, 0.5 c.c. diluted complement (two units as determined under standardization of the hemolytic system), 0.5 c.c. amboceptor (two units as determined under the standardization of the hemolytic system), and 1 c.c. saline. Incubate for thirty minutes at 37.5°C., add 0.5 c.c. of a 5 per cent. suspension of corpuscles, and incubate for one hour. The tube with the smallest amount antigen that shows complete absence of hemolysis represents one fixing unit. It is desirable to repeat this with three perfectly positive sera of cases in different stages of the disease, and to take the average of the four as the fixing unit.

The amount of antigen used in the actual tests should con-

tain at least twice the smallest amount of antigen that gives
complete inhibition of hemolysis in the test of the antigenic
property.   It is desirable that eight times this proper antigenic
dose should not be hemolytic and should not be anticomplementary.

In the case of cholesterin antigen, there is no difficulty in
obtaining an antigen that fulfills these requirements, but it
is practically impossible to secure a bacterial antigen that is
not anticomplementary in eight times the antigenic dose,
and it may be necessary to use an antigen that is anticompet-
mentary at twice the amount (four times the antigenic dose)
used in the test.   This is the shortest working distance that is
permissible.

The amount of antigen to be used in the test, as well as the
kind of antigen, differs much in various laboratories; but greater
uniformity exists since the advent of cholesterinized antigen.
It is usually found that 0.5 c.c. of this variety of antigen is about
one-fourth the anticomplementary dose.   This amount should
contain at least twice the antigenic dose.   Some workers specify
twice the antigenic dose as the amount to be used for each test,
but this amount of antigen may give in one serum a lipoid-antibody combination that absorbs a much greater or a much
less amount of complement than the lipoid-antibody combination formed in a second or third strongly positive serum.
This is illustrated by determining the fixing units or smallest
amounts of a strongly positive serum that will, with a definite amount of a given antigen, give complete inhibition of
hemolysis: 0.1 c.c. of A serum gives "positive $+ + + +$"
with 0.5 c.c. 1–10 emulsion antigen, while 0.01 c.c. of B serum
gives the same result.   When decreasing amounts of the same
antigen are added to tubes that contain 0.1 c.c. of A serum
(1 fixing unit) and 0.01 c.c. of B (1 fixing unit), it is found
that the first combination remains perfectly positive with
0.4 c.c. of antigen, and the second one with only 0.1 c.c.   An
exact titration of antigen, therefore, is not possible by this
method.   By pooling a number of perfectly positive sera an
"average fixing unit" may be obtained.   An antigenic dose is

the amount of antigen required to give complete inhibition of hemolysis when used with one fixing unit of the pooled sera.

Corpuscles.—Five-tenths c.c. of a 5 per cent. suspension of washed sheep's corpuscles is used for the actual test. In a sterile pint Mason jar containing glass beads collect the corpuscles of slaughter-house lambs. Collect half full, and then shake for ten minutes until completely defibrinated. Keep on ice until used. To prepare the corpuscles filter the defibrinated blood through muslin, and with a 10-c.c. pipet transfer 10 c.c. of the filtrate to each of two sterile 50-c.c. centrifuge tubes. Make up to 50 c.c. with the saline, balance on suitable balances, and centrifuge for five minutes; remove the supernatant fluid by a *permanent siphon* made by joining the glass cock of a broken buret to a piece of glass tubing bent into a U. The liquid may be removed by means of a sterile capillary glass tubing attached to the usual water suction-pump. Add saline to the 50-c.c. mark and repeat three or more times until the supernatant fluid is clear after centrifugation. After the supernatant fluid becomes clear, centrifuge for thirty minutes at the same speed used to throw down the corpuscles in five minutes, and carefully pipet off all the supernatant fluid. Place 10 c.c. of the corpuscles in a 250-c.c. Erlenmeyer flask and add 190 c.c. saline. Keep on ice. Use a 10-c.c. pipet graduated in tenths for measuring out the corpuscles. For each test use 0.5 c.c. of the 5 per cent. suspension of corpuscles.

Some workers prefer to *sensitize the corpuscles.* This is done by adding 0.5 c.c. amboceptor that contains two hemolytic units to 0.5 c.c. of the 5 per cent. suspension of corpuscles, incubating for one-half hour at 37.5°C. and using 1 c.c. of the sensitized corpuscles instead of the two units of amboceptor and 0.5 c.c. of corpuscles added separately. There appears to be no theoretical reason for or against such a sensitization of the corpuscles, and whether the test be a positive or a negative one, it makes little difference because the hemolytic amboceptor remains free during the first incubation of the test and it is certainly not injured by the incubation.

9

For a limited number of Wassermann tests it is often preferable to remove the blood from the jugular vein of a sheep kept for this purpose. One person places himself astride the sheep, holding its chin up, while the other clips off the wool and inserts in the jugular vein a small platinum-iridium needle attached to a 20-c.c. syringe. Defibrinate the blood in a 150-c.c. Erlenmeyer flask containing disks of wire-gauze. Without doubt the corpuscles from citrated blood are satisfactory and 9 c.c. of blood may be added to 6 c.c. 3.8 per cent. sodium citrate in a 15-c.c. centrifuge tube. Wash in 15-c.c. centrifuge tubes. When washing, a siphon pipet is very convenient for removing the supernatant liquid. To 0.5 c.c. washed corpuscles in a 15-c.c. centrifuge tube add sufficient saline to make 10 c.c. Vary the technic of making up the corpuscle suspension as little as possible. No changes whatsoever in the corpuscle suspension, are permissible after the complement and amboceptor units are determined. If a sheep is kept for Wassermann tests it should not be allowed to become anemic.

Saline.—Such an amount of saline (1 c.c. in test and 1.5 c.c. in anticomplementary control) is used in the actual test so that each tube from which a reading must be made may contain within 0.1 c.c. of 3 c.c. of fluid. Add 8.8 gm. sodium chlorid (Merck) to a liter of distilled water. Autoclave. The size of the flasks containing saline will vary according to the number of tests to be performed. A 10-c.c. pipet, graduated in tenths, is used for measuring the saline.

Method of Combining the Six Liquids for the Test.—Under each of the six liquids used in the test the exact amount required is indicated. In performing the test on a single serum, all that is required is that 0.1 c.c. patient's serum, 0.5 c.c. antigen, 0.5 c.c. complement, 0.5 c.c. amboceptor, and 1 c.c. saline be placed in a test-tube and incubated for one-half hour at 37.5°C.; whereupon it is removed from the incubator, 0.5 c.c. sheep's corpuscles is added and, it is again incubated for one hour. At the same time that the test is run a control is made. The control is identical with the test, except that it contains no antigen and has in it 0.2 c.c. patient's serum instead of 0.1 c.c.; 1.5 c.c. saline is added. The chief use of the control is to detect anticomplementary properties in the patient's serum. Minor modifications of technic are very numerous, but the general principles of the test are much the same in all laboratories where the most painstaking care is used. In a reaction where the technic is so complicated, the introduction of any factor which may increase the chance of error should be avoided.

In the test six liquids are placed together in a single test-tube: patient's serum (0.1 c.c.), dilute complement (0.5 c.c. equals two units), amboceptor (0.5 c.c. equals two units), antigen (0.5 c.c.), saline 1 c.c., and 0.5 c.c. corpuscles.

If a patient's serum is positive, there is present during the first incubation of thirty minutes: patient's serum with its syphilitic antibody (amboceptor), antigen, complement, and antisheep hemolytic amboceptor. During this incubation the first three combine with loss of complement present, the last one remaining free and inactive. When the corpuscles are added and, the second incubation of one hour made, the antisheep hemolytic amboceptor unites with the sheep corpuscles but there remains in the tube no complement to unite with the corpuscle-antisheep hemolytic amboceptor combination to bring about hemolysis. Hemolysis is incomplete or entirely absent, depending on the amount of syphilitic antibody present.

If the patient's serum is negative, there is no syphilitic antibody (amboceptor) of any kind; and there is no union between any of the ingredients during the first (thirty minutes) incubation. During the second (one hour) incubation carried out after the corpuscles have been added the antisheep hemolytic amboceptor unites with the sheep corpuscles, and the necessary complement is present to bring about solution of the sensitized corpuscles (antisheep hemolytic amboceptor corpuscle combination).

Standardization of Hemolytic System.—Place the test-tubes (80 by 10 mm.) in the front row of a three-row metal rack,

and to each of these add the amounts of amboceptor, complement, corpuscles and saline indicated in the table below. The
racks of the galvanized sheet iron are made to fit the tubes
selected and have three rows of holes with ten holes in a row.
Incubate in the water-bath for half an hour at 37.5°C. The
amboceptor is so diluted that 0.25 c.c. of the dilution contains
one unit, or somewhat more provided the strength is the same
as it was when the rabbit was bled, and the strength of the
serum determined. That is, this dilution is based on the bulk
amboceptor titration.

The smallest amount of complement that gives complete
hemolysis when combined with one unit of amboceptor (bulk
amboceptor titration) is one *complement unit*. Twice the smallest
amount that gives hemolysis (two units) is used in the test.
If more than 0.25 c.c. of 1–10 complement is required to give
complete hemolysis it is better to discard the complement
and secure fresh. If 0.2 is required, two units are contained
in 0.4 c.c. of the 10 per cent. dilution or in 0.5 of an 8 per cent.
dilution and a sufficient amount of saline is added to the 10
per cent. complement to make an 8 per cent.

One *amboceptor unit* is determined by using varying amounts
of amboceptor with a given amount of complement which is
known to be sufficient for hemolysis. In the appended table
0.4 c.c. amboceptor contains two units, and this must therefore
be diluted to 80 per cent. so that 0.5 c.c. will contain two
units.

The determination of the complement and the amboceptor
unit is a relative one. The titration of both amboceptor and
complement is of value because it shows the activity of these
with the particular ingredients to be used in the actual test.
Always note that amounts of amboceptor and complement,
smaller than those to be used in the actual test, when combined
produce complete hemolysis. The preliminary dilutions of
complement (1–10) and amboceptor (0.25 equals two units according to bulk titration) may be made up in 100-c.c. graduated
cylinders and the correct amount of saline added to each after
the titration.

TABLE FOR STANDARDIZATION

No. of tube	Amboceptor (0.25 c.c. did contain 1 unit)	Complement (10 per cent.)	Corpuscles (5 per cent.)	Sterile saline (0.88 per cent.)	Model results	
1	0.25 c.c.	0.5 c.c.	0.5 c.c.	2.0 c.c.	Complete hemolysis	
2	0.2 c.c.	0.5 c.c.	0.5 c.c.	2.0 c.c.	Complete hemolysis	Amboceptor titration
3	0.1 c.c.	0.5 c.c.	0.5 c.c.	2.0 c.c.	Moderate hemolysis	
4	0.25 c.c.	0.4 c.c.	0.5 c.c.	2.0 c.c.	Complete hemolysis	
5	0.25 c.c.	0.3 c.c.	0.5 c.c.	2.0 c.c.	Complete hemolysis	
6	0.25 c.c.	0.25 c.c.	0.5 c.c.	2.0 c.c.	Complete hemolysis	Complement titration.
7	0.25 c.c.	0.2 c.c.	0.5 c.c.	2.0 c.c.	Moderate hemolysis	
8	0.25 c.c.	0.1 c.c.	0.5 c.c.	2.0 c.c.	No hemolysis	
9	0.5 c.c.	0	0.5 c.c.	2.0 c.c.	No hemolysis	
10	0	0.5 c.c.	0.5 c.c.	2.0 c.c.	No hemolysis	Controls
11	0	0	0.5 c.c.	2.0 c.c.	No hemolysis	

Technic of the Actual Test.—The patient's sera, the complement, amboceptor, antigen, corpuscles and saline having been prepared and standardized, are now ready for the tests.

1. For each Wassermann test to be made, place a tube (80 by 10) in the front row of a rack. Reserve the first three holes in the front row. The first one is for a positive control (with 0.1 c.c. of a "positive + + +" serum), the second one for a negative control (with 0.1 c.c. of a known negative serum) and the third one is for an antigen control (with no serum).

2. Add to the fourth, fifth, sixth, etc. tubes of this front row 0.1 c.c. of serum (inactivated thirty minutes at 55°C.) of patients A, B, C, etc. For measuring, use a pipet graduated

in hundredths to the very tip. Place a pipet in each tube of serum or a single pipet may be used and washed four times with saline between each serum.

3. To each tube add 0.5 c.c. amboceptor, 0.5 c.c. complement, 0.5 c.c. antigen (1–8) and 1 c.c. saline.

4. Place tubes in the second (middle) row and add to each exactly the same as was added to those in the front row, except that 0.5 c.c. antigen (1–10) is added instead of 0.5 c.c. antigen (1–8).

5. Place tubes in the third (rear) row and to each add exactly the same as was added to those in front; except that no antigen is added, 0.2 c.c. patient's serum is used instead of 0.1 c.c., and 1.5 c.c. saline employed instead of 1 c.c.

6. Incubate in water-bath for one-half hour at 37.5°C.

7. Add 0.5 c.c. 5 per cent. sheep corpuscles to each tube. Those that prefer sensitized corpuscles do not add the amboceptor as indicated, but in this step add 1 c.c. sensitized corpuscles

8. Incubate in water-bath for one hour at 37.5°C.

9. Read results.

When the reaction does not proceed in the usual way, it is important to trace the source of error. Hemolysis takes place gradually, and when complete in less than fifteen minutes the reaction is faulty at some point. Corpuscles may have an abnormal tendency to dissolve, in which case, there would be hemolysis in the control, known "positive + + + +;" corpuscles more than seventy-two hours old are not used when preserved as indicated above. It also occasionally appears that exceptionally active complement, although carefully titrated may produce too rapid hemolysis.

Hemolysis may remain incomplete as the result of anti-complementary action of the patient's serum, both test and control showing incomplete hemolysis. If considerably more than the usual amount of amboceptor is found to be required when the titration for amboceptor unit is made, the corpuscle suspension may be too strong, in which case it should be diluted and another titration carried out. It is also possible that corpuscles may be met with that hemolyze with unusual difficulty. It must be remembered that an abnormal weakness of complement may be met with, but this usually appears in the titration. Complement older than forty-eight hours is not used. Only amboceptor with a high titre is used.

Combinations to Save Ingredients.—As noted under antigen, all sera negative with 0.5 c.c. antigen (1-8) are also negative with 0.5 c.c. antigen (1-10). It is, therefore, entirely unnecessary to employ second (middle) row tubes on sera that are negative in the front row. Again, there is no indication for the employment of an anticomplementary test (third row) on sera that are negative. A very serviceable method is to make an antigen (0.5 c.c. of 1-8)—complement (0.5 c.c.)— ambceptor (0.5 c.c.)—saline (1 c.c.) combination, and then to add 2.5 c.c. of this and 0.1 c.c. patient's serum to the front row tubes, to incubate for one-half hour, to add 0.5 c.c. corpuscles, and again to incubate for one hour. Those that are positive are tested with the antigen (1-10) and an anticomplementary fest made on each. If the number of biweekly tests reaches trom 50 to 100, a saving of almost one-half in complement and amboceptor may be made in this way.

If a *gonococcus complement-fixation test* is to be made on any of the sera, the tubes are usually numbered and set up in a separate rack in order not to interrupt the sequence of numbers in the other racks. The test is identical with the Wassermann except that only one amount of antigen is used. Controls with positive and negative sera and the antigen are required and, of course, the anticomplementary control of each positive serum. The comparatively high anticomplementary property of the antigen should be constantly in mind. The antigen consists of portions of the bacterial cell and if the test is positive the individual has an active gonorrheal process. A negative reaction proves nothing. The practical difficulty in applying these statements is that the inhibition of hemolysis is usually not complete, owing to the presence of smaller amounts of antibody than are present in syphilitics. In cases with evidence of a marked active inflammatory process not on a superficial mucous membrane such as the anterior urethra or vagina, the reaction is positive in about 50 per cent.　The common lesions are chronic salpingitis in the female and posterior urethritis, prostatitis and epididymitis in the male.　Most cases of gonococcic arthritis are positive.

The *complement-fixation test in glanders* is now extensively used instead of the agglutination reaction for the diagonsis of the disease in horses and mules.　The preparation of antigen is the same as the preparation of gonococcic antigen except the bacilli are grown on glycerin agar and as in the case of gonococcus test the most important part of the test is the preparation and standardization of the antigen.

Typhoid antigen is prepared in exactly the same way except the bacilli (several strains) are grown on plain agar.　Unfortunately the reaction becomes strongly positive only late in the disease.

A large number of tuberculosis antigens have been prepared but so far the results obtained by the complement fixation test in this disease have been indefinite and irregular.

BACTERIOLOGIC EXAMINATION OF BLOOD

There is no bacteriologic method of greater diagnositc importance.　With simplified and improved technic, a bacteremia is now being found in infectious diseases in which it was not suspected a few years ago.　With very little inconvenience to the patient, blood may be drawn by the syringe method, using a fine, platinum-iridium needle.

To make a blood culture carefully, not only is the inoculation of media in tubes and flasks usually required but also the plating of the blood.　Since the separation of fibrin and bacteria takes place in blood added to bouillon, it is necessary to make all cultures at the bedside or to add oxalate or citrate to the blood to prevent coagulation.　If the former method is employed and all media carried into the wards, this part of the routine of a hospital laboratory is time consuming and laborious.

In the collection of blood for Wassermann tests, in which perfect asepsis is not obligatory, a needle is inserted into the arm

vein and the blood run directly into a sterile tube. It is the
ease and speed with which a large number of specimens of blood
may be collected for this test that prompted the use of a tube
with oxalate solution in it and a needle attached.

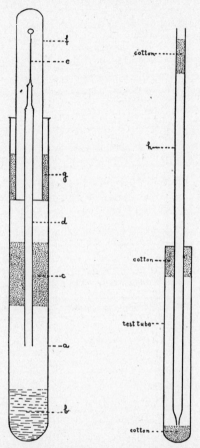

Fig. 19.—Blood tube (McJunkin).   Reproduced with permission from Mallory and Wright's Pathological Technique.   *a*, Extra large test-tube; *b*, oxalate
solution; *c*, cotton; *d*, 3-mm. soft rubber tubing; *e*, large needle provided with a
large stilet; *f*, small test-tube; *g*, cotton; *h*, a sterile 5-c.c. pipet for transferring the blood to the various media.

Blood Tube Method (McJunkin; Fig. 19; Journal American
Medical Association, Vol. lxii, p. 774).—The preparation of the
tube is simple, a number may be kept on hand for use and the

blood from several patients may be collected during one trip through the wards.   After the needle has been inserted into the vein, a few seconds are required for the blood to pass through the tubing.   The lower cotton plug eliminates all chances of contamination and, when it is removed in the laboratory, the upper end of the tube is flamed and the diluted blood transferred with

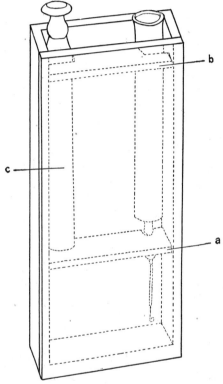

Fig. 20.—Twenty-five slide box (B. & L. O. Co.).   The upper end has been removed, two strips of wood, *a* and *b*, put in place and the cover fastened firmly with small tacks.   In the drawing the cover has been removed to show position of syringe.   Twenty-c.c. syringe with ground-glass plunger, *c*.   Autoclave as shown except that the box is placed on its side at an angle of 30 degrees.

a 5-c.c. sterile pipet to the media that are indicated.   The tubing and the needle are cleansed by forcing through them a few cubic centimeters of water from a syringe, after which they are placed in a saturated solution of borax in a quart Mason jar.

Syringe Method for Blood Cultures (McJunkin; Fig. 20).—
The objection to carrying melted agar and troublesome apparatus
to the bedside of the patient may also be met by sterilizing
sufficient sodium citrate in the syringe to prevent coagulation
of the blood when drawn into it.   This method has the advantage that a small platinum-iridium needle may be used with
little pain to the patient.   For a 20-c.c. syringe, one-fifth gram
of sodium citrate is sufficient.   A two-piece syringe (single-
piece barrel) with ground-glass plunger is selected, and several
of these (for a large hospital, six) are kept in boxes sterilized
and ready for use.   The wooden boxes are satisfactory but
ones made from copper or even from galvanized iron are more
satisfactory.   The syringe is sterilized by placing the box
(wrapped in muslin to protect from dust) in the autoclave in
such a way that the syringe forms an angle of 30 degrees with
the bottom of the autoclave.   When the air is expelled from
the autoclave, the condensing steam dissolves the citrate; and
later, when it dries, the powder is left in the lowermost portion
of the barrel.   The plungers are dipped in sterile saline or water
and inserted before leaving the laboratory.   After filling the
syringe it is replaced in the sterile box and carried to the
laboratory in the horizontal position.   If there has been no
contamination of the needle the blood is forced through it
into the various media or the needle may be removed and the
glass needle tip of the syringe carefully sterilized in the flame before forcing the blood out through it.   In this way a number of
specimens of blood may be collected by one person during one
trip through a ward.   Owing to faulty organization of the work
or to the burdensome requirements used in collecting the blood,
frequently blood cultures are not made even when they are the
only key to a diagnosis.   The importance of blood cultures in
infections such as the many common pyogenic infections, puerperal infection and pelvic inflammation, appendicitis and inflammations in the peritoneal cavity, pneumonia and inflammation
in the pleural and pericardial cavities, typhoid fever, paratyphoid infections, infections with the dysentery bacillus, colon

bacillus infections, anthrax, glanders, etc., cannot be over-emphasized.

Large numbers of cultures show that oxalate and citrate in quantities merely sufficient to prevent coagulation affect the vitality of organisms slightly or not at all.   The action of anti-bacterial bodies in the whole blood is of more importance, and the minimum time is consumed between the collection of the blood and the making of cultures.   This should certainly be less than thirty minutes.

Inoculation of Media.—In all cases 10 c.c. is inoculated into a flask containing 150 c.c. bouillon and the remaining 10 c.c. inoculated into a flask or bottle of sterile melted plain agar (100 c.c.) for five plates.   After making Gram's stain the broth may be used for serologic tests.   See pages 192, 218, 219 and 307 for the identification of typhoid, dysentery, pneumococcus and streptococcus.

To prepare a monovalent *antityphoid serum*, give a rabbit four intraperitoneal injections at three- or four-day intervals, starting with one-half of an 18-hour agar slant culture suspended in 10 c.c. saline and increasing one-half slant at each dose. Bleed from the carotid ten days after the last injection.   The bacilli are killed by placing in a water-bath at 55° C. for one hour.   The sterile serum is preserved in 1-c.c. vaccine vials. The two *antiparatyphoid sera* are prepared in exactly the same way, except only one-half as much of the culture is injected. The *polyvalent* serum is made by giving one-sixth slant of typhoid, paratyphoid A and paratyphoid B at the first injec-tion, and increasing one-sixth at each subsequent injection.

The best polyvalent *antidysentery serum* is obtained by immunizing a horse against the Shiga and Flexner groups and is now commercial as a therapeutic serum.   A monovalent serum for each of the two groups is made by giving a rabbit on three successive days $\frac{1}{100}$, $\frac{1}{75}$ and $\frac{1}{50}$ of a live culture on agar by the intravenous route.   After one week, repeat giving $\frac{1}{10}$ of a slant.   Bleed in ten days.   The three sera should have titres of 1–10,000.

The three (1, 2 and 3) types of *antipneumococcus* horse

serum may be obtained. There is no agglutinating serum for the organisms of type 4.

The commercial *antimeningococcus serum* 1–100 is the polyvalent serum for the agglutination of pure cultures from nasopharynx, 1–50 normal horse serum being used as a control. To prepare the monovalent regular and the monovalent para inject rabbits in exactly the same way as with dysentery, growing typical agglutinable strains on plain glucose agar. Agglutinate glucose agar cultures in dilutions 1–50, 1–100, 1–200 and 1–500 with the monovalent sera, making a saline control and a 1–50 horse serum control. Set at 55° C. overnight. A certain number of meningococci agglutinate with both types of sera (irregulars). The nasopharynx of at least 2 per cent. of adults yields agglutinable cocci while in regions of an epidemic this carrier rate may rise to 40 per cent. At present polyvalent serum is administered regardless of the type of organism. The cultivation of meningococci from the spinal fluid is more difficult and only about half of the cases yield positive results by the present methods. It is now advocated that the desiccator containing plate or tube cultures be exhausted to 76 mm. negative pressure and atmospheric pressure be restored by introducing carbon dioxid. In all cases the blood agar must be warm and the cultures immediately placed in the incubator.

SPUTUM, SEROUS FLUIDS, AND EXUDATES

In this chapter are included the common bacteriologic methods employed in determining the bacterial content of excreta, fluids, and pus but a systematic consideration of all pathogenic bacteria has been avoided. Special bacteriologic methods are also given under blood, urine, feces, and surgical tissue and the whole may be grouped and presented, together with the serologic methods, as a special short course of study in *medical bacteriology;* or they may be included in the subject of clinical microscopy. The need of well-defined instruction in the practical application of bacteriologic technic to the diagnosis of the more common infectious processes is coming to be better recognized. In general the bacteriologic examination of sputum and of fluids obtained from the various body cavities is usually of greater importance than the cytologic, so that the material is sent to the bacteriologic division of a hospital laboratory.

SPUTUM

Since the saliva and the mucous secretions from the nose, mouth, and throat, as well as the material coming from below the larynx, are often spoken of as sputum, it is important to be very certain that the specimen to be examined was raised through the larynx of the patient by an expiratory effort, and at the same time to caution him against expectorating nasal, oral, and pharyngeal secretions into the receiving cup. A wide-mouth vessel for collection of sputum is absolutely essential; many of the sanitary cups are satisfactory. To obtain a specimen as free as possible from the nasal and oral secretions, it is usually best to collect material expectorated during the morning, since exudate from both bronchi and cavities is most likely to be expectorated at this time.

Amount.—The normal individual will, by expiratory effort, expel daily from the larynx a very small amount of mucus-containing dust that is free and in endothelial leukocytes. Unless the air breathed is excessively dust laden, this expulsion of mucus occurs when such person arises in the morning, and is brought about by a "hemming" effort rather than by coughing. Such sputa have a slightly alkaline reaction, but on standing may become acid. The foreign particles are carried by the cilia at least as far as the bifurcation, and are expelled with the mucus.

Pathologic sputum is usually raised by coughing, and when not expectorated from a large cavity has an alkaline reaction. In some cases of severe pulmonary inflammation, such as lobar pneumonia, caseous pneumonia, or the earliest stage of apical tuberculosis, violent coughing takes place but no sputum is present; while in bronchiectasis, tuberculosis with cavity formation, and sometimes in bronchitis or in gangrene of the lung, a large amount (1 liter in bronchiectasis, 150 c.c. in tuberculous cavity formation) of sputum is the rule. In non-inflammatory edema of the lung, in circulatory disease, and after withdrawal of large amounts of pleural fluid, an abundant (500 c.c.) frothy sputum (albuminoid sputum) is frequently present. An expectorant such as ammonium chlorid may be given as an aid in obtaining sufficient sputum for examination.

Color.—When sputum raised from the lungs is blood red in color, the usual indication is hemorrhage per rhexin (aneurism, tuberculous cavity, gangrene or other process causing rupture of the larger vessels). Since small to large amounts of blood not infrequently escape from the naso-pharyngeal mucosa, this source of blood must always be considered. The derivatives of hemoglobin arising in blood from capillary hemorrhages may take on any shade of green, yellow, red or brown. The *rusty* sputum of lobar pneumonia affords a good example of the color produced by extensive capillary hemorrhage. In incipient tuberculosis the capillary hemorrhage may cause mere brownish flecks in the sputum or a considerable brownish discoloration. In pulmonary gangrene, cancer, and certain pneumonias, the sputum is more fluid and the blood pigment brown to black (prune-juice sputum). Green sputum may occur in jaundice (bile pigment), or in resolving lobar pneumonia (hemoglobin derivative), caseous pneumonia, and abscess. In severe chronic passive congestion of the lung (mitral disease) sufficient hemosiderin may be present to color particles of the sputum yellow. Less commonly, bile pigment tinges the sputum yellow (egg-yolk sputum). Anthracosis, siderosis, and calcicosis are the common pneumokonioses, and give rise to a black, a rusty, and a chalky sputum, respectively.

Consistency.—"Serous" "mucoid" "muco-" or "seropurulent," and "purulent" are terms applied to sputa. Unless expectorated from cavities, the sputum is usually *frothy;* and this admixture with air is especially marked in the abundant serous sputum formed in edema of ·the lungs. Pus appears white to yellowish green and lessens the tenacity due to mucus. Caseous material has the same effect. Although the tenacious rusty sputum of fibrinous pneumonia contains considerable hemoglobin, large amounts of blood lessen the tenacity of sputum.

Gross Particles (Fig. 21).—Sputum is now usually sent to the hospital laboratory in one of the many varieties of paper cups provided for this purpose, while special sanitary cases are provided by Boards of Health for transportation. After the color and consistency of a specimen have been noted, it is emptied into a glass finger-bowl (10 cm. diameter) and the empty cup filled with 10 per cent. formalin or completely immersed in a large vessel containing formalin. Against a black table top, the sputum in the finger-bowl is examined for gross structures. After the examination has been completed the dish is filled with 10 per cent. formalin.

Pin-head to larger caseous masses of a yellow to white color may be found in tuberculous sputa. In non-tuberculous cases of putrid bronchitis, pulmonary gangrene, and bronchiectasis, there may be found masses of this size, but these are more apt be to the shape of a bronchus (Dittrich's plugs). They are made up of masses of organisms and fat crystals and have a putrid, rancid odor. Particles answering this description more or less closely are dislodged from the crypts of the tonsils. The latter have little clinical significance and must not be confused with masses from the bronchi. *Casts of bronchioles* are found in pneumonic sputum as small short cylinders scarcely visible,

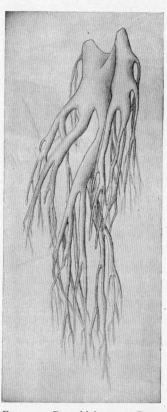

Fig. 21.—Pathologic macroscopic findings in sputum. About natural size. *a*, Casts from bronchioles from a case of fibrinous pneumonia; *b*, cast from bronchus from case of bronchial asthma; *c*, Dittrich's plugs; *d*, caseous masses; *e*, Curschmann's spiral from case of bronchial asthma.

Fig. 22.—Bronchial cast. Drawn from one of a number of casts from one case of bronchial asthma. It is suspended in Kaiserling preserving fluid.

but in certain cases of bronchitis they may appear as threads several centimeters long. *Casts of bronchi* (Fig. 22) are found in chronic fibrinous bronchitis. They may occur as a tree-like structure measuring several inches. *Curschmann's spirals* (Fig. 24), sometimes found in bronchial asthma, are

10

about the size of the larger casts of the bronchioles; but when
placed under the microscope a distinct central spiral arrangement may be seen.

Yellowish to greenish masses of alveolar epithelium, consisting mostly of fat, may be visible to the naked eye.   Corpora
amylacea 1 mm. in size are rarely seen.

Calcification is a common process in tuberculous necrotic
material in dilated bronchi and in the lung parenchyma.   The
calcified masses may be expectorated with the sputum.   They
are irregular, varying in size from a millet-seed to that of a

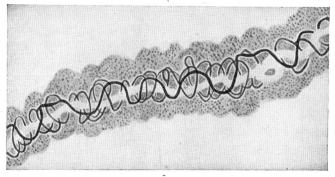

FIG. 24.   Curschmann's spiral (after Emerson).   A refractive central fiber (probably dense mucus) surrounded by a mantle of mucus, cells and detritus.

bean, and are known as *bronchioliths* or *pneumoliths* according
to their origin.

Actinomycotic granules, 1 mm. in diameter, have a distinctive glistening appearance.   The sputum in pulmonary actinomycosis closely resembles tuberculous sputum.

Fresh Microscopic Preparations.—At the time of making the
gross examination of sputum, it is often desirable to examine
selected particles under the microscope.   To do this, material
is removed from the bowl by means of a platinum loop, transferred to a slide, and a square cover-glass applied; the preparation is examined with the low-power, high-dry or oil-immersion
lens according to the structure to be examined for.   These
fresh preparations are later dropped into the formalin solution.

Red Blood Corpuscles.—If from a fresh hemorrhage these are normal in appearance and are arranged in rouleaux. In vomitus, gastric contents, feces, and inflammatory exudates corpuscles rarely present a normal appearance, since the gastric juice and other liquids quickly destroy them; but in sputum they are preserved for a considerable time. Their presence in endothelial leukocytes is extremely important, as it shows that hemorrhage has taken place into a bronchus or a space connected with a bronchus, usually an alveolus. It is possible that phagocytosis might take place in vitro at room temperature but this does not appear likely. If the hemorrhage is of some days' duration, hemosiderin may be present in endothelial leukocytes ("heart-failure" cells). If the hemorrhage is a large one hematoidin crystals may be found. These may form *in vitro*. The numerous sources (nasopharynx, abrasions about teeth and lips) for a few corpuscles must be kept in mind.

White Cells (pus cells, eosinophiles, or endothelial leukocytes).—The neutrophiles (pus cells) may contain fat, glycogen, hemosiderin, particles of coal dust or bacteria; their size remains about twelve microns. In bronchial asthma almost all the cells present are eosinophiles.

Endothelial leukocytes ingest by phagocytosis red blood corpuscles, pus cells, lymphocytes, dust particles and certain bacteria. The incorporation by endothelial leukocytes of corpuscles is especially common in all conditions in which capillary hemorrhage takes place. Since these leukocytes are especially numerous in incompensated valvular lesions (mitral stenosis), they have been spoken of as *"heart-failure" cells*. At first, the dissolved portions of the corpuscles (hematoidin) do not give the iron reaction, but later the test for iron (hemosiderin) is positive. In microscopic sections, the epithelial cells definitely lining the air-sacs are found not to have incorporated any corpuscles, and there is no reason to think that they do so after desquamation. Again, leukocytes morphologically identical with the "heart-failure" cells are found in sections of such lungs in the alveolar walls and about blood-vessels where they have migrated by ameboid activity. By the leukocytic granule stain these cells color in the same way as endothelial leukocytes found elsewhere. The endothelial leukocytes that contain carbon are spoken of as "dust" cells.

Epithelial Cells.—The pavement is usually from the outer portion of the nose and from the throat, while cylindrical cells may come from the nose and bronchial tree. The small, flat, epithelial cells of the alveoli with fine fat droplets in their cytoplasm, may be present in pneumonic sputa. The endothelial leukocytes with large fat globules, hemosiderin, carbon, corpuscles, and neutrophiles incorporated in their cytoplasm, are often erroneously regarded as epithelial cells.

Elastic Fibrils.—To test, treat the suspected particle from the finger-bowl under a cover-glass with 10 per cent. potassium hydrate, in which the fibrils are insoluble and examine with the low-power and high-dry lens. The fibrils may occur singly or in small groups. The small groups are about at the limit of vision. The fibrils are refractive, have a uniform diameter, and curl somewhat at the ends. Before the demonstration of tubercle bacilli, the presence of elastic fibrils constituted the most important sign of tuberculosis to be found in the sputum. They are also found in abscess and gangrene of the lungs.

Charcot-Leyden crystals are most numerous in bronchial asthma and they stain pink with eosin. They appear to be a product of the eosinophiles, and certainly result from these cells *in vitro*. They are examined for with the oil-immersion lens.

Hematoidin and *fatty acid crystals* may be present in putrid bronchitis, bronchiectasis, tuberculosis, and gangrene. They are pointed, and are soluble in caustic potash. These crystals may be found after expectoration if the substances giving rise to them are present in the sputum.

Stained Preparations.—If there is a good reason for examining a sputum, the macroscopic examination is usually not sufficient. In actual work the microscopic study of stained preparations is the most important sputum examination but there is little question that the microscopic examination of fresh unstained particles carefully selected by the naked-eye is not practised as much as it should be. If cultures are to be made,

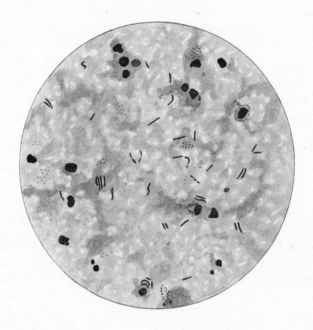

Fig. 23.—Tubercle bacilli in sputum stained by the Ziehl-Neelsen method; few pus cells present.

the dish used for the gross examination should be sterile and the cultures made without any undue manipulation. For making preparations of sputum, slides are best. The commonest examination is for the tubercle bacillus, but it is often necessary to examine for penumococcus, bacillus influenzæ, bacillus mucosus capsulatus, actinomyces, and other organisms, as well as for red blood corpuscles, leukocytes and epithelial cells.

Ziehl-Neelsen Stain for Tubercle Bacilli (Fig. 23).—With a platinum loop, cover three-fourths of a slide with selected particles of the sputum, leaving one end of the slide and the entire margin uncovered. Warming the slide slightly over a flame facilitates the spreading out of a tenacious sputum. After drying the preparation, apply the stain: (1) carbol-fuchsin (page 196) for two minutes, steaming gently; (2) wash with water, and then with Czaplewsky solution (page 196) until the thinner portions of the smear are a faint pink (about one-half minute); (3) wash with water, and counter-stain (one-half minute) with Loeffler's methylene blue; (4) wash with water, dry in air, and with the oil-immersion lens examine for tubercle bacilli. The bacilli are a bright red; other structures blue.

Antiformin Method of Making Smears.—This treatment is of greatest value for reducing homogeneous blood clots, masses of tissue, fibrinous clots, etc., to such a state that stains for tubercle bacilli may be made. It is also of use in preparing sputum and other material for cultures since the treatment for from one to two hours kills most bacteria other than tubercle bacilli. Thoroughly pulverize 100 gm. fresh chlorinated lime, add the powder to 750 c.c. water, shake and filter. To the filtrate add 150 gm. sodium carbonate dissolved in 250 c.c. water, and again filter. To the sputum, add an equal volume of the antiformin prepared in this way; mix, allow to stand for one hour and centrifuge. Smears are made from the sediment and stained in the usual way. Instead of using the Petroff medium, cultures may be made from the sediment on Dorset's egg medium. Cultures have not proved of much value in the diagnosis of pulmonary tuberculosis. Place all glassware used in a large crock containing 50 per cent. sulphuric acid to which 5 per cent. potassium bichromate has been added; this not only kills the tubercle bacilli but removes them from the glassware.

Blood Stain for Cells in Sputum.—It is frequently desirable to make accurate observations on the morphology of the cells present. A perfectly fresh specimen of the sputum is secured, a smear made on a slide which is supported on the top of a small bottle, 8 drops of a polychrome blood stain applied for one minute, diluted with 16 drops of 0.0015 N sodium carbonate and allowed to stain for ten minutes, washed with water for about one minute, and dried in the air. Eosinophiles, neutrophiles, endothelial leukocytes with hemosiderin ("heart-failure" cells), lymphocytes and red blood corpuscles are well brought out.

Gram's stain and capsule stains (described on page 194) are often required for the differentiation of bacteria found in the sputum. Streptococcus, staphylococcus, pneumococcus, tubercle bacillus, influenza bacillus, bacillus pertussis, bacillus mucosus capsulatus, bacillus diphtheria, bacillus pyocyaneus, bacillus typhosus, bacillus coli, bacillus anthracis, bacillus aerogenes capsulatus, bacillus pestis, micrococcus catarrhalis, micrococcus tetragenus, sarcines, yeasts, moulds, blastomyces, oidium immitis, oidium albicans, actinomyces and echinococcus are the names of important organisms found in the sputum.

Pulmonary Tuberculosis.—In early apical tuberculosis there may be little sputum with no bacilli present in it for months. However, the initial lesion is a focus of tuberculous pneumonia in a bronchiole usually in an apex and as soon as the inflammation spreads with production of a small area of necrosis, the caseous material tends to be discharged through the small bronchi and form a cavity. In this necrotic material there are tubercle bacilli. In acute miliary tuberculosis the bacilli are not present unless an older open pulmonary lesion exists. An acute pneumonia that does not end by crisis is suspected of being acute tuberculous lobar pneumonia (galloping consumption), and the tubercle bacilli may be absent during the first days of such a pneumonia. During the course of chronic ulcerative tuberculosis, the bacilli in the sputum may appear and disappear as the disease progresses; and for this reason repeated examinations from day to day are necessary. Elastic tissue is sought for without staining by examining the small caseous masses under the high-dry lens.

First examine the small caseous masses for tubercle bacilli. At least half a dozen bacilli should be found. If not found, the sputum may be digested according to the method of Petroff (see page 192), or by the antiformin method, and stained preparations of the sediment examined. It is often desirable to state to the patient when reporting one negative examination that biweekly specimens may be required for three weeks. If the examinations are repeatedly negative, and the number of streptococci are not too great, a guinea-pig may be injected. Acid-alcohol-fast bacilli in the sputum are almost sure to be tubercle bacilli. Smegma, timothy hay, milk and butter, and sewage acid-fast bacilli are best excluded by using care in collection and in the materials used in making the stains. Precautions in regard to the distilled water are given on page 196.

Lobar Pneumonia (Pneumococcus).—Except in the very young and in the very old, a tenacious mucoid sputum first appears which becomes bloody in four to five days and soon takes on the typical rusty appearance. At the crisis it is likely to present a muco-purulent character. A green color may indicate tuberculosis. A "prune-juice" appearance with a fetid odor indicates gangrene; but without the odor it may mean simply a relative abundance of serous fluid. Minute fibrin casts of bronchi may be found in the rusty sputum. To examine for pneumococci, the sputum must be expectorated immediately before examination; for it is only the number of organisms that has any significance in the direct examination, since pneumococci, influenza bacilli, pneumobacilli, and others, are commonly present. Isolation of the pneumococci, and a determination of the type (see page 220), is important not only in prognosis but also in the serum treatment of cases. Although

the pneumococcus is the chief cause of a lobar pneumonia, the
tubercle bacillus, typhoid bacillus, and pneumobacillus may
produce this variety of consolidation.

Influenza.—Bacillus influenzæ causes a lobular pneumonia
but the bronchitis usually predominates. In the sputum they
occur in clumps that are intracellular and extracellular. Smears
are stained with dilute carbol-fuchsin (page 196). For its
certain identification the compact particles containing the
greatest number of organisms are washed in sterile saline, and
by the streak method (Fig. 29) are inoculated on the surface of
the blood-agar plates or slants.

Bacillus Mucosus Capsulatus Pneumonia (Friedländer or
pneumobacillus).—This bacillus causes a lobular or lobar
pneumonia that is likely to persist and finally cause the death
of the patient. There is frequently a septicemia and blood
cultures should be made. In the sputum the organism is frequently found in neutrophiles and in endothelial leukocytes.
A Gram's stain and a capsule stain are made. Mice may be
injected and the organism obtained in pure culture from the
organs of the animal. Often bacilli of this group are present
in pulmonary processes as secondary or more or less unimpor-
tant invaders with the result that the pathogenicity of the
pneumobacillus has been discredited but it produces an important clinical variety of pneumonia.

Pertussis.—The amount of sputum expectorated at each
paroxysm is small and the consistency tenacious. In children
it is frequently impossible to obtain sputum not contaminated
by gastric and other secretions. In such cases it is necessary
to recognize the particles that come from the respiratory tract.
The bacillus pertussis is present in large numbers in the sputum
during the earlier stages of the disease but otherwise the scanty
sputum shows nothing characteristic. Unlike the influenza
bacillus, this organism may be grown on hemoglobin-free media.
It is best grown on Bordet's potato agar which is made by
autoclaving 200 c.c. 4 per cent. glycerin with 100 gm. potato
finely ground in a meat-chopper and adding to the filtrate 150
c.c. normal saline and dissolving 5 gm. agar. A small amount

of sterile defibrinated human blood is added to each sterile tube, as in making blood agar. Direct smears and smears from cultures are stained with dilute carbol-fuchsin.

Pulmonary Actinomycosis (Fig. 121).—In this disease the sputum is purulent, or it may be watery and abundant. It is necessary to find the granules, which are the size of a millet-seed. If these are found, the diagnosis is quickly made by crushing them out and staining with Gram's stain. The organism consists of very narrow branches but in sputum from the human lung it does not show the marked clubbing present in the *lumpy-jaw* of cattle and commonly pictured in descriptions of the *ray-fungus*. In cattle the greater resistance to the growth of the organs seems to cause the formation of the capsules which give the club appearance.

Pulmonary Blastomycosis and Coccidioidal Infection.—The sputum often closely resembles the sputum of tuberculosis. Purulent particles are stained, and examined with the oil-immersion lens. Budding forms, the capsule, spores, and the shape and size make possible an identification of the organisms. It now appears that the *blastomyces* (true yeasts; Fig. 55 [e]) multiply in the tissues by budding so that if typical buds are found the organism may be diagnosed as blastomyces. The majority of cases reported have been from the vicinity of Chicago. *Oidium immitis* (Fig. 55 [f]) which causes the cocci-diosis of the Pacific coast does not divide in the tissue by budding but forms spores. The cultural differentiation is not so simple.

Echinococcus Infection (Fig. 81).—In the fresh preparation hooklets are searched for with the high-dry lens. Hemorrhage and secondary infection are the rule. These cases have usually been diagnosed as tuberculosis.

Bronchial Asthma.—During the paroxysm, small, firm masses of very tenacious mucus may be raised; and some of these, on being teased out and examined with a low power, may show Curschmann's spirals (Fig. 24). The central fiber of very dense mucus which is definitely spiral is only a few microns in diameter, while the attached mucus is often 1 mm. in diameter.

Charcot-Leyden crystals when present are frequently in proportion to the number of eosinophiles. In a sputum that has a large eosinophile count, these crystals are formed on standing. Endothelial leukocytes, with large amounts of hemosiderin, may be present.

The attack consists of severe dyspnea with the greatest difficulty in expiration. There is much proof of a clonic contraction of the involuntary muscles of the smaller bronchi, together with an active hyperemia of the mucosa. The association of these two changes cause the characteristic symptoms and the peculiar formations of mucus found in the sputum. The majority of these cases are hypersensitive to certain proteins, usually of vegetable origin as well as to certain bacteria. Since the bacteria may be found in the sputum, it may be of importance in such cases to determine the presence of the predominating organism and to isolate it.

The second step is to determine whether or not the individual is hypersensitive to the dermal injection of the specific bacterial products. The *vegetable proteins* are now on the market and these patients may be tested with them. Improvement has been reported to follow vaccine treatment whenever staphylococci or subtilis bacilli predominate.

Bronchiectasis.—The action of emptying the cavity occurs more often in the morning, when a half liter or more of mucopurulent fetid sputum is expectorated. Microscopically, fatty acid crystals, pus cells, and great masses of bacteria are present. Dittrich's plugs are common. The great majority of cases of *putrid bronchitis* come under this head.

Acute and Chronic Bronchitis.—The character of the sputum varies with the cause of the bronchial inflammation. In chronic fibrinous bronchitis, the cause of which is unknown, fibrinous casts or moulds of the bronchial tree are coughed up at intervals. They consist of fibrin or of mucus.

Chronic Passive Congestion.—Expectoration of the mucoid and frothy sputum with rusty streaks occurs in the morning. The amount of sputum varies with the cardiac incompensation present. The brown or red streaks show enormous numbers of endothelial leukocytes filled with hemosiderin ("heart-failure") cells). Mitral stenosis causes the extreme degrees.

SEROUS FLUIDS

The chief serous cavities lined with mesothelium are the subarachnoidal (endothelial? lined), peritoneal, pleural, and pericardial. There are also fluids from various pathologic cysts. In general, it is possible to distinguish between *transudates* (accumulations of fluids in the cavities as a result of circulatory disturbances, and analagous to the stagnation edema of tissues) and *inflammatory exudates*, but the tendency is to designate the cavity and qualify the fluid according to its characters. In general, it may be said that transudates have a low specific gravity with a minimum amount of albumin and fibrinogen and contain few cells of any kind. The cells, microörganisms, and substances in solution are the objects of investigation, and these vary with the cavity from which the fluid is obtained and with the cause of the accumulation of fluid.

CEREBROSPINAL FLUID

Introduction.—Recent work carried out by a number of different investigators has brought forth conclusive proof that the cerebrospinal fluid is not lymph, which, indeed, is a fluid contained in definite closed vessels—the lymphatic vessels— that are not present in the central nervous system. Cerebrospinal fluid is contained within a space lined with flattened cells. There is less uniform agreement in regard to the name of the cells, but perhaps "endothelial" is preferable to "mesothelial" since these cells differentiate from mesenchyma, while the mesothelial cells of the body cavities differentiate from mesoderm. Many consider this layer of endothelial cells, which lines the dura and extends more or less perfectly over the pia to form a sac, as a part of the dura; in which case the arachnoid consists only of the connective-tissue prolongations that extend between the two layers of mesothelium. More, however, prefer to speak of the arachnoid as a structure not only comprising these prolongations but also as including the layers of endothelium. Whether there is a more or less definite endothelial lined subdural sac separate from the endothelial lined subarachnoidal space must be considered unsettled at this time. With this conception, the cerebrospinal fluid is subarachnoidal rather than subdural, where it is confined in the connecting *subarachnoidal spaces*. The fluid passes into these spaces from the ependymal-lined ventricles and central canal of the cord through actual openings or through very thin membranes in the roof of the fourth ventricle, in which it is secreted by the choroid plexuses. The passage of the cerebrospinal fluid from the subarachnoidal space takes place for the most part through the arachnoidal villi (Pacchionian villi), which are villous-like extensions of the arachnoidal endothelium that come into intimate contact with the venous sinuses in the dura.

Disturbances of the mechanism regulating the *pressure of the cerebrospinal fluid* causes an initial compensatory expansion of the dura of the cord, the appearance of headaches, choked disks and, later when the arteries are compressed stupor, epileptiform convulsions ensue. If there is no excess fluid, the amount of cerebrospinal fluid obtained by puncture is usually less than 5 c.c.

Not all the subarachnoidal fluid comes from the ventricles for some passes from the vessels in the substance of the cord and brain into the surrounding perivascular tissue and reaches the subarachnoidal space. The *amount of fluid* is increased in inflammatory processes involving the meninges, syphilis of the central nervous system, tumors of the brain, internal hydrocephalus, certain cases of chronic alcoholism, and other conditions. In these cases the pressure is usually increased (normal average about 150 mm. of water).

Cerebrospinal fluid is obtained by *lumbar puncture*. To do this insert a 10-cm. needle provided with a stylet, and having a 10-cm. piece of rubber tube attached, into the subdural space exactly in the median line and between the spinous processes of the third and fourth lumbar vertebræ. A 30-cm. piece of glass tubing, for determining the pressure under which a fluid escapes, is also often attached to the needle. The glass tubing has a 1-mm. lumen and a millimeter scale. The needle, rubber tubing, and graduated glass tubing are connected and for 20 minutes autoclaved at 110°C. All tests except the Wassermann reaction are made at once. Two cultures on Loeffler's blood serum are made at the time of puncture by running about 1-c.c. of the fluid directly in the tubes.

Cytologic Examination.—*To determine the number of cells*, Hayem's solution, with sufficient dry acid fuchsin (15 mg. to 100 c.c.) added to give the solution a very distinct cherry red color, is drawn up to the 1 mark in the white hemocytometer pipet; the fresh cerebrospinal fluid is, after vigorous shaking, drawn up to the 11 mark; the mixture is shaken, and the number of cells in 1 c.mm. determined. If fibrin in any form has separated, the result is not satisfactory. The surface of the ruled part of the chamber is 9 sq.mm. and the depth one-tenth millimeter. The number of cells counted in the nine squares are, therefore, contained in nine-tenths cubic millimeter, but 10 parts of the mixture contain 9 parts of cerebrospinal fluid, the 1 part of cerebrospinal fluid in the pipet not entering into the dilution. The number of cells counted in nine-tenths cubic millimeter times $1\frac{1}{9}$ times $1\frac{1}{9}$ gives the number of cells in 1 c.mm. of the fluid. The number of cells in 1 c.mm. of normal fluid (cell-count) never exceeds 20, and since the number present in usually less than 5, any number above 10 is considered pathologic. In a clear tuberculous spinal fluid the count may be as low as 10 but is likely to be greater; while in the same condition the fluid is frequently cloudy and the cell count above 500. In cerebrospinal syphilis, the number is likely to fall between 10 and 50, which is above that met with in non-infectious, low-grade inflammations of the meninges such as chronic alcoholism, uremia, epilepsy, and forms of insanity.

In general, it may be stated that in non-bacterial inflammatory processes (such as those mentioned in the foregoing paragraph and in arteriosclerosis, nephritis, chlorosis, tumors) which produce an excessive accumulation of cerebrospinal fluid with a normal and increased protein content, there is no material increase in the number of cells per unit volume. In pyogenic infections involving the inner meninges, the fluid appears purulent on macroscopic examination and a cell count is not required. In less acute infections such as syphilis and tuberculosis, there are fewer cells. In infantile paralysis, the character of the spinal fluid varies greatly. Blood interferes with the cell-count; but if the hemorrhage is fresh the number of corpuscles may be computed and a corresponding number of leukocytes deducted. It is better to secure a specimen free from blood. Under normal conditions an occasional white blood cell may migrate from the vessels of the brain and cord substance and reach the cerebrospinal fluid in this way; and in such conditions as cerebrospinal syphilis it appears that the increase in lymphocytes is due to such additions.

To determine the kind of cells present, stained preparations are examined. The fresh fluid is centrifuged in a sterile 15-c.c. centrifuge tube, and if a culture has not already been made it is now made from the sediment. The clear fluid is decanted into a second sterile tube, to be used for other tests; and the sediment in the bottom of the centrifuge tube is shaken up with normal saline, and again centrifuged. The supernatant saline is siphoned off after the second centrifugation, the sediment placed on cover-glasses with a capillary, spread like blood films, dried in the air, and stained with blood stain in the same way that blood films are stained except that the diluted stain is allowed to act for ten minutes. Well-stained preparations, free from precipitate, are secured by making the preparations on cover-glasses. A differential analysis of the cells present is of value, but accurate morphologic studies in many conditions are lacking.

If no blood is present in the fluid, cloudiness suggests meningitis. In tuberculous meningitis, the fluid is clear or slightly cloudy, and the cells are neutrophiles (early) or lymphocytes (late). A web-like coagulum in a tube of clear fluid that has stood overnight is very suggestive of tuberculous meningitis. In meningitis due to the meningococcus the fluid is usually moderately cloudy but in some cases it may be quite clear. In a meningitis due to streptococcus, pneumococcus, staphylococcus, or to the influenza bacillus the fluid is much more likely to be purulent. If the cell count is moderately high and the cells on microscopic examination are found to be almost entirely lymphocytes and plasma cells, cerebrospinal syphilis should be suspected.

Bacteriologic Examination.—Owing to the number and importance of the infectious agents involving the central nervous system and its meninges, a determination of the bacterial content of this fluid is of importance in diagnosis and may be required for treatment of the case.

Bacillus Tuberculosis.—The demonstration of tubercle bacilli in meningitis is especially important in children. The simplest method of direct examination, and the one perhaps that gives the highest percentage of positive results, is the staining, by the Ziehl-Neelsen method, of the web-like coagulum that forms in the tube of fluid from cases of tuberculous meningitis, on standing overnight in the refrigerator. The coagulum is removed with a platinum wire and spread out on a slide held some distance above the flame to aid in spreading the material. By this method, more than one-half the tuberculous cases yield positive results and this percentage is increased by repeating the examination. If negative, as much of the fresh sterile fluid as possible may be centrifuged at high speed and the sediment injected into a guinea-pig as indicated on page 205.

Meningococcus.—In all cases of meningococcus meningitis, the cocci are always found in the spinal fluid during the early stages of the disease and may be present in considerable numbers during the late stages. The cultures may be made by running 1 c.c. of the fluid directly from the needle into tubes of plain blood agar, or the fluid may be centrifuged in sterile tubes and cultures made from the sediment on this medium. Small translucent colonies appear in twenty-four hours at 37.5°C., but not at room temperature. The best way to rule out a contaminating growth of Gram-negative saprophytic cocci is to make a Gram's stain of the sediment within one-half hour after it has been withdrawn. The cocci during the earliest stage of the disease are found both inside and outside the neutrophiles, but later they are almost entirely intracellular, and great variations in the size of the individual cocci are seen. If necessary, the agglutinating properties of the cocci from cultures are determined with the serum of a rabbit immunized against several strains of meningococcus; agglutination is most often required in cultures from the pharynx. The therapeutic antimeningococcus serum has considerable agglutinating properties. A majority of all cases recover.

Pyogenic Cocci.—Streptococci, pneumococci, and staphylococci are the three Gram-positive pyogenic cocci most commonly met with. The spinal fluid is either seropurulent or purulent. The number of cocci appearing in the smears is usually not large, so that cultures are required in the diagnosis of the infection. Cultures of the fluid, if purulent, or of the sediment, if seropurulent, are made on glucose agar slants and on blood agar. If the infection is widely distributed over the meninges, the termination is fatal.

Infantile Paralysis.—The character of the fluid varies greatly. From cases that are typical clinically, a Gram-positive coccus that appears to be a mild streptococcus of low virulence, may be present. In such cases the fluid is cloudy and there is evidence of meningitis. In other cases the spinal fluid may show little clouding and prove negative on culture. In such cases there is only moderate hyperemia of the meninges. Flexner and others have isolated in cultures a minute organism from the cord and other tissues.

Influenza Bacillus.—In severe epidemics a meningitis due to extension of the infection from nose or middle ear to the meninges is not rare. Cultures of the sediment are made on blood agar. If no other organisms are present, the prognosis is said to be favorable but frequently other bacteria have been found to accompany the infection with the influenza bacillus.

A culture of the *gonococcus* may be obtained on Loeffler's blood serum, but hydrocele agar is a better medium. This infection of the meninges is rare. Examination of the cerebrospinal fluid has not usually been carefully made in cases of *blastomycosis* involving the meninges, brain and cord. In *syphilis*, the treponemata are not sought in the spinal fluid. In several severe septicemic conditions, such as anthrax, the organisms appear in the spinal fluid.

Serologic Examination.—The protein content is usually increased when the pressure is abnormally high, but in certain non-inflammatory conditions accompanied by increased intracranial pressure such as hydrocephalus, the percentage of protein is normal, or even below the average. In most non-infectious inflammatory processes, the amount of protein is slightly increased; in mild infections such as syphilis or tuberculosis the protein is moderately increased; while the greatest amount of protein is found in the acute infections. Accurate chemical estimations have not been extensively applied in investigations of the nitrogenous constituents of the spinal fluid.

Of the soluble substances, globulin is the most important. To make the *globulin test* (Noguchi), to a test-tube containing 0.2 c.c. of the clear, blood-free, supernatant fluid from the first centrifugation, add 0.5 c.c. 10 per cent. butyric acid (pure Merck), and while hot add 0.1 c.c. normal sodium hydrate. Boil, and allow thirty minutes for the formation of a precipitate. A control is made by heating the reagents without the addition of the spinal fluid. In children it is not unusual, in the absence of infectious processes, to find the pressure of the cerebrospinal fluid increased well above 150 mm. of water. In these cases the globulin test is negative. In tuberculous meningitis, it is always positive; and this is significant where the tubercle bacilli are not found. The test is positive in almost all cases of general paresis, and a majority of the cases of tabes show an excess of globulin. A colloidal gold solution is being employed for quantitative globulin determinations, and it may prove to be of greater value than the less delicate globulin test given but has not done so yet.

For a *Wassermann test* of the spinal fluid 0.5 c.c. are employed, instead of 0.1 c.c. which is the usual amount of blood serum used for this test. Inactivation is not required. One c.c. is used for the anticomplementary control. In suspected syph-

11

ilis of the central nervous system, the spinal fluid is frequently positive although the blood serum is negative. In cases that suggest tabes or general paresis with a diagnosis in doubt, the test is made on the spinal fluid. The treatment of these cases with salvarsanized serum should be followed by repeated tests on the fluid.

ASCITIC FLUID

Serous fluid in any considerable amount in the peritoneal cavity is spoken of as ascitic fluid and the condition as ascites. The relation between the lymphatics and the mesothelial-lined peritoneal cavity is usually said to be very close, but there is little evidence of any compensatory drainage through the lymph vessels in the cases of portal congestion with no involvement of the general venous or lymphatic channels. If the fluid contained in the cavity is purulent or small in amount, it is spoken of as an exudate rather than ascites. *General venous obstruction* (cardiac or renal) and *portal obstruction* (cirrhosis of the liver, thrombosis of splenic or portal vein) are the two conditions causing a majority of the cases of ascites. The clear or opalescent fluid of *specific gravity* below 1.018 has a slight straw color, and contains only a few cells which may be obtained by the centrifugation of large volumes of the fresh fluid. A large, soft, gelatinous coagulum may form in the fluid on standing, but this usually does not occur. Small flakes of *fibrin* are so common that a large aspirating needle is necessary for abdominal taps. Such a simple transudate is recognized by its negative characters on bacteriologic and cytologic examination period. Such fluid may become infected.

In metastatic tumors involving the peritoneum or in tumors that infiltrate the peritoneum, fluid may accumulate in the peritoneal cavity; and examination of this fluid is not, as a rule, of great importance in diagnosis of the condition. In involvement of the cavity by malignant disease or tuberculosis, *hemorrhage* into the fluid takes place more commonly than it does into simple transudates. It is recognized by a red to brownish tinge of the fluid, and microscopically by the presence of corpuscles. Bits of tissue from a tumor may pass through the needle, but much difficulty is encountered in the histologic diagnosis of these.

In tuberculosis the number of cells (lymphocytes, neutrophiles, and endothelial leukocytes) is greater than in simple transudates, and the specific gravity is higher. These points are not sufficiently conclusive for a positive diagnosis of tuberculosis. To examine for tubercle bacilli, 100 c.c. of the fluid drawn into a sterile 350-c.c. Erlenmeyer flask is treated with 20 c.c. pepsin solution and placed overnight at 37.5°C. The fluid is centrifuged in a 100-c.c centrifuge tube at a high speed, the sediment placed on a slide, dried in the air, fixed in the flame and stained for tubercle bacilli. This method is named *inoscopy*. The pepsin solution is prepared by adding 2 gm. pepsin, 10 c.c. glycerin, 10 c.c. concentrated hydrochloric acid, 3 gm. sodium fluorid to 1000 c.c. distilled water. In the majority of cases of peritoneal tuberculosis, such an examination does not reveal the presence of tubercle bacilli. The sediment obtained in this way or by the centrifugation of the citrated fluid may be injected into a guinea-pig, but the fluid in tuberculous peritonitis often proves negative for the bacilli.

The term *cytodiagnosis* has been applied to the examination of the cellular elements of serous fluids. The fresh fluid is centrifuged in sterile centrifuge tubes, the clear fluid decanted, sterile saline added, and the whole is again centrifuged. Smears are made on cover-glasses, dried in air, and stained in the same way as blood smears (page 150). Clotting is always a serious disadvantage; and in cases where the identification of the cells is important, it is better to prevent clotting by drawing the fluid into flasks that have in them at the time they are autoclaved 1 gm. sodium citrate per 100 c.c. of fluid to be added. A marked relative and absolute increase of lymphocytes in the peritoneal fluid may be taken as an indication of tuberculosis, but neutrophiles may predominate in cases of peritoneal tuberculosis.

In seropurulent fluids and purulent fluids, pyogenic cocci, bacilli of the colon group, gas bacilli and other bacteria are encountered.   Frequently the infection is a mild one.   A putrid fluid occurs in cases in which putrefactive bacteria gain access to necrotic tissue.   In these cases, cultures are required; but direct smears of the fluid, or of sediment stained by the Gram's stain and obtained by centrifugation, show the relative number of the various organisms present.

In *chylous ascites* the fluid is milky.   The accumulation of chylous fluid in the peritoneal cavity may be brought about by parasites especially filaria bancrofti blocking the large lymphatic vessels and the lymph vessels of the mesentery. The condition may also be due to the blocking of the lymph vessels by malignant tumors and other processes, such as in- flammations.   To determine that the clouding of an ascitic fluid is due to fat and not to something else in suspension, dry the fluid on a slide, and stain with a saturated solution of scharlach R or extract 100 c.c. fluid with 10 c.c. ether; evaporate the ether on a slide, and stain for fat.   Lipoids, are not uncommonly present in the fluid in malignant growths involving the peritoneal surfaces whether they block the large lymph vessels or not, and the clouding of the fluid is not due to fat or cells but to lipoids, probably lecithin.   The same thing is often true in cirrhosis of the liver and in chronic tuber- culosis of the peritoneum.

PERICARDIAL AND PLEURAL FLUIDS

Hydropericardium and *pleurisy with effusion* correspond to the transudates met with in ascites.   As in the peritoneal transu- dates, the fluid in these transudates is clear or opalescent, the specific gravity is low, the protein content is small, and only a few mesothelial cells or endothelial leukocytes are encountered. Hemorrhage into pleural fluid not uncommonly occurs in malig- nant disease.

Acute seropurulent and *purulent exudates* are met with in cases where an inflammatory process has extended from the lungs, and for this reason pneumococcus is a common invader of these cav- ities, and streptococcic pleuritis and pericarditis are almost as common.   A determination of the exact variety of coccus present is frequently of importance in both prognosis and treatment. For this reason, collection of the fluid must be carefully performed, and painstaking cultures made on blood agar, ascitic agar, and blood serum. Streptococci of a low virulence infecting the pericardial cavity not only grow with difficulty on artificial media but die out rapidly in the cavity itself. In tuberculous pleuritis, neutrophiles frequently predominate, as they often do when the infection involves an epithelial or mesothelial surface. Actinomyces may set up a process closely resembling tuberculosis.

Cyst Fluids

The character of the fluid from cysts varies so greatly with the nature of the process and with the tissue in which the cyst formation takes place, that only those that are likely to be aspirated are mentioned. **Ovarian cysts** frequently become very large. The contents of simple cysts (dilatation of follicles, corpora hemorrhagica, or embryonic structures in the broad ligament) have a clear or slightly blood-tinged fluid of low specific gravity (1.005). The fluid obtained from papillary cyst adenomas (true tumors) is frequently gelatinous and contains pseudomucin, which is precipitated by alcohol but not by dilute acetic acid. Before making the precipitation test with alcohol, any albumin present should be removed from the diluted or undiluted fluid by the heat-and-acetic-acid method and filtration through paper. The specific gravity is high. Epithelial cells from the lining of the cavities and endothelial leukocytes containing much fat may be found microscopically. Hemorrhage may take place into such cystic tumors, giving the fluid a brownish or chocolate color.

Hydrocele fluid has a rather marked straw color, with a specific gravity above 1.010. A chylous fluid fills the sac in filaria infection. A few leukocytes may be found; fibrin flakes may be present; spermatozoa may gain entrance to the fluid in several ways. A purulent exudate indicates infection. The fluid is contained within the tunica vaginalis, and hemorrhage may take place into it. In spermatocele, the cystic dilatation is within the epididymis; and a careful search must be made for spermatozoa in all cases in which it is suspected. If spermatozoa are found the anatomic relations serve to show whether the fluid is in the tunica vaginalis or in the epididymis.

Synovial fluid is clear, or slightly cloudy and viscid. This fluid is greatly increased in many inflammatory conditions. In these cases careful cultures are required, since the organisms may be present in large numbers and difficult to grow. In severe arthritis with extensive acute exudation of pus, a long-chain streptococcus may frequently be grown without difficulty on simple media such as glucose agar; but in rheumatic fever, careful cultures on blood agar are required during the first days of the disease, since the cocci present appear to die out rapidly in the tissue. If due to gonococcus, a positive complement-fixation (Schwartz test) may be secured. The fluid present in a hydrosalpinx resulting from this infection becomes clear and of a low specific gravity as the infection subsides. If tuberculosis is suspected, the fluid may be injected into a guinea-pig; but if the material is only that obtained from a "cold abscess," such injection often proves negative. By diluting such fluid, treating it with antiformin, centrifuging it, and staining the sediment by the Ziehl-Neelsen method, acid-fast granules (Much granules) may be found. Material from tophi in cases of gout show biurate needles, which on treatment with hydrochloric acid form uric acid crystals.

Renal Cysts.—The cysts of sclerosed kidneys due to distention of the capsular space or subtending tubule usually do not reach such a size as to be aspirated. The contents are colloidal in character. Multiple cysts are present in congenital cystic kidney. These are filled with fluid containing urea and uric acid at first, but these substances may disappear in the older cysts in which they are no longer being added to the contents. The fluid is clear in the cases in which hemorrhage has not taken place. In hydronephrosis the fluid contains the usual urinary constituents unless the kidney substance has been compressed and destroyed to such an extent that secretion into the fluid no longer takes place. In pyonephrosis pus cells are present in larger numbers unless tuberculous when caseous material fills the cavities.

The fluid of **echinococcus cysts** is usually free from albumin and contains sufficient sodium chlorid to make the specific gravity more than 1.010. It is often impossible to demonstrate hooklets (Fig. 81) in puncture fluid. The antigenic properties of the cyst fluid may be determined, and the serum of the patient is tested with echinococcus antigen. Such cysts occur especially in the liver but also in the lungs, kidneys, spleen, omentum and rarely in the central nervous system.

Fluid from **pancreatic cysts** may be obtained at surgical operations. It is at once tested for its ferments by placing in the incubator for thirty minutes 10 c.c. of the fluid in each of three tubes mixed with dilute starch solution, a piece of albumin tube, and an emulsion of neutral olive oil. Test the starch solution by Fehling's method, and the acidity of the oil emulsion with litmus paper.

EXUDATES—BACTERIOLOGIC TECHNIC

No set of rules can be laid down for the examination of bacteriologic and other specimens coming from patients in hospital wards since constantly varying conditions are arising and there may be a number of entirely different methods of arriving at equally satisfactory results. However, there is need to emphasize the advantage to the patient and to medical science of not placing a chemist in charge of some difficult microscopic examination, a specialist in serology in charge of the diagnosis of surgical tissue, etc.

Personnel of Hospital Laboratories.—Aside from the immediate clinical value of bacteriologic examinations, important advances in the science have been made in hospital laboratories. The source of pathogenic bacteria, the infected human tissue, is most accessible to the laboratory of the hospital, and the best effort should be made to provide for efficient handling of this work. If possible, a highly trained bacteriologist who gives his undivided attention to it should have charge. If this is not possible, then one of less training should perform the work under supervision. It is usually required that a director of a laboratory be guided in his plan of organization by varying conditions, but the possibilities and limitations of both individuals and equipment must be kept in mind. In general, specimens of greatest importance must receive the most careful attention, and those requiring the most skill in examination should be left to the persons best trained.

Recent additions to medical knowledge, especially through chemical analysis of blood, urine and other fluids, and of tissues, show the injustice of diverting all blood, urine, feces, gastric contents, and sputum specimens into a department of clinical pathology where the examinations are performed by the least experienced members of the staff. It is true that many of these examinations are very simple and may be executed by internes and others of little technical experience, but the plan of work should be such that the important and difficult tests of these specimens may be made by the direction of one suitably trained in the microscopic or chemical technic required in the examination. In organizing the laboratory of a hospital of two hundred beds, or even less, an orderly division of work must be arrived at. If it is not possible to place highly trained workers in charge of the necessary laboratory departments, then properly trained technicians (usually not graduates in medicine) should be selected for the technical work of these departments, and should be supervised by the director. Desirable departments are pathology (surgical and autopsy specimens), bacteriology (sputum, body fluids, smears, cultures), chemistry (urine, feces, gastric contents, chemical blood examination) and serology (Wassermann and other complement-binding reactions, Widal and other agglutination tests, preparation of vaccines, etc.). Frequently a bacteriologist is a trained serologist. It seems desirable that all hospital internes receive a certain amount of laboratory training, and the simplest examinations in each of the departments may be done correctly by internes.

Personnel of Hospital Laboratories of Medical Schools.— In hospitals housed with medical schools, a more satisfactory distribution of specimens is usually possible. Each clinic should have its own laboratory and laboratory staff, for it is here that the greatest interest in the specimen centers. The training of those in charge of these laboratories will necessarily vary with the clinic; for the specimens from the gynecologic clinic, for example, will be quite different from those of the clinic of internal medicine. Under this arrangement it will also be possible for the laboratories of the various clinics to pass certain problems on to the chemical, bacteriologic, pathologic, physiologic, or anatomic departments of the Medical School.

B.	Diagnosis:
Material:	
Name:	Service:
Clinical Diagnosis:	
Smear (Stain):	Date:
Agar or Blood Serum:	
Litmus Milk:	
Other Media:	

FIG. 25.—Index card (5 by 7 inches) for bacteriologic records. All cards for indexing are this size.

With this division of work the autopsies are usually performed by the department of pathology, but they should be done in close association with the clinic to which the case belongs.

Numbering the Specimens and Recording the Findings.— Several systems for recording and numbering specimens are in use. Perhaps the simplest one is to indicate bacteriologic specimens by B, surgical specimens by S, and autopsy specimens by A, and to place the last two numerals of the current year after these letters to show in what year the specimen was received. If the laboratory is so organized, C, may be used for chemical and

W for serologic specimens.   If this system is used, the first bacteriologic specimen received in 1918 bears the number B 18.1, and the 515th specimen bears the number B 18.515, and so on.

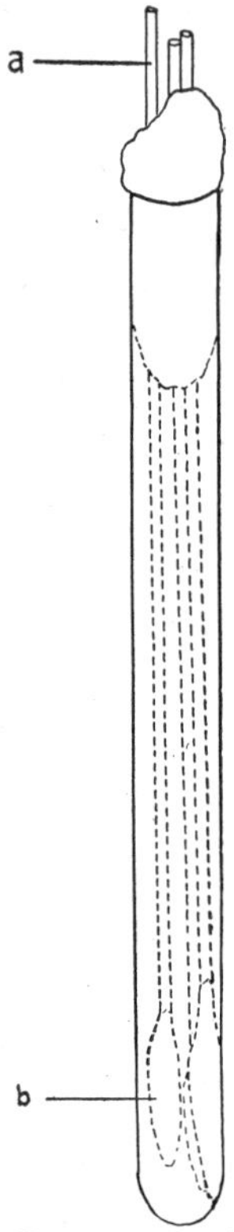

At the time the brown slip is removed from about the specimen, the bacteriologic number is written on the bottom of the slip.   The number is ascertained from the card index which is on the table at hand.   There must be a card for every consecutive number.   The number is also placed on a card for the laboratory record and this card inserted at the front in the card index. The brown slips are kept on file in consecutive order until the diagnosis is made, when they are immediately returned to the clinician.   There is a brown slip for all specimens except autopsy specimens. .   The data is recorded on the card for the laboratory record.   The cards (Fig. 25) are kept during the current year in a card index case in the order of the numbers on them.   The cards for previous years may be tied together and filed away.   There must be a card for each number.

FIG. 26.—Sterile cotton swabs. Dry-heat sterilize and then autoclave. Use one swab for making a culture and one for making a smear on a slide. a, Wooden applicators (16 cm. long) which may be obtained in boxes; b, small amount of cotton firmly wrapped by rotating a.

Bacteriologic Examination of Autopsy Specimens.—The methods for the bacteriologic examination of specimens other than urine, blood, feces, and sputum considered elsewhere are outlined in this chapter.   The heart's blood, various exudates, spleen, liver, lungs, kidneys, and meninges are the organs most commonly cultured, and the thoroughness with which this is done will depend largely on the simplicity of the methods.   A potato-knife or other thin-bladed knife set in a wooden handle is provided for searing the surface of the organ from which the cultures are to be made.   A fine-pointed scalpel sterilized in a flame is used for cutting through the seared surface, and it must be kept sharpened. The material is removed from the incision with a sterile swab, or with a sterile bulb pipet, carried to a Bunsen flame, and inoculated into the media selected. Loeffler's blood serum, dextrose agar, ascitic agar, blood agar, lactose bile, and dextrose bouillon, are the media most often employed.

Smears are made on slides at the time the cultures are taken. Both cultures and smears bear the autopsy number and the name of the tissue or organ from which the cultures are made. The culture tubes bear a white label on which the numbers are placed. *Culture of the heart's blood* is made from all cases, and cultures of other tissues and organs as indicated.

The card bearing the record of the bacteriologic examination of the autopsy specimens receives a regular bacteriologic number but in addition the autopsy number is placed after it. After the examinations have been completed, the diagnoses are written on cards, and these are filed away in the bacteriologic index. From these cards the bacteriologic findings are copied into the typewritten autopsy protocol.

Examination of Routine Specimens other than Autopsy Specimens.—As a routine *two swabs* (Fig. 26) are sent to the laboratory. With one of these, a smear is made on a slide and stained by Gram's method. With the other, a culture is made first on a slant of Loeffler's blood serum by gently rubbing it over the surface, and then in a tube of litmus milk. Other media are used if indicated.

The bacteriologic number—for example B 18.515, or just 515— is written on each inoculated tube, with a pencil. The cultures are placed in a rack with the blood serum cultures in the front row. The rack is placed in the incubator at 37.5°C. The following morning a smear is made from each blood serum slant and each milk culture, and stained by Gram's method. In examining colonies from a plate or a large number of tube- or flask-cultures, it is very convenient to make eight or ten preparations on a slide (Fig. 27), marking the exact position of each with a wax pencil at the margin of a slide. Place the first preparation at the left end of a slide.

Sterile swabs are best prepared by wrapping firmly with

cotton one end of a wooden throat applicator, placing two or three of these in a test-tube, and plugging the upper end of the tube with cotton. The tubes are dry-heat sterilized, and then autoclaved. The lower ends of the applicators reach the bottom of the tubes with the upper ends 1 inch or more above the top. One of the swabs is used for making direct smears on slides, and the second is used for making cultures.

If *throat cultures* for a contagious hospital are sent to the laboratory, they are examined separately, and separately tabulated. Exclusive of such cultures, the majority of those received come from surgical clinics and are best sent on swabs, as indicated. If, for example, a large pus cavity is opened, it is preferable to make immediately two swabs from the material, rather than to fill a test-tube or other container which frequently

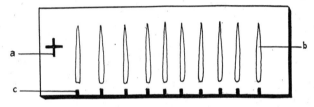

FIG. 27.—Slide with ten preparations. *a*, Cross made with wax pencil next to which is placed number one; *b*, ten small drops water placed on the slide with pipet to which are added portions of the cultures with a platinum loop. Spread each out as indicated and mark the exact position of each preparation on the margin, *c*, with a wax pencil. If the material is not from a growth on solid media, the droplets of water are omitted.

results in contamination of the specimen. If smears are made by members of a clinical staff, they should be examined by them. It is usually unsatisfactory to make a diagnosis from a smear made by someone else. In all cases where the macroscopic examination may be of first importance, material should be brought to the laboratory in a sterile tube or other sterile container; for example, pus from actinomyces infection, in which the demonstration of the organism depends largely on searching out the actinomycotic granules in the pus, should be sent to the laboratory in a sterile container. Specimens of urine, blood, sputum, or of feces are collected as indicated under these specimens.

For routine diagnosis, the culture media and the stains should be made as simple as possible. The details of the preparation and the application of the media and stains should be thoroughly understood.

Cultivation of Bacteria.—The number of bacteria present may be so small that they cannot be found in smears of the material; it may be impossible to identify organisms from smears alone; or it may be desirable to keep the bacteria alive in order to test their biologic characters, and for other purposes such as the preparation of vaccines, antigens, and

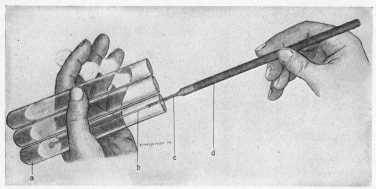

Fig. 28.—Dilutions in agar for plating. The tubes, *a*, and the cotton plugs are held in the left hand as indicated. *b*, 20-gauge platinum wire 3½ inches long firmly inserted into a syringe needle (platinum-iridium needle preferred), *c*, which is firmly slipped on the end of a wooden teasing needle holder, *d*.

the like. In such cases, the organisms must be grown on media in cultures, and often in pure cultures.

The material of which a culture is to be made is placed in the sterile media by means of the sterile platinum loop. For the simplest cultivation of bacteria, there are required special media in sterile closed containers, a platinum loop, and a Bunsen or alcohol flame. The loop is made by bending into a circle one end of a 3-inch piece of 20-gauge platinum wire and inserting the other end into a melted glass rod or other holder (Fig. 28). It is sterilized in the Bunsen flame by heating the entire wire to redness. If the loop is filled with a liquid that contains bacteria, the loop is first inserted into the central cool portion of the flame and allowed to dry before it is heated to redness.   The glassware is dry-heat sterilized in the dry-heat oven, by heating for one hour at 180°C.   After the media are placed in the tubes, they are autoclaved for twenty minutes at 110°C. (7 lb. pressure).

Additional apparatus is necessary for the isolation of pure cultures, and for the usual routine work coming to a hospital laboratory.

Isolation of Pure Cultures.—For the isolation of bacteria in pure cultures, the individual cells are mechanically separated from one another to a distance of at least 1 cm.   This may be done by the streak method, by which the bacteria-containing substance is rubbed over the surface of a solid medium (Fig. 29); or the same result may be obtained by mixing the infected substance with melted agar (agar melted at 100°C. and cooled to 45°C.) that becomes solid on cooling.   The melted agar, after inoculation, is usually poured into a 9-cm. Petri dish so as to obtain a flat surface.   The single separate bacterial cells multiply in the medium sufficiently to give rise to a macroscopic mass—a colony.   Such a colony of course consists of a single kind of organism, since the single bacteria are scattered about in the solid agar well separated from one another.   A method that has little practical use lies in picking out a single organism from a liquid under the high-power of the microscope and placing it in the culture medium.

Streak Method (Fig. 29).—By this method, as explained above, the bacteria are planted on a solid surface.   Culture on Loeffler's blood serum must be made by this method—since that medium cannot be melted—and may be made as indicated under nose and throat cultures for diphtheria bacilli.   If the bacteria-containing substance is solid material, like tissue, it may be held in sterile forceps and drawn in successive streaks across the surface of a solid medium in a Petri dish.   If fluid, the material is usually taken on a blunt and slightly curved glass rod and rubbed across the plate to make successive parallel streaks.   It is usually better to use two Petri dishes with at least twelve streaks.   Agar slants in extra large test-tubes also provide a surface for this method.

Plate Method.—In the usual plate method (Fig. 28), four tubes of agar, numbered 1, 2, 3, 4 with a wax pencil, are melted in a water-bath at 100°C. and kept for ten minutes in a copper rack (Fig. 30) in a water-bath at 45°C. Two tubes of the melted agar are placed between the thumb and index finger of the left hand, the cotton plugs are removed, and the mouths of the tubes are carefully passed through a Bunsen flame. Keep the tubes as nearly horizontal as possible, to prevent particles

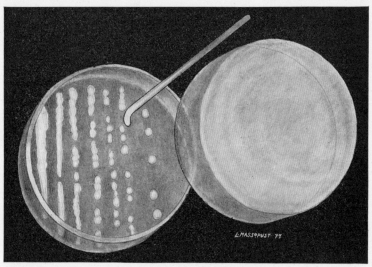

Fig. 29.—Streak method for isolating bacteria. The last of the successive streaks on the right show separate colonies. The glass rod has been drawn out slightly in the flame, curved, broken off and the broken blunt end perfectly rounded by heating in the flame. In plating streptococcus, pneumococcus, and meningococcus it is desirable to deposit a small amount of the material at a point in the periphery of a plate and then spread over the plate from this point with a clean platinum loop with the loop itself bent to such an angle that the flat of the loop lies on the surface. It is an advantage to place all plates inverted in a desiccator jar containing water for incubation.

of dust from the air from falling in and hold the cotton plugs between the fingers of the left hand in such a way as to protect the sterile portion of the plugs. With a sterile loop, pick up a loopful of the infected material and thoroughly mix it with the agar in *tube* 1. After mixing *tube* 1, carry the loop into *tube* 2, and thoroughly mix. Sterilize the loop, insert the plug in *tube* 1, and replace it in the water at 45°C. Remove the plugs from *tubes* 3 and 4, sterilize the mouths, and place them with *tube 2* between the thumb and index finger of the left hand. With a sterile loop, carry a loopful from *tube 2* to *tube 3*, mix, and carry a loopful from *tube 3* to *tube 4*. Insert the plugs and return to water at 45°C.

If the bacteria have been taken from a solid growth such as the colony, or from a solid growth on a slant culture, the smallest visible mass of growth should be taken. In such a case only *tubes 2, 3,* and *4* are poured into Petri dishes, because the number of bacteria in *tube 1* is so great that separate colonies could not be expected. To pour into the sterile Petri dishes, the cotton plug is removed from *tube 2,* and the mouth of the tube sterilized by rotating it in the very periphery of the flame. Pour its contents into Petri dish marked 2, the cover of which

FIG. 30.—Circular copper rack for melting agar tubes. The rack is placed in a half-gallon pail in which the water is boiled.

has been raised at one side just enough to admit the end of the tube. The cover is quickly replaced, and the dish carefully rocked until the agar spreads evenly over the entire bottom. The tube and plug are separately placed in a two-gallon jar of 1–1000 bichlorid or other disinfectant. Plates 3 and 4 are made in the same manner. If the material to be plated is liquid and is thought to contain only a moderate number or a few bacteria, then *tubes 1, 2* and *3*, but *tube 4* need not be made.

It may be more convenient to have at hand a box made of galvanized iron to receive all tubes and plates containing bacteria and infected material. Such a box is 30 by 12 by 12 inches, and is provided with a hinge-lid. Two boxes are provided, and at the end of each day the box with lid open is placed in the autoclave and for one hour sterilized at 120°C.

Method of Fishing Single Cells (Barber).—On a fat-free slide make a large, shallow hanging-drop of a suspension of bacteria so thin that only a single organism appears in the high-dry field. The Abbé condenser is removed, and the hanging-drop, with the preparation side down, is placed over the opening in the stage. A very fine sterile capillary pipet, mounted in a substage-holder, is brought into the drop and the bacterial cell drawn into it. It is then inoculated into the proper medium. The slide is moved by means of a mechanical stage, and the capillary raised and lowered by the substage screw. The very fine capillary is made by drawing glass tubing into a capillary which is heated and drawn out into a second capillary.

Transferring Bacteria from Colonies to Media in Tubes.— The plates, when solid, are inverted and placed at $37.5°$ C. until colonies have developed. To examine a colony a surface one is placed under the low-power objective and a portion removed with a sterile platinum wire (fishing) and rubbed up with a small drop of water on a slide. If the colony proves to be made up of the organism sought, it is often desirable to carry a part of the colony from the plate into a tube of sterile medium. A culture made from a culture is known as a subculture. To make this, another portion of the same colony, or the remainder of the colony if it is small, is removed with the sterile wire and inoculated on the surface of the medium chosen.

Tube Cultures.— For obtaining cultures that are not necessarily pure and for making subcultures from colonies and other pure cultures, media in tubes are usually employed. It has been pointed out that in routine work pure cultures as a rule are not necessary for diagnosis, and media in tubes are inoculated directly with the swabs.

Cleaning and Plugging Test-tubes.— Before sterilizing glassware it must be clean. Old tubes containing living bacterial cultures are first autoclaved for one hour at $120°$C. (15 lb. pressure). The tubes are then placed in a basin of hot water and the media removed with a test-tube cleaner. Place the tubes in a 2 per cent. soapine or other alkaline solution, and boil for thirty minutes. Rinse in several changes of water, and set aside in a wire basket to drain and to dry overnight. If the tubes are especially dirty, wash off the alkali and place overnight in a 50 per cent. sulphuric acid in which 5 per cent. sodium or potassium bichromate has been dissolved. Wash out the acid, and set aside to dry. Petri dishes are treated in the same way.

12

Non-absorbent cotton is used to cotton-plug test-tubes. A square of the correct size and thickness is folded in from two of its sides so that two free margins meet in the middle. It is then folded in the median line where the margins meet, and rolled into a firm plug from a third side. A second method of making plugs is to force the square of cotton into the upper end of the tube by pressing down the center with a glass rod.

Dry-heat Sterilization.—This method is limited almost entirely to the sterilization of glassware. It may be desirable to subject metallic apparatus to the action of dry heat to render

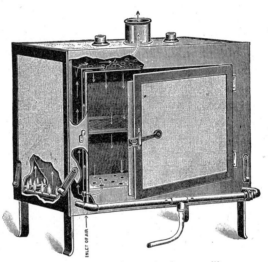

FIG. 31.—Lautenschlaeger dry-heat sterilizer.

it germ free. All apparatus subjected to dry heat must be free from moisture.

The glassware, after being covered or plugged, is placed in the hot-air oven (Fig. 31) and the temperature raised to 180°C., at which point it is maintained for one hour by lowering the flame the correct distance. Do not open the oven door until the temperature falls to 100°C. or lower. Sterile Petri dishes and other glassware may be wrapped in paper before sterilization to protect them from dust. All fabrics, including cotton plugs, are placed at least 2 inches from the sides and bottom of the oven.   The thermometer bulb reaches the center of the inside space of the oven.

Moist-heat Sterilization.—Materials containing moisture are sterilized by heating in water or steam.   The common media, except gelatin and those containing carbohydrates, and all the other materials used in bacteriologic work that are not dry-heat sterilized, are sterilized by subjecting them to live steam under pressure in an autoclave (Fig. 32) for ten minutes, at 110°C. (7 lbs. pressure).   A very satisfactory autoclave is a horizontal one in which the water is heated in a container by means of a gas burner underneath.   In sterilizations in which the additional heat is not objectionable a temperature of 120°C. (15 lbs. pressure) instead of 110°C. is used.

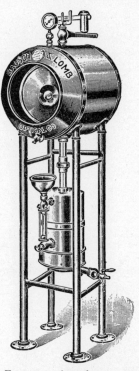

Immersion in water at 60°C. for from ten minutes to one hour kills vegetative bacteria while water at 70°C. kills in from five to fifteen minutes.   Boiling water at 100°C. kills in from one to five minutes. Surgical instruments may be sterilized in boiling water; but instruments used in making cultures should never be so sterilized, because boiling is not a practical way in which to kill spores and resistant forms of bacteria.

FIG. 32.—Autoclave. The steam may be admitted from a high-pressure boiler or a gas burner may be used to generate it.

Gelatin and media containing carbohydrates are sterilized in an Arnold sterilizer (Fig. 33) by heating for thirty minutes, after the steam begins to escape freely, on three successive days.   During the time between heatings, the media are kept at room temperature.   This is known as *fractional sterilization*.   *Pasteurization* is a term applied to the heating of milk at 145°F. This kills or inhibits the growth of many pathogenic bacteria.

Sterilization by Filtration.—Bacteria and other particles in suspension may be removed from a liquid by passing it through a Pasteur-Chamberland or a Berkefeld porcelain filter. The entire apparatus is sterilized before use by autoclaving for one hour at 120°C. (15 lb. pressure).

Disinfectants.—In distinction to sterilization which consists of killing all microörganisms present, disinfection implies only the destruction of pathogenic bacteria in the material

FIG. 33.—Arnold sterilizer for fractional sterilization.

disinfected. *Germicide* is a common term given to chemical disinfectants in solution. A disinfectant in a more dilute solution may prevent the multiplication of bacteria present without destroying them. A substance acting in this way is known as an *antiseptic* or *preservative*. The effectiveness of disinfectants varies with material treated.

Tincture of iodin (8 gm. iodin in 100 c.c. 95 per cent. alcohol) is the best disinfectant for small areas of skin. The freshly prepared solution is painted on the dry skin surface previously cleansed with alcohol. A dilute non-alkaline hypochlorite solution (Carrel-Dakin) is efficient in deep, infected, lacerated wounds. Two per cent. *boric acid* used as a wash on a mucous membrane acts as an antiseptic. *Oil of eucalyptus* in the naso-pharynx exerts an antiseptic action. In general, chemicals that are germicidal are also poisonous to the tissue cells. The action of quinin on malarial parasites, that of arsenobenzol on treponemata and trypanosomes, and of *thymol* and *santonin* as vermifuges, are examples of substances that act on specific organisms more strongly than they do on the protoplasm of cells.

Sputum, vomitus, soiled clothing, urine, and feces are dis-infected by adding *phenol, cresol,* or *sulphonaphthol* to make a 2 per cent. solution and allowing it to act for two hours or longer. *Chlorinated lime* in sufficient quantity to make 10 per cent. of the mass to be disinfected is used for the disinfection of cess-pools, latrines, and the like. Dental instruments or clinical thermometers must remain for two hours in a 5 per cent. solu-tion of phenol.

The *hands* must be scrubbed with green soap and placed for five minutes in 1 per cent. permanganate followed by 2 per cent. oxalic acid for one minute, or they may be placed in a 1–1000 bichlorid solution for five minutes. One per cent. solu-tion of cresol in green soap is as germicidal as a 2 per cent. aqueous solution of cresol. Seventy per cent. alcohol has some germicidal action, while absolute has practically none. A 3 per cent. commercial solution of hydrogen peroxid in water is useful in the mouth and in wounds. Commercial hydrogen peroxid contains 3 per cent. by weight of the gas. One per cent. *benzoate of soda* acts as a preservative of foods. Thymol is especially useful in preventing the growth of moulds. Less than a milligram of *chlorin* in a liter of water kills most patho-genic bacteria. *Ozone* is also used for the disinfection of water.

For *gaseous disinfection of rooms* formaldehyd is used. Ten ounces of formalin for each 1000 cu. ft. of space are placed in a 2-gallon galvanized pail, and 5 oz. of potassium permanga-nate added. The temperature should be 18° to 20°C.; the floors should be sprayed with water, and all openings about windows and doors plugged with cotton. The room is kept closed for eight hours. Insects and most small animals are not killed. For the disinfection of warerooms, cellars, base-ments, and holds of ships, where it is desirable to kill small animal life, 5 lb. sulphur per 1000 cu. ft. are burned. The sulphur is placed in a large iron pot, spread over the bottom and 1 oz. of alcohol is placed in the center and ignited.

Culture Media.—Bacteria require carbon, hydrogen, nitro-gen, oxygen and other food elements. Meat extract, peptone, and salt furnish suitable food for most bacteria, and these form the base for most media. An organism may require a very special kind of food such as hemoglobin. Such special foods are usually added to one containing the above ingre-dients. Substances are also added to media to make the growth of the organisms characteristic. The media must be placed in glassware that has been sterilized in a hot-air oven and then subjected to moist-heat sterilization.

Agar.—Dissolve 3 gm. Liebig's meat extract, 5 gm. salt, and 10 gm. peptone in 1000 c.c. of water at 55°C. Titrate to PH 7.4.

With the peptones now in use the old method of phenol-phthalein titration is inaccurate due to the varying phosphate content of the different peptones. It is desirable to determine the hydrogen ion concentration. To do this, place 5 c.c. of the medium in a test-tube and add 20 c.c. hot freshly distilled water and 10 drops of 0.01 per cent. phenolsulphonphthalein. Run in one-fiftieth normal sodium hydrate until the color exactly matches the tube with a value of PH 7.4 (page 103). Add an amount of normal sodium hydrate sufficient to give the remainder of the liter this reaction. The tube used for the titration and the standard should be of the same diameter.

After adjusting the reaction, add 20 gm. pulverized agar, or 15 gm. unpowdered agar, boil until the agar is dissolved (ten to thirty minutes), cool the medium to 45°C., and stir in very thoroughly the whites of two eggs. Boil gently and carefully for ten minutes over a flame with asbestos gauze beneath vessel, and during this time do not agitate the mix-ture in any way. The egg coagulates in large masses, and the clear fluid readily runs through muslin placed in a large funnel provided with a cork at its opening (Fig. 34). A thin layer of cotton is placed over the muslin. Make up to one liter in an agate ware measure and pour the hot agar upon the filter only so fast as it filters through. Substitute asbestos for cotton and filter paper to retain vitamines.

For slants, fill the tubes from the funnel used for the tubing of media (Fig. 34) to such a height that the upper edge of the slant lacks 1 inch of reaching the cotton plug, while the bottom

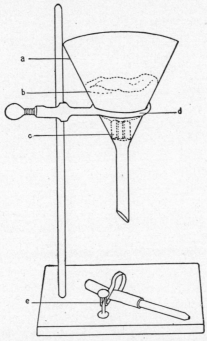

FIG. 34.—Funnel for filtering media. *a*, 22-cm. funnel; *b*, thin layer of cotton; *c*, large cork notched with knife; *d*, iron ring supporting funnel; *e*, pipet with cock to be attached to the funnel for tubing media.

o. the tube is not completely covered with medium. In preparing agar, that is to be used for plates, or for *stab cultures*, the tubes are almost half filled. A stab is made by pushing a platinum wire without a loop (needle) to the bottom of the tube. Tubes of media are placed in wire baskets of suitable size (Fig. 35).

Glycerin and Dextrose Agar.—To make glycerin agar from the plain agar, add 2 per cent. of twice-distilled glycerin to the desired quantity of melted agar in a flask; mix, and tube.   For dextrose agar, add 2 per cent. dextrose.

Blood, Ascitic, and Hydrocele Agar.—To prepare blood agar from the plain sterile slants, add about 20 per cent. sterile defibrinated rabbit, or human blood from a pipet, to the agar tubes melted and cooled to 45°C.   Thoroughly mix by rolling. Slant.   The sterile non-defibrinated blood from the arm vein of a patient may be added directly from a syringe.

For the growth of most bacteria it is preferable to use dextrose instead of plain agar.   As much as 3 c.c. to 5 c.c. of blood may be obtained by pricking the finger with an automatic

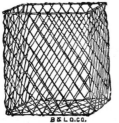

blood lancet.   If the finger is painted with tincture of iodin and wiped off with 95 per cent. alcohol, the sterile blood may be dropped directly into the tubes.   An added precaution in securing sterility is to coat the finger over with thin celloidin after the alcohol dries.

FIG. 35.—Wire baskets for culture tubes.

To prepare hydrocele or ascitic agar, add these fluids in the same way that blood is added.   Hydrocele and ascitic fluids are collected under sterile conditions, but, if accidentally contaminated, they may be made sterile by passing them through a porcelain filter.   All slants should be placed in the incubator for twenty-four hours to test their sterility, and they should be kept permanently in the slanted position and undisturbed until used.   The preparation of these media differs from the preparation of glycerin and sugar media in that the material added must be sterile.   To do this, a sterile bulb pipet is very useful but sterile 10-c.c. pipets may be used to transfer the liquid to the tubes.

Bulbs, Pipets and Blood Tubes for Handling Sterile Liquids.— Some technic in glass blowing is required even for simple bacteriologic work.   The sterile bulb pipets referred to above are prepared from large or small caliber glass tubing, according to the size of bulb desired.   Glass tubing with outside diameter of 6 mm. and inside diameter of 4 mm. is a very desirable size to work with. All flasks, tubing, and pipets are plugged with cotton, and dry-heat sterilized. The position of the plugs will depend on the part to be sterilized.

Collecting Sterile Blood from Laboratory Animals.—To bleed a *rat* or a *guinea-pig*, a defibrinating pipet is prepared from a test-

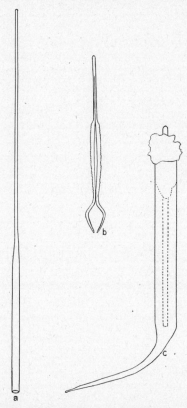

Fig. 36.—*a,* Wright measuring pipet. The large end may be expanded for a nipple by heating in flame and jamming against asbestos pad; *c,* guinea-pig heart pipet (Novy.) To make this pipet heat the bottom of a test-tube in the blow-flame, place a small glass rod against the melted bottom and allow to cool. Use the glass rod as a handle and evenly soften the tube near the bottom, draw out, curve, and seal in the flame. Break the tip off and round in flame before puncturing the heart. Place a small glass defibrinating rod in it, plug with cotton and sterilize. *b,* Forceps for holding the heart while making the puncture of the auricle with the pipet.

tube (Fig. 36). The tip is broken of, sterilized in a flame, and inserted first into the auricles and the beginning of the veins, and then into the ventricles, while the suction is made with the mouth. A rat is etherized by placing it in a tightly covered battery jar, with cotton on which ether has been poured covering the bottom. As soon as the animal falls over, it is removed and tied by its four legs to an animal board (Fig. 37). It may be given additional ether by means of a small cone. Guinea-pigs are etherized by the use of a small paper cone made from a bit of heavy paper held in shape by a small pin.

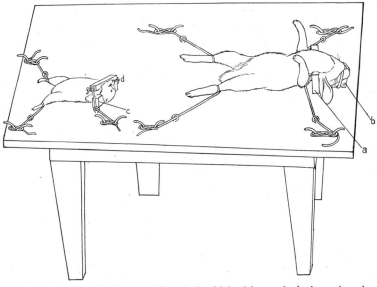

Fig. 37.—Animal holder on table 40 inches high with top of 1-inch maple 30 b 60 inches. *a*, Neck elevation 6 inches wide for rabbit made of ¾-inch wood 2½ inches high at ends and 1½ inches high at center with the semicircular ring; *b*, 1½ inches diameter (brass cover lifter) for rabbit's mouth; *c*, yolk 4 inches wide with a 1¼-inch opening for neck of guinea-pig to be closed by top bar which is supported by a hinge, *d*. Animal legs except front legs of guinea-pig are held by 4-mm. paraffined window-cord passing through eye-screw to cord fastener. The rabbit holder is also suitable for dogs under 15 kilos.

To obtain the blood from a *rabbit* the canula of a sterile pipet is inserted into the carotid and held there tightly by means of a silk thread, or a sterile canula (Fig. 38) not attached to a sterile pipet is inserted and the blood allowed to flow into a sterile Erlenmeyer flask. The rabbit is held in a suitable holder (Fig. 39). As soon as all the blood is obtained from

either a rat, a guinea-pig, or a rabbit, it is defibrinated by means
of a glass rod that passes into the pipet.

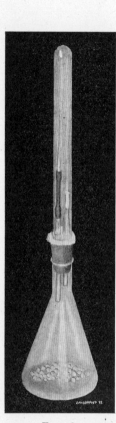

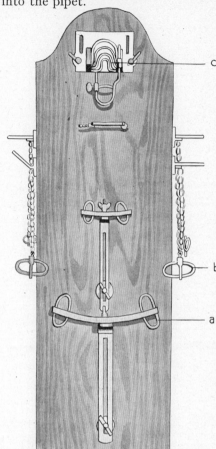

FIG. 38.   FIG. 39.

FIG. 38.—Flask used in bleeding rabbits.   Glass beads are placed in a 350-c.c.
Erlenmeyer flask with a two-hole rubber stopper through which two pieces of
glass tubing project.   One of these is cotton plugged while to the other is attached
rubber tubing bearing a 2-mm. glass capillary with end rounded in flame for
insertion into the carotid.   A test-tube is placed over these, plugged with cotton
about the rubber stopper and the flask autoclaved at 120°C. for twenty minutes.

FIG. 39.—Latapie rabbit board.   Hind legs are clamped in *a*, and the animal
turned on its back when the forelegs are clamped in *b* and the ring, *c*, placed behind the incisor teeth.

Bouillon.—Dissolve 5 gm. Liebig's beef-extract, 5 gm. salt,
and 10 gm. peptone in 1000 c.c. water.   Boil fifteen minutes,

make up to 1 liter, titrate to 0.8 per cent. acid, autoclave for twenty minutes at 110°C., place in the ice-box to cool, and when cool filter through filter paper. Place in flasks or tubes, and autoclave for twenty minutes at 110°C.

Beef Infusion.—For the cultivation of many of the pathogenic bacteria, it is desirable to obtain the meat extractives directly from the meat which insures a more luxuriant growth of those that do not grow readily. In cases where the laboratory facilities are good it is advisable to use chopped beef as a routine in making up all media. To do this, substitute the words [1000 c.c. beef infusion] for the words [5 gm. Liebig's beef, extract] in the directions for the preparation of agar, bouillon- etc. and also omit the words [1 liter of water] since the correct amount of liquid is contained in the infusion.

Beef infusion is prepared by adding 1000 c.c. of water to 500 gm. spice-free lean beef ground in a sausage grinder, and by placing it in the ice-box for twenty-four hours, and then filtering it through muslin. The filtrate is the "beef infusion." Another way of preparing the "beef infusion" is to heat the beef and water for one hour, at 50° to 55°C., instead of allowing it to stand in the ice-box for twenty-four hours.

Unheated Bouillon.—Heat may remove from the infusion substances desirable for certain purposes. The heat may be dispensed with by adding peptone and salt to the infusion, correcting the reaction, and then passing the whole through a Berkefeld filter.

Sugar-free Bouillon.—Inoculate the "beef infusion" with bacillus coli and place it in the incubator overnight (eighteen hours). Proceed in the same way as with the "beef infusion." This medium is better for the indol test than Dunham's solution. It must be used for making up accurately the various strengths of sugar media, and for the production of diphtheria toxin.

Sugar and Glycerin Bouillon.—One per cent. dextrose, lactose, saccharose, mannose, or inulin, may be added to sugar-free bouillon just before filtering; or 2 per cent. glycerin may be added.

Calcium Carbonate Bouillon (Bolduan).—Prepare the sugar

bouillon as above, and place it in tubes that contained a small chip of marble at the time of dry-heat sterilization. As acid is produced it is removed by the marble. Pneumococcus and streptococcus grow well on this medium.

Potato Tubes.—Scrub, and carefully remove the skin from a large potato. With a cork-borer, cut cylinders; with a knife divide the cylinders diagnonally into halves, and immediately place these in running water. Leave thus overnight, and then place them in sterile test-tubes. Autoclave.

The bacillus of glanders is grown on potato. At the same time that the purulent material is inoculated on the potato it is plated on glycerin agar. A pure culture of any Gram-negative granular bacillus obtained is inoculated intraperitoneally into a male guinea-pig. The testicles swell (Strauss reaction), and the animal dies in a week. The growth on potato is heavy and brownish.

Egg Medium (Dorset).—To 300 c.c. of well-beaten egg add 200 c.c. of dextrose bouillon; slant, coagulate, and sterilize in the same way as Loeffler's blood serum. The eggs are measured before being beaten. After being beaten a small amount of ether may be added to dissipate the air bubbles. It is useful for the cutivation of tubercle bacillus and for diphtheroid bacilli.

Litmus Milk.—To 1 liter of fat-free milk, add sufficient 1 per cent. azolitmin (Merck) to give the desired blue. The milk must be perfectly fresh, or it will coagulate when sterilized.

Gelatin.—To 1000 c.c. water add 3 gm. Liebig's beef-extract, 100 gm. gelatin (Gold label), 5 gm. salt, and 10 gm. peptone, and dissolve at 55°C. Titrate the gelatin to a reaction of PH8 (see titration of agar); cool to 30°C., and thoroughly stir into this the white of one egg; without stirring, raise just to the boiling point for fifteen minutes; filter through muslin and a thin layer of cotton. Tube.

Dunham's Solution.—To 1000 c.c. water add 10 gm. peptone and 5 gm. salt. Dissolve with heat, and filter through paper. Autoclave.

Bile.—Autoclave 1 liter fresh ox-bile; filter; place in tubes and flasks, and again autoclave.

Semisolid Carbohydrate Media.—Make sugar-free agar using 5 gm. unpowdered agar instead of 15 gm.; add 1 per cent. Andrade indicator (100 c.c. 0.5 per cent. acid fuchsin plus 16 c.c. n/1 NaOH); place 5 c.c. in small tubes; and autoclave. Add 0.5 c.c. of the desired sugar from a sterile 10 per cent. solution (page 191 for reactions).

Russell-Lead Acetate Medium.—To sugar-free agar add 1 per cent. Andrade indicator and auto-clave; add 1 per cent. lactose (glucose free and sterile) and 0.1 per cent. glucose (sterile); cool to 60°C., and add 0.05 per cent. basic lead acetate; place 4 c.c. in sterile Wassermann tubes. The glucose is only sufficient to show acid production and the reddening is not great enough to be con-fused with the intense red color caused by lactose fermentation. The typhoid and paratyphoid B blacken the lead acetate; dysentery bacilli and paratyphoid A do not. The tubes are slanted slightly and a stab made near the shallower margin and the surface of the slant inoculated.

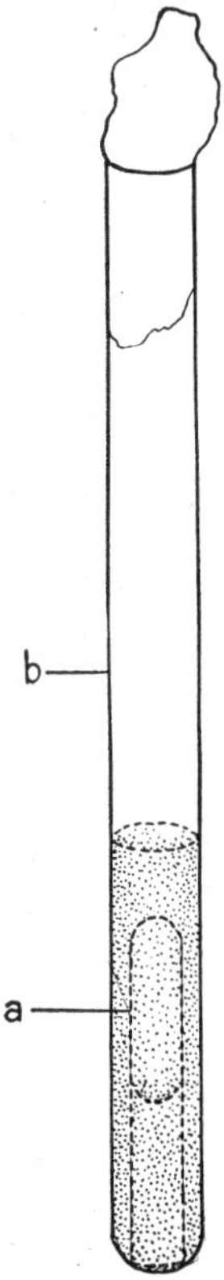

Loeffler's Blood Serum.—To 250 c.c. 1 per cent. glucose bouillon, add 750 c.c. clear, hemo-globin-free, calf- or pig-serum. The pig-serum is less expensive and just as satisfactory. Tube; slant; place in an incubator or an inspissator; slowly raise the temperature to 85°C. and maintain that temperature for two hours. Autoclave for twenty minutes at 110°C.

Fig. 40.—Fer-mentation tube. Place a 55 by 7-mm. test-tube, *a*, upside down in bouillon in a 155 by 16-mm. test-tube, *b*, before ster-ilization. The air is driven out of *a* during the steril-ization. Minute bubbles in both in-dicate gas pro-duction.

To store media such as Loeffler's blood serum it must be protected against evaporation. This may be done by dipping the plugs and the upper ends of the tubes of solid media in the melted paraffin. More care should be exercised in preserving valuable cultures from evaporation by sealing the tubes with sealing-wax.

To preserve cultures, after the inoculated tubes have been

TABLE OF BACTERIAL FERMENTATION OF CARBOHYDRATES

	Inulin	Saccharose	Lactose	Mannose	Dextrose
B. proteus...................	o	Gas	o	o	Gas
B. cloacæ....................	o	Gas	Gas	Gas	Gas
B. edematis maligni..........	.o	Gas	Gas	Gas	Gas
B. aerogenes capsulatus......	o	Gas	Gas	o	Gas
B. coli......................	o	Few strains	Gas	Gas	Gas
B. mucosus capsulatus........	o	o	Acid	Gas	Gas
B. enteriditis...............	o	o	o	Gas	Gas
B. paratyphosus B...........	o	o	o	Gas	Gas
B. paratyphosus A...........	o	o	o	Gas	Gas
B. typhosus.................	o	o	o	Acid	Acid
B. dysenteriæ (Hiss).........	o	o	o	Acid	Acid
B. dysenteriæ (Flexner)......	o	o	o	Acid	Acid
B. dysenteriæ (Shiga)........	o	o	o	o	Acid
Micrococcus meningitidis.....	o	o	o	o	Acid
Strep. pyogenes..............	o	Acid	Acid	Acid	Acid
Strep. of subacute endocarditis	o	Acid	Acid	Acid	Acid
Strep. mucosus cap...........	Acid	Acid	Acid	Acid	Acid
Strep. pneumoniæ............	Acid	Acid	Acid	Acid	Acid
Staph. pyogenes aureus.......	Acid	Acid	Acid	Acid	Acid

incubated the desired length of time, the plugs are cut off square with scissors, seared, pushed into the tubes to a distance of 1 cm. and covered over with sealing-wax melted from large sticks.

Endo's Medium.—To 100 c.c. sterile sugar-free agar with a reaction of PH 7.8 contained in a 4-oz. bottle, add 5 c.c. 20 per cent. sterile lactose and 1 c.c. indicator. The bottle is rotated to mix its contents and the medium poured into Petri dishes. To prepare the indicator (reduced fuchsin), add 1 gm. anhydrous sodium sulphite in 10 c.c. of water (freshly dissolved), to 1 c.c. of a saturated solution of basic fuchsin in 95 per cent. alcohol, and heat for twenty minutes in an Arnold sterilizer. This must be prepared immediately before use. The lactose solution is sterilized in the same way as the indicator.

In typhoid fever, the bacilli may be isolated from the stools in 60 per cent. of the cases. This is practically the only procedure in carrier cases, and in determining the release of convalescents.

One large loopful of feces is emulsified in 5 c.c. of broth containing 1–200,000 brilliant green and the broth culture incubated one to two hours. Plate the supernatant liquid on two endo-plates by the streak method (page 175). Incubate for twenty-four hours and mark at least ten small translucent colorless colonies by ringing them with wax-pencil on bottom of plate. Each colony is agglutinated by emulsifying it in a drop of saline on a slide and this drop at once mixed with a drop of 1–100 dilution of a very strong antityphoid serum. Five colonies may be agglutinated on one slide at the same time, the drops of saline and serum being placed opposite each other before adding the bacteria. There should be a macroscopic agglutination in five minutes. Let the preparations dry down and stain them with Gram's stain. Transplant each of the positive colonies to a Russell tube (page 190), incubate overnight, emulsify with saline, and agglutinate using dilutions of 1–1200, and 1–2400 of a strong serum together with a saline control.

Petroff Medium.—To about 25 c.c. of the material (sputum) in a centrifuge tube of suitable size, add accurately 25 c.c. normal sodium hydroxid from a 50-c.c. buret; stir thoroughly, and place in the incubator for thirty minutes at 37.5° C. Add accurately 25 c.c. normal hydrochloric acid from a second buret, to neutralize the normal alkali used. Both alkali and acid are made up with water immediately after distillation. Centrifuge, and make smears or cultures from the sediment.

To prepare the medium, add 15 c.c. glycerin (twice distilled) and 0.03 gm. methyl violet to 200 c.c. whole eggs and 100 c.c. beef infusion. Mix thoroughly and heat in inspissator at 85°C. until coagulated and then for one hour on two successive days at 75°C. Inoculate with the sediment obtained by digestion with caustic soda.

Potato-blood Agar for Bacillus Pertussis.—Dissolve 15 gm. agar and 1.5 gm. salt in 300 c.c. water, and to this add 100 c.c. potato extract made by boiling for thirty minutes 100 gm. potato ground in a food chopper in 200 c.c. 4 per cent. glycerin. Boil, filter, and place in tubes (about 3 c.c. in each). Autoclave; cool to 45°C., and add 1.5 to 2 c.c. of defibrinated human or rabbit blood. Slant. To make the culture, bronchial mucus from an early case of whooping cough is washed in sterile saline and inoculated on the surface of a number of tubes. *Bacillus influenzæ* may be isolated on this medium or on plain blood agar. *Bacillus pertussis*, after repeated transplants, may be grown on ascitic agar without hemoglobin, while the influenza bacillus cannot be grown in this manner. From cases of pink-eye, the *Koch-Weeks bacillus* may be isolated on this medium. See page 152 for Bordet's potato agar.

Bacteriologic Stains.—The number of stains employed should be made as small as possible in order that the worker may familiarize himself with every detail of the stains used. A ten-

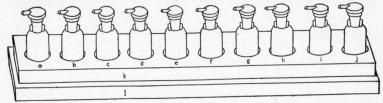

FIG. 41.—Block for stains. Bottles (B. & L. O. Co.) hold 30 c.c. and are provided with a snout leak. The block consists of the lower ¾-inch board 3.5 by 25 inches, *l*, on which there is tacked a board, *k*, that has in it ten 1.5-inch holes for the bottles. *a*, Gram's staining solution; *b*, Gram's iodin; *c*, 95 per cent. alcohol; *d*, pyronin for one-tenth per cent. basic fuchsin; *e*, Ziehl-Neelsen solution; *f*, Czaplewsky solution; *g*, Loeffler's methylene blue; *h*, distilled water; *i*, polychrome protozoon stain; *j*, polychrome blood stain.

hole block (Fig. 41) for ten 30-c.c. staining bottles with snout-leaks is very convenient for routine work. This block is kept on a desk or table near a sink with the following solutions in it: (1) Gram's staining solution, (2) Gram's iodin, (3) Pyronin, (4) Loeffler's methylene blue, (5) Ziehl-Neelsen, (6) Czaplewsky, (7) 95 per cent. alcohol, (8) Polychrome blood stain, (9) Polychrome protozoon stain, and (10) Distilled water.

Most dyes are more soluble in alcohol than in water. Three grams of fuchsin (basic) dissolve in about 100 c.c. alcohol, 1½ gm. in about 100 c.c. water; 4½ gm. of gentian violet dissolve in 100 c.c. alcohol, and almost this amount in 100 c.c. of water. Unless a given dye of a reliable manufacturer is

13

specified, it is not possible to make a general statement about solubilities. Variations in the quality of dyes are perhaps less serious than in histologic work, but care should be exercised in making purchases, and uniformity must be insisted on.

Protection of Labels.—Write the labels, and when dry apply thin celloidin with a camel's hair brush. As soon as this is dry, paint over with balsam damar in xylol. (The balsam damar already dissolved in xylol may be obtained from Bausch & Lomb Optical Co.)

Fixation of Bacteria.—Unless otherwise directed, all bacterial preparations are fixed in the flame. Proper fixation must be acquired by experience. To fix a smear on a cover-glass, hold the cover-glass in forceps for ten seconds with the preparation side up, and at a distance of 5 inches above a Bunsen burner flame 4 inches high. If the preparation is on a slide, hold 3 inches above the top of the flame for the same length of time.

Loeffler's Methylene Blue.—This stain is used for staining diphtheria bacilli, since it brings out as much detail in the morphology of this organism as any of the special stains. It is also the best of simple stains for routine work; but dilute carbol-fuchsin is more useful for a few organisms that stain with some difficulty. It stains in a few seconds, and does not readily overstain.

To 1485 c.c. distilled water, add 500 c.c. of a saturated alcoholic solution of methylene blue and 15 c.c. 1 per cent. aqueous solution of potassium hydroxid. Grübler's methylene blue (Koch for bacteria) is the best for this purpose. To saturate the alcohol with methylene blue, place a bottle containing 1000 c.c. absolute alcohol and 70 gm. methylene blue in the paraffin oven for several hours and shake repeatedly.

Gram's Stain.—This double stain serves to seperate bacteria into two groups, of which one stains violet (Gram-positive) and the other red (Gram-negative). This separation is so important that Gram's stain is the routine stain used for staining smears and cultures containing unknown bacteria. Its chief disadvantages are that there is more or less black precipitate formed in smears that contain cellular detritus or protein material, and that small organisms are not heavily stained. Owing to this tendency to precipitate protein, it is often advisable to make also a Loeffler's methylene blue stain of intracellular bacteria, such as gonococcus; or fix in methyl alcohol. The albumin should be removed from sediments by re-centrifuging with saline whenever possible. A few bacteria, such as bacillus pyocyaneus, may stain negative or positive; but this is not true for the common pathogenic bacteria that color with simple stains.

Two stock solutions are required. Solution A is made by adding an excess of methyl violet to 330 c.c. absolute alcohol and 90 c.c. anilin oil in a 500-c.c. glass-stoppered bottle. Solution B is made by adding an excess of methyl violet to 400 c.c. distilled water in a 500-c.c. glass-stoppered bottle.

To make the staining solution (*Gram's staining solution*), add 2 c.c. of A to 18 c.c. of B in a 30-c.c. staining bottle provided with a snout-leak. The Gram's staining solution keeps two weeks. For this reason it is necessary once in two weeks to make the solution up fresh from the two stock solutions. Solutions A and B are permanent.

The heat-fixed preparation is covered for three minutes with the Gram's staining solution. Wash off with water, and for thirty seconds, apply *Gram's iodin* (iodin 1 gm.; potassium iodid 2 gm., and water 300 c.c.). Wash the iodin off with water and for thirty seconds run 95 per cent. alcohol over the preparation. Wash with water, and stain for one minute with *pyronin* (pyronin 2 gm., 10 per cent. formalin 10 c.c., and water 90 c.c.). In cases where a Gram-negative organism that stains with difficulty is suspected, it may be advantageous to counterstain with dilute carbol-fuchsin instead of with pyronin. Wash, air-dry, and examine with the oil. Each one employing the stain must test the time for each step with the particular solutions being employed by him by using slides that have on them both Gram-negative and Gram-positive bacteria.

Dilute Carbol-fuchsin.—This is preferable to Loeffler's methylene blue for staining influenza, pertussis, Koch-Weeks bacillus and other bacteria that stain with difficulty. It also gives good results with both the plague bacillus and micrococcus melitensis. It is prepared by adding 10 c.c. carbol-fuchsin to 90 c.c. distilled water.

Ziehl-Neelsen Stain for Tubercle Bacilli.—This stain is a specific one for the group of acid-fast bacteria, and its chief application is in the identification of the tubercle bacillus. The leprosy bacillus is the other pathogenic acid-fast organism. Both bacillus tuberculosis and bacillus lepræ are alcohol- and acid-fast; that is, an acid alcohol acting for the usual length of time does not remove the fuchsin from these bacilli.

Some bacteria (for example, smegma bacillus) are much more readily decolorized by alcohol and by certain organic acids than are either tubercle or leprosy bacilli; but since this staining difference is relative, methods (animal inoculations) giving absolute results are employed for this differentiation.

To 450 c.c. 5 per cent. carbolic acid in a glass-stoppered bottle, add 50 c.c. of a saturated absolute alcohol solution of fuchsin (neutral, basic). To saturate the absolute alcohol with fuchsin, place a tightly stoppered bottle containing alcohol and an excess of fuchsin in the paraffin oven and shake. A stock bottle of the saturated absolute alcohol solution of fuchsin should be kept on hand. The 5 per cent. carbolic acid is made up with distilled water immediately after distillation. Tap water is used in making the smears and in no other part of the technic is distilled water used. *Acid-fast organisms* may proliferate to an astonishing extent in distilled water and lead to serious error.

Czaplewsky's solution for decolorizing stains of the tubercle bacillus is made by adding 5 c.c. concentrated hydrochloric acid, 5 gm. sodium chlorid, and 200 c.c. water to 1000 c.c. 95 per cent. alcohol.

The smear properly fixed on a slide is placed on a staining support and the Ziehl-Neelsen solution dropped on and heated by occasionally waving a Bunsen burner flame beneath it, so as to cause gentle steaming for from two to five minutes. Apply fresh stain as often as necessary. The slide may also be heated by placing it across the rings of a boiling water-bath. Wash off the stain by flooding the preparation with water. By dropping the Czaplewsky solution from the bottle, it is now run over the preparation until the thinner parts of the smear are a faint pink.

Wash with water, and stain for one-half minute with Loeffler's methylene blue. Wash, air-dry, and examine with oil-immersion lens. The tubercle bacilli (or other acid-fast bacilli) are red, while all other parts of the preparation are blue, unless there are heavy masses in the smear which may retain the red.

Capsule Stain (Rosenow).—A clear zone about bacteria may suggest capsules, but this is not conclusive because a retraction zone produced by drying or fixation may give a similar appearance. Conclusive proof of capsule formation is obtained by differential staining. Occasionally, this is seen in the usual Gram's stain and in polychrome protozoon stains, but uniform results cannot be obtained with them.

Make the smear on a cover-glass, and as it becomes almost dry in the air cover for twenty seconds with 10 per cent. tannic acid. Wash with water, dry in the air, and follow with freshly prepared Gram's staining solution. Counter-stain with 60 per cent. alcohol saturated with Grübler's yellowish water-soluble eosin. Mount in colophonium-xylol. The capsules stain pink, and the bacteria blue or violet.

Flagella Stain (Loeffler).—Inoculate 10 c.c. of sterile saline with so small a number of the bacteria that only a slight cloudiness is produced. Incubate for one hour at 37.5°C. Place 1 drop on a fat-free cover-glass, and let dry in the air (Kendall). Cover the preparation for one minute with the mordant and gently heat, but do not boil. The mordant is prepared by adding 5 c.c. saturated alcoholic solution of fuchsin (basic) and 25 c.c. saturated ferrous sulphate to 50 c.c. 10 per cent. aqueous solution tannic acid. Filter before using. This solution does not keep. Wash off the mordant with water, and stain for two minutes over a boiling water-bath with freshly prepared carbol-fuchsin to which 0.1 per cent. potassium hydrate has been added. Wash, dry in the air, and mount in colophonium-xylol.

If the flagella are attached to the bacteria and are visible at all, they are usually distinct. Although flagella may be seen with dark-field illumination, a stain is required for their certain identification on an unknown organism.

Spore Stain.—Uniformity in the shape and position of spores usually makes their presence quite certain, but portions of the protoplasm of bacterial cells other than spores may remain entirely unstained with the simple stains so that true spores are simulated closely. For this reason, it is frequently desirable to apply a specific double stain.

The age of the culture is important in staining spores. In general, the preparation should be made as soon as possible after spore formation begins. First examine the culture with a simple stain to ascertain if spore formation has taken place. Make a cover-glass preparation with the cells well separated, fix in the flame, and treat for ten minutes with 5 per cent. chromic acid. Wash, blot off the excessive water, apply freshly prepared carbol-fuchsin and gently steam for ten minutes. Wash with water, and examine in water. If the spores are red, drop 60 per cent. alcohol on the preparation for about one-half minute. Wash with water, and examine in water. If the spores appear as distinct red spherules, counterstain for fifteen seconds with Loeffler's methylene blue. Wash, air-dry, and mount in colophonium-xylol. The spores are red, and the remainder of the cell blue.

Serologic Methods for the Identification of Bacteria.— Such methods as complement-fixation, agglutination, and bacteriolysis are important in both diagnostic work and original investigations. Some of the methods may be used either for the identification of an unknown serum using a known organism, or of an unknown organism, using a known serum. The Widal reaction is an example of the former application (page 105). Other specific methods are given under bacteria described in connection with feces and blood.

Agglutination.—Bacteria placed in specific agglutinating sera

become motionless, gathered into clumps, and often partially
dissolved. The specific serum is prepared as indicated on
page 140; or it may be obtained from an infected patient. Typhoid fever, paratyphoid infections, bacterial dysenteries,
Malta fever, infections in cattle with bacillus abortus, and
infections in horses with glanders bacillus, are some of the
diseases in which a diagnosis may be made by an agglutination
test. Controls with normal sera are always required. Both
microscopic and macroscopic methods af agglutination have
been described under Widal test.

Precipitin Test.—The *in vitro* test for pneumococcus type
which depends on the precipitin reaction is made by adding
0.5 c.c. thoroughly washed sputum to a centrifuge tube containing 5 per cent. blood—1 per cent. glucose broth, shaking
and incubating for five hours. Sediment the corpuscles, add
3 c.c. of the supernatant liquid to 1 c.c. of ox bile in a second
tube, incubate 15 min., and to 0.5 c.c. of the clear liquid in each
of three serum tubes add 0.5 c.c. of each of the three types of
sera (Avery). For urine add 0.5 c.c. to 0.5 c.c. sera.

Bacteriolysis.—The reaction is not as simple as agglutination
and precipitation. Unheated immune serum added to the
specific organism produces solution, but after the serum is heated

FIG. 42—Concave slide for hanging-drop preparations.

at 55°C. solution does not take place unless fresh serum is
added to the heated serum. This shows that two factors enter
into the phenomenon: the one present in normal serum and
sensitive to heat is complement; while the specific one, present
only in an immune animal and stabile to heat, is amboceptor.
Both of these are necessary to bring about solution of the bacteria. The reaction may be carried out *in vitro* or *in vivo*.

In *Pfeiffer's reaction*, a bouillon culture or a suspension of
the organism in saline is injected into the peritoneal cavity of a
guinea-pig that has been hyperimmunized against the organism.
At the end of five, ten, thirty and sixty minutes, peritoneal exudate is withdrawn, and examined in hanging-drop preparations (Fig. 42) under the microscope for agglutination, bac-

teriolysis and phagocytosis.   Smears may be made on the slide
and stained with a polychrome blood stain.

Complement-fixation Test.—In this test, the principle of cyto-
lysis (solution of a given variety of cells by specific amboceptor
and complement) is made use of.   Its practical and most important application is given under the Wassermann test.
Complement-fixation is of value in the diagnosis of certain
forms of gonorrhea (Schwartz test), echinococcus infection,
and glanders infection in horses.   It has been applied in tuberculosis and typhoid fever with indifferent results.   In experimental work, the reaction has been of some help in showing
the relation of certain organisms to a clinical disease.

Inoculation of Animals for the Identification of Bacteria.—
The use of experimental animals in the development of bacteriology is unquestioned.   Small laboratory animals are now
indispensible in the routine methods of diagnosis, while larger
animals are required for the preparation of sera and attenuated
viruses used in the treatment and prevention of certain infections.   Some of the uses of large animals are in the preparation
of diphtheria antitoxin, tetanus antitoxin, gas bacillus antitoxin, antimeningococcus serum, and antipneumococcus serum
from the horse; small-pox vaccine, and serum for media from
cattle;   and corpuscles for the Wassermann test from sheep.
Small animals are used in diagnosis to detect small numbers of
bacteria (tubercle bacilli in urine sediment), to identify an infectious organism quickly (gas bacillus), to determine the
strength of an antitoxin, to test the virulence of bacteria
(bacillus diphtheriæ), and to obtain a pure culture of bacteria
(pneumococcus).   They are also employed for the application
of the third (infection of an animal) and fourth (recovery of
the organism from the infected animal) *rules of Koch.*   The
first rule of Koch states that the organism be present in all
cases of the disease, and the second that it be obtained in pure
cultures.

The usual routes selected for administering the bacteria
are subcutaneous, intravenous, and intraperitoneal; but the
animals may be infected by rubbing bacteria on the skin or

on the nasal mucosa, by the introduction of these into the stomach or rectum, into the pleural or the intracranial cavity, the anterior chamber of the eye, the spinal canal, or the testicle, or by insufflation into the trachea. Guinea-pigs while being kept under observation should be conveniently at hand and in suitable cages (Fig. 43).

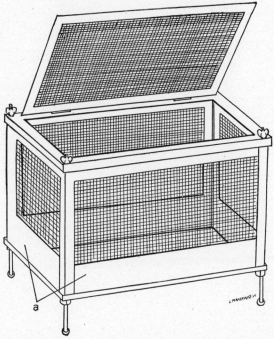

Fig. 43.—Vaughan animal cage for guinea-pigs and rabbits. (Eberbach & Sons, Ann Arbor, Mich.). *a*, Galvanized sheet iron to keep hay or shavings off the floor.

Rabbits are inoculated intravenously through the marginal ear vein (Fig. 44). Liquid may be given to rabbits through a small catheter (No. 8 French of composition) inserted into the stomach, the thumb and index finger of the experimenter's gloved left hand being used in each case to hold the animal's mouth open. It is not necessary to fasten the rabbit to the board for either of the afore mentioned injections, but it is necessary to do so if it is to be bled.

Guinea-pigs are used in routine diagnostic work. The injections are usually subcutaneous or intraperitoneal, and when given into the blood stream the injection is made into an ear

FIG. 44.—Intravenous injection of a rabbit. Place animal in wire basket or better secure it firmly on board (Fig. 38), shave ear, paint with tincture of iodin and inject into the marginal vein (thin edge of ear) just in front of the left thumb with which the ear is held.

vein with a fine needle or directly into the heart. In any case, the hair at the area of injection is clipped with scissors or hair clippers and may be shaved. The skin is wiped off with alcohol,

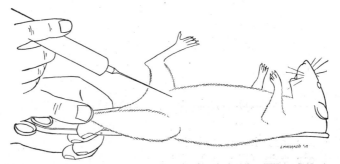

FIG. 45.—Inoculation of rats. Hold rat in left hand with long (30-cm.) ovum-forceps while injection is made with the right hand.

and wiped thoroughly with a swab moistened with tincture of iodin. To make the subcutaneous injection, the skin over the abdomen of the animal, which is firmly held on the board, is raised by means of the thumb and index-finger of the left hand, and the needle is pressed through at an angle of 60 degrees to the surface. To give guinea-pigs material by the mouth, the tip of a graduated glass pipet is placed well back in the mouth while the liquid is slowly forced out by means of a medicine dropper bulb on the upper end of the pipet.

White rats are held in forceps (Fig. 45) and inoculated intraperitoneally or subcutaneously; while *white mice*, with the

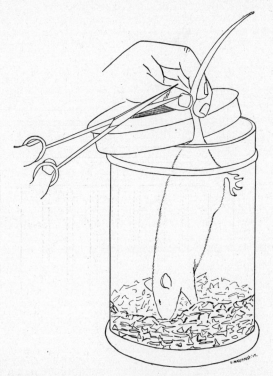

FIG. 46.—Battery jar provided with leaded gauze covers for rats. To examine the blood, pull up the tail with forceps, clip off the very tip with scissors and touch a cover-glass to a small drop of the escaping blood.

tail projecting through the small end of a tin cone, are inoculated intravenously into the tail vein, or subcutaneously at the root of the tail To examine the blood of a rat, its tail is pulled out between jar (Fig. 46) and cover until the rear of the rat is firmly held against the side of the jar, the very tip of the tail clipped with the scissors, and a cover-glass applied to the small drop of blood.

*Dog*s are readily inoculated subcutaneously or intraperitoneally, with the aid of an assistant. For intravenous injection into the ear vein it is better to anesthetize them (Fig. 47) for after a failure to enter the vein a resection may be required. For inoculation either by the mouth or subcutaneously, *cats* are pressed into long cylindrical boxes (Fig. 48).

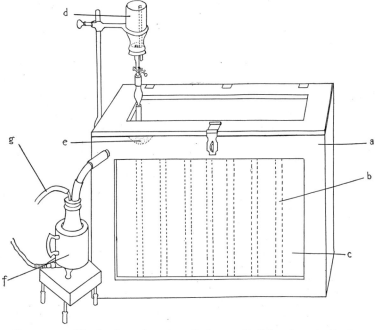

FIG. 47.—*a*, Wooden box 4 by 3 by 3 ft. for anesthetizing dogs or other large animals (drawn from apparatus designed by Dr. B. F. McGrath*). b*, Wooden strips inside the glass to protect glass front, *c*, from animal. The ether is contained in a pint milk bottle, *d*, that is provided with a glass air tube that reaches almost to the bottom of the bottle. The ether escapes on cotton in the metal screen cage, *e*. For more rapid anesthesia the ether bottle is placed in an electric heater, *f*, and the vapor forced into box by a current of air coming through *g*.

Bacteriologic Examination of Milk.—To sterile, widemouthed bottles containing 99.5 c.c. of sterile water, 0.5 c.c. of milk collected in sterile test-tubes are added.

The milk is placed in the test-tubes by pieces of sterile glass tubing (3 ft. long) kept sterile by wrapping in sterile muslin. These long pieces of tubing are used for stirring the milk in the can before the sample is placed in the sterile test-tubes in which the samples are taken to the laboratory.

One cubic centimeter of this 1–200 dilution is added to one tube of melted agar cooled to 45°C. After mixing, pour into a Petri dish and incubate for forty-eight hours. Two-tenths cubic centimeter of a diluted milk is used for making a second plate. Count the colonies after forty-eight hours of

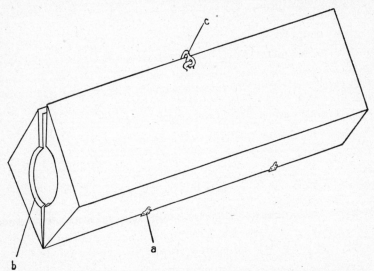

FIG. 48.—Cat holder. 14 by 6 by 6 inches outside measurements made from ¾-inch boards. The box opens on hinges, *a*. The cat is placed within, a wooden block that fits the interior placed behind it, the 2½-inch opening, *b*, closed around its neck and the box fastened by the hook, *c*.

incubation. Report the number of colonies per cubic centimeter of milk. In counting the colonies, rule the bottom of the plate into 9 parts by means of a wax pencil (Fig. 51). Many city and state Boards of Health provide that 1 c.c. must not contain more than 500,000 bacteria. As a routine, examine small translucent colonies for streptococci.

To examine for tubercle bacilli, inject 10 c.c. subcutaneously into the two groins of a guinea-pig, and autopsy in six weeks. On Petroff medium make a culture from caseous masses found in the guinea-pig organs, and inoculate a rabbit with the pure culture. The *bovine type of the tubercle bacillus* is very pathogenic for rabbits, while the human infects this animal very slowly or not at all. The human type produces a permanent acidity in glycerin bouillon, and the bovine type a permanent alkalinity.

If *Malta fever* is suspected, after four days' incubation very minute colonies on the milk plates are examined for micrococcus melitensis by agglutinating with a hyperimmune serum. The lesions in the mouth and between the clefts of the hoofs are quite characteristic of foot and mouth disease. Suspected milk may be injected into a small pig. For typhoid and dysentery bacilli, the milk should be plated on Endo's medium, but statistical information of the spread of these diseases is the most important task.

Bacteriologic Examination of Water and Sewage.—The American Public Health Association standard prescribes that no colon bacilli be contained in three 10-c.c. samples and that not more than 100 colonies appear after an incubation of forty-eight hours at 37.5°C., on a plain agar plate inoculated with 1 c.c. of the water.

The samples are collected in sterile 4-oz. bottles in such a way that the water is exactly representative of that used for drinking purposes; the examination is made within an hour after collection.

To examine for the number of bacteria, pour a tube of agar at 45°C. into a Petri dish, add 1 c.c. of the water from a pipette, mix thoroughly, allow to solidify and incubate for forty-eight hours at 37.5°C. Count the colonies (Fig. 51).

To examine for the presence of colon bacilli, inoculate three extra large fermentation tubes (Fig. 40) containing lactose broth with 10 c.c. each, a fourth one with 1 c.c. and a fifth one with 0.1 c.c. If there is gas production, plate out on Endo medium; test red colonies for gas formation on lactose broth and for indol in Dunham's solution. Colon is the only organism fermenting lactose with gas production that grows aërobically; the few anaërobes that produce gas from lactose do not grow well outside the small tube. Sewage is examined in the same way except that $\frac{1}{10}$ and $\frac{1}{100}$ of the above amounts are inoculated into the media.

Bacteriologic Examination of Meat for Bacillus Botulinus.—
Sausage poisoning (botulism) results usually from eating meat, but may be due to vegetables infected with the bacillus. This form of food poisoning must be distinguished from ptomaine poisoning on one hand in which there is a formation of basic poisons as the result of putrefaction, and from infection with bacillus enteritidis Gärtner (often called "meat poisoning") on the other hand. In neither case is it possible to demonstrate gross changes in the infected food. Although the symptoms which consist especially of paralysis of the cranial nerves with absence of intestinal symptoms are thought to be due to preformed toxins in the meat, the infected individuals do not show symptoms for twenty-four hours or more. To make a diagnosis, crush 20 gm. of the suspected meat in a mortar with 20 c.c. sterile saline, filter through sterile filter paper, and inject subcutaneously into a 250-gm. guinea-pig. If positive, the guinea-pig after one day will show paralysis of the motor centers in the brain and in the cord, and death usually follows. At the same time that the guinea-pig is inoculated with the filtrate, sear the surface of some of the meat, and inoculate a minute bit into a fermentation tube of glucose

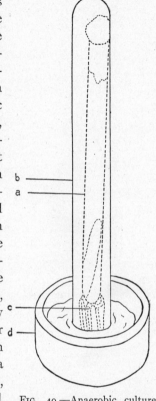

FIG. 49.—Anaerobic culture cylinder. Place the culture tube, *a*, within the inverted 100-c.c. test-tube or graduate, *b*, and insert mass of filter paper, *c*, in which is wrapped 1 gm. pyrogallic acid and a 1-inch piece of caustic soda so as to support the culture tube. Dip the filter-paper end of the tube in water, invert in a Stender dish, *d*, and pour 52-degree paraffin into the dish. To examine melt the paraffin and remove culture tube.

bouillon that has a small

piece of sterile kidney or liver in it, and make the culture anaerobic (Fig. 49). Examine the cultures for a Gram-positive bacillus with rounded ends, about the size of the anthrax, and inoculate a second guinea-pig with the bouillon. If there are a number of cultures the *Novy jar* (Fig. 50) is required.

Ptomains.—Unlike the soluble toxin of b. botulinus, ptomains are basic substances formed by the putrefaction of protein, fat, and carbohydrate foods. Make plates on gelatin, and cultures in glycose bouillon in a fermentation tube, and examine for proteus, colon, and other putrefactive bacteria.

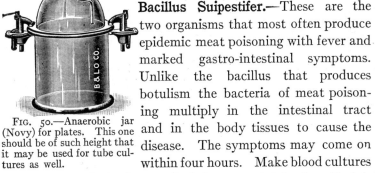

FIG. 50.—Anaerobic jar (Novy) for plates. This one should be of such height that it may be used for tube cultures as well.

These basic substances are rather thermostabile. They may be produced in perfectly refrigerated foods.

Meat for Bacillus Enteritidis or Bacillus Suipestifer.—These are the two organisms that most often produce epidemic meat poisoning with fever and marked gastro-intestinal symptoms. Unlike the bacillus that produces botulism the bacteria of meat poisoning multiply in the intestinal tract and in the body tissues to cause the disease. The symptoms may come on within four hours. Make blood cultures and cultures of the feces and of the suspected food on Endo's medium, and agglutinate the suspicious colonies with strongly positive sera. Bacillus betaparatyphosus less commonly produces meat poisoning; while the bacillus paratyphosus alpha develops much more slowly, producing paratyphoid fever which resembles Gärtner bacillus infection less yet. Highly agglutinating sera of these four organisms should be kept on hand.

Cultures of Bits of Surgical Tissue.—The disposition of bacteriologic specimens from autopsies and the general disposal of routine specimens have already been described (page 170 and page 171). The cultural and bacteriologic examinations of sputum and serous fluids, blood, urine, gastric contents, and feces are indicated in the respective chapters dealing with these subjects. It remains to indicate the bacteriologic examination of surgical tissue and certain special specimens.

The technic of making cultures from surgical specimens of pus, fluids, and of other liquid material has been detailed (page 172) and is simple. Bits of tissue are more difficult to handle without contamination; and, in addition, the specimens are frequently contaminated during or immediately after removal. Instruments, rubber gloves, gowns, and the like, cannot be sterilized bacteriologically by boiling; steaming at

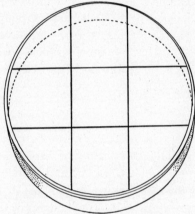

Fig. 51.—Petri dish showing the wax pencil ruling for counting colonies in the examination of milk and water.

110°C. for twenty minutes or direct sterilization in the flame is required. It is certain that taking tissue with instruments "sterilized" surgically from trays that have been likewise "sterilized" surgically, and placing this into culture media may give growths of bacteria not present in the tissue before operation. Such technic may rarely lead to errors when well known pathogenic organisms are dealt with, but the possibility of error is sufficient that it should never be used for the investigation of a disease of unknown etiology.

To make a culture of tissue, a large piece is always desirable. Cauterize the entire outer surface with a spatula heated in a flame and immediately applied to the tissue before cooling

14

has taken place. With small scissors sterilized in a flame, cut from beneath this surface a small cube of tissue, and with forceps sterilized in like manner drop this tissue into the culture tube. The bit of tissue should not be so large that it becomes necessary to use force to push it into the tube. The tissue may be crushed with special long-handled forceps after it has been placed in the tube. The mouth of the tube must of course be thoroughly sterilized in the flame.

Pus or Curetings for Bacillus Aerogenes Capsulatus (Fig. 54).—This organism has been spoken of as b. enteritidis sporogenes, and is commonly known as the gas bacillus. It is a constant inhabitant of the intestine, and may invade the tissues after death or shortly before death. It may be distributed through the body as a septicemic process with widespread subcutaneous emphysema and with no evident primary focus of infection, but most commonly it spreads from a deep, lacerated wound. The soluble toxin is elaborated by the bacilli growing in the infected tissue.

Smears show a Gram-positive bacillus about the size of the anthrax. The bacilli rarely form long chains, and capsules are frequently demonstrable. The earliest possible diagnosis is imperative. If the material is plentiful, inject 0.5 c.c. rubbed up in saline into the ear vein of a rabbit; kill the animal after five minutes, and place its body in the incubator for twelve hours. Nail to a board and perform an autopsy. If the gas bacillus is present, the organs (liver and muscles, especially) and body cavities will contain large amounts of gas.

If only a swab has been sent for diagnosis, inoculate two tubes of litmus milk and two of glucose agar. Place the litmus milk cultures in the incubator for twelve hours under anaerobic conditions (Fig. 49). After twelve hours, inject 5 c.c. of the litmus milk into the ear vein of a rabbit, kill, incubate as above, and examine. To inoculate dextrose agar, melt, cool to 45°C., agitate the melted agar thoroughly with the infected swab, let it solidify, and place in incubator without making anaerobic.

Agar is torn apart by gas bubbles, and the curd of the coagulated milk shows bubbles. In plain bouillon it forms spores.

The *bacillus of malignant edema* is often decolorized by the Gram method, forms long chains, has no capsule, and forms spores but no gas in milk.

Material for Tetanus.—The tetanus bacillus remains localized at the point of inoculation and produces a strong toxin that passes to the central nervous system, where it produces symptoms and often death.   It may happen that the site of infection cannot be ascertained; but usually there is a puncture wound or a wound produced by powder grains or by the highly infected material.

Examine smears for the Gram-positive pin-shaped bacilli. Inoculate two dextrose bouillon fermentation test-tubes, or, better still, inoculate such a tube that has at the bottom a small bit of sterile organ from a guinea-pig or a rabbit (Theobald Smith), and make two dextrose agar stabs.   Make the cultures anaerobic by placing them in a Novy jar or as indicated in Fig. 50.   Examine one tube daily until a diagnosis is made. As soon as a growth is demonstrated, inject subcutaneously 0.5 c.c. of bouillon culture into a mouse.   If the bouillon contains the toxin, after eight hours the muscles of the mouse will show a continuous spasm.

It is not often required to obtain the bacillus in pure cultures. Before attempting to isolate the organism which is difficult, suitable apparatus should be at hand.   Place a bouillon-sterile-organ culture, showing many of the bacilli, in a water-bath for one hour at 60°C.   Transfer 2 c.c. of this heated culture to a second bouillon-sterile-organ tube, make anaerobic, and incubate for five days.   Heat this culture, transfer, and incubate.   Heat, make ten glucose agai plates, make anaerobic, incubate for five days, and microscopically examine suspicious colonies.   Transplant pure cultures of bacillus tetani to gelatin, and incubate at 37.5° C.

Nose and Throat Cultures for Diphtheria Bacilli.—In eighteen-hour throat cultures on Loeffler's blood serum a diagnosis consists of finding a bacillus of a certain size with dark blue granules havine light spaces between them (Fig. 52).   With a swab, rub the suspicious portion of the mucous membrane and with the infected material on it inoculate a tube of Loeffler's blood serum. Incubate overnight, and stain the eighteen-hour growth with Loeffler's methylene blue.

In careful comparisons of the bacillus with diphtheroid organisms, it is desirable to make a *Neisser stain.* To 100 c.c. distilled water, add 5 c.c. glacial acetic acid, 2 c.c. 95 per cent. alcohol and 0.1 gm. methylene blue. For ten seconds stain the preparation in this solution, and then wash and stain for ten seconds in 0.2 per cent. Bismark brown. The granules (metachromatic) stain blue, while the remainder of the protoplasm stains brown. Bacillus hoffmanni (pseudodiphtheria bacillus) found in the throat ferments neither dextrose nor saccharose, while bacillus xerosis found in the eye and nose ferments both. True diphtheria bacilli ferment dextrose but not saccharose. These two bacilli are thicker and shorter than bacillus diphtheriæ, and the light-staining portion is regularly in the center. Non-virulent diphtheria bacilli are morphologically like virulent ones (Fig. 52). Non-pathogenic bacilli, morphologically identical with the *Klebs-Loeffler* organism are common in nature. Some of these *diphtheroid bacilli* grow rapidly and luxuriantly, while others grow slowly and with difficulty.

Where a large number of cultures are examined daily, one may make eight or ten preparations on a slide. A pipet with a double curve is very convenient for placing on the slide the small drops of water to which the bacteria from the surfaces of the tubes are added by means of a platinum loop. Always use new slides, and do not use the stain a second time.

Test of Virulence.—Cultural differences between virulent and non-virulent diphtheria bacilli may exist, but these have not proved of practical value. Both ferment dextrose, but not saccharose. When the diphtheria bacilli persist in the nose or throat for more than six weeks, a test of their virulence may be desirable. To do this, make a swab from a culture that shows numerous bacilli of typical morphology, and thoroughly wash the swab off in the water of condensation at the bottom of a tube of blood serum. Tubes that are of the same length, but twice the diameter of an ordinary test-tube, are the best for this purpose. Repeat the process with the same swab on tubes numbered 2, 3, 4, 5, and 6, passing from one tube to another with the same swab. After making the dilution, flood with the water of condensation the surface of the medium of each tube, and then incubate overnight in the upright position.

Microscopically, examine smears from a number of translucent colonies from the surface of those slants that show well isolated colonies, and inoculate five separate tubes of blood serum from the same number of positive colonies. The diphtheria colonies are determined by making smears on slides (eight or ten on a slide) and staining with Loeffler's methylene blue.

After twenty-four hours, inoculate each of the tubes that contain pure cultures into a 350-c.c. Erlenmeyer flask containing 50 c.c. of sugar-free bouillon. After forty-eight hours' incubation, subcutaneously inoculate a small guinea-pig with 0.5 per cent. of its weight of the forty-eight-hour flask culture.

If the guinea-pig dies within five days, go back to the original five tubes containing the five pure cultures, and inoculate another flask of bouillon with these. Incubate for forty-eight hours, and inject a second guinea-pig with 0.5 per cent. of its weight; but, along with the toxin, inject 0.5 c.c. of antitoxin. If the animal lives for five days the bacilli are diphtheria bacilli.

The adrenals of a guinea-pig, dead of diphtheria toxin, are reddish-brown rather than yellow and microscopically present hemorrhages; but such changes do not warrant a diagnosis without an injection of toxin together with a neutralizing dose of antitoxin.

Examination of the Oral, Pharyngeal, and Laryngeal Mucous Surfaces for Organisms other than the Klebs-Loeffler Bacillus. —In all cases, the smears or cultures must be made accurately and definitely from the diseased focus. In routine diagnostic work, a culture from this region is rarely indicated unless a definite disease process can be made out. Smears from a *mucous patch* are stained by a protozoon stain, or, better still, examine by means of dark-field illumination.

Tuberculous ulcers must be lightly cureted and these smears stained by the Ziehl-Neelsen method.

Oidium albicans is found in the areas characteristic of thrush. The material is placed on a slide, and a drop of 2 per cent. acetic acid added, when the budding, yeast-like organisms are observed under the high-dry lens.

In *actinomyces* infection, the narrow branching Gram-positive threads are found in the granules pressed out from the sinuses connecting with the infected tissue.

The pathogenicity of the *bacillus* and *spirillum* of *Vicent's angina* is questionable. Smears are stained with protozoon stain or with methylene blue. The finding is frequently positive in extensive gangrenous processes about the oral and pharyngeal cavities. An examination of the crypts of the tonsils for pyogenic cocci may throw light on general infections with these organisms.

Amebæ are often found when material from cases of pyorrhea alveolaris is examined on a warm stage. Endothelial leukocytes have not infrequently been mistaken for amebæ, owing to their active ameboid motion.

Eye, Ear, and Nose.—In the *eye*, gonococcus, Koch-Weeks bacillus, pneumococcus, and influenza bacillus are the most important. A Gram-negative intracellular diplococcus of typical shape and placement in the cell, which is sufficient for positive diagnosis in the male urethra, can, in smears from the conjunctiva, only be diagnosed as gonococcus in connection with the clinical picture of gonorrheal ophthalmia. Careful cultures should be made on potato-blood agar, or on plain blood agar, for the other three organisms mentioned. A chronic conjunctivitis is said to be due to the Morax-Axenfeld bacillus, which is much like bacillus mucosus capsulatus but has no distinct capsule.

Infection of the *middle ear* is due to streptococcus, pneumococcus, staphylococcus, and less commonly to such bacteria as the colon and influenza bacilli. Aspergillus and mucor are moulds that may grow in the external ear where they set up a mild inflammation.

Nasal diphtheria is common. Tuberculosis infection is uncommon in the *nose* but leprosy infection starts there.

Injection of a guinea-pig induces tuberculosis in the animal if tubercle bacilli are present, while an injection with secretion containing bacillus lepræ is negative. Acid-fast saphrophytic bacilli found in the nasal secretions grow readily on glycerin agar, but the leprosy and tubercle bacilli do not. Bacillus rhinoscleromæ found in rhinoscleroma and the closely related bacillus ozenæ found in ozena belong to the mucosus capsulatus group. Pneumococcus, streptococcus, and the influenza bacllius may be found in acute coryza. In purulent putrid secretions, bacillus proteus should be suspected. By careful cultural methods meningococcus may be demonstrated in the nasal secretion. By filtration of the nasal secretions and injections of the filtrate into monkeys the virus of acute poliomyelitis has also been demonstrated in nasal secretions.

Pus.—This term has been limited by many to inflammatory exudates containing neutrophiles; but it may be applied to fluid or semifluid necrotic material, or to any inflammatory cellular exudate. Bacteria, producing neutrophilic exudates are termed pyogenic.

A *"cold* or *white" abscess* is filled with a thick yellowish or greenish-white material free from cells and bacteria. Tubercle bacilli cannot be found on microscopic examination of this necrotic material, but guinea-pigs are infected. Small acid-fast granules known as *Much granules*, that are frequently present, may represent the tubercle bacilli. In purulent material from sinuses about the mouth, from bones and from lungs, *actinomycotic granules* should be looked for. They are the size of a millet seed, a steel grey to yellow color, perfectly smooth and glistening, and when crushed out and stained by Gram's method show fine, Gram-positive, branching threads.

Blastomycetes, oidia, and certain forms of *moulds* (hyphomycetes) are to be kept constantly in mind in the case of material from skin lesions. In the tissue, the two first organisms named are always found in spherical form; while in one kind of mould infection (sporotrichosis) the organism also exists in the shape of small round spores. A careful direct microscopic examination in such cases may reveal one or another of these organisms and lead to a successful cultivation of the infecting agent.

·*Staphylococcus aureus* (Fig. 53) is found as a secondary invader in many processes such as "cold" abscesses, but it is present as a primary infecting organism in pustular acnea, furunculosis, and pyogenic osteomyelitis. For diagnosis, the finding of Gram-positive cocci in typical clusters on the blood serum slant is sufficient. Several days are often required of,

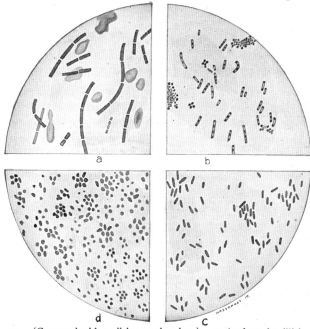

FIG. 52.—(Camera lucida; oil-immersion lens). *a*, Anthrax bacilli in splenic smear; *b*, diphtheria bacilli from a throat culture on Loeffler's blood serum; *c*, bacillus mallei; *d*, bacillus pestis from an agar slant culture.

the formation of the golden pigment of the staphylococcus aureus. Staphylococcus albus produces no pigment, is less pathogenic for man, and the cultures liquefy gelatin more slowly than the aureus. The citreus produces a yellow color and is met with only at rare intervals. Potato slants and blood serum give good pigment production. Staphylococcus epidermidis albus which may be found in very mild skin infections such as stitch abscesses in aseptic wounds, is only slightly virulent, and does not liquefy gelatin.

Staphylococci produce almost a pure neutrophilic reaction, but, owing to the necrosis and rapid liquefaction of the leukocytes frequently nothing but fragmented nuclei are found in the pus. Since staphylococci so commonly secondarily infect

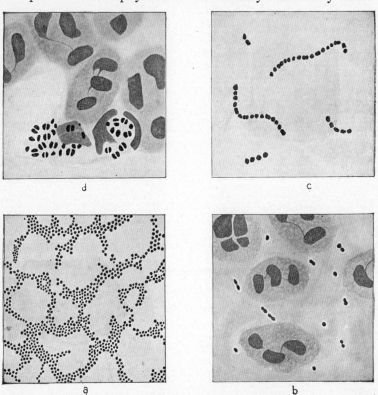

FIG. 53.—Pyogenic cocci. (Camera lucida; oil-immersion lens.) *a*, Staphylococcus pyogenes aureus from an agar slant culture; *b*, pneumococcus (capsules) from pus; *c*, streptococcus pyogenes from bouillon culture; *d*, gonococcus from urethral discharge.

a tissue already infected with another organism, a knowledge of the primary lesions produced by staphylococci is important in interpreting the laboratory results. *Micrococcus tetragenus*, Gram-positive, is somewhat larger than the staphylococcus and appears in groups of four.   It is found in the mouth and, although it may be present in cavities in the lung, its pathogenic properties are limited.   *Enterococcus*, Gram-positive, is morphologically like the pneumococcus, but it neither hemolyzes blood agar nor produces a greenish color on this medium.   It is found in the intestinal tract and its pathogenicity is doubtful.

Streptococcus pyogenes (Fig. 53) is not so easily recognized in simple routine work as the staphylococcus, since it does not grow so readily on artificial media.   The culture of infected material in litmus milk, however, usually shows chains.   As staphylococci frequently grow in pairs and short chains, chains of 12 units or more from a liquid medium are of first importance in diagnosis.   With a clinical diagnosis of streptococcus on the brown slip, usually an additional culture should be made on a blood agar plate by rubbing material from the swab within a wax-pencil ring at one side of the plate and this material spread by means of a platinum loop.   In the examination for carriers of hemolytic streptococcus the plate only need be made from a tonsil swab.

An extreme variation in toxicity and character of lesions produced exists in streptococcus pyogenes but attempts to associate the tissue lesions with a type of streptococcus manifesting definite biologic properties have not been entirely satisfactory. The streptococcus most often met with produces a light zone of hemolysis about the colonies on blood agar.   This strain is known as streptococcus hemolyticus or longus in distinction to streptococcus viridans (brevis) which produces a green color on blood agar but no hemolysis.   The latter is found in less virulent forms of certain lesions such as the subacute endocarditis of Poynton and Payne.   The hemolytic streptococcus appears to produce a peculiar variety of focal pneumonia.   A streptococcus producing a mild toxin (streptococcus rheumaticus) appears to be associated with rheumatic fever.   The cultural characteristics of this variety of streptococcus are not well known; in the lesions such as the verrucous vegetations of the heart valves and Aschoff's bodies of the heart muscularis the cocci rapidly die out. The usual so-called streptococcus mucosus is a pneumococcus, type 3; rarely a true streptococcus mucosus that is insoluble in bile may be found.

After twenty-four hours incubation, colonies with a wide hemolytic corpuscle-free zone are transferred to plain bouillon and as soon as there is visible growth examine microscopically; test the hemolytic properties of the organism by adding 0.5 c.c. broth culture to 0.5 c.c. 5 per cent. washed rabbit corpuscles and incubating two hours; and determine its bile solubility by adding 1 c.c. of the broth culture to 0.2 c.c. sterile ox bile and incubating one hour.

The viridans variety of streptococcus produces no hemolysis but the colonies are smaller than pneumococcus and are bile insoluble. All streptococci are likely to agglutinate more or less with antipneumococcic sera. A secondary zone of hemolysis outside the ring of methemoglobin may appear about old pneumococcic and viridans colonies.

The short-chain streptococcus (strep. viridans) grows slowly, is usually recovered from slightly toxic lesions and, since it exhibits a green zone about the colony on blood agar, is spoken of as the viridans variety. At present it is important to determine that a streptococcus comes from a human case for there is no definite proof that the so-called bovine streptococcus commonly found in dairy products is pathogenic for man.

Otitis media, meningitis, and peritonitis may be due to the streptococcus; it is also the cause of erysipelas, and is found in the joints in articular rheumatism. A dangerous wound infection may resultf rom the streptococcus, which is the most important organism producing secondary infections.

Pneumococcus (Fig. 53).—This organism is the cause of 90 per cent. of lobar pneumonia, and of other common infections. Gram, capsule, and Ziehl-Neelsen stains are made on sputum and the type of organism determined as indicated below. When the peritoneal cavity of the mouse is first opened smears are made and a loopful of the exudate inoculated on one-half of a blood agar plate; the heart's blood is streaked over the second half of the plate and a tube of plain bouillon inoculated.

The next day a confirmatory agglutination is made on the bouillon culture. Pus, pleural and other fluids are plated (see streptococcus), colonies transferred to broth and the type of pneumococcus determined. In all cases the solubility in bile of the organism is determined at the same time that the agglutination test is made by adding 0.5 c.c. of the bacterial suspension to 0.5 c.c. of bile (page 189). Type 1 is found in about 33 per cent. of the cases with a mortality of 25 per cent.; type 2, 31 per cent. with 32 per cent. mortality; type 3, 12 per cent. with 45 per cent. mortality; type 4, 24 per cent. with 16 per cent. mortality. Serum treatment has reduced the mortality in type 1 infections to about 7 per cent. (Dochez, Stillman, Avery and others).

To identify the pneumococcus type, a fresh particle of sputum is collected, mixed with as little saline as possible, and 0.5 c.c. injected into the peritoneal cavity of a white mouse. In twelve hours the mouse is killed and the peritoneal exudate removed to a 15-c.c. centrifuge tube by means of a bulb pipet. The cavity is washed out with saline to make the fluid up to about 12 c.c. Centrifuge slowly for ten minutes to throw down cells and coarse débris, pipette the somewhat cloudy fluid containing the pneumococci and centrifuge this at a high rate of speed. The sediment of cocci is removed with a fine capillary, saline is added and 0.5 c.c. of the suspension in saline mixed with 0.5 c.c. of agglutinating serum prepared from each of the three types. Type 4 is a mixed group. A negative result indicates the organism belongs to this group. A *precipitin test* made by adding the specific sera to a few hours growth of the organism is now being used for a rapid diagnosis.

To make the precipitin test 0.5 c.c. of the clear supernatant liquid is substituted for 0.5 c.c. of the coccus suspension. In both reactions incubate for one hour at 37.5°C.

Meningococcus.—The presence of Gram-negative coffee-bean-shaped diplococci in purulent spinal fluid is sufficient for a positive diagnosis of epidemic cerebrospinal meningitis. The organisms are usually in leukocytes. In infantile paralysis showing symptoms of like severity, the spinal fluid is clear or almost so.

To identify meningococcus from the nasopharynx, a culture is made from the posterior nares on a cotton-swab wire passed behind the palate, inoculated on a glucose blood agar plate (page 175), incubated overnight and colonies (not green, hemolyzed or opaque) carried to a blood agar plate ruled with wax pencil on bottom into eight sectors. The sectors are stained and one loopful rubbed off in 1 c.c. polyvalent serum (page 241), a second loopful is emulsified in 1 c.c. 1–50 normal horse serum and a third loopful of known meningococcus in 1 c.c. of the agglutinating serum. The tubes are incubated overnight at 55°C., shaken and examined for clumps. The type of organism should later be determined by monovalent type agglutinating sera (page 241).

Gonococcus (Fig 53) infection in the male urethra is diagnosed by the finding of Gram-negative intracellular diplococci of typical shape (coffee-bean) and placement (discrete diplococci in the cells). This morphologic finding indicates gonorrhea with less certainty when the smears are made from the vagina, and with still less certainty when made from the eye. In making a diagnosis of gonorrheal vaginitis or ophthalmia the clinical symptoms are taken into account.

Anthrax material may be sent to the laboratory as a swab of pus or as curetings of tissue. A direct stain shows large Gram-positive bacilli with square ends (Fig. 52). If the smear shows such bacilli, inoculate a small guinea-pig intraperitoneally and at the same time make a culture on an agar slant. Also inoculate a melted tube of glucose agar, as the infection may be caused by gas bacillus or bacillus of malignant edema. At the end of twenty-four hours the culture on agar should show chains of bacilli in some of which there are round or oval spores. In forty-eight hours an infected guinea-pig shows the bacilli in the heart's blood. Unless the amount of pus is considerable, it is better to inoculate the guinea-pig from a culture. The malignant pustule is the skin form of the disease. The bacilli are present in the sputum, in the pulmonary form of anthrax; in the intestinal form, they appear in the feces. Anthrax is a disease chiefly confined to cattle, sheep, horses, and swine;

and in man such infection comes largely from wool and hides from South America and Africa.

Bacillus mallei (Fig. 52) in pus is recognized by the Strauss test (swelling of testicles of guinea-pigs after intraperitoneal inoculation) and by the slimy brownish growth on potato. In the horse, the disease may be present as a general infection beginning in the nasopharynx, or as a localized fistulous skin lesion (farcy). It is usually fatal to human beings, and is a Gram-negative bacillus resembling diphtheria bacillus somewhat in morphology. Stain with dilute carbol-fuchsin.

Pyocyaneous produces a greenish pus. It does not react typically to the Gram stain, but on agar slant its growth is typical, since a yellowish-green color is imparted to the agar beneath the surface.

Ducrey bacillus is found in pus from the soft chancre (chancroid) and bubo. It is a very minute Gram-negative bacillus forming chains in the tissue which sometimes may be quite long. Care should be taken not to break up these chains in making smears, which is a procedure not easily accomplished in the case of ulcers. If smears are spread from the pus coming from a bubo, however, and stained with dilute fuchsin, very narrow rods will be found running parallel to a depth of a half dozen bacilli, although these rods are not exactly end to end. Positive cultures from the bubos may be obtained on blood agar.

Cholera vibrio (Fig. 54) is a short, slightly curved, actively motile rod found in the feces in great numbers in cases of the disease. Inoculate a tube of Dunham's solution with five loopfuls of feces; and at the end of six hours in the incubator transfer a loopful from the very top of the first tube to a second; and after six hours transfer from this tube to a third. The vibrios from the third tube must agglutinate in a dilution of 1–2000 of hyperimmunized rabbit serum. Agglutination may be tried at the end of the first six hours. This simple technic is very useful in examinations for carriers. The *indol test* is performed on one of these cultures by adding 1 c.c. of concentrated hydrochloric acid and stratifying 1 c.c. to 2 c.c. of 2 per cent. solution of paradimethylaminobenzaldehyde in alcohol on the surface. If positive, a purplish ring forms. If agglutination and indol formation are positive, a probable diagnosis may be made. The greatest difficulty is encountered in the identification of this vibrio because of the occurrence of similar vibrios under the same conditions and in the same material.

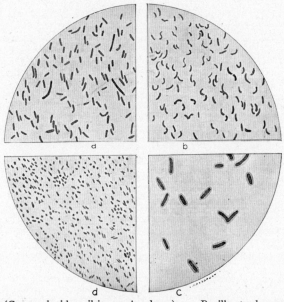

FIG. 54.—(Camera lucida; oil-immersion lens.) *a*, Bacillus typhosus; *b*, vibrio of Asiatic cholera; *c*, bacillus aerogenes capsulatus; *d*, bacillus influenzæ.

Bacillus pestis (Fig. 52) occurs in human plague as a short, ovoid, Gram-negative bacillus in the enlarged lymph-gland. This finding, together with a typical clinical picture, is sufficient for a diagnosis. Inoculate a rat or a guinea-pig subcutaneously, or by rubbing the infected material on the shaved skin. At autopsy, the animal shows hemorrhages in the liver, spleen, and especially in the large inguinal and cervical lymph-glands. In inoculating experimental animals, care must be exercised to guard the experimenter against accidental infection. In the pneumonic cases the sputum is used for the inoculations.

Moulds (fungi) differ from bacteria in not being simple uni-

cellular protoplasmic masses that reproduce by simple fission
(Fig. 55). They are multicellular, and certain cells differentiate to form special reproductive cells. The limits of the group
are not uniformly agreed upon. They differ from the yeasts
in that they do not reproduce by budding. *Actinomyces
bovis* is a low form of mould. Its relation to the organism of

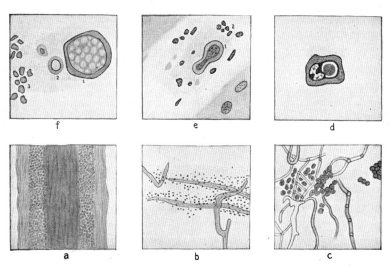

FIG. 55.—*a*, Trichophyton tonsurans (spores outside dark hair-shaft) in hair of
beard that has been treated under cover-glass with 20 per cent. sodium hydrate,
washed with water, cover removed, dried, and the preparation mounted in balsam; *b*, achorion Schönleinii (typical branching) from scrapings of scalp from a
case of favus; *c*, microsporon furfur (not in relation to hairs) from scrapings of
skin of back. These three preparations were obtained by the writer in the
dermatologic clinic of the N. Y. Post-graduate Hospital and drawn with camera
lucida and oil-immersion lens; *d*, phialophora verrucosa (after E. M. Medlar)
showing yeast-like form of this fungus in an endothelial leukocyte; *e*, blastomyces (from a specimen coming from Montreal General Hospital) (1, budding
yeast and 2, leukocytes) in a small lymph-vessel in a section of lung; *f*, oïdium
immitis (1, sporulating form, 2, form in which most of the organisms are present
and 3, red blood corpuscles) in section of lung. The organisms are present in
great numbers. Note comparative size of parasite and cells in both *e* and *f*.

farcin and Madura-foot has not been clearly established.
Sporothrix is as yet a group that forms spores in the tissue, and
mycelia with spore-organs in cultures. *Oïdium albicans* may
grow as mycelial threads. *Achorion schönleinii, trichophyton
tonsurans*, and *microsporon* are typical moulds. *Aspergillus
umigatus* occasionally proliferates in the external ear, and still

more rarely in the lungs. Glycerin agar, without the addition of meat extract or alkali, is best for the cultivation of typical moulds. To examine material containing fungi, place it under the high-dry lens with 10 per cent. sodium hydrate. Branching forms and groups or masses of spores are the two most striking things.

Yeasts (Fig. 55) in the tissue divide by budding. The *blasto-myces* of blastomycosis multiplies in this way, while *oïdium immitis* (found on the Pacific coast in chronic local and general infections that closely resemble tuberculosis) certainly forms spores in the tissue but may also divide by budding. Both of these organisms form mycelial threads in cultures.

Accurate botanic terminology should be employed in the determination of the specific names of pathogenic plant forms; but once names have been determined, it is unnecessary to emphasize complicated botanic classifications.

Filterable virus is applied to an organism passing through porcelain filters of a certain grade of fineness. The filterable viruses of pleuropneumonia of cattle and of acute poliomyelitis have been seen, but others (typhus fever, yellow fever, foot and mouth disease, trench fever) are ultramicroscopic.

Unknown viruses produce small-pox, chicken-pox, measles, mumps, dengue, rabies, and trachoma; while there is still a doubt in regard to scarlet fever and Rocky Mountain spotted fever. All of these are definitely transmitted from one infected individual or animal to a non-infected one, and in some of them the exact manner of conveyance of the virus is known. It is very possible that other diseases presenting less evidence of infection may be due to infectious agents.

Bacterial Vaccines.—The local infections of considerable dur-ation and the general infections that become localized and chronic react most favorably to vaccine therapy. At present, it appears that an autogenous vaccine—one in which the bac-teria are obtained from the patient treated—is the best. In the preparation of a stock vaccine, all available strains (poly-valent vaccine) should be used.

To prepare a vaccine, open up the lesion freshly and make a

15

swab with which an agar culture is inoculated.   If the culture is contaminated with organisms that are not desired in the vaccine, make a swab from the surface of the mixed agar culture; and with this swab make dilutions on the surface of five agar slants—as was done on ten blood serum tubes in testing the virulence of the diphtheria bacillus (see page 212)—or by rubbing the swab over the surface of the slants in succession.   The tubes are placed in the incubator.   The following day colonies are examined and agar subcultures made from those selected. After incubation overnight, the tubes are filled half full with saline and the growth rubbed off with a platinum needle. Transfer the suspension to a sterile test-tube, draw out the portion of the tube above the liquid in a flame, and seal.   For ten minutes shake vigorously in a mechanical shaker.   Immerse completely in a water-bath, and heat for one hour at 60°C., open, and make a culture to test the sterility of the suspension.

To determine the number of bacteria in the suspension, place about 1 c.c. of the sterilized suspension in a watch crystal; and fill the blood pipet, used for counting the red blood corpuscles, to the 0.5-mark with the suspension; and then fill the pipet to the 101 with Hayem's solution to which sufficient acid fuchsin (dry) has been added to give the solution a distinct red color. After the preparation on the slide has stood for one hour, count the bacteria in the same way as the red blood corpuscles are counted.   If the vaccine is to be injected intravenously it should be filtered through a sterile filter paper to remove any gross particles present.

Dilute the suspension with normal saline, so that 1 c.c. contains, for example, 1000 million bacteria per cubic centimeter; add 0.5 per cent. phenol, and place the whole in 10-c.c., square, sterile bottles, and cover these with a rubber cap.

Before using, this rubber cap is wiped off with lysol, and the needle of a long 2-c.c. tuberculin-syringe inserted through it, and the desired amount of vaccine drawn into it.   In dispensary work, the needle may be sterilized by sticking it into an oil with a high boiling point heated to a high temperature.

The *therapeutic use* of *vaccines* in many infections such as acne is firmly established. In local streptococcus infections especially about the nasopharynx a vaccine may or may not have some effect on the lesion. The use of a pneumococcus vaccine is questionable. Some cases of gonococcic epididymitis and prostatitis appear to be benefited and without question cases of arthritis have been improved. Typhoid vaccines have been injected during the disease both subcutaneously and intravenously but their value is in dispute. Mixed infections with pyocyaneus and proteus appear to be benefited by vaccines. B. ozenæ vaccine has been used in ozena and b. rhinoscleromæ vaccine in rhinoscleroma. The therapeutic use of vaccines in tuberculosis is very doubtful.

The *prophylactic use* of typhoid vaccine is certain. The "lipoid" vaccine now in use contains two and one-half billion of bacillus typhosus and a like number of each of the paratyphoids. The bacteria are grown on agar slants in flat bottles, removed, dried, and suspended in olive or almond oil that contains 10 per cent. lanolin. The amount indicated is injected subcutaneously at a single dose. To sterilize the bacteria are heated at a temperature not to exceed 55°C. The vaccine is tested by culture aërobically and anaërobically and for toxicity by animal inoculation. Plague and cholera vaccines have value during epidemics. Prophylaxis by vaccines against meningococcus infections is doubtful. The prophylactic value of pneumococcus, bacillary dysentery and influenza vaccines is now in a very active stage of determination.

URINE

For convenience in collection of specimens the patient may be supplied with a 3-liter narrow-mouthed bottle which is provided with a funnel and contains 10 c.c. toluol, this preservative being used in preference to chloroform which interferes with some chemical tests and is not entirely driven off by heat. A 4-oz. sample taken from the 24-hour urine collected in a bottle is sent to the laboratory for chemical analysis. A second bottle of freshly voided urine is collected for microscopic examination. If the sample for microscopic purposes cannot be sent to the laboratory soon after it is voided, a small amount of 10 per cent. formalin is added and the addition marked on the label, since urine to which formalin has been added is not suitable for chemical analysis.

Normal urine when freshly voided is usually clear; but occasionally in strongly alkaline urine there is a cloudiness due to precipitated phosphates and carbonates. Soon, however, a cloud (nubecula) is formed by the collection of epithelial cells on the mucin present. In chyluria the urine is milky. The *color* varies from colorless to dark amber. Blood, bile, the products of phenol poisoning, melanin, hematoporphyrin, and alkaptone bodies may cause more or less blackening (smokiness) of the urine. The *amount* is from 800 c.c. to 3000 c.c. Amounts below and above these figures are spoken of as oliguria or anuria and polyuria respectively. A pathologic increase is commonly met with in diabetes mellitus and in vascular nephritis. In a number of conditions the period in which abnormal amounts are voided is of greater significance than in total quantity. An alkaline *reaction* in fresh urine is due to alkaline (disodium) phosphates and to carbonates, while the usual, acid reaction results from an excess of di-hydrogen phosphates. There may be such a combination of phosphates that the reaction is amphoteric. When urine stands for any length of time, an ammoniacal odor may result from the decomposition of urea. The *specific gravity* is taken with the urinometer (Fig. 56). It has a normal variation of from 1.005 to 1.035. Glucose is the commonest cause of a high specific gravity in a urine of greatly increased volume.

A *quantitive determination of the acidity of the urine* (Folin) is made by adding 5 gm. potassium oxalate to 25 c.c. urine in an Erlenmeyer flask, shaking for one minute, and immediately titrating with decinormal alkali, using phenolphthalein as an indicator. The number of cubic centimeters of decinormal solution required multiplied by four gives acidity per cent. in terms of the strength of the alkali (normal, about 25 acidity per cent.). The addition of the oxalate precipitates calcium and eliminates the error due to the presence of acid phosphates, also diminishing the error due to the effect of ammonia on the indicator.

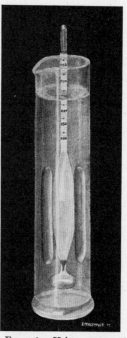

FIG. 56.—Urinometer. If conical cylinders (Fig. 60) are used for obtaining sediment, the specific gravity is taken in them.

In the examination of urine, as in the examination of other hospital specimens, some method of procedure is followed which will in the great majority of cases lead to the detection of any important abnormal condition. The color, odor, reaction, and specific gravity are recorded. Albumin and glucose are tested for, and the sediment examined microscopically. The indications for additional tests may be clinical, or they may arise from the routine findings.

ALBUMIN

This term as used in connection with urine examinations is more or less indefinite. The usual abnormal protein substances in urine included under this heading are serum albumin and serum globulin, but so-called nucleoalbumin (page 237), albumose, and mucin are other proteins that may be present but are not commonly classed as albumin. There are other substances, present normally or accidentally, that may with some tests react like albumin. The commonest of these are urates, uric acid, urea, bile acids, and resins.

Albuminuria.—Only substances in solution pass into the urine from the blood and tissues, unless there is an interruption in the continuity of the lining epithelium, or unless leukocytes in inflammatory processes migrate into the urine by ameboid motion. These inflammatory conditions are discussed in detail under organized sediment. However, cells may desquamate from the surface of the kidney tubules and the lower tract for in the sediment obtained by centrifugation of normal urine, there are present desquamated epithelial cells, which have found their way into the urine more or less accidentally from the urinary and genital tracts. It appears that these cells may dissolve to add minute traces of protein to the urine, especially in the form of mucin and nucleoalbumin.

The substances passing into the urine in solution may be normal or abnormal. Those that are normal constitute the greater part of the body waste products. There may be present a pathologic amount of a normal constituent, or substances not normally present in the urine may make their appearance. Of the latter, albumin is one of the most important.

Functional Albuminuria.—"Functional" is used in the sense that there has been established no morphologic basis for the condition. By the usual tests, normal urine contains no albumin. By using special methods, however, such as concentration of large volumes, a trace of albumin which appears to be derived from the blood by filtration through the glomeruli may be demonstrated. After violent exercise or emotions, cold baths, or heavy protein meals, traces of albumin may appear in the urine (physiologic albuminuria) but the amount should not exceed 0.5 gm. per liter. Casts also appear under these conditions. Occasionally, there is a person who continuously or at intervals shows distinct traces of albumin in the urine, and yet so far as can be made out has no morphologic kidney lesion.

Closely related to these rare sporadic cases, there is a type of albuminuria found in cases of constitutional weakness during the period of adolescence. The albumin appears in large quantities during the mornings, when the patient first arises, and is spoken of as *orthostatic albuminuria*. It is probably due to local circulatory disturbances. At autopsy, no lesion is demonstrable in these cases.

Causes of Albuminuria.—The usual case in which the routine examination shows the presence of albumin in the urine is nephritis. In general, it may be said that the normal renal epithelium does not permit the passage through it of the albumin and globulin present in the blood. Since the endothelium of the blood-vessels allows the passage of these substances, as shown by the albuminous character of lymph, transudates and exudates, the impermeability must lie in the renal epithelium. The usual albuminuria, therefore, is due to a lesion of the kidney epithelium. The exact nature of all lesions at this time is not fully understood, for in many cases of albuminuria no anatomic lesions are present at autopsy.

Circulatory changes may cause an albuminuria. An increased pressure within the urinary passages may cause an *anemia* of the kidney by pressing the blood out of the capillaries and arterioles with the production of an albuminuria. Increase in the general venous pressure (cyanotic kidney), or a local interference with the renal circulation by pressure on the renal vein or by infarction, may lead to the appearance of albumin in the urine.

Toxic injury to the kidney is of first importance. The poisons may be non-bacterial, such as bichlorid of mercury, lead, chromium salts, uranium nitrate, cantharadin, and poisons elaborated during pregnancy; or they may be of bacterial origin. The pneumococcus, streptococcus, diphtheria bacillus, and others are organisms that produce soluble toxins acting on the kidney. The part of the kidney units acted upon by these poisons may be the arteries and arterioles, the tuft capillaries, the capsular epithelium, or the epithelium lining the tubules. For example, the injury done by mercury is chiefly upon the tubular epithelium; lead works its havoc with the arteries; while pneumococcus and streptococcus toxins cause their severest injuries to the tuft capillaries or to the capsular epithelium.

Infectious processes due to the localization and proliferation of bacteria in a kidney substance may produce an albuminuria. It is often difficult to determine to what extent the escape of albumin into the urine is due to the infection in the kidney, or to what extent to the toxins elaborated by the bacteria and carried to the kidney through the circulation.

Excluding the functional albuminurias discussed above, there is present, then, an anatomic change in the kidney as a basis for the escape of albumin. The lesion is commonly spoken of as nephritis, but *nephropathy* is also used as a term to include all kidney lesions. As already mentioned, these lesions result from circulatory disturbances, soluble poisons, and infectious agents, and are referred to again under organized sediment of the urine.

Tests for Albumin.—If the urine is not *clear*, filter it before testing; and if filtration does not clear it, add a minute amount of kieselguhr, and filter. It should be remembered, however, that kieselguhr and other precipitant may remove small amounts of albumin from solution. Lead acetate is not suitable for clearing urine for albumin tests.

In all tests, the technic is developed with the idea of determining the presence or absence of the substance under consideration. This implies that other substances may be present which are differentiated by the procedure. There is usually a choice of methods; and as long as the results obtained are equally correct, it cannot be said that one method is better than another. It is always advantageous to know the exact way in which the test acts on the specimen under consideration. In clinical laboratory work the source of the specimen is inquired into, and the way in which it has been handled before reaching the laboratory should be known. This is important, because most tests are carried out on the assumption that unusual or accidental contaminating factors have not been introduced.

If a test for albumin is positive, it is determined as accurately as may be that the precipitate is serum albumin or globulin; and an idea of the amount of albumin present is obtained

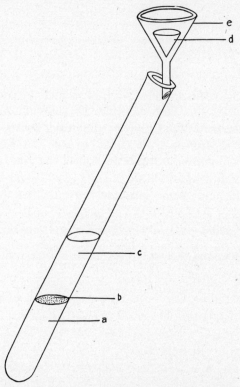

FIG. 57.—Heller's test. *a*, Nitric acid; *b*, precipitate at surface of contact; *c*, filtered urine; *d*, filter paper; *e*, 5-cm. funnel. The tube may be stood upright after the urine has filtered through. The test-tube is heavy glass with non-flaring mouth 155 by 16 mm. outside measurements. A medium-size tube for Wassermann work, etc., measures 80 by 10 mm. A small serum tube measures 55 by 7 mm. (Test-tubes of this size may be obtained from B. & L. O. Co., Rochester, N. Y.)

from the amount of precipitate. In the interpretation of a positive test, functional, circulatory, toxic, and infectious causes are considered. A searching examination of the patient may fail to determine the cause of albumin present. The character of the sediment, which is discussed under organized sediment, may indicate the cause of the albuminuria.

Heller's Test (Fig. 57).—Place 5 c.c. concentrated nitric acid in a test-tube, and stratify the urine above the acid by slanting the tube and allowing 5 c.c. clear urine to trickle down its side from the funnel employed for filtration. A white ring formed within two minutes at the surface of contact between acid and stratified urine may be due to albumin. When Heller's test is positive, protein substances other than albumin are ruled out by further observations and tests. Nucleoalbumin and mucin produce a ring several millimeters above the surface of contact, and on gentle agitation this clouding ascends as the acid diffuses upward. If due to albumose, gentle heat causes the ring to disappear. Therefore, to rule out nucleoalbumin mucin, and albumose in cases in which the ring is obtained, agitate and apply gentle heat.

As regards non-protein substances, if resins are suspected add a few drops of hydrochloric acid to 10 c.c. of the original clear urine, and shake. Resins are precipitated, and are important because of the frequency with which they are administered internally in gonorrhea and other conditions. The remaining substances—urates, uric acid, urea, and bile acids—do not give Heller's test unless the urine is concentrated. Of these substances, a precipitate of urates is most often met with; it disappears on the application of heat.

Heat-and-acetic-acid Test.—If a ring is obtained with Heller's test, the heat-and-acetic-acid test is applied, not only to confirm the presence of albumin, but to enable one to rule out with greater certainty the substances that may be precipitated and that are not albumin. To 10 c.c. urine in a test-tube add 5 drops 10 per cent. acetic acid and 2 c.c. saturated solution of sodium chlorid. If it is certain that a cloudiness is due to phosphates, the urine need not be filtered because the addition of the acetic acid will dissolve precipitated phosphates. Boil the upper half of the contents of the tube by heating the surface of the liquid gently in a low flame; compare the upper half with the lower unheated portion which serves as a control; then boil the entire tube. A clouding indicates albumin. The sodium chlorid keeps the nucleoalbumin and mucin in solution, while albumose is soluble in the heated liquid. Urates, uric acid, urea, and bile acids are not precipitated. If a precipitate of resins is suspected, cool, and shake vigorously with 10 c.c. of benzol. Any precipitate of resins goes into solution in the benzol.

Albumose (and Bence-Jones' protein) form a coagulum at about 60°C. in t e heat-and-acetic-acid test; but the precipitate, unlike that due to albumin, almost entirely disappears when the boiling point is reached. The Bence-Jones' protein is found in cases of multiple myeloma and in other varieties of malignant disease in which there are extensive metastases in the bone-marrow. The small amount of albumose (deutero-albumose so called), that is found not infrequently along with albumin, is precipitated in the same way as the Bence-Jones' protein; but since considerable amounts of albumin are also present, the precipitation of these obscures the disappearance of a part of the precipitate on boiling. Boil, as in the heat-and-acetic-acid test (page 234); filter; with caustic soda make a part of the filtrate alkaline, and add a few drops of 1 per cent. copper sulphate. A red color (biuret test) signifies albumose. The remainder of the filtrate is allowed to cool, and is then examined for precipitate. In cases of *multiple myeloma*, if albumin as well as Bence-Jones' protein is present, this procedure is followed. The presence of deutero-albumose is said to have little significance. The exact characterization of Bence-Jones' protein, which has great significance, is not simple; but its presence is easily established.

Quantitative Estimation of Albumin by Gravimetric Method. —Precipitate by the heat-and-acetic-acid method exactly 10 c.c. of clear urine contained in a perfectly clean 15-c.c. centrifuge tube that has been dried for one hour at 100°C. Centrifuge; decant; make up with boiling water containing a few drops of acetic acid; centrifuge and decant a second time. Add 50 per cent. alcohol; centrifuge and decant a third time; dry for one hour at 100°C., after rolling the tube to distribute the precipitate; cool, and weigh. Subtract the weight of the tube in order to ascertain the weight of albumin in the 10 c.c. of urine, which is the difference. Record as grams per 100 c.c. of urine, or express in per cent.

Quantitative Estimation of Albumin by the Turbidity Method (Folin).—If the standard protein solution is prepared accurately, this method is easily applied and the results found reliable in specimens that are not highly colored with bile or blood pigments. It is applicable to fluids other than urine.

To prepare the standard solution, add from 25 c.c. to 35 c.c. of either clear hemoglobin-free fresh beef, pig, or human serum to 1500 c.c. 15 per cent. sodium chlorid (Merck Reagent); mix, and filter. Determine the total nitrogen of this solution. (The protein is estimated by multiplying the total nitrogen by 6.25.) Add sufficient 15 per cent. saline so that 1 c.c. will contain 2 mg. protein; and place the whole in a glass-stoppered bottle with 20 c.c. chloroform as a preservative.

To make the determination, place about 75 c.c. water and 5 c.c. 25 per cent. solution of sulphosalicylic acid in each of two 100-c.c. volumetric flasks. To one flask add 5 c.c. standard protein solution; and to the other add, by means of an Ostwald pipet, 1 c.c. of urine at a time until the turbidity seems to be about that of the standard. Mix by carefully inverting. Make both flasks to volume with water. In the colorimeter, the turbidity of one is compared with that of the other, and the amount of albumin computed in grams per 100 c.c. of urine.

The nitrogen of urine albumin may be determined by taking the difference between the total nitrogen and the nitrogen after precipitation and removal of all albumin by the heat-and-acetic-acid test, as determined by the biuret test.

Rough Estimation of Albumin by Esbach Method (Fig. 58).— Fill the albuminometer to the mark U with acidified urine, and to the mark R with Esbach's reagent (picric acid 1 gm; citric acid 2 gm; and distilled water 200 c.c.). Stopper; thoroughly mix by inverting, and set aside in a test-tube rack for twenty-four hours. The reading on the tube that corresponds to the upper surface of the precipitate is the number of grams of protein per liter of urine. Less than 0.5 gm. per liter will not sediment. This estimation of protein is not accurate and has a doubtful value.

True Mucin and Nucleoalbumin.—These two substances have physical properties in common, react to some tests in the same manner, and thus have sometimes been confused. True mucin is derived from the intact epithelial cells lining the genitourinary tract, and may entangle cells and other material to form the nubecula. Although the secretion of mucin by the epithelium lining the genitourinary tract is small compared with that secreted by epithelium of the alimentary tract, it is generally stated to be secreted by the former. Mucin contains a carbohydrate group but no phosphorus. It is precipitated by dilute phosphoric acid, but is soluble in excess of acetic acid. Sodium chlorid keeps it in solution.

Nucleoalbumin, on the other hand, is formed by the disintegration of the nuclei of desquamated cells and possibly by cells from other sources. It contains phosphorus, and is not dissolved by an excess of acetic acid. Since the chemical constitution of important nucleins has been determined the term nucleoalbumin is passing into disrepute and appears to have very little use.

Fig. 58.—Esbach albuminometer. The tube held in wood base is filled to U with urine and to R with reagent.

It appears that mucous membrane inflammatory processes are apt to produce an increase in both of these proteins.

CARBOHYDRATES

Dextrin may appear in the urine in diabetes mellitus, but does not do so commonly. If it is present, boiling the glucose-free urine with Fehling's solution produces a greenish color. Sugars other than dextrose (glucose or grape-sugar) may appear in the urine, and owing to their different responses to chemical tests it is necessary to recognize their occurrence. Among the less common carbohydrates levulose and the pentoses have attracted most attention.

Levulose.—On a carbohydrate-free diet, this sugar may appear in the urine in severe cases of diabetes mellitus and has by some been regarded as a grave sign. A careful quantitative estimation of sugar present is made by the fermentation test, and again by the polariscopic method. The difference in the percentage indicates approximately the levulose present. Glycuronic acid and beta-oxybutyric acid are levorotatory but non-fermentable. To determine the character of levorotatory substances present, ferment a sample of urine and test its polarization before and after fermentation.

Pentoses.—There are rare occurrences of these sugars in the urine of individuals who appear normal (idiopathic pentosuria). They may occur after the ingestion of fruits (blueberries, plums) rich in pentoses (alimentary pentosuria). A negative fermentation test and a positive Fehling's test in non-diabetic urines should lead one to perform a phenylhydrazin test. The pentose osazones have melting points very close to 160°C. Arabinose, xylose, and rhamnose are the ones found.

Lactose.—This sugar is not abnormal in the urine of lactating women. Fehling's test with lactose is positive (reduction is slow), while the fermentation test is practically negative. In the presence of other sugars it is not possible to detect small amounts of lactose. The osazone has a melting point of 200°C.

Maltose.—This is not uncommonly found in cases of diabetes. The dextrorotatory properties of maltose is two and one-half times as great as that of glucose, and where the fermentation test or Fehling's test indicates a distinctly less amount of sugar than is indicated by the polariscope, the presence of maltose should be suspected and its osazone formed (melting point 207°C.).

Saccharose (Cane-sugar).—This sugar is not found in urine.

It may find its way into urine accidentally or it may be added by malingerers. It does not reduce Fehling's solution but gives the urine a high specific gravity. After boiling with dilute hydrochloric acid a urine that contains saccharose reduces Fehling's solution.

Glycuronic Acid.—This acid is formed by the hydrolytic splitting cf glucose, and in the urine it is present only in combined forms—the glycuronates. On rather prolonged boiling, the glycuronates reduce Fehling's solution; but they do not react with phenylhydrazin unless previously boiled with a mineral acid. With the usual procedure, the glycuronates give either a greenish reduction with Fehling's solution, much like the reduction given by the pentoses, or a mere trace of glucose. Indoxyl and skatoxyl are largely eliminated with sulphuric acid as ethereal sulphates, but they are also found in combination with glycuronic acid. The glycuronates occur in traces in the normal urine and may be greatly increased in diabetes. Since an increase in glycuronates is usually accompanied by the presence of glucose, the specific rotation of the acid urine may be determined, the urine precipitated with basic lead acetate, and the rotation of the acid urine again determined. The glycuronates which are levorotatory are precipitated in acid urine by basic lead acetate, and large amounts of glycuronates may be detected by increases in dextrorotatory properties after their precipitation in this way. *Glycuronic acid* (Tollen) may be tested for by adding a minute amount of phloroglycin from the point of a knife blade, and 5 c.c. hydrochloric acid to 5 c.c. urine, boiling for one minute, cooling, and extracting with 10 c.c. ether. The ether turns a faint purple with the usual normal amount, and a dark blue or violet with increased amounts. Pentoses and lactose give a similar reaction.

Homogentisic Acid.—Although not a carbohydrate, this compound reduces Fehling's solution. A fresh, light-colored specimen of urine from an individual affected with alkaptonuria darkens on standing—a change which is hastened by the addition of alkali. Such a urine does not reduce bismuth, does not ferment, and crystals are not formed with phenylhydrazin.

Individuals with *alkaptonuria* continue in excellent health for a great many years. The condition is frequently inherited, and for this reason is looked upon as being a chemical defect in the protoplasm of the germ cells. The hemogentisic acid may be obtained from the urine and purified by repeated crystallizations.

Glucose (Dextrose, Grape-sugar).—The significance of the appearance in the urine of carbohydrates other than glucose is not well enough understood to warrant a detailed discussion. Practically, glycosuria and glucosuria are used synonymously at the present time. About one-twentieth per cent. of glucose is present in normal urine; but this amount does not react with the usual tests.

The percentage of glucose in the blood in health remains almost constant at from 0.1 to 0.12 per cent.; and, if for any reason the amount in the plasma rises above this, more sugar appears in the urine than the traces normally present, and a glycosuria is said to exist. There are several conditions that may lead to an excess of sugar in the blood, and therefore several forms of glycosuria exist.

Alimentary glycosuria is due to a hyperglycemia produced by the ingestion of large amounts of sugar. Since dogs with an Eck fistula—which diverts the blood from the portal vein directly into the ascending vena cava and prevents the venous drainage from the intestine passing through the liver—show a diminished tolerance for sugar, it seems that increased percentage of glucose in the blood results from a deficient removal of sugar from the blood by the liver. If sugar reaches the venous circulation through the large lymphatic trunks, the same thing will be accomplished as in the case of an Eck fistula and this by some is said to explain alimentary glycosuria. Normally, sugar passes by way of the portal vein to the liver and is there dehydrated and polymerized to glycogen. This process is reversed, and glucose passed into the blood plasma by hydrolysis of the gylcogen in the liver cells, whenever the percentage in the plasma falls below normal. In disease of the liver there is usually no tendency to alimentary glycosuria. Some cases that readily show alimentary glycosuria develop a true diabetes; but the majority do not, and care must be exercised in drawing any conclusions when there is a tendency to this form of glycosuria. It cannot be produced by the administration of an excess of starch.

Phlorhizin glycosuria is an experimental condition produced by the administration of the glucoside, phlorhizin. This poison appears to exert a toxic action on the renal cells rendering them incapable of holding back a normal amount of glucose present in the blood. This is, therefore, one form of glycosuria in which there is no hyperglycemia.

Renal diabetes is a term that has been applied to glycosuria in cases of nephritis with hypertension but without marked hyperglycemia. It is entirely possible that there may be a retention of a poison acting like phlorhizin in such individuals but certainly in the usual case of severe chronic nephritis there is an increase in blood sugar.

Epinephrin glycosuria results from the introduction of an excess of epinephrin into the circulation, either experimentally or through the normal mechanism by which an excess is liberated by the adrenals due to a stimulation through the sympathetic nervous system. Since the higher centers may act on the sympathetic system, a glycosuria may be psychic in origin. The epinephrin liberates glucose from the storehouse of glycogen in the liver and in the muscles. The glycosuria that may be present in Graves' disease and in other affections of the glands of internal secretion may be closely related to epinephrin glycosuria.

Transient glycosurias, lasting a short time, are observed in a number of different intoxications (morphin, strychnin, cocain) and infections (pulmonary tuberculosis) and in injuries of the central nervous system. An example of the last is experimental puncture of the floor of the fourth ventricle (piqûre of Claude Bernard). The glycosurias resulting from such puncture as well as those seen in brain tumors, apoplexy, head trauma, tabes, general paralysis, and cerebrospinal meningitis are probably of the epinephrin type.

Diabetes mellitus is a condition in which there is a marked

16

disposition to glycosuria, which persists indefinitely. In many of the cases coming to autopsy no well-defined lesion can be demonstrated histologically in the pancreas or elsewhere. The cause has not been established definitely, and the pathologic basis for the disease may be found to vary in different cases. The most definite histologic change is the deposition of a hyaline material about the capillaries of the islets of Langerhans which compresses the cells and causes their atrophy. A change not so well defined consists of a greater or less sclerosis of the islets. It is possible that in certain cases the kidney, the liver, or the thyroid, or other organ is at fault.

In the definition just given, however, only the clinical findings are considered. That the sugar is excreted by the kidneys because of a *hyperglycemia* that results from the inability of the liver to store the dextrose brought to it, offers a plausible theory. In the severest forms of the disease there is also an inability of the body cells to use sugar; but this may, so far as can be judged from present knowledge, be due to the absence of sufficient *glycogen* in the cells in which oxidation takes place. That the liver, heart muscle and striated muscles are deficient in glycogen in diabetes mellitus has been established. There is at hand a certain amount of proof to show that the islet cells secrete a substance that enables the liver cells and the striated muscle syncytium to dehydrate and polymerize the glucose to form glycogen. Because no changes are demonstrable in the pancreas with existing histologic methods is not proof that a lesion of this organ does not exist in all cases of diabetes mellitus.

Formerly, mild and severe cases of diabetes were differentiated on the ground that in light cases withdrawal of carbohydrates from the diet caused sugar to disappear from the urine. Individuals with diabetes may secrete greater amounts of sugar than are taken as carbohydrates in the food, which indicates that sugar in the body is derived from fats and proteins. The sugar formed from the keto-acids, after the splitting off of ammonia, is no different from that derived from carbohydrates, and the liver can store it no better.

As just mentioned, there is frequently in severe cases (above 5 per cent. of sugar) a diminished ability of patients to oxidize sugar. This is shown by the reduction of the respiratory coefficient. In the combustion of carbohydrates, the volume of carbon dioxid given off is equal to the volume of oxygen consumed; that is, the ratio is one, while in the burning of fats and proteins the ratio of carbonic acid gas to oxygen is seven to ten. When fats and proteins are the main source of energy the ratio of carbon dioxid to oxygen falls.

As the result of the uselessness of carbohydrates to diabetics, they must take excessive amounts of proteins and fat or become emaciated. Certain organic acids—especially beta-oxybutyric and diacetic—are formed in excessive quantities, which give rise to an acidosis or abnormal decrease in the alkalinity of the blood that is most marked in cases of diabetic coma. The source of these acids has not been definitely established.

The increased amount of sugar in the blood (See under blood sugar, page 87) favors the growth of bacteria in the tissues, which with other factors explains the existence of gangrene, tuberculosis, furunculosis, and stomatitis as common complications. The cause of the frequent arteriosclerosis, which may lead to the familiar diabetic gangrene of the extremities, is not clear. There is often an intense thirst. The amount of urine may reach fifteen liters in twenty-four hours. Once the presence of glucose in the urine has been established, further information is sought to ascertain whether or not the case is one of diabetes mellitus. A marked polyuria (more than 20 liters per day) may occur in cases with cerebral lesions and is occasionally met without demonstrable lesion (diabetes insipidus).

Tests for Glucose.—Some methods of sugar determination are based on its physical properties, but most are chemical tests. As mentioned, normal urine contains a minute amount of glucose, and the uric acid and creatinin have reducing power, but the total reduction by these substances is not great enough to lead to mistakes in the practical tests used to determine the presence of sugar in the urine. Albumin, when present, is removed by means of the heat-and-acetic-acid test. For polariscopic deter-

minations lead acetate is added and the urine filtered. Urine
to which formalin has been added is never used for sugar tests.
Chloroform must be removed as completely as possible from
urine to which it has been added as a preservative. Toluol is
the most satisfactory preservative for urine to be used for chemical tests.

Fehling's Test.—Place 5 c.c. Fehling's solution A (copper
sulphate, Merck reagent, 34.65 gm. (accurate), distilled water,
q.s. ad. 1000 c.c. in a 1-liter volumetric flask) and 5 c.c. Fehling's
solution B (Rochelle salts 173 gm., sodium hydrate 125 gm.,
distilled water, q. s. ad 1000 c.c. in a 1-liter volumetric flask)
in a test-tube, and boil. Remove from flame, and at once
add less than 1 c.c. urine, and allow a few minutes for reduction to take place. A reduction is shown by the appearance
of a brick red precipitate. Do not heat for ten minutes after
the addition of urine. If no reduction has taken place in this
time sugar is not present. The mixture may again be boiled
to ascertain if heat will develop any reducing substances in the
urine. If positive, apply Nylander's test.

Nylander's Test.—To prepare Nylander's reagent, dissolve
20 gm. Rochelle salt in 500 c.c. warm 10 per cent. sodium hydrate and add 10 gm. bismuth subnitrate; shake, cool, and filter
into a dark-colored bottle. To 10 c.c. urine in a test-tube from
which all albumin has been removed add 1 c.c. of the reagent,
and place the tube in boiling water in a water-bath for five
minutes. If positive, the urine darkens and a black precipitate
settles out during the heating. Uric acid, creatinin, and the
alkaptone bodies may produce a dirty yellow (atypical reaction)
with Fehling's test, but they do not react to Nylander's test.

Haines's Test.—This test is not given for the purpose of
supplementing Nylander's or Fehling's, but rather as one that
some workers prefer to substitute for Fehling's. Dissolve
12 gm. copper sulphate and 45 gm. potassium hydrate in
1000 c.c. distilled water, and add 90 c.c. glycerin. Make fresh
once in two months or oftener. To use, place 10 c.c. of the
solution in a test-tube, boil, and immediately add less than
1 c.c. of urine. A positive reaction is the same as Fehling's.

Phenylhydrazin Test (Fig. 59).—If the reduction (Fehling's, Nylander's) is not altogether typical, and it is desirable to determine accurately whether glucose is present, this test is applied. If the specific gravity of the urine is high, the sample is diluted until it is below 1.020. Even in urine with a high specific gravity, 0.2 per cent. sugar gives a positive test. To 5 c.c. urine in a test-tube add 5 drops pure phenylhydrazin base (Merck) and 10 drops glacial acetic acid. Boil for one minute. Add 5 drops 15 per cent. sodium hydrate, (the liquid

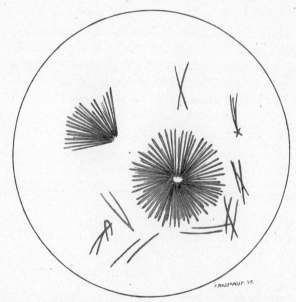

FIG. 59.—Phenylglucosazone crystals drawn with the high-dry lens.

remains acid); heat again for a few seconds, and set aside to cool. The yellow sheaf-like crystals appear at once, or within twenty minutes. The crystals obtained with a pipet from the bottom of the tube are examined with the high-dry lens.

Since the test is made only in cases where there is doubt in regard to the presence of sugar, the steps are carried out with care. The glucosazone crystals may be filtered out, dried in the paraffin oven, and 60 per cent. alcohol added drop by drop to the crystals contained in a tube held over a flame until solution occurs. Cool, and filter off the crystals. Again, crystallize from hot alcohol and dry. Place the dry crystals in a small glass tube sealed at the bottom. This tube is placed in concentrated sulphuric acid, alongside a thermometer, and the temperature gradually raised. If phenylglucosazone, the crystals melt at 204°C. Levulose gives a glucosazone with the same constitutional formula; but the crystals dissolved in equal parts of absolute alcohol and pyridine rotate polarized light to the left. In the concentration found in urine, lactose gives no reaction. Maltose gives crystals melting at 207°C. The compounds resulting from the pentoses have much lower melting points.

Provisional Examination of Urine for Anesthesia.—Urine should be examined before a general anesthetic is administered. In hospitals where there are large surgical wards urine examinations may become burdensome. In such cases, rather than that the urine should be carelessly examined, the above technic may be altered somewhat. Urine cylinders (Fig. 60) with a cone at the bottom (A. H. Thomas and Co., Phila.) are placed on a table, and all the urine emptied into these before beginning the tests. Re-move the slip from the bottle in which the urine is sent to the laboratory and place it

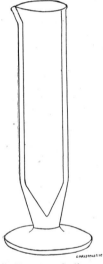

FIG. 60.—Sediment-ing cylinder.

under the cylinder at the time the urine is poured into it. To test for albumin, use a modified Heller test (page 234) by substituting a piece of glass tubing a foot long, with a 3-mm. lumen, for the test-tube. Lower the tubing into the urine to a depth of 1 in. and retain the urine in it by pressing the index finger against its top. Lower the pipet into a graduate containing concentrated nitric acid—taking care to keep the finger on top of the tube until it is sunk to the level of the urine—and when 1 in. of the acid is forced into the tube, again place the finger in position and remove the pipet, examining against a black background for a white ring at the zone of contact.

To test for sugar, add to a test-tube containing Fehling's solution a few drops from each of about five samples of urine, and perform a Fehling's test in the usual way. If positive, then go back and determine which urine gave the positive test.

To obtain sediment from the bottom of the cone, lower the small glass tubing to the bottom, holding the finger over the top, and allow the desired amount (1 cm.) of sediment to flow

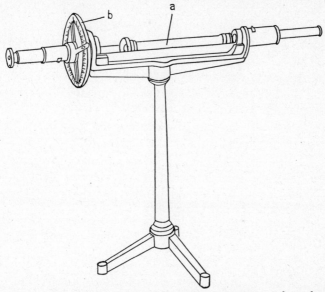

Fig. 61.—Polariscope provided with glucose percentage scale and sodium lamp (Eimer and Amend). Add 1 gm. basic lead acetate to 100 c.c. urine, shake, filter and fill tube, a. Add one or more drops to the tube in the upright position to bring the level of the liquid above the tube in order that the glass cover may be applied with no air bubbles beneath it. Take reading from milled adjustment, b.

into it. Place a drop of the sediment on a glass slide large enough for at least five sediments. This method of examination is used only when a more careful examination is prohibitive.

Polariscopic Determination of Glucose (Fig. 61).—Two grams of lead acetate are added to the 24-hour sample of urine. After filtering, make acid, and fill the 189.4-mm. glass tube with the clear urine; apply the glass disk, being careful not to get an air bubble beneath it, and screw on the metal cap. Place the tube in the polariscope which is focused against a sodium light; and, starting at zero, turn the handle until the field is equally illuminated. The percentage of sugar is read directly from the vernier, provided the instrument is made for sugar estimation only (saccharometer).

Quantitative Estimation of Glucose by Fehling's Method.— Place 10 c.c. (accurate) Fehling's A (10 c.c. of this solution contain 0.3465 gm. copper sulphate) and 10 c.c. Fehling's B (approximate) in a 300-c.c. Florence flask of Jena glass, and dilute with about 50 c.c. of water. (If the specific gravity of the urine is 1.030 or over, dilute 1–5 with water.) Heat to boiling, and from a buret run in less than 1 c.c. of the diluted urine, and again boil. The hot flask is conveniently moved about by folding a sheet of strong paper into a 1.5-in. band which is carried once about the neck. Repeat this until no blue color remains. Examine for this end point (absence of bluish tinge) by looking against a white sheet of paper on the clear line 3-mm. below the top of the meniscus. A yellowish change in the red precipitate indicates that too much urine has been added. For the reduction of this amount of Fehling's, 0.05 gm. of glucose is required. For example, if 8 c.c. of the 1–5 dilution—or 1.6 c.c. of the undiluted urine—are necessary to discharge the blue color, this amount of urine contains 0.05 gm. glucose; 1 c.c. of the undiluted urine contains 0.032 gm.; 100 c.c. contain 3.2 gm., or 3.2 per cent.

A simple method for computing dilutions is to express the strength of each in terms of percentage. By a 10 per cent. solution or a solution of 1 in 10 (1–10) is meant such a dilution that in ten parts of it there is one part of the original liquid and nine parts of water. To make a given strength of a solution from a stronger one, reduce both to percentages, and take of the stronger solution the number of cubic centimeters that represents the dilution desired, and make up to the number that represents the stronger solution. For example, to make a 3 per cent. solution from a 1–8 solution, take 3 c.c. of the 1–8 and make up to 12.5 c.c. with water.

Quantitative Determination of Glucose (Benedict).—Weigh out accurately 18 gm. (accurate) copper sulphate (Merck reagent) and dissolve in about 200 c.c. distilled water in a 1000-c.c. graduated flask. Weigh out approximately 200 gm. crystallized sodium carbonate, 200 gm. sodium citrate, and 125 gm. potassium sulphocyanate, dissolve in about 500 c.c. distilled water and slowly pour with stirring the solution into the volumetric flask containing the copper sulphate; add 10 c.c. 5 per cent. potassium ferrocyanid solution, and make up to volume. Of this solution 25 c.c. are reduced by 0.05 gm. glucose, 0.052 gm. levulose or 0.067 gm. lactose.

To use, measure 25 c.c. of the reagent into a 4.5-in. evaporating dish, add 10 gm. sodium carbonate, and boil vigorously. Now add urine diluted as in Fehling's test, boiling after each addition until the last trace of blue color is discharged. Five divided by the amount of undiluted urine used gives the per cent. of sugar. This method may be substituted for Fehling's method. The end point is sharp, and this is the advantage the method has over Fehling's test.

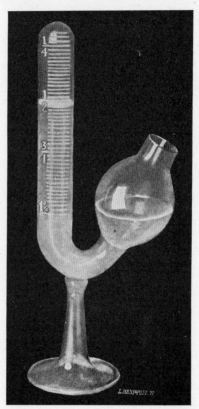

FIG. 62.—Saccharometer (Einhorn). The undiluted urine used in the test shown here contains one-half per cent. fermentable sugar.

Quantitative Determination of Glucose by Fermentation (Fig. 62).—Dilute the urine so that the specific gravity is below 1.008, and the percentage of sugar below 1 per cent. The test-tube that comes with the Einhorn saccharometer should now be filled to the mark with the diluted urine, whereupon a knife-point of compressed yeast should be added. Shake well; fill the saccharometer, displacing all air in the closed end, and place in the incubator for twenty-four hours. The percentage of sugar is indicated on the blind arm by the amount of gas

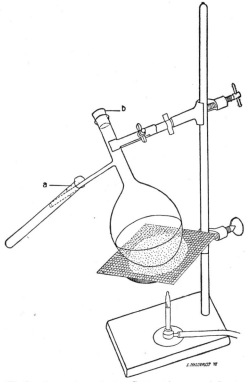

Fig. 63.—Distillation for acetone test. Cotton is pressed in at *a*, to hold the collecting test-tube firmly; *b*, rubber stopper.

present. To get the percentage of sugar, multiply this by the dilution.

This method gives only an approximate result and is not used in careful work for quantitative determinations. This test cannot be substituted for either the polariscopic or titration methods just given; but it is frequently of value as a qualitative method in the differentiation of some sugars.

Acetone (Lange) (Fig. 63).—In diabetes there is always a tendency to acidosis, which is characterized by the appearance in the urine of acetone followed by diacetic acid, and in the severest cases by beta-oxybutyric acid. Most tests for acetone react equally well to diacetic acid but the significance of these two compounds is much the same. The daily output of acetone which is always small reaches about 1 gm. before beta-oxybutyric acid appears. Acetone appears in many febrile conditions in which the diet is greatly restricted but especially in scarlatina and diphtheria. The so-called alimentary acetonuria is met with in individuals on a rich protein diet containing a minimum of carbohydrate.

For the detection of acetone in the urine, to 15 c.c. in a test-tube add 1 c.c. 10 per cent. acetic acid that contains 10 per cent. sodium nitroprossuid; mix, and on the surface stratify a few cubic centimeters of strong ammonia. If a violet color appears at the surface of contact and persists, it is most likely due to acetone. *To stratify any liquid*, slant the tube and carefully let the lighter liquid flow down the sides of the inclined tube. If positive, apply the Gunning test.

Acetone (Gunning).—Place 100 c.c. urine in an extra large test-tube or in a small Erlenmeyer flask, and add 1 c.c. concentrated hydrochloric acid. Stopper with a rubber cork carrying a glass tube 2 ft. long curved at an angle of 45 degrees. Boil, and collect the first 10 c.c. of distillate in a test-tube. To 5 c.c. of this add 5 drops ammonia, and then iodin solution (iodin, 4 gm.; potassium iodid, 6 gm.; and water, 100 c.c.) until the black precipitate that forms does not immediately dissolve. The black precipitate soon goes into solution, and if acetone is present a yellow precipitate of iodoform quickly collects and the iodoform is easily detected by its odor and by microscopic examination. Before recording as negative, let the distillate stand overnight. Examine the precipitate for hexagonal crystals, using the high-dry lens. A positive test is produced only by acetone.

Quantitative Determination of Diacetic Acid and Acetone (Folin).—In a perfectly fresh specimen of acetone-containing urine there is several times as much aceto-acetic acid as acetone and, since the formation of acetone from the diacetic acid is so irregular and the two substances are so closely related, there is little indication for their separate estimations.

To about 1 c.c. 10 per cent. sulphuric acid contained in a large Jena test-tube add an amount of urine (0.5 to 1 c.c.) that contains 0.3 to 0.7 mg. acetone and connect (Fig. 67) with a second tube containing 10 c.c. fresh 2 per cent. sodium bisulphite solution. Place the first tube in water at 37.5°C. and aspirate for fifteen minutes (very slowly at first). Transfer the sulphite-acetone solution to a 100-c.c. volumetric flask and add 50 c.c. distilled water. To each of two other 100-c.c. volumetric flasks add 10 c.c. standard acetone solution, 10 c.c. 2 per cent. bisulphite solution, and 40 c.c. distilled water. To each of the three flasks add 15 c.c. clear Scott-Wilson reagent, make up to volume with distilled water and let stand twelve to fifteen minutes. Place the two standard acetone solutions in the cylinders of the Duboscq colorimeter, and, using the colorimeter metal screen, adjust the instrument until 20 mm. of the two suspensions are equal. Replace the contents of one cup with the second standard suspension and the contents of the other with the unknown; make a turbidity comparison with the standard set at 20 mm. Twenty times 0.5 divided by the reading gives in mg. the amount of acetone in the urine used for the test.

To prepare the standard acetone solution, place 2.5 gm. acetone-sodium bisulphite (Merck) in a 1000-c.c. volumetric flask, dissolve in 50 c.c. water and make to volume with dilute (1–5) hydrochloric acid. Place 25 c.c. of this solution in a small Erlenmeyer flask, add 20 c.c. tenth normal iodin, and after five minutes titrate the surplus iodin with tenth normal sodium thiosulphate which gives the sulphur dioxid content of the solution. Again place 25 c.c. of the acetone-bisulphite solution in a flask, add 50 c.c. tenth normal iodin, after five minutes 10 c.c. 40 per cent. sodium hydrate and five minutes after the addition of the alkali add 18 c.c. concentrated hydrochloric acid. Titrate the liberated iodin with thiosulphate. From the 50 c.c. of iodin subtract the number c.c. used for titration of the liberated iodin and from this result subtract the sulphur dioxid content of 25 c.c. determined by the first titration. The remainder represents the acetone content. From this standard stock solution make such a dilution that 5 c.c. of the dilute solution contain 0.5 mg. acetone. To prepare the iodin, add 6.4 gm. iodin to 50 c.c. water— in which 12 gm. potassium iodid has been dissolved—contained in a 500-c.c. volumetric flask. After solution of the iodin make up to volume. To prepare the thiosulphate solution, dissolve 24.85 gm. sodium thiosulphate in a small amount of water contained in a 500-c.c. volumetric flask and make up to volume. To determine the strength of the thiosulphate, place 20 c.c. deci-normal iodin in a flask, add 100 c.c. water and run in thiosulphate solution from a buret until the liquid assumes a straw color; add a few drops starch paste and continue to run in the thiosulphate until the blue color is lost.

To prepare the Scott-Wilson reagent add 10 gm. mercuric cyanid dissolved in 600 c.c. water to 180 gm. caustic soda dissolved in 600 c.c. water and cooled to room temperature. To this mixture contained in a heavy jar add slowly 2.9 gm. silver nitrate dissolved in 400 c.c. water with vigorous stirring. The solution keeps several months. Remove from the tiop of the bottle with a siphon.

Diacetic Acid (Gerhardt).—Diacetic acid is tested for in perfectly fresh urine, since some of it may change to acetone. To 10 c.c. urine add 10 drops 10 per cent. ferric chlorid solution; filter to remove phosphates, and add a few drops more of the ferric chlorid solution to insure an excess. If diacetic is present a red color appears. Place 10 c.c. urine in a second test-tube, boil for five minutes and proceed with the test in exactly the same way. If the red color was due to diacetic acid, it should be much less intense or entirely absent in the boiled urine, since the boiling will have changed any diacetic acid to acetone which does not produce a red color with ferric chlorid. Certain common drugs give the red color obtained before boiling, but the acetates and formates are the only ones that react after boiling. If diacetic acid is present there is found a considerable amount of acetone, and beta-oxybutyric acid is usually present. It occurs in much the same conditions as acetone. The detection of this compound in cases of suspected acidosis is significant.

Beta-Oxybutyric Acid (Black).—Evaporate 50 c.c. urine in a small porcelain dish to about one-fourth; acidify with a few drops of hydrochloric acid, and with a spatula add plaster of Paris to a thick paste. When the mass begins to harden, break up into a meal by means of a spatula; add 30 c.c. of ether, and mix. Decant the clear ether into a dry evaporating dish; evaporate the ether over a water-bath and dissolve the residue in 10 c.c. water. Neutralize with an excess of dry barium carbonate; pour into a test-tube; add a few drops of hydrogen peroxid, which oxidizes beta-oxybutyric to diacetic acid, and 5 drops 10 per cent. ferric chlorid. A red color indicates beta-oxybutyric acid. A quantitative estimate may be made by placing the meal in a Soxhlet apparatus and extracting with ether for several hours. After evaporation of the ether, the residue is thoroughly extracted with small amounts of distilled water, and the washings finally made up to 25 c.c. in a volumetric flask. This liquid is placed in a polariscope and its levorotatory properties determined.

If fermented urine is strongly levorotatory this substance is likely present. When it appears in a diabetic urine the amount is likely to increase and large amounts may be eliminated in the twenty-four hours.

CHEMICAL TESTS FOR RENAL INSUFFICIENCY, FOR URINARY PIGMENTS, AND FOR CERTAIN INORGANIC SALTS

RENAL INSUFFICIENCY

Many general facts in regard to changes in the chemical constituents of the urine, such as the diminished amount of nitrogenous urinary solids in uremic poisoning, were known before accurate and practical methods were developed for their quantitative determination. Likewise it was shown that the freezing point of blood plasma is lowered in uremia, owing to an increase in the number of molecules in it (non-protein molecules containing nitrogen) before the estimation of the total non-protein nitrogen of the blood was carried out in the routine examination of these cases.

In conditions in which the kidneys fail to excrete substances that they should there is an increase in non-protein (residual, non-coagulable) nitrogen in the blood. Artificial substances in great numbers have been introduced into the circulation of man and experimental animals with defective elimination, in order to determine the part of the kidney unit affected; but this attempt to localize the lesion within the kidney has not been successful. The failure may be due to the fact that except during the early active stage of the lesion the process is diffused and the entire kidney unit is involved.

The experimental work in determining the rate of excretion of many different substances in normal and pathologic conditions has developed tests of practical value for determining the functional condition of a kidney as a whole; and of these phenol-sulphonephthalein is most used. This substance is a triphenyl-methane dye that is quantitively excreted by the kidneys after artificial introduction. The rate of excretion of this dyestuff is quite uniform in normal individuals, and a decrease without question throws some light on the functional condition of the kidney. With improved technic in ureteral catheterization, a unilateral kidney lesion may be detected by estimating the phenolsulphonephthalein output of the two kidneys separately.

Phthalein Test (Rowntree and Geraghty).—Let the patient drink a pint or more of water, and inject intramuscularly 1 c.c. of a sterile solution that contains 6 mg. phenolsulphonephthalein. To prepare this solution for this injection, add 1 c.c. normal sodium hydrate and 100 c.c. saline to 0.6 gm. phenolsulpho-nephthalein. Of this solution give 1 c.c. or one ampule (Hynson, Westcott and Co., Balto.) which contains 6 mg. The bladder is emptied with a catheter which is left in place, and the urine allowed to flow into a container in which a drop of strong sodium hydrate has been placed until the first red color appears (ten minutes normally), when the catheter is removed. If the time for the appearance of the dye in the urine is not desired the catheterization may be dispensed with. At the end of the first hour the patient urinates into a clean container, and at the end of the second hour into a second container. Place the first- and second-hour specimens into two separate 1000-c.c. cylinders; add 20 c.c. normal sodium hydrate, and distilled water to 1000 c.c. The two vessels in which the specimens are collected are washed with small amounts of distilled water, and the water is then added to the respective cylinders previous to making them up to volume. Compare these with standard samples in ten tubes containing respectively 0.1, 0.2, 0.3, 0.5, 1.0, 2, 3, 4, 5, and 6 mg. per 1000 c.c., and estimate the percentage eliminated during the two hours. The standard tubes are kept permanently in a wooden frame provided for the purpose. Kidneys functioning normally excrete practically all during the first two hours, and one-half during the first hour; while the excretion may be only one-half this amount if a moderate nephritis exists, and frequently the elimination is only 25 per cent. or less.

Micro-method for Total Nitrogen in Urine (Folin and Farmer) (Fig. 64).—Place 5 c.c. urine in a 50-c.c. graduated flask, and dilute to volume. To 1 c.c. of the diluted urine, measured into a 25 mm. by 200 mm. test-tube (Jena) provided with a fume-absorber, add 1 c.c. sulphuric acid by means of an Ostwald·pipet, 1 gm. potassium sulphate, 1 drop 10 per cent. copper sulphate, 1 drop of caprylic alcohol, and 4 glass beads. With the fume-absorber in place, boil over a micro-burner for from five to ten minutes until digestion is complete. Cool until viscous; detach the fume-absorber; and, while shaking, slowly add 6 c.c. of water. Add 3 c.c. 40 per cent. sodium hydrate and 1 drop caprylic alcohol, and at once start the suction to aspirate the ammonia into the 250 c.c flat-bottomed flask. The suction should be slow at first, and then continued more rapidly for fifteen minutes in order to aspirate all the ammonia into the flask, which contains 10 c.c. one-fiftieth normal hydrochloric acid, 3 drops alizarin red solution, and 30 c.c. water. At the end of fifteen minutes wash the delivery-tube, and titrate the excess of acid in the flask with one-fiftieth normal sodium hydrate until the end reaction is reached, which is a red color. Each cubic centimeter of one-fiftieth normal acid neutralized by the aspirated ammonia is equivalent to 0.00028 gm. nitrogen. Estimate the number of grams nitrogen in 100 c.c. urine. Specimens are always examined in duplicate.

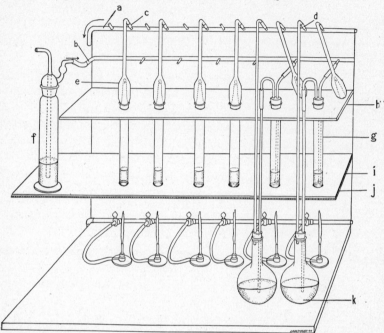

FIG. 64.—Nitrogen determinations. *a*, Three-fourth-inch pipe and twelve connections of soft metal for suction. The six connections, *c*, are large enough for the end of the large fume absorber, *e*, to slip inside of it while the remaining six smaller connections, *d*, are for rubber connections to be slipped over them. The two sets (Jena test-tubes 200 by 20 mm.) on the left are being digested with the microburners beneath them while the ammonia is being aspirated from the third set (duplicate samples) on the right. The air is drawn through sulphuric acid in *f*, and through a one-half-inch soft metal pipe, *b*. The apparatus is best placed over a side table provided with gas. *h*, is a three-fourth-inch wooden shelf; *i*, heavy sheet of asbestos; *j*, sheet of coarse wire gauze through which the lower ends of the tubes project.

Kjeldahl method for Total Nitrogen in Urine.—For those who have not had an extensive experience in chemical technic there is less chance for error in the estimation of total nitrogen by the Kjeldahl method. To exactly 5 c.c. urine in a 500-c.c. Kjeldahl

17

flask add 15 c.c. ammonia-free sulphuric acid and 2 c.c. 5 per cent. copper sulphate. Boil thirty to forty-five minutes under a hood with a good draft. After the oxidation is complete and the liquid colorless, it is allowed to cool and added to a 1000-c.c. round-bottomed flask of Jena glass that contains about 200 c.c. distilled water. Rinse out the last traces of the acid and add the washings to the large flask. Cool, and add sufficient 40 per cent. caustic soda to make the solution alkaline (the amount should be determined approximately by titrating 15 c.c. of a concentrated acid with the alkali to be used). At once connect the flask with a condenser—the tip of which dips into a solution consisting of 25 c.c. decinormal hydrochloric acid, 3 drops alizarin red and 50 c.c. water contained in a 350-c.c. Erlenmeyer flask. Shake the flask to mix alkali and acid, boil briskly until the distillate is no longer alkaline to litmus paper (about thirty minutes). Titrate the excess of acid with decinormal hydrate. The number of cubic centimeters of acid neutralized by ammonia multiplied by 1.4 gives the number of mg. nitrogen in the 25 c.c. urine.

Urea Nitrogen (Marshall).—Measure into a flask 25 c.c. one-fiftieth normal hydrochloric acid, 3 drops of alizarin red, and 1 drop of caprylic alcohol. In a tube place 5 c.c. urine diluted 1–10, 1 c.c. 15 per cent. urease dissolved in water (the urease is obtained from Arlington Chemical Co., Yonkers, N. Y.) and 1 drop of caprylic alcohol. Stopper the tube and flask, as shown in Fig. 64 , and allow them to stand for fifteen minutes, and then pass air for fifteen minutes; proceed as in micro- method for total nitrogen. Each cubic centimeter of one-fiftieth normal acid neutralized is equivalent to 0.00028 gm. nitrogen. Find the number of grams nitrogen that would be liberated from 100 c.c. of urine; and from this amount subtract the number of grams of ammonia nitrogen in 100 c.c. of urine; and the remainder will be the number of grams of urea nitrogen in 100 c.c. of this urine.

Rough Determination of Urea by Ureometer (Fig. 65).— Add to the small side tube of the ureometer (Doremus-Hinds) 1 c.c. urine, allowing it to flow in through and to fill the opening in the glass cock. Close the cock, and with water wash out any urine that has run into the bulb portion of the instrument, after which it is ready for addition to the hypobromite solution filling the blind arm and a portion of the bulb.

To prepare the hypobromite solution, place in a large test-tube 13 c.c. Rice's solution A (bromin 10 c.c.; potassium bromid 31 gm.; distilled water ad. 250 c.c.) and add 13 c.c. Rice's solution B (40 per cent. caustic soda). Pour the mixture into the bulb portion of the apparatus; incline so as to displace the

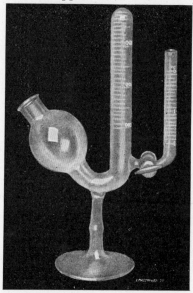

FIG. 65.—Ureometer. (Doremus-Hinds). 1 c.c. of urine is delivered accurately from the short arm.

air from the blind arm and to fill it with the hypobromite mixture. Allow exactly 1 c.c. urine to flow slowly from the small side-tube into the bulb portion. Each large division of the blind arm represents 1 per cent. urea. The large divisions are divided into tenths. For example, if the column of gas in the blind arm measures 0.014, then the percentage of urea is 1.4.

The determination of urea by this method, even when most carefully carried out, is not an accurate one; so that it has a doubtful use.

Ammonia Nitrogen (Folin-Macallum).—Place 2 c.c. urine in a large test-tube, and add 0.5 c.c. ammonia reagent (15 gm. potassium carbonate; 15 gm. potassium oxalate; 100 c.c. water) and 2 drops caprylic alcohol. Connect up at once, and proceed as in the total nitrogen determination by the micromethod (page 257). Estimate the amount of ammonia nitrogen in 100 c.c. urine.

Formalin Method for Ammonia Nitrogen (Ronchèse).— To 20 c.c. urine taken from a twenty-four hour sample, which is contained in a 150-c.c. Erlenmeyer flask, add 5 drops 0.5 per cent. phenolphthalein and 20 c.c. neutral saturated potassium oxalate solution. Shake for one minute, and at once run in decinormal sodium hydrate to a faint pink. Add 5 c.c. neutral formalin, which changes ammonium salts to hexamethylene tetramine, and titrate to a faint pink. To make the formalin and oxalate solutions neutral, add a few drops of phenolphthalein and carefully run in decinormal hydrate until the faintest trace of pink appears. Since the formalin combines with ammonia to set free acid equivalent to the amount of ammonia present, each cubic centimeter of difference between the two titrations represents 0.0014 gm. ammonia nitrogen. Determine the amount in the twenty-four hour sample. It should be noted that the first titration gives a "total acidity" which is of significance in diabetic urines. The ammonia and the total acid curves run parallel in both normal and diabetic urines. This test is not accurate enough for metabolic work.

Determination of Uric Acid in Urine (Folin).—To 2 to 5 c.c. urine in a 15-c.c. centrifuge tube, add distilled water to 6 c.c. and 5 c.c. silver lactate solution (a solution containing 5 per cent. silver lactate and 5 per cent. lactic acid); stir with a very small glass rod, wash the rod with a few drops of water and centrifuge the mixture. Add a few drops of the silver solution to the tube and if a precipitate occurs add 2 c.c. more of this solution, mix and again centrifuge. Decant the supernatant liquid and from a buret add 4 c.c. 5 per cent. sodium cyanid solution (highly poisonous) to the precipitate. Add 5 c.c. water, stir until clear, pour the contents into a 100–c.c. volumetric flask and wash the centrifuge tube and glass rod adding the washings to the flask. Pour in water to the flask to bring the volume to about 40 c.c. and add 4 c.c. uric acid-phenol reagent. In a second flask place 20 c.c. of a standard uric acid solution that contains 1 mg. of uric acid and add 4 c.c. cyanid solution, 20 c.c. water and 4 c.c. uric acid-phenol reagent. Add 20 c.c. 20 per cent. sodium carbonate to each of the two flasks. At the end of twenty minutes make both to volume and read the unknown against the standard at 20 mm. in the colorimeter. Twenty divided by the reading of the unknown gives the number of mg. of uric acid present in the amount of urine used. Albumin must be removed by the heat-and-acetic-acid test. To prepare the uric acid-phenol reagent, dissolve 100 gm. sodium tungstate, and 20 gm. phosphomolybdic acid in 750 c.c. water and add 50 c.c. 85 per cent. phosphoric acid and 100 c.c. concentrated hydrochloric acid. Boil gently for two hours with funnel in mouth of flask, cool and make up to one liter. To prepare the standard uric acid solution, place exactly 250 mg. pure uric acid in a small beaker and dissolve in 40 c.c. 0.4 per cent. lithium carbonate. Transfer to a 500-c.c. volumetric flask with repeated washings, make to volume and mix. Transfer 100 c.c. of this liquid to a 1000-c.c. volumetric flask, add about 500 c.c. water, 10 c.c. normal hydrochloric acid and make to volume. Transfer to a bottle, add 5 c.c. chloroform and mix. Twenty cubic centimeters of this solution contains 1 mg. uric acid.

To test deposits qualitatively for uric acid, place the powder in a small porcelain dish; add a few drops nitric acid; and during ten minutes evaporate off the acid, holding the dish well above the flame. The dry, yellowish deposit gives a reddish color on the addition of a few drops of 1 per cent. ammonia (murexid test).

URINARY PIGMENTS

Bile Pigments.—The bile pigments occurring in human urine are *bilirubin* and its oxidation products. *Choluria* is caused by the failure of bile to escape to the intestinal canal (hepatogenous icterus), or by a failure of the liver to transform all liberated hemoglobin into bilirubin, and to excrete it (hematogenous icterus). Normally, the bilirubin passes into the gut, where it is reduced to form *urobilinogen* and is excreted as *urobilin* in the feces. Urobilin results when urobilinogen (colorless) is exposed to the air. Urobilinogen absorbed from the intestine is said to be changed somewhat and excreted in the urine as *urochrome*, which is also spoken of as urobilin and is the normal coloring matter of urine.

To test for urobilin in the urine, add 5 drops Gram's iodin to 10 c.c. acid urine; mix with 10 c.c. saturated absolute alcohol solution of zinc acetate, and filter. A green fluorescence indicates urobilin. On spectroscopic examination (Fig. 66) this fluid shows the absorption spectrum of acid urobilin

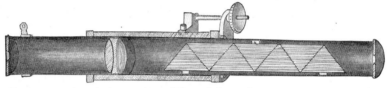

FIG. 66.—Hoffman's Spectroscope (Eimer & Amend). This model meets all the requirements of routine analysis.

(Schlesinger). When urine is first passed it is a much lighter color than it is after standing a few hours, and the pigment is said to be present as urobilinogen which is changed to urobilin (urochrome) on standing and by the iodin in this test.

Stratify the urine above concentrated nitric acid taken from a bottle in which a pine shaving has been placed. If bile pigment is present, a greenish to reddish color appears at the surface of contact (Gmelin).

To confirm this test for bile pigment, add 95 per cent. alcohol to tincture of iodin until it is a straw color, and stratify the dilute iodin solution on the urine. A greenish color at the contact indicates bile pigment (Smith).

Bile Acids.—Glycocholic and taurocholic acids may appear in the urine in obstructive jaundice. If large amounts of these acids are present, they may be tested for by adding 1 c.c. of saccharose and 1 c.c. sulphuric acid to 10 c.c. of the purified acids in a test-tube and warming to a temperature below 70°C.

(Pettenkofer). A reddish color appears at once or after several days. To obtain the purified acids 200 c.c. urine are evaporated to dryness on a water-bath, 20 c.c. hot absolute alcohol added, and the alcoholic extract filtered. The filtrate is measured in a graduated cylinder and 15 volumes ether added. The precipitate is filtered off, dissolved in 20 c.c. distilled water and shaken with a small amount of animal charcoal. The charcoal is filtered off and the filtrate tested for bile acids.

Indican.—This substance is an alkali salt of indoxyl sulphate which on oxidation yields indigo blue. Since it is normally present in the urine, definite amounts of all reagents are used regularly in the tests employed, so that an excessive elimination of indican may be detected.

Indican results from bacterial activity. This may take place parenterally as in empyema, gangrene of the lung, appendiceal abscess, or pelvic abscess from putrefactive change; but more commonly an increase is associated with augmented intestinal putrefaction following, on one hand, hypochlorhydria, or achlorhydria, and on the other an inhibition of the peristalsis of the small intestine such as occurs in ileus and in local or general peritonitis. In health, indican is formed almost entirely in the large intestine.

Jaffé's Test for Indican.—To 2 c.c. chloroform in a test-tube add 5 c.c. urine, 5 c.c. concentrated hydrochloric acid, and 2 drops of a strong calcium hypochlorite suspension (10 gm. in 100 c.c. of water). Shake. A blue color in the chloroform is positive. Iodids may give from a confusing red to a purplish color. If their presence is suspected, add a few drops of sodium hyposulphite solution and shake, which removes any color in the chloroform due to iodids.

Obermayer's Test for Indican.—To 5 c.c. filtered urine to which 20 per cent. by volume of a 20 per cent. lead acetate solution has been added before filtration, add 5 c.c. Obermayer's reagent (2 per cent. ferric chlorid in concentrated hydrochloric acid) and shake with 2 c.c. chloroform. Normally, the chloroform is colorless or a light blue. A darker color indicates an amount of indican above the average.

Uroerythrin.—As stated under bile pigments, *urochrome*, which gives the normal yellowish color to urine, is probably derived from or is identical with absorbed urobilinogen. The pink color of urates and the bright red color of uric acid deposits are ascribed to a rather indefinite coloring matter—uroerythrin —which is said to be absent in perfect health and to reach its maximum in cases of chlorosis, carcinoma, and chronic passive congestion of the liver.

Pathologic Blood Pigments.—*Hemoglobin* is tested for by the guaiac, aloin, and benzidin tests, and by spectroscopic examination. The coloring matter is usually present as methemoglobin. Although hematuria, which is characterized by the presence of red blood corpuscles in the urine, is common, hemoglobinuria is rather uncommon; but it may be produced by hemolytic poisons such as potassium chlorate, anilin derivatives, carbon monoxid, and hydrogen sulphid, and is present in hemorrhagic exanthemata as well as in paroxysmal hemoglobinuria. Absorption spectra (Fig. 67) of hemoglobin derivatives are of the greatest value in their identification.

Melanin is often present in large amounts in cases of melanoblastoma. Such urines darken on standing; and if such darkening is due to melanin, a black precipitate is formed by the addition of 10 per cent. ferric chlorid.

In *alkaptonuria* the urine becomes dark on standing, and the addition of alkali darkens it immediately.

Phenol causes urine to darken on standing. It is seen after the administration of phenol or salicylic acid, and may be tested for by adding 2 c.c. of nitric acid to 10 c.c. urine, boiling and adding 1 c.c. bromin water, which produces a precipitate. Smaller amounts are present when there is a great increase of indican.

Diazo Reaction (Ehrlich).—In typhoid fever and measles the reaction is almost constantly present; in numerous acute infections, such as acute miliary tuberculosis, scarlet fever, or erysipelas, it is often present, while in chronic tuberculosis, chronic kidney lesions, and in a few other diseases, it may occasionally be positive. To 10 c.c. sulphanilic acid solution

(5 gm. sulphanilic acid; 50 c.c. hydrochloric acid; 1000 c.c. water), add 0.5 c.c. of 0.5 per cent. sodium nitrite solution and 10 c.c. urine. Mix, and stratify with concentrated ammonia.

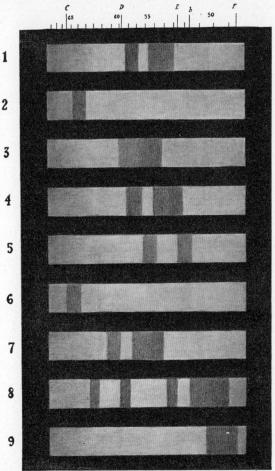

FIG. 67.—Absorption spectra. 1, Oxyhemoglobin; 2, methemoglobin; 3, reduced hemoglobin; 4, carbon monoxid hemoglobin; 5, reduced hematin; 6, hematin in acid solution; 7, hematoporphyrin in acid solution; 8, hematoporphyrin in alkaline solution; 9, urobilin.

If positive, a pink ring forms at the surface of contact, and when the mixture is shaken the foam appears pink (not yellowish or brownish red).

INORGANIC SALTS

Chlorids (Volhard).—To 5 c.c. urine (albumin-free) contained in a small Erlenmeyer flask add 20 cc.. distilled water, 10 c.c. silver nitrate solution (29.075 gm. pure silver nitrate in 1 liter water), and 2 c.c. indicator (30 c.c. water; plus 70 c.c. uncolored nitric acid, whose specific gravity is 1.2; plus excess of ferric ammonium sulphate; filter). Now run into the filtrate a standard ammonium sulphocyanate solution until the first red appears and persists when stirred. One c.c. of the silver nitrate solution is equivalent to .01 gm. sodium chlorid. The number of cubic centimeters of silver nitrate required to precipitate completely the chlorids present is 10 c.c. less the sulphocyanate added. Determine the amount of sodium chlorid in the twenty-four-hour specimen of urine. To prepare the sulphocyanate solution, dissolve 13 gm. pure ammonium sulphocyanate in water and make up to 1 liter in a volumetric flask. One c.c. of this solution is exactly equivalent to 1 c.c. of the silver nitrate solution against which it is titrated when first prepared.

The normal excretion of chlorids lies approximately between 5 gm. and 25 gm. daily, and a reduction below the minimum may by experience be determined by adding two drops of 10 per cent. silver nitrate to 10 c.c. urine in a test-tube, and noting the amount of precipitate. An excess is less readily determined in this way. In febrile conditions the chlorids are decreased and in severe fevers they are less than 2 gm. per day. A decrease below 2 gm. is especially constant in lobar pneumonia before the crisis, with a rapid rise after the crisis. In most chronic diseases chlorid elimination is decreased, but a decrease below 2 gm. is a bad prognostic sign. In the interpretation of chlorid elimination the amount of salt ingested in the food must be known.

Sulphates (Folin).—To 25 c.c. urine in a beaker add 5 c.c. concentrated hydrochloric acid, and boil very gently for fifteen minutes in order to convert ethereal sulphates into inorganic sulphates. Cool; make up to 100 c.c. with water and keeping at the boiling point, add drop by drop 15 c.c. barium chlorid (5 gm. barium chlorid; 100 c.c. water). Allow to stand for one hour; decant the clear supernatant liquid and filter the remaining liquid through a dry Gooch crucible that has been ignited, weighed on an analytical balance, and washed a number of times with 1 per cent. hydrochloric acid and finally with distilled water. Dry the precipitate; ignite, and weigh the crucible; the increase in weight is due to barium sulphate. In the twenty-four-hour specimen calculate the total amount of sulphates as sulphuric anhydrid.

The *inorganic sulphates* are determined in exactly the same way as the total sulphates, except that the boiling after the addition of the hydrochloric acid is omitted and 10 c.c. 20 per cent. sodium chlorid are added before the addition of the hydrochloric acid in order to decrease its ionization. The difference between the total sulphates and the inorganic sulphates equals the *ethereal sulphates*.

The sulphates are the product of protein metabolism and are, therefore, increased when there is an augmentation of protein destruction. The normal output varies from 1.5 gm. to 3 gm. daily. The ethereal sulphates are about one-tenth of the total.

Phosphates.—A quantitative determination of phosphates in the urine may be made by the uranium acetate method. To 50 c.c. urine in an Erlenmeyer flask add 5 c.c. of a sodium acetate solution (100 gm. sodium acetate, 100 c.c. 30 per cent. acetic acid, water ad. 1000 c.c.). Boil the mixture and run in from a buret a standard uranium acetate solution. The mixture is boiled and the uranium acetate added until no distinct precipitate is formed. Now add the uranium acetate drop by drop and test the solution after each addition by adding one drop of it to a few crystals of potassium ferrocyanid on a porcelain surface. The first appearance of a brownish red color indicates the end reaction. The uranium acetate solution is prepared by dissolving 34 gm. uranium acetate in water, adding 50 c.c. glacial acetic acid and making up to 1000 c.c. To standardize, substitute 50 c.c. of a monopotassium phosphate of such a strength that 50 c.c. contain 0.1 gm. phosphorous pentoxid for 50 c.c. urine and proceed exactly as above. The amount of uranium acetate required is equivalent to 0.1 gm.

phosphorous pentoxid. One-tenth gram divided by the amount of uranium acetate required gives the value of 1 c.c. of the uranium acetate; this value is recorded on the label of the standard solution.

Phosphates are present in the urine in amounts varying between 1 gm. and 5 gm. (phosphorous pentoxid). The ratio of the alkaline phosphates to the earthy phosphates is about 2 to 1. The elimination of phosphates is decreased in acute febrile conditions and in many chronic diseases. In conditions in which the total volume of urine is increased the total output of phosphates may be increased (so-called phosphatic diabetes). In conditions such as osteomalacia, osteoporosis, rickets, tetany, and other pathologic states associated with disturbed calcium metabolism, there is little accurate information in regard to phosphorous excretion in the urine.

Lead.—It may be desirable to examine urine for poisons. To test for lead, place for several hours a bright strip of lead-free magnesium in a flask of the urine. If the magnesium becomes coated, place the strip in dilute nitric acid for one-half hour; filter; and evaporate the filtrate to dryness. Dissolve the dry residue in 1 c.c. distilled water contained in a small serum tube, and add 2 drops potassium iodid solution which gives a yellow precipitate. For a careful determination, the lead from the twenty-four-hour sample is separated, purified, and weighed.

Mercury.—Place a coil of bright copper wire in a flask with 500 c.c. urine, 100 c.c. hydrochloric acid, and 5 c.c. potassium chlorate, and boil for one minute. If the copper tarnishes, place it at the bottom of a test-tube, and heat when the mercury condenses as globules on the cold glass above. In important cases, the qualitative test is confirmed by more accurate chemical methods, and the amount of mercury in the twenty-four-hour sample determined.

URINARY SEDIMENT

Most of the solid waste material of the body is excreted in the urine; but the solids are in solution at the time they pass into the kidney tubules, and under normal conditions usually remain in solution until voided. Thus the only morphologic elements present in normal urine when voided may be considered as accidental and to come from the lining of the genito-urinary passages. The presence of extraneous material introduced into the urine through handling must be kept in mind (Fig. 69). When voided, a perfectly normal urine may be slightly alkaline and cloudy from precipitated phosphates present. This is seen especially after ingestion of large amounts of vegetable acids.

The collection and preservation of urine to be examined, and the method of obtaining sediment must be carefully performed; and since the organized sediment is first affected by careless technic, these points are taken up under that heading.

The Unorganized Sediment of Acid Urine.—The reaction of the urine is the important factor in determining the precipitation of the inorganic constituents. Usually, freshly voided urine is slightly acid owing to the presence of acid phosphates. On standing a short time, there separates out—in addition to the nubecula, which consists of mucin and accidental cells—biurates (quadriurates?) of sodium (and potassium), and, later, uric acid. The separation of calcium oxalate is common, but very irregular in its occurrence. Calcium sulphate and monocalcium phosphate are other inorganic constituents that may separate out. Of these, uric acid and oxalates are crystalline, while calcium sulphate and monocalcium phosphate may rarely be present as rosettes of needles.

Urates (biruates [quadriurates?] of sodium and potassium) are likely to be present in a concentrated urine that is acid at the time of examination. The amorphous deposit due to urates is yellowish or reddish yellow, owing to the absorption of uroerythrin from the urine; while phosphate deposits are white or slightly darkened. On warming, urate precipitates dissolve; while phosphate precipitates remain unchanged by the heat but are dissolved by the addition of a small amount of acetic acid. Under the microscope the urates appear as fine granules which may present a slightly brownish tinge.

Uric acid (Fig. 68) occurs in concentrated acid urine as a deposit that is smaller, denser, and redder than a urate deposit. Such a deposit does not dissolve on warming, but is immediately brought into solution by the addition of a few drops of normal sodium hydrate. Urate and uric acid deposits are often present in the same urine. Under the microscope, whetstone crystals are most common. By applying the murexid test to uric acid deposits a deep purple is obtained. The kind and amount

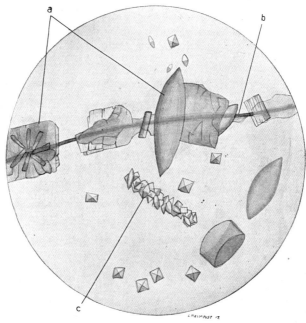

Fig. 68.—*a*, Uric acid crystals which have formed on a cotton thread, *b*; *c*, calcium oxalate pseudocast many of which are present in this urine sediment.

of inorganic sediment in the urine gives no clue to the amount of these substances that is excreted. For example, a large sediment of uric acid and urates, may form in a urine, while at the same time the urine itself may contain a diminished amount of uric acid. An individual who continuously excretes a urine from which uric acid separates out has at least one of the elements usually present in the formation of vesical and renal calculi.

Calcium Oxalate.—The colorless octahedral crystals are characteristic, occasionally the crystallization is less typical and hour-glass like forms are assumed. The crystals are dissolved by dilute mineral acids but not by dilute acetic acid. Monosodium phosphate and magnesium are accredited with the property of holding the oxalates in solution; certainly it is constantly being excreted in the urine (25 mg. per day) and only at rare intervals forms crystals. The oxalates are ingested in vegetables such as tomatoes and spinach and in fruits and grains. They pass into the urine in solution and if precipitation takes place, the crystals are formed in the urinary

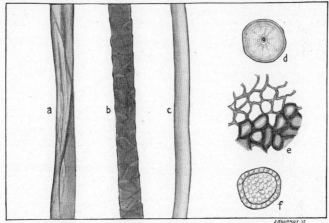

FIG. 69.—Vegetable cells and fibers drawn with high-dry lens. *a*, Cotton fiber; *b*, wool fiber; *c*, silk fiber; *d*, cork cell; *e*, vegetable cells; *f*, lycopodium spore.

tract. That the formation of crystals may take place in the kidney tubules is strongly suggested by the shape of some crystalline masses. In about one-fourth of vesical calculi oxalate crystals are present and some calculi consist almost entirely of the crystals. Aside from calculus formation, *oxaluria* is of little significance. Oxalic acid is estimated quantitatively by repeated crystallizations as calcium oxalate which is determined gravimetrically as calcium oxid after ignition.

Calcium sulphate in the form of elongated plates or needles may precipitate from very acid urine. This salt is not soluble in dilute acids; it is only occasionally present.

Monocalcium phosphates are found in highly acid urines only. They are colorless, and are soluble in dilute acetic acid.

Creatinin.—Besides the inorganic salts, certain other unorganized substances may be present in acid urine. Creatinin has been observed in the urine as lozenge-shaped crystals after violent muscular exercise.

Hippuric acid crystals may appear after the administration of benzoic acid as needle-like crystals arranged in sheaths, insoluble in dilute acetic acid.

Cystin.—This is one of the amino acids and occurs as hexagonal plates soluble in hydrochloric acid, which distinguishes them from uric acid crystals. Like alkaptonuria, cystinuria is usually looked upon as a metabolic anomaly. The excretion of cystin predisposes to calculus formation. The crystals may be present in neutral or alkaline urine.

Leucin and *tyrosin* have been found in the urine in acute yellow atrophy and in phosphorous poisoning; less constantly, in severe small-pox; and especially in yellow and typhoid fevers. Tyrosin occurs as needles, and leucin as refractive spherules. The leucin spherules show a radiating appearance about the periphery that differentiates them from fat globules. *Homogentisic acid* (Fig. 70) which is probably derived from tyrosin or phenylalanine does not separate from urine as crystals.

Fat globules present may result from decomposition of fat-containing epithelial cells or leukocytes. In chyluria it is present in a very fine state of division.

Cholesterin has on rare occasions been found in the urine in cystic conditions of the kidney.

Hematoidin is probably the same as bilirubin, and crystals are not uncommonly present in a deeply icteric urine.

The Unorganized Sediment of Alkaline Urine.—In urine that, when voided, has an alkaline reaction not due to ammonia, there is apt to be a clouding due to di- and tri-calcium and magnesium phosphates, and to calcium and magnesium carbonate. These compounds are amorphous. On application of heat the clouding is increased somewhat due to the changing of acid salts into more basic forms. Dilute acetic acid dissolves the precipitate; carbonic acid gas is evolved from the carbonate granules.

On standing for several hours, especially in a warm place, urine undergoes alkaline fermentation and becomes alkaline in reaction from the ammonia formed by the decomposition of urea. In ammoniacal urine, in addition to the inorganic substances mentioned as occurring in urine made alkaline by fixed alkalies, ammonium biurate and ammonium-magnesium phosphate deposits are present. It is this ammoniacal fermen-

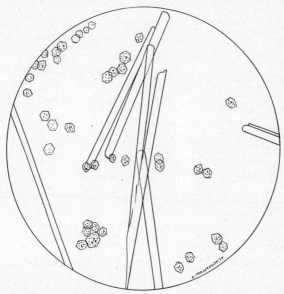

FIG. 70.—Hexagonal and needle-like crystals of homogentisic acid purified from the urine of a case of alkaptonuria. (Drawn from a preparation loaned by Prof. C. J. Farmer.) On standing the needles disappear and the six-sided crystals become much larger.

tation that destroys organized sediments so rapidly. Often in inflammatory conditions of the bladder such fermentation may take place before the urine is voided. In fresh urine in cases of acidosis large amounts of ammonium salts may be present.

Ammonium biurate is the only urate deposit found in alkaline urine. The deposit is usually amorphous, but thorn-apple spherules frequently form. Such a deposit is normal in urine that is not fresh.

Ammonium-magnesium phosphate crystals (coffin-lid or triple phosphate crystals) indicate that the specimen after being voided has undergone an alkaline fermentation or that this fermentation has taken place in the genito-urinary tract. The only exception is the occasional presence of the crystals in the freshly voided acid or alkaline urine of individuals suffering with a severe acidosis. They are, therefore, only of clinical significance in urine immediately after it has been voided.

Tri- and di-calcium and tri- and di-magnesium phosphates may form *amorphous phosphate* precipitates in ammoniacal urine as well as in urine made alkaline by fixed alkalies. Calcium carbonate is also amorphous, but the addition of acid causes the evolution of gas from it.

Urinary Concretions.—Uric acid calculi (large) or gravel (small) comprise about three-fourths of the urinary concretions. They are usually rather small and have a yellowish or reddish color. Calcium oxalate concretions may be small, jagged, and of a dark color due to the presence of blood, or they may be larger mulberry-like masses; while the phosphatic calculi found in the bladder are quite likely to be larger and rather soft. Cystin stones are common in cases of cystinuria.

Organized Sediment.—As mentioned previously, the urine as it passes into the kidney tubules contains solids in solution only. It has also been shown in the preceding pages how certain of the unorganized solids may precipitate out in the lower passages, or after the urine is voided. In distinction to unorganized sediment, that which is organized includes tissue cells and morphologic structures, such as casts or cylindroids. Owing to the great variations in size and shape of the various elements that may be present, it is important to distinguish extraneous matter that may be present such as fibers, vegetable cells, and the like (Fig. 69). Contaminations from the rectum (see under feces) are common. Scratches on a cover-glass or slide, or other artefacts, are constantly kept in mind while making microscopic examinations.

In the passage of the urine from the glomerulus to the external urethral meatus certain formed elements may normally wash into it, namely, mucus, epithelial cells, an occasional leukocyte, and spermatozoa. Pathologically, neutrophilic and endothelial leukocytes, red blood corpuscles, and parasites may pass into the urine from the vessels or casts may be formed in the kidney tubules.

Examination of Urinary Sediments.—Chemical urinary examinations were formerly of greater importance in metabolic studies of normal and pathologic conditions than they are at the present time. This is due to the advent of a number of satisfactory methods for the quantitative determination in the blood plasma of substances excreted through the kidneys. As a result, aside from tests for albumin and sugar the most to be gained from a urine examination is in regard to conditions in the genito-urinary apparatus, and local changes here frequently lead to the introduction of abnormal morphologic elements into the urine.

The *tonicity of urine* has a wide range of variation; and, since non-living elements present undergo rapid changes with these variations, it is important to examine urine as soon as possible after it has been excreted by the kidney. Specimens obtained by ureteral catheterization are always of interest if brought directly to the laboratory. If it is not possible to secure a fresh specimen, formalin may be added; but it is better to have the patient urinate into about 1-oz. of Hayem's solution contained in a perfectly clean 4-oz. bottle. Urine preserved in this way cannot be used for albumin tests. If cultures are to be made, the bottle must be sterile and no preservative is permissible.

To examine microscopically, centrifuge the fresh specimen in a 15-c.c. centrifuge tube. With a small capillary pipette remove the sediment by holding the finger over the upper end of the tube until a small amount of sediment has entered the tip of the pipet and place a single drop on the center of a clean slide. Apply a No. 1, 22-mm. square cover-glass, and examine with the high-dry lens after swinging out the substage condenser and cutting the light down to a twilight. Such an examination of fresh unstained sediment usually serves for the identification of the elements present.

To stain, centrifuge, pipet off the supernatant urine; add saline; shake, and again centrifuge. Repeat the washing twice; make smears on cover-glasses by placing a bit of the sediment on one of the covers by means of a capillary pipette and proceeding as with blood films except that the diluted stain is allowed to act for ten minutes (page 49); or, better still, dry in the air; fix for ten minutes in methyl alcohol or in absolute alcohol-ether, and stain with protozoon stain. Since cells may undergo rapid changes in morphology in urine, the patient should be given a pint of water, the bladder emptied and the first urine collecting in the bladder at once voided into a small beaker.

Preservation of Urinary Sediments.—The preservation of unorganized urinary crystals is not easy, but is of some importance in teaching. A large amount of the urine is centrifuged at a high rate of speed in 100 c.c. centrifuge tubes, and the sediment evaporated to dryness in a vacuum. The dry sediment is pulverized and placed in a tightly stoppered tube. By using different specimens, all the precipitates found in an acid urine may be combined and preserved in this way. For student study, a small amount of the dry sediment is added to acid urine and examined. In the same way the precipitates of alkaline urines may be obtained and preserved. To make permanent microscopic preparations, the dry powder is placed with a drop of glycerin beneath a cover-glass and the cover-glass ringed with asphalt.

To preserve casts and other organized sediment, large amounts of the urine are centrifuged, the urine is decanted, and a number of volumes of Müller's fluid added. After two weeks it is centrifuged, water is added, and it is then centrifuged again. The water is siphoned off, and 50 per cent. glycerin that contains 2 per cent. phenol is added. A small drop of the sediment may be placed on a slide under a cover-glass, ringed with asphalt and kept permanently.

Epithelial Cells.—It is not possible to name the source of all the separate epithelial cells found in urine sediment, and too positive statements in this regard are frequently not convincing. A great increase in the number of examinations of specimens obtained by ureteral catheterization has made possible the separation of certain types of cells coming from the kidney tubules and from the kidney pelvis and ureters. The cells from the uriniferous tubules are about one-third larger than neutrophiles (pus cells), while those from the pelvis of the kidney and ureter are about twice the size of pus cells. In sediment of voided urine, cells from the glands of the prostate are identical with those from the ureters. The former are abundant in prostatitis, and the latter are numerous in inflammations of the pelvis such as ·those due to renal concretions. Cells from the seminal vesicle are small, narrow and non-ciliated, and those from the ejaculatory ducts are small, narrow, ciliated cells. When a pathologic condition is suspected, these two varieties of cells, as well as those from the prostate, are examined for in urine passed after thorough prostatic massage, which is compared with that obtained before massage. In the female, cells like those from the prostate may come from the Bartholinian glands, and small ciliated cells may come from the uterus.

From the larger cavities, the flat epithelial cells from the bladder are larger than those from the urethra, while those from the vagina are largest of all. Caudate cells from the bladder, ureters, or pelvis of the kidney are said to be increased in inflammations of these surfaces. Since the same type of cell may vary greatly in size in different specimens of urine, relative sizes are always studied rather than actual measurements.

Pus.—An occasional leukocyte may be found in almost any sediment, but the presence of a few pus cells indicates some inflammatory process. The leukocytes are usually neutrophiles (pus cells), and they have finely granular cytoplasm with polymorphous nuclei that are well brought out by allowing 2 per cent. acetic acid to flow under the cover. Usually the leukocytes present abnormalities, and in alkaline urine they quickly break up forming sticky gelatinous masses if many are present. If a large amount of pus is present, the condition is spoken of as *pyuria*. Without doubt, endothelial leukocytes appear in the sediment in those genito-urinary inflammations, in which this is the chief reacting cell. This variety of leukocyte containing blood pigment unquestionably is present at times. Lymphocytes are said to be present in chronic Bright's disease. In studying the morphology of cells in the urine a more careful technic than that ordinarily used must be employed (page 276).

It is desirable to determine the source of the pus, and this is best cleared up by cystoscopic examination, ureteral catheterization, massage of the prostate, and so forth. An accurate study of the variety of leukocytes in the urine has been neglected. In cases of urethritis, pus may be pressed from the urethra; while massage of these seminal vesicles and prostate may force pus from the structures into the urethra. In the female, contamination of the specimen with leukorrheal discharge is common unless it is obtained by catheterization of the bladder. In the absence of contradictory evidence, casts indicate that pus comes from the kidney, and the character of the epithelial cells may aid in determining the source of the pus. If a considerable amount of pus is present, albumin at least in traces may be demonstrated. It is stated that 0.1 per cent. albumin results from the presence of 100,000 leukocytes per 2. c.c. urine (Posner). The 24-hour sample is preserved with formalin, shaken and the leukocytes counted in the blood counting chamber. An additional amount of albumin is due to Bright's disease.

Suppurative nephritis, non-suppurative nephritis, pyelonephritis, pyelitis, pyonephrosis, renal calculus, renal tuberculosis, tuberculous and non-tuberculous cystitis, vesical stone, and gonorrheal infections of the genito-urinary tract are conditions in which pus is present in the urine.

Blood.—During the menstrual discharge, the red blood corpuscles usually find their way into the urine but, except for such accidental contamination, blood in the urine is abnormal. A cloudiness (smokiness) is produced by small amounts of blood, but a reddish tinge follows the mixture of many corpuscles with the urine. Plasma escapes with the corpuscles, and the albumin content of the urine increases with the blood present. If a certain amount of hemoglobin (about one-sixtieth of the total) is in solution in the plasma (hemoglobinemia), it appears in the urine (hemoglobinuria) where it may be detected by the chemical reactions for blood.

Hematuria implies the escape of blood in the urine, shown, on microscopic examination, by the presence of corpuscles. If the urine is alkaline, the corpuscles must be identified soon after they pass into it, for their solution is rapid. Fibrin and small clots are commonly found in fresh hemorrhage per rhexin such as may be produced by a renal calculus.

Acute toxic nephritis, acute infectious nephritis, renal calculus, renal tuberculosis, trauma, and tumors of the kidney are common causes of the escape of blood into the upper part of the urinary tract; and it is in the two first-named conditions that blood casts of the tubules are more likely to be present. Embolism, mechanical injury, and intoxication with cantharides and turpentine may cause bleeding. In cases of vesical stone, bladder tuberculosis or cancer, hemorrhage from the bladder is common. The cystoscope and ureteral catheterization usually clear up the source of blood.

Casts (Fig. 71).—They are formed from substances within the tubules of the kidney. The source of the cementing substance, or of the substance that does not clearly consist of morphologic elements such as red blood corpuscles, is probably not the same in all cases. For instance, in many cases of chronic nephropathies the cells of the uriniferous tubules contain very large spherules of colloid, which correspond in structure and tinctorial reactions to the substance of *hyaline casts*, and this hyaline material is found in sections properly fixed and stained to protrude from the cell and to merge into typical casts filling the tubules. In some granular casts a reaction may be obtained for fibrin, and it appears that such casts may result from a disintegration of blood corpuscles, pus, and epithelial cells that have been glued together in the tubules by a fibrinous coagulation of blood constituents. A common view of the *origin of some casts* is that they result from a precipitation of albumin, and it is not definitely established that colloidal substances may not be precipitated by the salt concentrations present within the tubules.

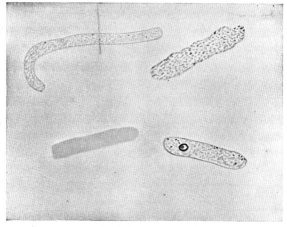

a

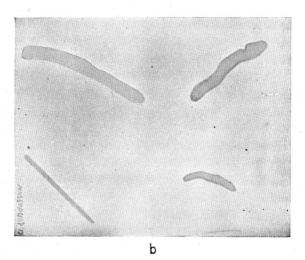

b

FIG. 71.—Sediment from a case of acute nephritis (high-dry lens). *a*, Three granular and one hyaline cast; *b*, four hyaline casts.

The appearance of casts may follow the slightest injury that can be done to the kidney, and over long periods of time an occasional cast may be present in the urine sediment of individuals who show no nephritis at autopsy. But owing to the fact that casts are not found in the vast majority of individuals in usual health, their presence always deserves careful consideration; and, of course, in most cases they signify some degree of nephritis. A few casts may be present without albumin. It is only in cases of nephritis that large numbers of casts are for many days present. In general it may be said that casts are more numerous in acute nephritis and in *chronic parenchymatous nephritis* (so called; see page 422) than in *chronic interstitial nephritis* so called.

The type of cast may throw some light on the nature of the affection. Hyaline casts alone are more common in cases of arteriosclerotic kidneys and in scleroses following glomerular affections, but are present in large numbers along with *cellular casts* (blood, epithelial, and granular) in acute nephritis. Granular casts often become more numerous after the lesion has persisted for a few weeks. One would expect to meet with epithelial casts more commonly in cases of tubular nephritis (mercury, diphtheria). Pus casts, as well as blood casts, occur in those cases in which these elements exist in the urine in greatest abundance. *Waxy casts* are more refractive than hyaline casts and may give the amyloid reaction. They are present in amyloid disease and in cases of marked sclerosis, and are not commonly found in acute and subacute lesions. There is probably a waxy cast of a composition different from that of a hyaline cast but in the usual untreated fresh preparation it is not easy to differentiate the two. *Fat casts* may be formed in cases in which there is a large amount of fat in the pus and epithelial cells escaping into the tubules.

Cylindroids are hyaline in character, but differ from casts in that one or both ends taper, and also in their great length. They appear to be mucus from the upper urinary passages, and do not have entirely the same significance as casts; but they should be recorded when positively identified.

Mucous threads are present in normal urine and are best seen in the nubecula. They appear to be of the same composition as cylindroids, but are larger and longer, and they branch and are frayed at the ends. These are normal, while typical cylindroids are not.

So-called *false and pseudocasts* are more or less accidental formations, taking the shape of casts by adherence to mucous threads, cotton fibers, and in other ways. Urates are commonly found in yellowish masses that resemble casts somewhat, and phosphate deposits may be similarly grouped. Pus may be arranged in tubular form, and bacteria may mass together in urine that has stood for a while. Oxalate crystals not uncommonly form cylindrical masses.

Prostatic plugs with spermatozoa imbedded in them, together with *corpora amylacea* occur in the urine after prostatic massage. The latter color with iodine and show concentric lamellations. *Sago bodies* the size of a small pea, consisting of colloid material and spermatozoa, may come from the seminal vesicles. *Spermatozoa*, are present in large numbers in massage-urine.

Clap Threads.—These macroscopic shreds, 1 mm. in diameter and a number of millimeters in length, are from various parts of the urethral mucosa and may come from the prostate. They should be identified in urine immediately after being voided. They consist of pus and epithelial cells in varying proportions stuck together with mucus, are pathologic, and constitute an important sign of urethritis. Small masses, macroscopically similar to the above, may occasionally be found in normal individuals, but on microscopic examination they do not consist of pus cells.

There is little question but what *connective tissue* is voided with the urine in tuberculosis of the kidney, and in sloughing vesical cancers (malignant papillomas); and particles resembling connective tissue, when found in carefully catheterized specimens, deserve a careful investigation. Tumor cells may also be voided with the urine, but their identification is practically impossible unless held together to form a small mass of tumor tissue.

Embryos of filaria and the eggs of Bilharzia (see under feces, page 312) may be found in the urine.

Bacteria in the Urine.—The catheterized specimen in a sterile container is centrifuged in sterile centrifuge tubes, washed with sterile saline, and the sediment examined. The amount of inorganic and organic salts in the urine is enough to interfere seriously with the staining of the sediment. It is advisable as a routine to decant as much of the urine as possible after centrifugation, fill the tube with sterile saline, and again centrifuge. Cultures are made before the centrifugation; smears for stains afterward. Gram's stain is used as a routine, but if a study of the cells is desired the sediment is stained with a polychrome blood stain. The pyogenic cocci, typhoid bacillus, and colon bacillus are some of the common organisms met with. Cultures on Endo's medium are best for isolating typhoid and colon bacilli. The typhoid and paratyphoid bacilli do not change the color of the medium, while a pinkish zone appears about colonies of colon bacilli.

Tubercle Bacilli in the Urine.—In localizing the infection, specimens are frequently obtained by ureteral catheterization. "Right" or "left ureter" is written on the brown slip, as well as requests for guinea-pig inoculations. The specimen may be obtained by having the patient void into a sterile container after massage of the prostate. In all cases in which the urine is voided, care must be exercised in cleansing thoroughly the external genitals, if direct microscopic examination is to be depended upon for identification of the bacilli, and if the patient is a female, it is always better to obtain the specimen by catheterization. There is no question that smegma bacilli are less alcohol-fast than tubercle bacilli; but a relative factor that may vary with the thickness of the preparation and the degree of fixation can scarcely be relied upon for an absolute diagnosis.

To make the examination, centrifuge in a sterile centrifuge tube, decant the supernatant fluid; place the sediment on a slide, and stain by the Ziehl-Neelsen method. If no tubercle bacilli and few streptococci are found on microscopic examination, a guinea-pig may be injected. If streptococci are present in numbers, the sediment is diluted with sterile freshly distilled water and heated at 60°C. for ten minutes and again centrifuged.

In the right groin of a 250-gm. guinea-pig inject subcutaneously one-half a cubic centimeter of the sediment remaining in
the bottom of the centrifuge tube, and one-half a cubic centimeter
intraperitoneally. Autopsy at the end of six weeks. Examine
the tissue of the right groin, spleen, liver, lung and peritoneal
surfaces macroscopically and microscopically in celloidin sections
for tubercles; examine smears of these organs stained by the
Ziehl-Neelsen method for tubercle bacilli.

It is stated that satisfactory results are obtained if the tissues
in the groin are extensively crushed before injection by means
of hemostatic forceps, and the autopsy performed in three weeks
instead of six. Typical tuberculosis develops more rapidly if
the guinea-pigs are subjected to x-ray treatments. For convenience, the animal is given a single maximum exposure.

Guinea-pig inoculation is employed with material other than
urine, such as feces, surgical tissue, serous fluids, and the like,
either when the number of bacilli is too small to be recognized
microscopically, or when it is necessary to resort to the procedure to rule out acid-fast bacilli other than tubercle bacilli.
Such material usually requires preparatory treatment by the
antiformin or Petroff method. Tubercle bacillus is the only
acid-fast organism that produces tubercles in the guinea-pig.

Animal Parasites.—The embryos of *filaria bancrofti* may be
found in the urine. · Chyluria is usually present. The diagnosis
is confirmed by the examination of the blood. The ova of
schistosoma hematobium with their characteristic spine may be
found in Bilharzia infection. *Trichomonas vaginalis* may enter
the urine from the vagina, and occasionally from the urinary
bladder.

GASTRIC CONTENTS

GASTRIC JUICE AND TEST MEALS

The variety and quality of the food, as well as the changes it undergoes in its passage to the stomach, alter the character of gastric juice. Constant *insufficient mastication* resulting from stomatitis, poor teeth, or weakness of the muscles used in chewing may cause gastric disturbances, because the imperfectly masticated particles may mechanically injure the stomach mucosa, or the gross particles that cannot be acted upon by the ferments may give rise to irritating chemical substances. *Pathologic saliva* has a deleterious effect on gastric digestion. The diminished flow of saliva seen in fevers, in paralysis of the chorda tympani and in some cardiorenal cases, may reduce the quantity of starch digested, while ptyalism, such as occurs in mercurial poisoning, in bulbar paralysis, or from reflex nervous stimulation, may render the food too alkaline, neutralize the gastric juice to too great a degree and produce abnormal changes in this secretion.

The food may be interrupted in its passage to the stomach by stenoses from scar tissue or ulcers, from cancer, or from pressure from without by tumors, aneurism, or inflammatory exudates. Secondary dilatation followed by hypertrophy of the muscularis takes place above the stenosis. The regurgitated food in these cases differs from vomitus in that it shows no action of the gastric secretion. After the food reaches the stomach, the local conditions that alter its character are numerous, and there is scarcely any examination in which such a close correlation between laboratory and clinical findings is required as in examination of the gastric contents.

Vomitus may serve for the demonstration of blood, but its examination is not of much value otherwise. A mere trace of blood in vomitus may come from the mucosa as a result of the

285

violent muscular effort. In ulcers of the stomach, vomiting with relief of pain may occur at the height of digestion. During violent vomiting, bile is forced from the duodenum into the stomach, especially after the stomach has been emptied. Fecal vomiting occurs in complete obstruction of the ileum or colon.

FIG. 72.—Use of stomach tube. After insertion of the stomach tube lower the end *a*, compress bulb *b*, pinch off at *a*, and release bulb to make suction. Protect patient with rubber apron.

If food is vomited six hours or more after a meal the motility of the stomach is diminished.

Suitable material for chemical and microscopic examination is obtained by "passing" the stomach tube (Fig. 72). This is done in the morning before any food or drink has been taken (fasting stomach), one hour after a test breakfast (bread-water breakfast), or four hours after a test dinner (meat dinner).

Fasting Stomach.—Pure gastric juice can be obtained from experimental animals, but in man it is mixed with food particles. Occasionally in human cases with gastric fistulæ the secretion may be obtained quite pure and in such individuals the *amount* collected in twenty-four hours has been found to be about 1.5 liters and the acidity about 0.4 per cent. The *normal acidity* is due to hydrochloric acid, which is present as such, or is united more or less closely with basic substances, especially with proteins or hydrolytic protein products. Pepsin and rennin zymogens are secreted into the stomach, except in cancer, certain atrophic conditions, and certain neuroses. There may be present considerable mucus swallowed from the mouth. If more than 100 c.c. (8 to 50 in one case with permanent gastric fistula studied by Carlson) are obtained when the stomach tube is passed in the morning, there is retention or hypersecretion, and gross or microscopic food particles should be looked for. The maximum capacity of a normal stomach is about 1.5 liters. If the excessive amount is due to hypersecretion, few or no food particles are found. If *deficient motility* is suspected, a jam containing small seeds such as those of the raspberry may be given the previous night and the seeds examined for in the contents removed the following morning. Titrate the acidity and examine for lactic acid according to the directions given under chemical examination after a bread-water breakfast (page 290). The percentage of acid may be normal or decreased, but it is not increased above that found in normal individuals (0.5 per cent.).

Bread-water Breakfast.—Give one shredded wheat biscuit (Dock) and exactly 1 pint of water or weak tea without sugar or cream, and introduce the stomach tube at the end of one hour. One ounce of white (wheat) bread is by some substituted for the shredded wheat biscuit (Ewald). If there is any question of motor insufficiency the stomach is emptied by lavage the preceding night. With normal motility there is obtained less than 100 c.c. of odorless, colorless fluid containing particles of the carbohydrate food given.

Bile forced up from the duodenum gives to the contents a yellow or green color. Blood may be fresh, but more often is partially digested, and gives to the contents the "coffee-grounds" appearance so .commonly seen when blood is present in considerable amounts. A small amount of perfectly fresh blood of a bright red color may be present from mechanical injury produced by the tube. Lactic, butyric, and other organic acids give a sour odor. A putrid odor may result from necrotic stomach wall or from protein decomposition of retained food. An excess of mucus is shown by the tenaciousness of the material when the contents are poured upon the filter.

Meat Dinner (Riegel).—At noon give the patient a plate of clear broth, one-third of a pound of beefsteak, a small amount of mashed potato, and 1 roll. In four hours introduce a stomach tube. If the stomach has emptied itself in this time its motor power is good; and on the following day the tube is used three hours after the administration of a similar dinner.

Although the macroscopic examination is of little importance after a test-breakfast, the material recovered after a meat dinner shows the effect of gastric digestion and should be carefully inspected. Undigested meat indicates deficient gastric digestion, although there are only a comparatively few particles of it. In *achylia* many coarse pieces of meat are present. In *hyperacidity* there may be no meat fragments; but on sedimenting in a conical glass a granular layer of starch settles out at the bottom, while on the surface a foaming layer may be present, due to fermentation by yeasts and sarcines. Air-containing mucus from the respiratory tract must be recognized. In a normal stomach there may remain on chemical examination only a small amount of almost completely digested food with a trace of free hydrochloric acid. The chemical examination is carried out as in the case of a bread-water breakfast. Conclusions from single examinations are not reliable, and several test meals are given with variations to meet the existing conditions.

MICROSCOPIC EXAMINATION OF GASTRIC CONTENTS

Filter the entire amount of material obtained by means of the stomach tube into a 100-c.c. graduate, using a 10-cm. funnel. Make a microscopic examination of the sediment on the filter. *Starch granules* show concentric laminations. *Fat* globules are highly refractive. *Blood corpuscles* are not commonly seen, as they rapidly disappear in the stomach contents. The nuclei of *pus cells* may persist after the cytoplasm has disappeared. *Budding yeasts* and yeasts in large numbers are not normally present, while *sarcines* are abnormal. An abundant proliferation of microörganisms in the stomach is dependent almost entirely on stagnation of food there. If the amount of hydrochloric acid is normal—or only moderately decreased, as in benign stasis—carbohydrate fermentation by yeasts and sarcines, with liberation of carbon dioxid and hydrogen, takes place; while in malignant disease with a great diminution of hydrochloric acid, bacilli that produce lactic acid (Oppler-Boas bacilli) may be present, since they find suitable conditions for growth; putrefaction together with an enormous multiplication of many other varieties of bacteria may take place. A condition other than carcinoma, producing stagnation and anacidity, likewise gives a soil suitable for the growth of lactic acid-producing bacilli. Bacteria do not multiply to any great extent as long as the motility is normal, even if there is an anacidity. A diminution in the normal acidity of the stomach is one of the most potent factors in the production of increased intestinal putrefaction.

Portions of *carcinoma* may be removed through the stomach tube, but frequently the tissue is not large enough to enable a certain diagnosis. If a bacteriologic examination is to be made, the stomach should be thoroughly washed with a dilute carbonate solution; several hours later it is washed again with a small amount of the solution, which is centrifuged as soon as recovered and the sediment examined in smears. Cultures of the sediment may be made.

19

CHEMICAL EXAMINATION OF GASTRIC CONTENTS

One gram of the solid material on the filter and 1 c.c. of the filtrate are placed together in a test-tube and examined for *occult blood* by the guaiac test (page 303), while the remaining chemical tests are performed on the filtrate. Test the filtrate with blue litmus paper. The reaction is uncommonly alkaline for organic acids and acid salts as well as the hydrochloric acid reacts acid to litmus.

Günzberg's Test for Free Hydrochloric Acid.—Make a preliminary test for free hydrochloric acid by placing in the filtrate *Congo-red* paper, which is turned from a red to a blue color by free hydrochloric acid. Organic acids do not give a distinct blue. Günzberg's reagent reacts to a smaller amount of mineral acid than Congo-red paper, and is made by adding 5 drops of the filtrate to 5 drops of Günzberg's reagent contained in a small porcelain dish which is evaporated to dryness on a water-bath. A bright red color (obtained with 0.01 per cent. hydrochloric acid in water) shows the presence of a mineral acid. The reagent, which keeps for two months and must not be older, is prepared by dissolving 2 gm. phloroglucin and 1 gm. vanillin in 30 c.c. absolute alcohol.

Sahli's Test for Achylia.—Place a 3-mm. pill containing 0.05 gm. methylene blue held in extract of glycyrrhiza at the center of a small bit of dentist's rubber dam, twist the rubber into a neck, and tie the neck with three turns of oo catgut soaked in water until soft, leaving about 3 mm. of free rubber margin beyond the catgut. Give the pill with a full meal, and examine the urine in five, ten, and twenty hours later for a greenish color, or a greenish color after the addition of 20 per cent. acetic acid and boiling. The gut should be digested in twenty hours or less. This test is useful in such conditions as cancer or pernicious anemia when hydrochloric acid is absent, and, if positive, indicates achylia.

Quantitative Estimation of the Free Hydrochloric, Bound Hydrochloric, and Total Acidity.—

Phenolphthalein

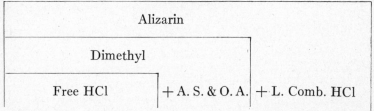

Place 5-c.c. gastric filtrate in a 30-c.c. Erlenmeyer flask which rests on white filter paper; add 1 drop (not more) dimethylamidoazobenzol (½ per cent. alcoholic solution), and run in decinormal sodium hydrate until the bright red color is lost and a yellowish color appears. If there is no free hydrochloric acid, no red color is developed when the indicator is added (Töpfer's test). If, for example, 1-c.c. tenth-normal alkali is required to discharge the red color, then 1 × 20 or 20 c.c. decinormal alkali would be required to neutralize 100 c.c. of the filtrate, using the dimethyl as an indicator. The amount of decinormal alkali required to neutralize 100 c.c. of the gastric juice is taken as the numerical expression of the acidity (so-called acidity per cent.), and in this case the free hydrochloric acid would be 20. Normally, it varies between about 20 and 40. Now add 1 drop phenolphthalein (½ per cent. alcoholic solution) and continue to run in the tenth-normal alkali until the first tinge of pink appears and persists. The presence of carbonates and ammonia introduces a large error. The number of cubic centimeters of alkali required to produce the pink multiplied by twenty represents the total acidity, and this lies between 40 and 70 as a rule.

To a second 5 c.c. of the filtrates add 1 drop sodium alizarin monosulphonate (1 per cent. aqueous solution), and run in the tenth-normal alkali until the first tinge of violet appears. This indicator titrates the organic acids and acid salts in addition to the free hydrochloric acid. The difference, then, between the alizarin titration and the dimethyl titration gives the organic acids and acid salts (A. S. & O. A.) (about 4). The estimation of the organic acids and acid salts by this method is of doubtful value and in the absence of free hydrochloric acid is often an entirely impossible one. Lactic acid reacts to the dimethyl and is the chief source of error. The difference between the total acidity and the alizarin titration gives the loosely combined hydrochloric acid (L. Comb. HCl).

If hydrochloric acid is absent by the Günzberg's test, the deficit of this acid may be determined by adding decinormal hydrochloric acid to 5-c.c. filtrate, until Congo-red paper is turned blue. The number of cubic centimeters required to produce this change in 100 c.c. filtrate may be used as a numerical expression.

Lactic Acid (Kelling).—If the total acidity is high and free hydrochloric acid is absent, organic acids are present; and of these lactic acid is the most important. Acetic, butyric, and valeric acids, as well as lactic acid, may be formed by bacteria in the stomach; and these acids may be recognized by their rancid odor, while lactic is odorless. They have the same significance as lactic acid. When the amount of hydrochloric acid is low or absent and the food remains in the stomach for an abnormally long time, varieties of long bacilli, including those of the *Oppler-Boas* type (Fig. 75) which split carbohydrates to form lactic and other fatty acids, find a favorable habitat in the stomach. Although there is an anacidity, these bacilli do not proliferate to any great extent provided the food passes through the stomach in the usual time.

To test for lactic acid, place 14 c.c. distilled water in a test-tube, and add 1 c.c. gastric filtrate and 1 drop 10 per cent. ferric chlorid. To a second tube of exactly the same size add 15 c.c. and 1 drop 10 per cent. ferric chlorid. If lactic acid is present, a canary-yellow color develops in the first tube. This is seen by looking straight into the mouth of the tube against a white background, and comparing this tube with the one that contains ferric chlorid alone. This test is delicate and lactic acid must be excluded from the test meal. Glucose, alcohol, citric acid, cane sugar, tartaric acid, and other less common substances, give the reaction. Bread-water breakfast cannot be used, but the Dock test breakfast (page 287) usually does not contain sufficient lactic acid to give a positive reaction.

Strauss' Test.—Perform the test as indicated in Fig. 73. If 0.1 per cent. lactic acid is present, a canary color appears in the water. The extraction eliminates most of the substances mentioned in the preceding paragraph which give the same color with ferric chlorid. If reasonable care is used in selecting the test meal, this reaction indicates a pathologic formation of lactic acid in the stomach. This test is more satisfactory than the older *Uffelmann's test,* which is made by mixing 15 c.c. 1 per cent. phenol, 2 drops 10 per cent. ferric chlorid, and 1 c.c. gastric filtrate in a tube, and examining for a yellow color against a white background.

Pepsin.—By suction, fill capillary glass tubes, 2 mm. in diameter and 20 cm. long, with egg white, and plug the ends with bread crumbs. Boil them for five minutes. Preserve the tubes in glycerin. To test for pepsin or its zymogen, dilute 1 c.c. gastric contents in a 30-c.c. Erlenmeyer flask with 15 c.c. twentieth normal hydrochloric acid, and place in it 2 cm. of the albumin tube shown in Fig. 74 (Mett's tube) after washing off the glycerin. Place in the incubator for twenty-four hours. The number of millimeters digested from the two ends in this time may be recorded, but the results are not to be taken as an exact quantitative determination of pepsin. This test, like the Sahli test, is applied in cases without free acid. In some cases of cancer, the pepsin is greatly decreased with only a slight decrease in acid.

Rennin.—Add 5 drops filtrate to 10 c.c. neutral milk, and place the mixture in the incubator for fifteen minutes. Coagulation shows

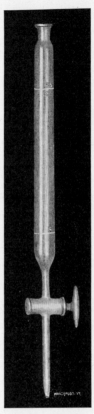

FIG. 73.—Strauss funnel for lactic acid. Fill to 5 with gastric filtrate and to 25 with ether. Shake and allow the aqueous filtrate to escape through the cock. Add water to the ether extract to 25; add two drops of ten per cent. ferric chlorid and shake. A greenish-yellow color in the water indicates lactic acid.

the presence of rennin. Proliferation of bacteria is rarely sufficient to cause coagulation in this time; but at the end of incubation it is well to test the reaction with blue litmus paper. The action of the rennin does not increase the acid present. Pepsin and rennin are decreased in about the same conditions and in the same ratio.

Rennin zymogen, which is changed to rennin by the acid of the stomach, is said to be much less sensitive to alkali than the zymogen (Riegel), and may be detected by adding 10 c.c. gastric filtrate—made alkaline with decinormal alkali—to 10

Fig. 74.—Capillary tubes filled with coagulated albumin for the determination of pepsin. The one at the top shows digestion at the ends.

c.c. neutral milk and 5 c.c. 1 per cent. calcium chlorid, and incubating for ten minutes. If the zymogen is present casein is precipitated.

Starch.—To 10 drops filtrate in a porcelain dish add 10 drops Gram's iodin. A blue color indicates starch.

To determine the degree of carbohydrate cleavage, the iodin is added a drop at a time because the hydrolytic derivatives (soluble starch, erythrodextrin, achroodextrin, maltose) have a greater affinity for iodin than starch itself. If the first few drops give a blue color, the starch has been acted upon to a very slight extent. At least 50 per cent. of the starch is rendered soluble by the saliva before the ptyalin is rendered inactive by the normal acid of the stomach, and as the action of the saliva is stopped by 0.12 per cent. hydrochloric acid, starch digestion is greatly interfered with in cases of hyperacidity.

Trypsin.—This enzyme which is secreted by the pancreatic cells has been demonstrated in the stomach in anacidity. It splits proteins further than pepsin, so that not only are *polypeptids* formed but also the constituent amino acids. To 10 c.c. gastric filtrate, made distinctly alkaline with decinormal sodium carbonate, add 1 gm. fibrin and a small crystal of thymol, and place in the incubator for forty-eight hours. Neutralize, filter, and examine the precipitate for crystals of tyrosin and leucin. Add very dilute bromin water to the filtrate, and if *tryptophane*—this amino acid, tyrosin, and phenylalanine are the three common amino acids with aromatic nuclei— is present a reddish color is produced. If trypsin is present a test for bile pigment is often obtained with the filtrate.

DISEASES OF THE STOMACH PRODUCING CHANGES IN THE GASTRIC CONTENTS

Increased Motility.—Increased peristalsis and a rapid emptying of the stomach often go hand in hand; but not necessarily so, since the passage of food into the duodenum is dependent upon the *pyloric play* which in turn is influenced by the acidity, physical condition of the food, pyloric spasms of nervous origin, mechanical obstruction of the pylorus, and other factors. Although hypermotility is frequently present in gastric ulcer, the emptying of the stomach is likely to be delayed in this condition and dilatation not infrequently results. In anacidity, emptying of the stomach is often accelerated, provided no pyloric stenosis is present.

Diminished Motility and Dilatation.—Mechanical pyloric obstruction from conditions within the cavity, such as cancer, cicatrix or spasm, or from compression from without, such as may be produced by gastroptosis, tight lacing or adhesions cause gastric dilatation; weakness of the wall itself such as a prolonged gastritis may result in dilatation (atonic dilatation). In some of these conditions, the motility is increased; while in others it is diminished; but as the dilatation progresses the motility is usually much diminished. *Antiperistalsis* with belching and vomiting are common in gastric dilatation.

The failure of food to reach the intestine may result in a serious lack of nourishment; and the material that does pass into the intestine has not been properly peptonized and has a bacterial content likely to set up intestinal inflammations. Decomposition products produced by bacterial growth and an abnormal quantity of peptones are present, and the absorption of some of these may possibly take place from the stomach and

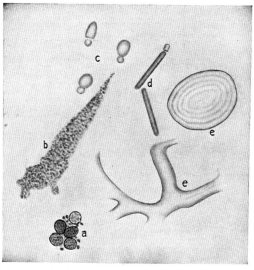

Fig. 75.—Microscopic findings in a case of gastric carcinoma. *a*, Pus cells; *b*, mass of débris heavily stained with hemoglobin; *c*, yeasts; *d*, bacilli (Oppler-Boas type); *e*, vegetable cells.

produce some of the symptoms observed in these cases. It is not possible, however, to demonstrate peptones in the blood by the methods now employed.

Salol Test for Motility.—In cases where the stomach tube is strongly contraindicated this test may be utilized. One gram of salol is given with a test-breakfast. The salol remains unchanged in the stomach, but in the intestine is split to phenol and salicylic acid. The latter should be present in the urine in one hour and a quarter as salicyluric acid, which gives a violet color on the addition of ferric chlorid. The test is carried out in the same way as for diacetic acid (page 253).

Cancer of the Stomach (Fig. 75).—The gastric juice frequently shows absence of free hydrochloric acid and the presence of lactic acid and the Oppler-Boas bacillus. Even in carcinomata that grow by infiltration of the stomach wall (so-called scirrhous cancer), some ulceration is almost always present with what is known as *"occult blood"* in the stools (page 303), this term being applied to blood that is present in such small amounts that it cannot be recognized macroscopically but has to be detected by a few useful tests that have been devised for that purpose. The vomiting of macroscopic blood ("coffee-grounds" vomitus) occurs in less than one-fourth of the cases coming under observation. If the growth is so situated that the pylorus is not obstructed, stasis with fermentation and dilatation will not occur, and the stomach may empty itself in less than the normal time, since sufficient acid is not present to maintain the pyloric action which normally prevents the passage of imperfectly digested food into the duodenum.

When cancer develops in a peptic ulcer, free hydrochloric acid may be present during the early development of the growth, but usually in gastric cancer this acid rapidly and completely disappears. The absence of free hydrochloric acid is usually accounted for by its neutralization after secretion, rather than by a complete cessation of its secretion. Complete anacidity (absence of free and loosely combined hydrochloric acid) oftener has a sudden onset in cancer than in chronic dyspepsias, where the lessening in acid is gradual. The presence of lactic acid is demonstrable in nearly all cases that have no free hydrochloric acid. Free acid may be absent in pernicious anemia, atrophic conditions of the mucosa, amyloid involvement of the stomach wall, cirrhosis of the liver, gallstones, ulcer, dilated stomach, miliary tuberculosis, cancer in various parts of the body, and many other conditions.

Microscopically, tumor fragments and bacilli of the Oppler-Boas type may be identified. Budding yeasts and sarcines are not common.

After middle life a definite onset of stomach symptoms (pain, vomiting, gastric formation, indigestion), with loss of weight and anemia, appears early in the disease. Not only must all the changes in the gastric contents ascertained by repeated examinations be considered collectively, but they must be taken in conjunction with the clinical signs such as the *x*-ray findings and the symptoms.

Gastric Ulcer.—Blood appears at intervals in the stomach contents of about 50 per cent. of the cases, and in the stools in an even greater number. Cirrhosis of the liver, chronic passive congestion, and cancer—as well as gastric ulcer—may give rise to the continued presence of blood in the stools and in the gastric contents. Hyperacidity, averaging about 50 (page 291) of free hydrochloric acid, is present in more than half of the cases; but the excess of acid decreases as the ulcers become chronic. After eating, pain and vomiting occur, followed by relief of the pain. If dilatation takes place, sarcines and yeasts multiply in the gastric contents. Here, as in cancer, examination of the stomach contents is of value only when considered in conjunction with a critical clinical analysis of the case.

Atrophy of Mucosa.—It is difficult to prove the existence of this condition microscopically, because any dilatation of the cavity thins the stomach wall, separates the glands to a greater distance and presses them out so that they are made shorter and appear atrophic. In cases where the dilatation is extreme, *achylia gastrica* is frequently present. In cancer of the stomach or of other organs, achylia (4) with a low total acidity may result. In functional and nervous achylia, the findings in the stomach contents may be the same as when organic disease exists.

FECES

Introduction.—The fresh specimen is sent to the laboratory in a covered container, and at once placed in the incubator until examined. The examination is made as soon as possible, and if cultures are required it is desirable to have a fresh specimen and the examination made at once. Cathartics are often administered; and in general a saline cathartic is preferable, since microörganisms and parasites are not injured by neutral salts. If the examination is to determine the efficiency of gastric and intestinal digestion, the patient is placed for three days on a diet consisting of milk, tea or coffee, butter, soft-boiled eggs, potato, and chopped lean beef.

The *consistency* of the stool (formed or soft) depends on secretion, absorption, and motility of the intestine; and a consistency that is normal for one individual may be abnormal for another. Small hard masses (scyboli) result from fecal material remaining in the large bowel too long. The hard masses may be covered over with mucus, or mucus may be present in fluid stools as small macroscopic or stringy masses. In diarrhea the stools are fluid.

The *color* is remarked. In adults, formed stools are brownish from the urobilin present; while in diarrhea in infants the unchanged bilirubin may be present and the stools yellowish or greenish. Stools containing large amounts of bismuth, iron, blood, and certain articles of diet such as blueberries, are black. Calomel frequently gives a greenish coloration and large amounts of chlorophyl may do the same. Clay-colored stools may result from entire absence of bilirubin derivatives (acholic), excessive reduction of the pigment to a leuko-compound by bacteria, or an excessive amount of fat may obscure the color.

Undigested food particles, substances escaping from the biliary tract, blood, and parasites are the usual things examined for, and the essential tests may be considered under these headings. When all examinations have been completed, the stool is covered with 10 per cent. formalin, and all slides and the like are disinfected.

UNDIGESTED FOOD PARTICLES

With a platinum loop place a small amount of the stool on the center of a glass slide; mix with water, if necessary; apply a cover-glass, and examine first with the low-power and then with the high-dry objective.

In faulty digestion, muscle fibers usually presenting a yellow-

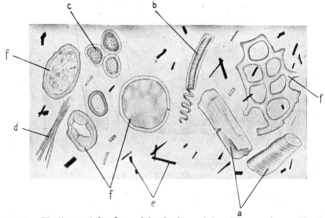

FIG. 76.—Undigested food particles in feces (after Emerson). *a*, Undigested muscle fiber; *b*, vegetable spiral; *c*, lycopodium spores; *d*, fatty acid crystals; *e*, crystals of bismuth oxide; *f*, vegetable cells.

ish tinge are numerous; and most of them have distinct striations and square rather than rounded ends (Fig. 76). If this condition (lientry) exists in a solid stool, it may suggest the acquisition of additional data in regard to proper functioning of the gastric, pancreatic, and intestinal juices.

Much *fibrous connective tissue* is said to indicate faulty gastric digestion. Care is necessary for its certain identification. *Vegetable cells*, spirals (the vessels of plants), and vegetable hairs are numerous in normal stools. The last may resemble embryos of worms but worms are motile and have structural characteristics.   Cells may have the appearance of the ova of intestinal worms, but vegetable cells of the same variety vary greatly in size, and the high-power lens shows differences in morphology.   *Curds* are frequently present in infants stools in indigestion and may be colored greenish.

Fat is present in acholic stools, in a tuberculosis of the mesenteric lymph-nodes that obstructs the lacteals, and in pancreatic disease especially.   Neutral fat is seen microscopically as small droplets; fatty acids appear as short curved or straight needles in compact masses; while soaps are in the form of very long needles.   Single phosphate and calcium soap crystals are of common occurrence, while calcium oxalate and cholesterin crystals may be present.

Quantitative Estimation of Fat.—In order to get the stool into such a state that it may be pulverized, mix about 100 gm. stool with 50 c.c. absolute alcohol and evaporate on a water-bath to dryness.   Again add 50 c.c. and evaporate to dryness. Thoroughly pulverize the dry feces, weigh out and place 5 gm. in a Soxhlet condenser, and extract for six hours with anhydrous ether.   Dry the residue at 100°C. and weigh it. The loss of weight is the weight of neutral fat and fatty acids.

Mucus.—In normal stools, mucin can only be detected chemically.   The mucus from the upper intestinal tract is intimately mixed with the feces.   When it can be distinguished microscopically, it appears as transparent irregular masses or shreds.   In mucous or *membranous colitis*, which usually affects women, jelly-like masses or strips more than a foot long are passed.   Mucus containing great numbers of leukocytes (pus) may signify ulcer or cancer.   Eosinophiles or Charcot-Leyden crystals may be demonstrable in cases of parasitic infections of the intestine.

SUBSTANCES ESCAPING FROM THE BILIARY TRACT

Gall-stones in the common or hepatic duct, inflammatory swelling of the walls of these ducts, or their occlusion by cancer within them or tumors compressing them from without, may exclude bile from the intestine and cause jaundice.   If no bile enters the intestine, 50 per cent. or more of fat fails of absorption, while the absorption of carbohydrates and proteins is but slightly affected.

To find gall-stones, the stool is tied up in a bag made of two thicknesses of surgical gauze, placed in a vessel, and the fecal material washed away under the tap. After washing out everything possible, cut the string with which the bag is tied, spread out the gauze with forceps, and examine for stones.

Stones from the gall-bladder often have facets, while those from the ducts are either rounded or have a mulberry-like appearance. When fractured, the stones show a concentric arrangement. Crush, dry, and powder. To determine the presence of cholesterin crystals, place a small amount of the powder on a slide, mix with water, and examine under the high-dry lens. To test for bile pigment, dissolve 1 gm. powder in 10 c.c. equal parts of absolute alcohol and ether. Evaporate off the ether on a water-bath, filter, and to the alcoholic filtrate add 5 c.c. 1 per cent. potassium hydrate, and to this apply Gmelin's test (page 262). Gall-stones are composed largely of cholesterin and a calcium salts of bilirubin. Stones made up mostly of calcium bilirubin are quite black. Gall sand in the stool is very questionable. Intestinal sand, the size of ordinary sand and consisting of a deposit of calcium about some organic material, is also uncommon. It usually proves to be small seeds from bananas.

Bilirubin, after escaping into the intestine, is reduced by the bacteria present to urobilinogen which on exposure to the air is changed to urobilin (brownish) by the absorption of oxygen and perhaps by an increase in size of the molecule by polymerization. Under normal conditions most of the chromogen disappears from the intestine and is said to be carried to the liver and destroyed. Some of it is excreted in the urine as urobilinogen or urobilin. To test for this pigment, rub up a gram mass in a mortar with 3 c.c. saturated aqueous solution of bichlorid of mercury; for twenty-four hours set aside to dry, powder, place the powder on a slide with water, and examine microscopically. The particles that contain urobilin are red, while those containing bilirubin are green (Schmidt). Bile acids do not appear in the stools, and they are said to be absorbed from the intestine.

In health bilirubin reaches the lower colon only in small amounts in vegetable masses, muscle fibers, and so forth. The more severe the diarrhea the more bilirubin there is in the stool and in the urine. There is difficulty in purifying the derivatives of bilirubin, and at present some difference of opinion prevails, especially in regard to its reduction products.

Hemoglobin, sugar, albumin, and other substances not normally present in bile, may be found pathologically in it, and in cases with fistula may be tested for. Typhoid bacilli, colon bacilli, pneumococci, and streptococci are frequently isolated from the bile.

OCCULT BLOOD IN FECES

Hemolysis takes place rapidly in the gastro-intestinal tract, rendering the blood invisible microscopically. In typical *melena* (tarry stools), the blood usually comes from the stomach or duodenum. In typhoid, red blood may appear. In peptic ulcer, blood frequently appears and disappears intermittently; while in cancer of the stomach it is more likely to be constantly present in small amounts. In tuberculous ulcers, blood is only occasionally present. In hemorrhoids, microscopic blood is present. Blood with mucus but with no fecal matter is passed in intussusception.

Guaiac Test for Chemical Blood.—With a glass rod, place 1 gm. feces in the bottom of a test-tube, add 5 c.c. glacial acetic acid and shake vigorously. A platinum loop may be used to transfer solid fecal material or, if fluid, a pipet may be required. Agitate by striking the lower end of the tube with the index finger. Extract with ether by adding 20 c.c. of ether to the tube and alternately inverting and righting it while holding the thumb firmly over the mouth; or the usual heavy test-tube that has a non-flaring mouth may be stoppered with a cork stopper and shaken.

Decant 5 c.c. of the clear, supernatant, ether extract into

a second test-tube, add an equal amount of distilled water, 1 c.c. hydrogen peroxid, and a knife-point of finely powdered guaiac, and shake. A blue color in the ether is a positive test. A blue color is given not only by hemoglobin but also may be produced by large amounts of red meats, green vegetables (they should be eliminated from the diet), pus, the heavy metals, and less commonly by certain other things. With the exception of the pus, these substances are eliminated from the diet before making the test as a matter of precaution, but it is seldom that they give a positive reaction with this test. A negative test shows the absence of blood.

The water with which the ether extract is shaken may be placed in a spectroscope and examined for the absorption bands of acid hematein (Weber's test).

Benzidin Test for Chemical Blood.—Place 1 gm. feces in a test-tube with 10 c.c. water, and bring to a boil. In a second test-tube place 1 c.c. glacial acetic acid, 0.1 gm. benzidin (Reagent Merck), and 3 c.c. commercial hydrogen peroxid, and examine for a blue color which denotes impurities or a contamination. If no color develops in the second tube, add a few drops of the feces suspension from the first tube to it, and examine for a blue to green color which indicates blood. Nothing short of a very distinct reaction is considered. This test is very delicate, and when positive the guaiac test should be applied. Before repeating these tests, the patient is placed on a milk, bread, and egg diet.

PARASITES PRESENT IN FECES

Examination of stools for intestinal parasites is of great importance, especially in the tropics where most natives show some sort of protozoon or worm infection. The specimens for examination are obtained by giving a saline cathartic.

Bacteria.—For convenience, bacteria are considered under this heading. The bacterial content of the gastro-intestinal tract has frequently been made the subject of investigation; but there are comparatively few organisms that are known to invade the intestinal wall and there produce specific lesions.

Considered as a body surface the intestinal lumen is the best habitat for the extensive growth of bacteria. The lining of the epithelium not only acts as a barrier against bacteria that are not able to proliferate in the human tissue, but also does not permit the absorption of the majority of toxic substances that may be formed in the intestine. Phenol, indol, skatol, and other simple compounds resulting from bacterial decomposition, do pass through the intestinal wall; and even more complex poisons may be absorbed under pathologic conditions (poisonous proteoses in intestinal loops in strangulated hernia, intussusception, and the like). *Enterogenous poisons* have been associated with the production of the so-called *autointoxications* that are frequently associated with nervous disorders. Phenol, skatol, and similar compounds are readily combined in the body, and there is no reason to suppose that their poisonous action is not completely neutralized. Owing to a failure to offer proof of a connection between poisons within the intestine and a more or less vague autointoxication, considerable doubt has been cast on the formation of intestinal poisons in general. There is now no question about the absorption of poisonous split-protein products (so-called endotoxins and products of non-bacterial origin). Therefore, aside from the bacteria that are definitely invaders of the living tissue, it is necessary to give some consideration to those that may give rise to poisons from a splitting of non-bacterial protein within the bowel. It is possible that poisonous products resulting from the activity of the normal enzymes may be absorbed under certain conditions.

Normal Intestinal Flora of Infants.—Bacillus bifidus and bacillus acidophilus comprise the great mass of bacteria in nursing infants. Micrococcus ovalis and bacillus coli are present. In artificially fed infants, the number of colon bacilli is much greater, and putrefactive bacteria are more frequently found.

Normal Intestinal Flora of Adults.—The stomach, as previously noted has few bacteria. The duodenum has comparatively few, and the number rapidly increases as the cecum is

20

approached. The cecum and ascending colon have the greatest number of living bacteria. About one-third of the normal stool dried at 100°C. consists of bacterial cells.

The majority of bacteria in the cecal region belong to the colon-proteus group. Bacilli of the mesentericus group, owing to their size and presence of spores, are most easily recognized. There is no question about the ability possessed by the bacteria that normally inhabit the intestine to split protein and carbohydrate; that this splitting is useful in the normal digestion of foods is questionable. It appears that the important service performed by the usual bacterial flora is the limitation of the growth of common pathogenic bacteria that are being constantly introduced into the intestine. In the case of intestinal loops, where there is an overgrowth of protein-splitting bacteria, there is unquestioned bacterial formation of poisons from protein. In other conditions, a pathologic effect may be exerted by an overgrowth of carbohydrate-splitting bacteria such as bacillus aerogenes capsulatus, bacillus mucosus capsulatus, and others.

Pathogenic Bacteria.—Certain bacteria constantly present in the intestine such as the colon bacillus, bacillus aerogenes capsulatus, and streptococcus may pass through the intestinal wall and set up processes in various organs and tissues. Other disease-producing bacteria such as the tubercle bacillus and the dysentery bacillus, are found in the intestine only in those with the infection or in carriers. The demonstration of *tubercle bacilli* is an indication of tuberculous ulcers of the intestine only when it is known that the patient has not swallowed tuberculous material coughed up from the lungs. Collect feces, after the administration of a saline cathartic, and treat with antiformin overnight. Centrifuge at high speed, and wash the sediment with freshly distilled water. In the usual way, stain the sediment for tubercle bacilli. If acid-fast bacilli are found, it is advisable to inject 1 c.c. of the sediment subcutaneously into a guinea-pig. It is said that contaminations with smegma bacilli may be largely avoided by cleansing about the anus.

To isolate *dysentery bacilli*, select a particle of mucus from a liquid and perfectly fresh stool and pass through three tubes of sterile saline; streak the mucus over two Endo plates. Incubate twenty-four hours and fish translucent colonies to serum tubes containing 1 c.c. 0.1 per cent. dextrose broth; incubate two hours and add 0.1 c.c. 1–5 polyvalent serum to those showing no gas bubbles; incubate one hour and retransplant those showing agglutination to Russel tubes. Next day emulsify and add 0.5 c.c. of emulsion to 0.5 c.c. 1–50 Flexner monovalent serum and to Shiga serum; incubate four hours at 56°C. All mannite fermenters are agglutinated by the Flexner serum.

Rhizopoda.—*Entameba histolytica.*—This ameba is the cause of amebic or tropical dysentery, and is the most important protozoon found in stools. To identify positively amebæ in the stools, it is very desirable that perfectly fresh specimens be examined and the extension of their pseudopodia be observed under the microscope. The stools of more than 50 per cent. of all inhabitants of tropical countries show amebæ; but recently only those individuals in which entameba histolytica is found are looked upon as being infected or as being carriers.

To identify amebæ in the stools, choose blood-stained mucus, if present, from the fresh warm stool; and place a small particle on a warm slide or a warm stage and apply a cover. In lieu of a warm stage the microscope may be placed on top of a radiator. With a high-dry lens this ameba has a clear ectosarc and in its cytoplasm there are often cells and usually bacteria. The nucleus is indistinct. This ameba is about five times the size of a red blood corpuscle.

The *entameba coli* is a common inhabitant of the human intestinal tract of individuals who dwell in the tropics, and is often present in the intestine of those residing in temperate climates. It is from two to three times the size of a corpuscle, has a distinct nucleus, and is only slightly phagocytic for corpuscles and other cells. It is not pathogenic. Similar amebæ (entameba buccalis) are found in the oral cavity especially in cases of pyorrhea about the inflamed gums.

Flagellata.—*Cercomonas hominis* is a small (12 microns) and very actively motile pear-shaped flagellate provided with a long tail-like flagellum at its broad end. The writer found during one summer this flagellate in large numbers in the stools of three consecutive cases of pernicious anemia. The *tricomonas intestinalis* (or vaginalis) has a distinct undulating membrane, and by some is said to have three to twelve flagella toward the blunt end. The *lamblia intestinalis* may readily be identified by a concavity on its inferior surface near the blunt end. These three flagellates have been found in the stools and less commonly in the vaginal, oral, vesical, and other mucous surfaces. They have not been shown to be pathogenic for man. They may be seen in fresh specimens with the high-dry lens.

Infusoria.—*Balantidium coli* is a pathogenic ciliate that produces ulceration of the colon and invades the wall of the gut. It may be found in the stools, and blood-stained mucus is selected in a search for it in the feces. Its pathogenicity is shown by the presence of the organism within the tissue. The ulceration produced by the infection is usually in the colon. The hog is commonly the carrier of this organism or one morphologically like it.

Nematodes.—A large number of the nematodes or round-worms are parasitic for man, and a much greater number for domestic and wild animals. *Uncinaria americana* (necator americanus) (Fig. 77) and *ankylostoma duodenale*, the New and Old World forms of the hookworm, are the most important of the nematodes found in the intestinal content. The American form differs from the European in that it does not have the buccal hook-like teeth. The adult worm which is usually quite firmly attached to the intestinal wall is present in the fresh stool only after treatment with thymol followed by castor oil. The European form is somewhat the larger, and the females (18 mm. maximum) are larger than the males. Embryo worms, obtained by placing ova-containing stools in the incubator for a few days, are seen with low-power lens, but their structure is best made out with the high-dry objective. The ova (about 30 microns short diameter) of the Old and New World forms of hookworm are not readily differentiated.

This variety of worm was known to be the cause of anemias (coolie itch, miner's anemia, bricklayer's anemia, Egyptian chlorosis) in Europe and Northern Africa many years before it was shown to be the cause of the anemic condition among the poorer of the white population of the Southern United States. The anemia is due in part at least to the loss of blood caused by

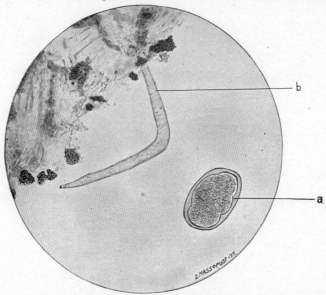

Fig. 77.—Uncinaria americana. *a*, Egg; *b*, embryo worm. Drawn with high dry lens from a single field of an incubated specimen.

the parasite when it attaches itself to the intestinal wall. A hemolysin has been extracted from the substance of the parasites. There is a difference of opinion in regard to the route by which the parasite enters the body. The ova hatch out and the embryo worms probably pass through exposed skin surfaces (feet and legs) producing the "coolie or ground itch" and passing to the intestine by way of the blood stream. In addition to the anemia infected individuals show a marked wasting, abdominal pains, and depressed mentality.

The eggs offer the chief means for diagnosis and frequently show segmentation. Examine by placing a small amount of the liquid stool on the center of a slide, applying a cover, and examining with a high-dry lens.

For a more searching examination, place about 1 oz. of feces in a urine-sedimenting cylinder, fill up with water and thoroughly mix with a glass rod. After sedimenting, pour off the supernatant liquid together with all material that floats, and repeat. Finally examine microscopically the layer of finest sediment.

Oxyuris vermicularis is the common pinworm or seatworm of children. The ova (about 50 microns) and the adult worms (3 mm. to 10 mm.) may be found in the feces. The former, with the embryos already developed within the capsule, are most often found in scrapings from about the anus, and this is the most important means of diagnosis. Scrape off the material with a dull scalpel, place on a slide with a very small amount of water and examine with the high-dry lens. In material obtained by giving an enema in the evening the adult worms are searched for with the low-power lens. This worm may cause a pruritis about the anus and vagina of children. A considerable number of appendices removed by surgical operation show a few pinworms; and occasionally an appendix is discovered well filled with these worms, and on microscopic examination the parasites are found to extend through the mucosa into the wall of the appendix where there is a cellular reaction about them.

Strongyloides stercoralis or *intestinalis* (anguillula intestinalis), which appears to cause a diarrhea prevalent in parts of China, is diagnosed by finding the embryos; since the eggs, which resemble those of the hookworm, are not commonly present in the stools. With the high-dry lens examine the water that settles out from fluid stools. The embryos which have a mouth with four distinct lips are about one-fourth as long as the adult worm, which may measure 2 mm. in length and is rarely present in the stools. It has been found in 0.5 per cent. of normal individuals, and its pathogenicity is doubtful. The adult worms are most abundant in the duodenum.

Trichocephalus dispar (trichuris trichiuria) or whipworm

(2 in. long) is found chiefly in the cecum, and rarely in the stools, except after treatment. In America, 10 per cent. of normal individuals may be infected; while in Southern Europe even 100 per cent. may have the worm in the intestine. It is diagnosed by finding in the feces the oval (25 microns across) ova, which have a plug in each end and are frequently stained brownish. It is usually harmless, but apparently it may in rare cases set up an enteritis.

Ascaris lumbricoides (common roundworm) is present in less than 1 per cent. of normal individuals. Both the adult worms (6 in. long) and the ova (50 microns breadth) inclosed in characteristic shells may be found in the stools. The latter may have ragged albuminous capsules or, less commonly, they may be naked. The adult worm may be removed from the intestine by the administration of santonin. It may be vomited and occasionally may work its way up into the pharynx and obstruct the respiratory tract. Its action appears to be merely mechanical.

Trichinella spiralis.—The mature males fertilize the females and die within a few days after they have developed from the encysted embryos of the infected pork; while the females (3 mm. long) persist in the intestine for several weeks, and may occasionally be demonstrated by obtaining sediment—as in the examination for hookworm ova—and examining it spread out in a Petri dish above a black background.

Filaria bancrofti.—Infection with this parasite is very common in certain parts of the tropics. The adult worm may measure as much as six inches, and is found in the thoracic duct and in the lymphatics elsewhere. The embryos (F. nocturna or F. sanguinis hominis) which measures 100 microns or more are present in milky (chylous) urines, and during the night they appear in the peripheral blood. They may be present in the feces. Urine and blood are examined with the high-dry lens, where they are easily recognized by their great motility. The urine may be centrifuged at a high rate of speed. Elephantiasis of the scrotum, labia, and lower extremities is often present.

Trematodes.—Infections with trematodes or flukeworms are not common in America, and the few cases are importations. Liver-flukes (distomum hepaticum) although common in sheep where they block the bile-vessels are practically never found in man.

Schistosomum hematobium (Bilharzia).—The eggs (60 microns across) of this parasite may be found in urine and occasionally in the feces. The adult worm (1.5 cm.) lies in the mesenteric vein and in the veins of the bladder and vagina. The ova, provided with a sharp spine, penetrate through the walls of the vessels causing papillomatous areas and hemorrhagic spots in the mucosa and reaching the lumen of the bladder and of the intestine. The infection with this worm (bilharzia infection) produces a severe hematuria, and when present in the stools is accompanied by blood. The infection is limited almost entirely to Northern Africa.

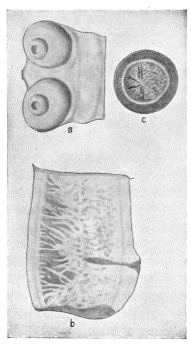

FIG. 78.—Tenia saginata. Drawn with low power of microscope. *a*, Head showing two of the four suckers; *b*, ripe segment showing at left margin the large number of branches of the uterus; *c*, egg which cannot be differentiated from eggs of tenia solium.

The Asiatic form (S. japonicum) occurs especially in the rice district of China. The ova have no spine and therefore resemble the ova of hookworm. This form is more commonly present in the feces; and to make a certain diagnosis the stool should be incubated overnight to allow the embryos time to develop and become free. The bladder is not affected. Infection of the lungs may occur and the ova appear in the sputum.

Cestodes.—Some of the tapeworms are intestinal parasites and are often diagnosed by the patient, who finds segments (links, proglottides) in the stools. Frequently it is necessary to use the proper vermifuge and to search for links and especially for the scolex in the feces.

Tenia saginata (beef tapeworm) (Fig. 78) infections are di-agnosed by discovering segments (5 mm. by 15 mm.) by the method used for finding gall-stones, or by coming upon the ova in the stools. If ingested, the ova will not infect man, since the cysticercus bovis· develops only in beef. The cu-boidal head (2 mm. across) has four suckers without hooks. The genital openings are at the margin of the segments, and the uterus may have three or four dozen dichotomous branchings that are very fine. This infection is com-mon and its distribution exten-sive. The worms occupy the small intestine and a sufficient number may be present to block the gut.

Tenia solium (pork tapeworm) (Fig. 79) differs from the saginata in the segments which have only two dozen or fewer lateral branch-ings. The ova, which may infect man directly, are similar to those

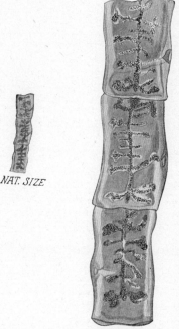

NAT. SIZE

X 4

FIG. 79.—Tenia solium (after Emerson). Note that there are only seven to ten coarse branches of the uterus to a side.

of tenia saginata. The 2-mm. dark colored head has four suckers and is provided with hooks. It is not common in this country. Raw pork is the common source of infections. The cysticercus may develop in the muscles of man.

The larval worms as they lie in the muscle appear as whit-ish areas (*measled pork or beef*) three to five millimeters in length and therefore distinctly larger than encysted trichinellæ.

Dibothriocephalus latus (fish tapeworm), like the two preceding tapeworms, is large. The eggs which have a cap on
one end and segments are both present in the stools. The
genital opening is on the side and the uterus is arranged about
this as a rosette. The anemia produced by this infection may
be indistinguishable from cases of pernicious anemia. The
majority of infected individuals show no anemia, and the
appearance of this condition in some cases and not in others has
not been explained. Removal of the worm effects a cure. In

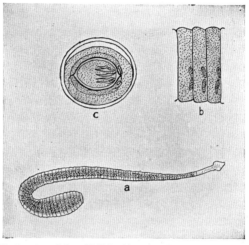

FIG. 80.—Tenia nana (after V. Jaksch). *a*, Adult worm (dwarf worm) which
is only about 1 cm. long; *b*, segments magnified; *c*, egg. The sharp process at
each end of the innermost of the two capsules characterizes it.

America most cases have been found in immigrants from
Northern Europe. The pike is the common source of infection.

Tenia nana (hymenolepis nana) (Fig. 80) is a dwarf tapeworm. It is found in children and is diagnosed by finding
the ova in the stools. The number of worms inhabiting the
intestine may be very great. The ovum (35 microns broad)
is usually oval, and from the inner of the two covering membranes that comprise the shell there are filamentous projec-
tions extending inward toward each pole. It inhabits the ileum
especially. The head is only one-fourth millimeter across,
but is provided with four suckers with hooks.

Tenia echinococcus (Fig. 81) infection in man is not common in America. Embryos or scolices develop in the intestine from ingested eggs and from here pass to the liver by way of portal vessels probably where cysts are formed. Such cysts may occasionally rupture into the intestine, bile vessels, or bronchi, with the escape of hooklets into these passages. Usually the material containing scolices, hooklets, and portions of the laminated wall are obtained at surgical operations.

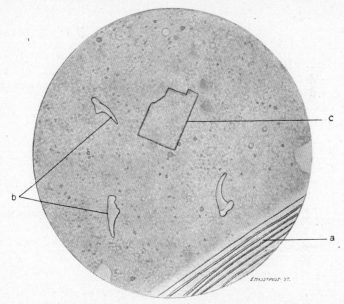

FIG. 81.—Scrapings from the wall of an echinococcus cyst of the liver. Oil-immersion. *a*, Lamellated wall of the cyst; *b*, hooklets from a scolex; the scolices (heads) are found within secondary cysts located on the wall of a large or primary cyst; *c*, cholesterin crystal.

The gross character of the cysts in man varies. In some cases extensive invaginations into the primary cavity and evaginations outward (*hydatid disease*) take place, while in others there are numerous separate small cysts (multilocular form). In all cases there is an extensive formation of new scolices. The adult worm develops in the intestine of domestic animals.

Preservation of Feces.—For class purpose and for other study, it may be desirable to preserve specimens of feces.

For the preservation of round worms, ova, muscle fibers, and tissue cells, it is best to add formalin to a fluid stool in such an amount that the diluted stool has a formalin content of 2 per cent. A crystal of thymol is placed in each container.

To make preparations of tapeworms, the selected portions are placed in a large volume of normal saline overnight and then pressed out between two microscopic slides to the extent desired when the slides are wrapped with thread to maintain the compression. The specimens are then treated in the same way as tissue is treated in the preparation of gross museum specimens (page 447), either by the Kaiserling or the Kaiserling-oil method. After fixation in the Kaiserling fixing solution, the slides may be removed. From the Kaiserling preserving solution or from oil the specimens may be mounted on a slide in glycerin jelly and the cover-glass sealed with a glass cement.

HISTOLOGIC AND AUTOPSY TECHNIC

The Histologic Work of a Hospital Laboratory.—There is no department of a hospital in which proper organization is of greater importance for efficient work than the hospital laboratory. The general principles for this organization are indicated elsewhere (page 167). The possibilities of personnel, building, and equipment determine the application of these principles.

Although in small hospitals it may be necessary to care for the bacteriologic specimens, the surgical and autopsy tissue, and the serologic work in the same room, a separate room is required for the chemical work. In this case the apparatus for the bacteriology and for handling the tissue should be separately placed in different parts of the room, and arranged so that large or small numbers of specimens may receive attention in an orderly way.

In larger hospital laboratories, aside from the chemical laboratory, there should be at least one large bacteriologic laboratory, one large room for tissue work, a room in which autopsies are performed, a small room for a technician, and a small room for an office and record room. The bacteriologic specimens are examined and the examinations recorded as indicated under that heading.

Equipment.—It is not practicable to set down details in regard to the plan of rooms, exposure, lighting, and so forth, since these will necessarily be dependent upon the local conditions under which the laboratory is established. Equipment is more easily controlled, and the purchase of apparatus must be made from first-hand knowledge of the articles to be purchased. Simplicity, durability, and efficiency usually go hand in hand in scientific apparatus. As a rule, supplies should be purchased to meet definite needs. It is the only way in

317

which serious delays in obtaining articles for immediate use can be prevented.

Diener and Technical Service.—No inconsiderable amount of important investigations has been done in laboratories with poor equipment and under great difficulties. Perhaps this is because those most capable of original investigation are able under adverse conditions to concentrate on a problem. The limits of the work that may be done by non-medical technicians should be kept clearly in mind. In general, any examination that does not vary to any great extent with each individual specimen may be done by a properly trained technician. For example the examination of throat cultures for diphtheria bacilli, sputum for tubercle bacilli, and the Wassermann test require no general medical knowledge; while potting and diagnosis of surgical specimens do require a familiarity with pathologic processes.

That the laboratory rooms be kept clean and orderly is important for the routine examinations and for careful research work. The amount of work required in keeping a laboratory clean and in order depends to a considerable extent on properly systematizing the daily routine. Not only must the floors and desk be kept clean, but containers used for bacteriologic cultures and for remains of surgical specimens must be emptied daily and disinfected with coal-tar dip.

Wood Stain.—Desk-tops, table-tops, blocks for staining-bottles, and other wood-work are stained black. To do this, apply with a brush a solution consisting of 125 gm. of copper sulphate and 125 gm. potassium or sodium chlorate dissolved in 1000 c.c. of water, and allow to dry. Cover with a second coat; allow this to dry, and apply a solution consisting of 150 gm. anilin hydrochlorid dissolved in 1 liter of water, and let this dry. Wash with soap and water; and after drying apply linseed oil which should be thoroughly rubbed in. Desks are cleaned off once a week with a cloth moistened with equal parts of linseed oil and chloroform. If anilin hydrochlorid is not in stock, anilin oil and hydrochloric acid in molecular proportions may be used instead.

Importance of Surgical Tissue.—The examination of all tissue removed at operation is of importance not only to the patient from which the tissue is removed, but it may lead to actual therapeutic and diagnostic advances in the treatment of individuals suffering from similar affections. From the standpoint of the pathologist, surgical tissue has the decided advantage that it may be fixed immediately postoperative. To appreciate this, one need only compare the perfect nuclear and cytoplasmic outlines of cells of a surgical specimen with those of autopsy tissue fixed even within two or three hours after death. On the other hand, in autopsy tissue the pathologist has before him all the ramifications and inter-relations of the disease process.

For histologic study, human tissue fixed within five minutes after its removal is most satisfactory. Tissue and organs from the lower animals may be required to illustrate the variations from the human; but such tissue cannot be substituted for human tissue in research study and in a systematic course in histology. Under suitable hospital conditions, fresh normal tissue can be obtained during the course of a few years from nearly all parts of the human body.

Disposal of Surgical Specimens.—A diagnosis on tissue removed during the life of a patient is often desired as soon as it can be made; while the ten days required for the slow paraffin method is no disadvantage in the case of tissue removed at autopsy. For this reason, tissue received at the laboratory is divided into surgical specimens that are removed during life and that receive a surgical number, and autopsy specimens that are removed after death and receive an autopsy number. The technic of handling surgical and autopsy tissue is often the same.

If the surgeon requests an immediate diagnosis while the patient remains on the operating table, frozen sections for immediate diagnosis are made. If an immediate diagnosis is not required, the tissue is fixed in formalin-alcohol for celloidin sections, or in formalin for frozen sections, so that a diagnosis may in every case be returned the following day. In addition, tissue may be fixed in Zenker's fluid, formalin, absolute alcohol, corrosive-alcohol, chrome-osmic acid solution, Müller's fluid, and other fixatives, as described under fixing solutions (page 340).

Histologic Methods.—In detailing the technic for surgical specimens, the histologic methods commonly employed in pathology are presented, whether they be used for surgical or for autopsy specimens. After *routine diagnostic methods* (pages 320 to 336), methods of *fixation* (pages 340 to 348) are given. These are followed by stains for *fibrils, fat, iron, glycogen, calcium bacteria, cytoplasmic granules, hyaline substances* and *nervous tissue structures* (pages 355 to 381).

Numbering the Specimens.—Surgical specimens are assigned a number as soon as they reach the laboratory and are disposed of according to their nature. Tags bearing consecutive numbers are kept on a file (Fig. 84) for this assignment of numbers. The uppermost tag is the number that the specimen receives, and it is placed on the Zenker-fixed material. If the tissue is not fixed in Zenker's fluid, the Z is scratched out, A or F added, and the tag attached to the bottle containing the formalin-alcohol or the formalin, as the case may be. The system is the same as that used for the bacteriologic specimens (page 170), S 16.231 being the 231st surgical specimen received during 1916. It may be advantageous to indicate the tissue or diagnosis on the tag, and time may be saved when specimens are discarded if the tag also bears the number of minutes postoperative that the fixation was made.

Care of the Tissue before its Delivery at the Laboratory.— As soon as the tissue is removed, it is wrapped in sterile gauze that has been moistened with sterile saline and oiled paper (1 ft. square), and is wrapped about the gauze. The brown slip is folded and slipped beneath the string. At the earliest possible moment the tissue is sent to the laboratory. To secure fixation of tissue for making differential stains and sections for instruction in pathologic histology, the tissue must be placed in the fixing solution within five minutes after its removal by the surgeon.

Rapid Diagnosis of Unfixed Tissue.—While the patient remains under the anesthetic, the tissue is removed and, without being wrapped up in gauze and oiled paper, immediately brought to the laboratory by an attendant. The sections that may be cut from the fresh tissue and the stains that may be made on the section give results inferior to those obtained by the celloidin or paraffin method. However, it is often possible to give the surgeon aid in arriving at a diagnosis, and usually a positive diagnosis can be made.

Cutting the Sections with a Hand-knife.—The attendant delivering the specimen should know the age of the patient, the clinical diagnosis, the site from which the tissue is removed, and the gross appearance of the field of operation. He should be able to assist the pathologist in choosing the part of the tissue from which the sections are to be cut. This choice is of the greatest importance and must be made without delay.

A drop of *dextrin solution,* which is 1.5 per cent. phenol to which dextrin has been added to the consistency of thin molasses, is placed on the disk of the freezing microtome. A piece of tisssue not larger than 2 cm. or thicker than 1 cm. is cut from the specimen delivered at the laboratory and placed in the drop of dextrin solution. The liquid carbon dioxid is allowed to flow into the copper tube by turning with a long-handled wrench the valve on the lower end of the cylinder.

If the cylinder is placed in a horizontal position, the liquid will reach the valve until the tank is one-half empty but after that the tube will be filled with gas and not with liquid. Expansion of the liquid directly beneath the disk insures more rapid freezing, and the tank should be placed upright if the position it occupies in the laboratory permits this. If placed in the horizontal position the tank must be firmly supported. In some cities the manufacturers allow enough sediment-containing water to remain in the cylinders to make their use in the upright position almost impossible, since the muddy water continues to run out for some time.

Before turning on the gas make sure that the block of tissue is depressed just below the knife-edge and that the shaft of the milled wheel is against the disk, so that there will be no loss of time in running up the milled wheel before it begins to elevate

21

the tissue.   Let the gas escape until the freezing zone shown by the whitening of the tissue just reaches the top of the block of tissue.

Holding the knife at an angle of 45 degrees, even off the upper surface to the place from which the sections are to be cut.   This may be done to advantage before the frost-zone has reached the top of the block of tissue.   If the tissue is not sufficiently

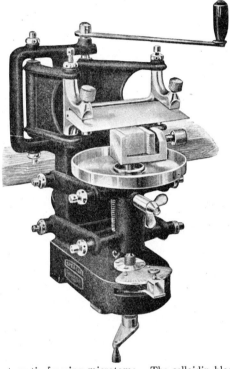

FIG. 82.—Automatic freezing microtome.   The celloidin block-holder shown in cut is replaced by a disk if frozen sections are to be cut.   Satisfactory celloidin sections are difficult to obtain with this microtome.

thawed, blow gently on the block; and just as soon as thawing begins on the surface, rapidly cut a number of sections by turning the milled wheel as the knife is rapidly slid back and forth. The sections are removed from the knife-blade by dipping the knife into a 1 per cent. salt solution contained in a finger-bowl. The finger-bowl must be wide enough to permit this.   Vary the distance that the milled wheel is turned, so that sections may be secured from tissue that holds together poorly and cuts with difficulty.

Cutting the Sections with an Automatic Knife (Fig. 82).— The method is the same as the one just given, except that the block is elevated and the knife brought across the tissue automatically by the small handle at the top. Sections are removed from the upper surface of the knife by means of the index finger and placed in the saline and agitated in order to unfold them. The block cut by this method must be smaller than the one cut by the previous method, the bit of tissue in this case being not more than 1 cm. in any direction. The point for emphasis is that the method chosen be practised until maximum efficiency is acquired.

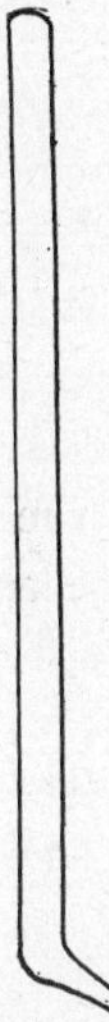

Staining with Unna's Polychrome Methylene Blue.—With glass rod (Fig. 83) that is drawn out and slightly curved at one end, remove the best section from the finger-bowl. Such a rod must be sufficiently large at the end to permit the section to be supported on it without its edges overlapping. In a small porcelain bowl of about the size of a thimble, which contains the polychrome methylene blue (Unna [page 359]), place the section for from ten to twenty seconds. Permit the section to spread out on top of the glass rod, but do not remove the rod from beneath the section during the staining. Wash in a 1 per cent. salt solution and clear in *Brun's glucose* (glucose, 240 gm.; distilled water, 840 c.c.; camphor, 60 gm.; and glycerin, 60 c.c.; filter), and mount in this solution by floating the section on a slide which must be kept exactly level as it is raised from the solution.

Fig. 83.—A glass rod 6 by 120 mm. for lifting frozen sections. When melting the glass in the flame and drawing it out, the curved portion must be large enough that the margins of the sections do not come in contact when they are placed on it.

Not more than five minutes is consumed in the whole procedure. The tissue left after the block has been cut for the frozen sections is treated as indicated under celloidin sections (page 333) so that the first diagnosis made from the fresh tissue may be confirmed by the examination of more perfect sections.

It is always desirable to check the first report by means of clinical data and more perfect sections made by other methods. The field of the pathologist in these cases is to lend assistance to the surgeon. If for one reason or another aid cannot be given, then the surgeon is told that he must exercise his best judgment. This is done rather than return an uncertain diagnosis.

Staining with McJunkin's Blood Stain.—This method gives somewhat better histologic differentiation, but care must be exercised to prevent a precipitate. The best section is removed from the finger-bowl by floating it on a 22-mm. square, No. 1 cover-glass held in cover-glass forceps. Remove the excess of saline with a small piece of filter paper. Stain, by dropping 2 drops of blood stain (page 53) from a dropping-bottle, and after one-half minute diluting these 2 drops with 4 drops of 0.0015 N sodium carbonate and staining for two minutes. Float the section off by placing in a second finger-bowl of saline the cover-glass that is held in forceps. After washing, float the stained section on a slide, straighten, remove saline from about it, drop on a square cover at the center of which a small drop of 50 per cent. glycerin has been placed, and examine with the high-dry lens. Other blood stains are satisfactory when their alkalinity is just right.

An *extramural diagnosis* of tissue at a private residence or a small hospital may be required. A small cylinder (2 in. by 24 in.) of carbon dioxid, a microtome and hand-knife, as well as the necessary staining dishes and stain, may be carried in a small hand-bag. An attachment is secured that punctures the cylinder when screwed into it. A portable microscope is convenient for this work.

Frozen Sections of Formalin-fixed Tissue for Routine Diagnosis.—For the routine diagnosis of surgical specimens either frozen sections of tissue formalin-alcohol fixed or celloidin sections of formalin-alcohol-fixed tissue or both, are used. The steps required are: (1) to make frozen sections of formalin-fixed tissue, cut frozen sections, using the technic given under fresh tissue (page 321) but cutting thinner sections; (2) 1 per cent. salt solution; (3) alum hematoxylin (dilute 1–5) twenty minutes; (4) saturated solution of lithium carbonate a few minutes; (5) 0.5 per cent. eosin ten seconds to one minute; (6) 80 per cent. alcohol ten seconds; (7) 95 per cent. alcohol one minute; (8) absolute alcohol or *carbol-xylol* (phenol 1, xylol 3) five minutes; (9) mount in colophonium-xylol. Absolute alcohol is preferable to carbol-xylol and must be followed by xylol before mounting in colophonium-xylol. If the hematoxylin tends to stain diffusely the sections should be differentiated in Czaplewsky's solution after step 3, and some prefer to do this as a routine.

In this way better preparations of certain tumors and organs can be secured than by the celloidin method. In addition to the hematoxylin-eosin stain, the fat stain and other stains described under formalin-fixation are made on the sections of formalin-fixed tissue. Either frozen sections or celloidin sections are superior to the rapid (forty-eight hour) paraffin method (page 354) in which acetone is frequently employed as a dehydrating agent, and they insure a diagnosis on the day following the removal of the tissue. It is better that the tissue remain in the formalin twenty-four hours, but overnight usually insures sufficient fixation to make good frozen sections possible.

Celloidin Sections for Routine Diagnosis.—Larger pieces of tissue may be imbedded in celloidin than in paraffin, and pieces even 2 cm. square and 1 cm. thick may be dropped into the formalin-alcohol. Just before moving into the 95 per cent. alcohol, it is often desirable to even up the surfaces with a sharp knife being careful not to cut away the essential part of the lesion. The specimens are moved back as indicated in Fig. 88, and blocked and cut as indicated under that heading. Proper staining is indicated under Fig. 84.

Celloidin sections are the best for the routine diagnosis of surgical specimens. By the celloidin method, the sections are stained, examined, and reported upon the morning following the day that the specimens are received. This method enables a technician to do the greater part of the work, and large numbers of specimens may be examined without burdensome labor or confusion.

It is of first importance that every surgical specimen that comes to the laboratory be examined microscopically. This may be of immediate value to the patient in revealing the malignancy of tumors, unsuspected syphilis, tuberculosis and the like. Furthermore, many interesting specimens are insignificant looking macroscopically. For example, a slightly enlarged ovary may show a rapidly growing embryoblastoma;

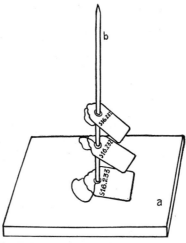

Fig. 84.—Surgical tag numbers. *a*, Small block of wood into which an extra-long wire-nail, *b*, has been driven. The tags are merchandise tags (white) measuring 2 by 1¼ in. The numbers on the tags of this spindle are consecutive. The fixation is indicated in the lower right-hand corner of each tag.

uterine curettings may reveal a chorionic carcinoma; or in necrotic material pressed out of a sinus there may be actinomyces. If frozen sections of formalin-fixed tissue are used, many specimens apparently uninteresting, are never examined. By the celloidin method every specimen is potted, which means that it must be examined or thrown away; and this method is recommended for routine diagnosis. It must also be remembered that it is difficult to make frozen sections of bone, dense fibrous tissue, necrotic material, and curettings.

Recording and Reporting of Specimens.—The report of the pathologic diagnosis goes back to the clinician on the brown

```
REPORT FOR THE PATHOLOGIST

    ,
    _____

                          Date......................

Name............................................................

Sex...............................Age.........................

..................................Service,Ward.........Bed.............

If not a hospital patient give name and address of physician.....

................................................................

Duration and Nature of Disease...............................

................................................................

................................................................

................................................................

Clinical.Diagnosis...........................................

Exact.Source.of Specimen or Specimens if more than one...........

................................................................

Diagnosis of Pathologist.......................................


                    ......................Pathologist


    ════════════════════════════════════════════════


            Instructions to House Officers.

All tissue is immediately covered with sterile gauze moistened

with saline and the whole wrapped with paraffined paper and the

brown slip.
```

FIG. 85.—Brown slip. The slip of light brown paper 6½ by 9½ in. is filled out by the clinician and sent to the laboratory with all surgical and bacteriologic specimens. As soon as a diagnosis is made it is written on this slip and returned to the clinician. If report is added to clinical history the diagnosis may be cut from the slip for this purpose, and pasted upon the regular history sheets.

slip that came with the specimen from him. Therefore, before this slip is returned, the clinical data must be copied from it. The clinical data, the gross description of the specimen, and the pathologic diagnosis are first recorded on the back of the brown slip and later transferred to a card for the laboratory record. The number on the tag (Fig. 84) at the top of the spindle is placed on the bottom of the brown slip. The brown slip (Fig. 85) is placed in a clip until the diagnosis is made. The brown slip with the diagnosis is given to a technician, who makes out the card (Fig. 86) for the laboratory record. The cards are kept in a card index case according to their number.

S-   Diagnosis:

Material: Date:

Name: Service:

Time p.o. and kind of fixation:

Clinical History:

Gross Description and Museum Number:

FIG. 86.—Index card (5 by 7 in.) for surgical records. All cards for indexing are this size.

The brown slip with the diagnosis written on it is at once returned to the clinician. The procedure adopted must be as simple as possible, and then rigidly adhered to in the case of every specimen coming to the laboratory.

Choice of a Fixative.—If a frozen section for immediate diagnosis is not asked for, the tissue is unwrapped, numbered, and the gross characteristics tabulated. If the specimen consists of uterine curettings or a bit of other tissue only large enough for a single block, all is placed in the formalin-alcohol bottle (Fig. 88) and the tag from the spindle placed on it. In this case, the Z on the tag is crossed off and A substituted.

Curettings are held together by placing them, by means of forceps, on a bit of filter paper 1 cm. square.

A method for routine diagnosis that may be spoken of

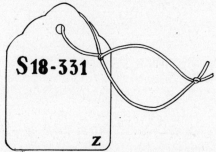

FIG. 87.—Tag for sections of surgical tissue. Merchandise tags 2 by 1¼ in. The symbol in the lower right-hand corner indicates Zenker fixation (Fig. 84). The thread is always tied into a slip-knot as shown here.

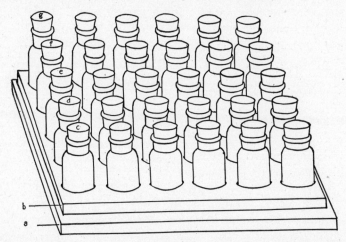

FIG. 88.—Block for celloidin imbedding. a, ¾-inch board; b, ¾-inch board 24 by 14 inches with holes for cork-stoppered bottles obtained from Whitall, Tatum Co., Phila. The outside diameter of the bottom of the bottle is 5 cm. and that of the upper part of the mouth is 32 mm. The bottles are 11.5 cm. high. c, Formalin (1 part)—alcohol 95 per cent. (9 parts) for one to two hours; d, 95 per cent. alcohol one to two hours; e, absolute alcohol for one to two hours; f, absolute alcohol and ether equal parts two hours; g, medium celloidin—overnight. Six specimens may be started at one time in this block. The following morning, all are ready to be cut. If tissue is added daily all bottles are cleaned and refilled at the end of each week.

as a rapid paraffin method is employed by some workers. There are a great many modifications, such as the use of acetone or glycerin as dehydrating agents, and they are all equally unsatisfactory. Formalin-fixed tissue is used, and it cannot be rapidly imbedded (one to three days) without serious shrinkage.

If there is enough of the specimen, pieces are always placed in a bottle of Zenker's fluid, unless it is an appendix, leiomyoma, or oviduct that is known to be of no interest.

The pieces for Zenker-fixation are cut after the pieces for diagnosis have been placed in the formalin-alcohol. The Zenker bottle receives the original number-tag and is set aside and put to wash after twenty-four hours. If it appears that a fat stain or a stain for bacteria may be desired, fix also in 10 per cent. formalin. Any very fresh tissue, or tissue that is likely to prove of interest, is fixed in formalin as a routine. The tag for this bottle bears an F in the lower right-hand corner.

Formalin-alcohol, Zenker's fluid, and formalin, therefore, are the three common fixing solutions when celloidin sections are used for the routine diagnosis. If frozen sections of formalin-fixed tissue are used for diagnosis, then of course formalin-alcohol is omitted. It must be remembered, however, that other fixatives are required in special cases. The use of the various fixing solutions is indicated under the methods of fixation (page 340).

Blocking and Cutting Celloidin Sections.—After the tissue has been selected and placed in the formalin-alcohol (Fig. 88), the remainder of the technic is very simple. The tissue with the tag is moved back with a pair of forceps 10 in. long. After fixation in the formalin-alcohol and before they are transferred to the next solution, blocks of tissue may be trimmed to the exact size and shape desired.

After remaining overnight in medium celloidin, the blocks of tissue are dipped by means of long forceps into *thick celloidin* (the thick is made like the medium, except that it has 2 oz. of celloidin to the 400 c.c. of alcohol-ether) and placed on a fiber block (Fig. 89) that has the surgical number written with a lead pencil on the reverse side. After a minute in the air, the blocks are dropped into a pint Mason jar which is half filled with chlo-

roform, where thay remain for one hour.   They are then transferred to 80 per cent. alcohol and sections may be cut im-
mediatley.   With a sliding microtome (Fig. 90), celloidin

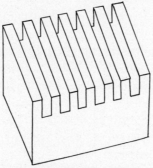

FIG. 89.—Fiber block for celloidin sections.   Fiber blocks 30 by 20 by 15 mm.
may be obtained from B. & L. O. Co.   Smaller blocks are not suitable.   The surgical numbers are written on the blocks with pencil.   To clean these blocks
remove celloidin by setting aside and letting dry forty-eight hours in the air.
Remove pencil marks with a moist cloth.

FIG. 90.—Sliding microtome for celloidin sections.   Slant the knife so that the
entire length of the edge is utilized in cutting off the sections.   Eighty per cent.
alcohol is dropped on the block from a bottle (Fig. 91).   A number of sections
are rapidly cut by drawing the knife back and forth.   With a teasing needle transfer the sections from the knife to a Stender dish containing water.   One of the best
sections is picked out and run through the stain (Fig. 94).

sections are cut 12 to 15 microns thick.   Eighty per cent.
alcohol is dropped onto the block from a large dropping-bottle,

to keep the block and knife wet (Fig. 91). By means of a teasing-needle, the sections are transferred from the knife to a dish of water. The number-tag is under this dish.

To make the *medium celloidin*, remove 1 oz. of celloidin (E. Schering) from the bottle, and blot off all water with filter paper, and dry in the air of a warm room. Place in a pint Mason jar containing alcohol-ether consisting of 200 c.c. of absolute alcohol and 200 c.c. of ether. Invert and right the jar on alternate days until solution is complete. *Thin celloidin*

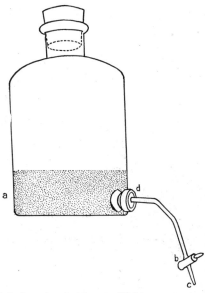

FIG. 91.—Alcohol dropping bottle. *a*, Eighty per cent. alcohol in a 4-liter bottle provided with a glass tube that has a cock, *b*. This tube is connected to the bottle by a rubber cork, *d*. The tip of the tube, *c*, comes directly above the celloidin block. This is done by placing the bottle on a support of the desired height.

which is made by adding an equal volume alcohol-ether to medium celloidin flows freely like water; the medium is syrupy, while the thick is with some resistance taken up on forceps. Celloidin, such as the pure pyroxylin of the Mallinckrodt Chemical Co. (St. Louis), may be used; but in making substitution it is essential that a sample of the substitute be first tried.

Slow Imbedding Process for Celloidin Sections.—In tropical countries under adverse conditions it may be impractical to cut paraffin sections. In military hospitals it is often advanta-geous to reduce the laboratory equipment to a minimum, with the elimination of such apparatus as a paraffin oven and an additional microtome. Further, the extra expense may render impossible the purchase by a small laboratory of the paraffin apparatus. Under any of these conditions, more perfect sections may be required than those obtained for routine diag-nosis in making celloidin sections by the rapid method.

To make the best sections by the celloidin method ten days are required. The tissue is placed for twenty-four hours in each of the following solutions; 80 per cent. alcohol: 95 per cent. alcohol; absolute alcohol; absolute alcohol-ether; and thin celloi-din (medium celloidin to which an equal volume of absolute alcohol-ether has been added). From the thin celloidin the tissue is carried into medium celloidin for from two days to one week, from which solution it is blocked. The sections are cut and stained in the usual way. For very large blocks, such as are used in embryologic work, it may be necessary to leave the sections in all solutions a double length of time in order to secure the best infiltration.

Staining the Celloidin Sections with Hematoxylin-Eosin.—
Hematoxylin (hematoxylin crystals 5 gm., dissolved in 25 c.c. alcohol by heating in a large test-tube; thymol 1 gm.; distilled water saturated with ammonium alum 500 c.c.) is most often used as a nuclear stain for celloidin sections, because many of the anilin dyes are taken up by the celloidin. The hematoxylin prepared in this way must be allowed to ripen for about two weeks before using; or it may be ripened for immediate use by the addition of 20 c.c. of 5 per cent. potassium permanganate. After a few months a hematoxylin begins to stain very diffusely. Such a stain may be improved by the addition of alum solution but it is better to make up fresh. Stender dishes are used for the solutions and the staining is carried out as indicated in Fig. 94. After clearing in origanum oil (cretan [Merck]) the sections are mounted in colophonium-xylol. Carbol-xylol is not so satisfactory for clearing.

The numbered tag is kept under the dish containing the

sections.   To do this it is moved forward with the sections from dish to dish.   Before the sections are placed on the slide by means of a spatula the slide is numbered (Fig. 92).   If the specimen from gross tissue to microscopic section is never separated from its written number a chance mixing of sections from different patients cannot take place.

Celloidin Sections of Tissue Fixed in Zenker's Fluid.— Celloidin sections may be made of tissue fixed in Zenker's fluid. After Zenker-fixation the tissue is placed directly in the 95 per cent. alcohol and not in the formalin-alcohol.   The sections of Zenker-fixed material are cut and placed in *iodin solution*

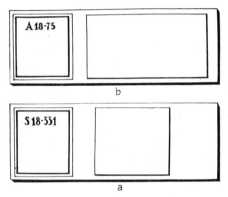

Fig. 92.—Slides for surgical and autopsy specimens.   *a*, Surgical specimen. The cover-glass is number 1, 22-mm. square.   Before mounting, the numbered labels are placed on the left end of the slide.   Labels (22-mm. square exact) are plain with a single narrow black or blue line border.   If for any reason a paraffin section is to be run and the Zenker-fixed material permanently preserved a "P" is placed on the label and on the index card at the time of examination; *b*, slide for autopsy specimen.   Cover-glass is number 1, 22 by 40 mm.

(iodin 5 gm.; 95 per cent. alcohol 500 c.c.) for fifteen minutes, and then in 95 per cent. alcohol until all iodin is removed (one hour or more).   The sections are stained in the hematoxylin for fifteen minutes instead of for from three to five minutes, the time required for the alcohol-formalin tissue.   The other technic is the same as for sections fixed in the formalin-alcohol.

Celloidin sections of tissue in 10 per cent. formalin are treated exactly like the tissue fixed in formalin-alcohol except that the tissue is placed directly in the 95 per cent. alcohol of the celloidin series (page 329) instead of the formalin-alcohol.

Decalcification and Staining of Bone.—With a small hacksaw (Fig. 107), saw the bone into pieces not more than 3 mm. thick; fix in Zenker's fluid, and decalcify for not more than forty-eight hours in a large volume of 5 per cent. nitric acid. Wash overnight; imbed in celloidin, and stain with hematoxylin and eosin.

Several stains are recommended to differentiate true bone from osteoid tissue, but none is satisfactory. Where this distinction is necessary, the tissue should be imbedded in celloidin and sections cut with an old knife and stained with hematoxylin and eosin. (Mallory and Wright's Pathological Technique.)

Examination of the Celloidin Sections.—The celloidin sections prepared in this way are examined and a diagnosis made if possible. To mark a microscopic area on a slide for future reference or study, the slide is fastened down firmly with a clamp, and if oil has been used this is removed with xylol. Then with the low-dry lens outline the area by drawing a ring with a pen dipped in *colored shellac*. The shellac is prepared by adding 10 gm. white shellac and 0.1 gm. methyl violet to 25 c.c. 95 per cent. alcohol. (Mallory and Wright.) The shellac is kept in a wide-mouthed 2–oz., glass-stoppered bottle, and 95 per cent. alcohol in a similar bottle. The pen is dipped in alcohol and cleaned before it is dipped in the shellac.

If a paraffin section of the Zenker-fixed material is desired, the P is placed on the label and on the record card, indicating that a bit of the Zenker-fixed tissue is to be cut and started through the paraffin series in order that more perfect sections may be cut and stained with eosin-methylene blue. The Zenker-fixed and the formalin-fixed material of all slides bearing the P mark is to be kept permanently. The Zenker-fixed material, as well as any formalin-fixed material of sections not so marked, is discarded. The celloidin blocks are kept for one week in one of the pint Mason jars containing 80 per cent. alcohol. The celloidin slides are kept for at least six months. The paraffin slides made from P tissue are kept permanently.

Slides are best kept by placing them in cloth-covered slide-boxes that hold one hundred slides. These boxes are labeled and filed away in order.

In those cases in which it is not possible to make a diagnosis from the celloidin sections, (or from a frozen section), and in cases where better sections are desired for study, paraffin sections of the Zenker-fixed material are made. For many of the differential stains, paraffin sections are necessary. In fact, celloidin sections are used almost exclusively for an initial diagnosis. Paraffin sections of Zenker-fixed material are used for all autopsy specimens.

To clean the slides and cover-glasses of discarded preparations, the slides are heated over a Bunsen burner, and the cover-glasses pushed off into a small dish containing an *acid cleaning fluid* consisting of 50 per cent. sulphuric acid in which 5 per cent. sodium or potassium bichromate has been dissolved. The slides are placed in a 5-gallon crock containing the same solution. After one week the acid is poured off and all acid removed from the slides by washing each separately under the tap. Wipe dry and set on edge in a drawer. Many prefer to boil the covers and slides separately in an alkaline soap solution and then to wash and place them in 95 per cent. alcohol from which they are wiped dry.

Clearing and Mounting Agents.—In general, paraffin sections are dehydrated in 95 per cent. alcohol and absolute alcohol, and cleared in xylol. Many exceptions occur as in the case of fat blackened by osmic acid which is soluble in xylol but is not soluble in chloroform. *Toluol* has a less solvent action on lipoidal substances than has xylol, and may be substituted for xylol in the removal of paraffin and in the clearing of the same sections. *Oil of bergamot* (green oil) will take up as much as 10 per cent. of water and may not affect some anilin colors. It has a questionable use in pathology. Celloidin sections are passed from 95 per cent. alcohol directly into *oil of origanum* (cretan [Merck]), or if stained with hematoxylin-eosin they may be passed from the 95 per cent. alcohol to *carbol-xylol* (25 gm. phenol crystals dissolved in 100 c.c. xylol). Carbol-xylol hardens and shrinks rapidly and extracts anilin colors; it should be avoided as much as possible. Other clearing agents that have a special application are indicated under the stains in connection with which they are used.

Canada balsam of commerce is a thick, tenacious, transparent liquid, and owing to its high acid-content is not suitable for mounting stained preparations. It may be evaporated in the paraffin oven until it becomes solid on cooling, and sufficient xylol added to this to give it the desired consistency (xylol-balsam). *Xylol-balsam*, however, contains acid and cannot be used for mounting specimens in which the chromatin is stained with methylene blue. To neutralize these acids, the balsam may in a large vessel be diluted with xylol to the consistency of water, treated with a large excess of sodium carbonate, and stirred for twenty-four hours with a mechanical stirrer. Carefully pour off the supernatant liquid, and in the paraffin oven evaporate to the desired consistency (*neutral balsam*). Pure white colophonium may be purchased at a low price, is sufficiently free from acids to answer most purposes, and is recommended as a routine medium for mounting histologic sections. It is pulverized in a mortar, and the fine powder added in excess to xylol in a liter bottle which is placed in the paraffin oven and shaken for several days. The *colophonium-xylol* is of a syrupy consistency. If too thin it is evaporated in the paraffin oven to the desired consistency; if it becomes too thick, xylol.is added to make it the proper thinness.

Injections.—Injections of vessels and ducts have a limited use in routine pathologic procedures, but may in special cases prove to be of considerable importance. Surgical specimens that may be obtained immediately after removal from the patient lend themselves best to this technic. For such injections, enough material to fill the vessel may be contained in a single large syringe. The needle of the syringe is inserted into the vessel selected and a small cord tied about the vessel to hold the needle firmly in place. In this way, a thick suspension of *white lead* in a thin paraffin oil may be injected into the artery of an extremity, and x-ray photographs made to show the relation of certain disease processes (infarction, for example) to the blood vessels.

Carmine Injection Mass.—This is the best injection mass for blood vessels. By gently warming, dissolve 200 gm. gelatin (Gold label) in 500 c.c. distilled water. Add 20 gm. carmine (Grübler) and 300 c.c. water and, while stirring, drop in enough concentrated ammonia, to bring about solution of the carmine. Add the carmine solution to the liquefied gelatin, and thoroughly mix at 45°C. To this, slowly add 20 per cent. acetic acid until the ammoniacal odor is lost. An excess of acid must be avoided. This must be observed carefully since an excess of acid will spoil the mass by precipitating the carmine. To use, place the organ in water at 45°C. and at this temperature force the injection mass into the arteries selected. At once place in cold water and after fifteen minutes fix as desired.

Berlin Blue Injection Mass.—This blue mass may be used for the injection of the venous system in tissue in which the arteries have been filled with a carmine mass. Make a 5 per cent. aqueous solution of Berlin blue, and add it to the gelatin— which is prepared in the same way as it is for the carmine mass— until a deep blue color is secured. Use in the same way as the carmine mass.

India Ink.—Black India ink (Higgins) is useful in the injection of the lymphatics of a tissue. Care and some experience are required in this technic. A very fine needle is used in making the injections, but it is not necessary to insert the needle into a lymph vessel, since the liquid ruptures into these vessels from the tissue spaces. Celloidin sections may be cut from tissue injected in this way and stained with hematoxylin-eosin; or it may be fixed in Zenker's fluid, paraffin sections cut and these stained with eosin-methylene blue.

Examination of Fresh Unstained Tissue.—In the routine gross examination of surgical and autopsy specimens, placing fresh tissue under the microscope necessitates only a brief interruption of the gross examination and is too often neglected. A microscope should always be at hand and fresh preparations made whenever indicated.

Scrapings of soft organs and of necrotic material are placed on a clean slide, covered with a square cover-glass, and examined with the dry objectives. A small drop of water may be added before applying the cover-glass, provided it is needed to thin the material. Two per cent. acetic acid may be drawn under the cover-glass by placing a bit of blotting-paper at the opposite side. This reagent dissolves albuminous granules but no fat, and gives a sharper contrast to nuclei. Soft cellular tumors such as a glioma may be diagnosed in this way. In the examination of unstained material the light is reduced to a minimum.

The *teasing* apart of firmer tissues, such as fibrous tissue and smooth and striated muscle, is required before the smaller structures can be identified. This is done by means of two teasing-needles after the addition of a drop of saline. Bits of tissue (encysted trichinella in muscle) may be cut sufficiently thin with scissors to permit its examination under the low-power lens. Ten per cent. caustic soda may occasionally be employed to *macerate* small bits of tissue. For the dissection of medullated nerves and all the tissues of the small embryos, the fresh tissue is placed in 5 per cent. hydrochloric acid in ice-water for twenty-four hours, washed in cold water and the dissection carried out (Longwell).

Frozen sections of fresh tissue may be used to advantage not only for the immediate diagnosis of surgical tissue, but also for microchemical tests: amyloid (1 per cent. methyl violet), glycogen (Gram's iodin), starch (Gram's iodin), colloid (1 per cent. methyl violet), fat (scharlach R or 1 per cent. osmic acid), urates (strong hydrochloric acid), calcium carbonate deposits with effervescence, and calcium phosphate without effervescence on the addition of 5 per cent. hydrochloric, and lead in tissue by treatment with 10 per cent. caustic soda through which a stream of hydrogen sulphid has been passed for five minutes.

Silver Nitrate for Cement Substance.—The boundaries of the cells of an endothelial or mesothelial surface are brought out by treatment with silver nitrate in such a way that the cell periphery appears as a black jagged line in contrast to the yellowish brown of the remainder of the cell. A bit of fresh unfixed mesentery may be tightly stretched over a microscopic slide and placed for ten minutes in a 0.5 per cent. silver nitrate. Transfer to normal saline and for ten minutes expose to direct sunlight. Pass through the alcohols, the xylols, and mount in colophonium-xylol, or examine at once in the salt solution. For endothelium, inject the solution into the artery; and after half an hour cut frozen sections and expose them to direct sunlight for ten minutes.

Fixing Solutions.—Living protoplasm is colloidal and does not color readily with the usual stains. At present, the living cells of animal tissue cannot be subjected to minute microscopic study. Since the unchanged living cells cannot be satisfactorily examined, they must be killed in such a way that they retain their form and a chemical composition that reacts best to stains.

Fixation consists of the precipitation of the colloids and this is brought about by placing the tissue in chemical solutions. The character of the precipitated colloids varies with the chemicals used in precipitating them. For this reason, it is necessary to know the way in which a tissue has been fixed in order to determine the kind of stain that is to be used. In careless histologic work, this correlation between fixation and staining is frequently disregarded. There is no one fixative that answers all purposes, and under the separate solutions the uses of the various fixatives are enumerated.

Zenker-fluid Fixation.—By this method the tissue is not only fixed (colloids precipitated) but it is hardened. With the hardening there is a shrinkage which may contract the tissue to two-thirds its original size. It is to the credit of the fixative, however, that further shrinkage does not take place during paraffin impregnation. It is not advisable to fix in Zenker's fluid very small bits of tissue, such as papules snipped from the skin. Such small bits of tissue should be fixed in formalin, and celloidin sections made; or they may be imbedded by the soap method, and sections made. At present, eosin-methylene blue brings out more general histologic detail than any other

stain. This stain, as well as the phosphotungstic acid-hematoxylin and the anilin blue stain, is made on Zenker-fixed
tissue. These stains require paraffin sections.

Since three of the most important stains (eosin-methylene
blue, phosphotungstic acid-hematoxylin, and anilin blue) in
the differentiation of cells can be applied to Zenker-fixed tissue

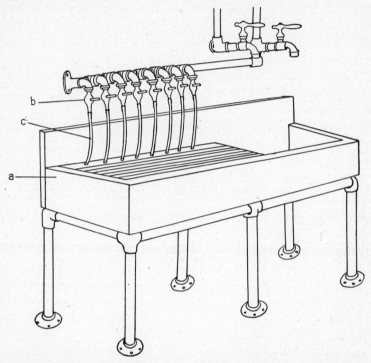

FIG. 93.—Sink for washing specimens. *a*, Sink of soapstone. The upper surface inclines and has shallow furrows in it; *b*, water-cock which carries a short
piece of rubber tubing, *c*. This tubing reaches into the bottle during the washing.
Small pieces of wire-gauze or muslin are placed over the tops of the bottles to
prevent the escape of bits of tissue.

only, it not infrequently happens that a diagnosis may be impossible because all the tissue has been placed in formalin or
alcohol. In such a case, the formalin- or alcohol-fixed tissue
is placed in Zenker's fluid (Zenkerizing formalin-fixed tissue).
If the original fixation was good this usually proves satisfactory.

Mercury must be removed from all Zenker-fixed tissue.

First, to remove the excess of mercury, chrome salt, and acid, the
pieces of tissue are washed in running water (Fig. 93) from overnight to twenty-four hours. Next, paraffin sections—after
the removal of the paraffin with xylol and the xylol with
alcohol—are placed for fifteen minutes in *tincture* of *iodin*
made by dissolving 5 gm. iodin in 500 c.c. 95 per cent. alcohol.
The iodin must be removed by allowing the slides to remain in
the 95 per cent. alcohol until all trace of the brown color has
been removed (from one to two hours). After the removal of
the iodin, the slides are covered with water and are ready for
the stain. Since celloidin sections are not attached to slides
they are removed from the microtome knife and immediately
placed in the tincture of iodin.

Zenker's fluid is prepared by adding 500 gm. mercuric
chlorid, 250 gm. potassium bichromate, and 100 gm. sodium
sulphate to 10 liters of water. Immediately before placing
the tissue in it, add 5 per cent. acetic acid. Zenker's fluid is
made up in a large 20-liter demijohn in the bottom of which
there is an excess of the bichlorid. For convenience in the
fixation of routine specimens, the Zenker's fluid, 10 per cent.
formalin, and 80 per cent. alcohol, are kept in bottles (10-
liter capacity) provided with cocks. The acetic acid is added
from a buret provided for the purpose. The amount of Zenker's fluid should be at least ten times the amount of tissue
placed in it.

This fixative is the best for general histologic work because
the most useful stains are made on Zenker-fixed material,
and paraffin sections are usually cut from tissue fixed in this
way. All tissues, except the most routine specimens such as
appendices, oviducts, fibroids, and the like, are fixed in Zenker's
fluid. The original surgical tag is placed on the bottle containing the Zenker-fixed tissue. Besides surgical tissue, all autopsy
specimens are fixed by this method.

For Zenker-fixation, the tissue is cut not more than 4 mm.
thick and the surface or flat side of the tissue must be the surface across which the microtome knife moves in cutting sections from the block. An exception is made to this in the case

of the brain, heart, or other large organ, from which a shaving
may be cut to show a superficial inflammatory process such
as a meningitis or pericarditis.   From the shavings, blocks for
paraffin sections are cut at right angles to the large surface.

The tissue remains in Zenker's fluid for twenty-four hours,
when it is washed in running water for twelve hours or
more, and then covered with 80 per cent. alcohol in which the
tissue remains permanently.   Sections cut after thirty years
in the alcohol stain well.   In such tissue, however, the mercury
is precipitated in a very insoluble form and special precautions
must be taken to remove it (overnight treatment of sections
with Czaplewsky's solution).

Formalin Fixation.—Ten per cent. formalin (4 per cent.
formaldehyde) is the strength for the fixation of tissue.   For-

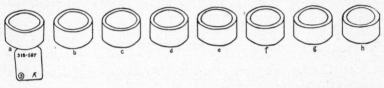

FIG. 94.—Stender dishes for staining celloidin section... *a*, Stender dish 6
cm. across and 3 cm. deep (inside).   For a few sections a dish 35 by 20 mm. (inside) is satisfactory.   The tag beneath *a* follows the section until the section is
mounted on the slide and the number recorded.   The symbol in the lower right-
hand corner denotes formalin-alcohol fixation and the number indicates that
there are three blocks of tissue; *b*, hematoxylin (page 333) for five minutes; *c*,
Czaplewsky for one minute; *d*, saturated solution of lithium carbonate; *e*, water;
f, ¼ per cent. eosin (yellowish, water-soluble) for one minute; *g*, 95 per cent.
alcohol for two minutes; *h*, origanum oil (cretan [Merck]) for five minutes.

malin and formol are commercial names for a saturated aqueous solution of the gas.   Forty per cent. of the gas is required
to saturate water.   Since the gas escapes on exposure to the
air, the formalin of commerce is usually somewhat less than 40
per cent.   As it stands in the laboratory, a white precipitate
may form about the opening of the bottles where the formaldehyde polymerizes to paraformaldehyde.   Normal saline has
been used instead of water in making up the 10 per cent. formalin, but this does not make the solution isotonic.   Lead carbonate may be placed in the bottom of the large bottle containing the 10 per cent. formalin to neutralize any acid present,

but this does not appear to be beneficial; calcium carbonate has been used for the same purpose.

For the demonstration of fat, frozen sections are cut from tissue fixed in formalin; and it has been remarked that in some laboratories the routine surgical diagnoses are made from frozen sections of formalin-fixed tissue stained with hematoxylin-eosin. Formalin-fixed tissue is also valuable for the demonstration of bacteria and protozoa present in tissue, calcium salts, various pigments, and for the indophenol reaction. All important specimens are fixed in formalin as well as Zenker's fluid. The tissue is kept in the formalin permanently, and satisfactory stains may be made after a number of years.

For the staining of organisms in the tissues, very thin sections are cut from paraffin blocks. No such shrinkage as happens in the case of Zenker-fixation occurs in tissue during the fixation in formalin, but during the paraffin imbedding process very serious shrinkage takes place unless special care is taken to prevent it. Formaldehyde acts differently on different tissues. It may harden the tissue somewhat, but frequently it does not do so.

Soap Method of Imbedding (McJunkin; Anatomical Record, 1918; in Press).—Two hundred grams transparent glycerin toilet soap are placed in a 500-c.c. Erlenmeyer or Florence flask that contains 200 c.c. distilled water. The flask is placed in the paraffin oven at 52°C. overnight in order to dissolve the soap. Remove it from the oven and place for three hours in an incubator at 37.5°C. The contents should be a syrupy liquid and should solidify when a small amount is poured into a paper boat and allowed to stand at room temperature for one-half hour. If solidification does not take place, 20 gm. soap should be added to the flask and the contents again melted in the paraffin oven. The toilet soap selected must be so hard that it is brittle and cracks apart when cut with a knife, otherwise the soap will not be of the proper consistency. After the correct consistency has been obtained the soap solution is placed in 100-c.c. wide-mouthed bottles with cork or glass stoppers, with about 50 c.c. to a bottle.

To imbed the tissue small pieces are taken from 10 per cent. formalin and dropped into the melted soap contained in one of the bottles which is placed at 37.5°C. two to three hours and occasionally shaken. The liquid soap in the bottles usually becomes solid after remaining at 37.5°C. for a day or more. To melt the solidified soap, the bottles are placed in the paraffin oven for an hour, the soap cooled to 45°C., the tissue added, and the bottles replaced in the incubator at 37.5°C. The soap solution with the tissue in it is emptied into a box of suitable size made from paper as in paraffin imbedding (page 349) and the tissue arranged on the bottom of the box with forceps. The box should be made from paraffined paper or the paper may be coated by pouring melted paraffin into it. At the end of about one hour the paper is removed, the solid soap trimmed with a knife to the desired size about the tissue and the blocks attached to a heated metal disk just as paraffin blocks are attached. The blocks after about one hour are dropped into a saturated solution of sodium chlorid in a pint Mason jar and the jar placed in the incubator at 37.5°C. overnight.

With forceps remove the block from the saturated salt solution, attach to rotary microtome and cut away the block until the tissue is reached. Carefully trim the block and allow to dry for from three to six hours until a ribbon 6 to 7 microns thick cuts perfectly. The disks may be detached from the microtome and attached after the proper drying so that the ribbon comes from the very surface of the block. The ribbon is placed in distilled water in a flat dish more than 6 in. in diameter and the sections floated on slides on which there is a thin coating of fixative made by adding 4 c.c. of a very thick syrupy celloidin (page 330) to 16 c.c. oil of cloves. The preparations after being pressed out and carefully blotted with filter paper are placed in the paraffin oven for fifteen minutes when they are removed, washed in 95 per cent. alcohol for thirty seconds and placed in distilled water where they remain less than five minutes.

Ionization in the large volume of water in which the soap sections are first placed develops only a slight alkalinity and in the thick soap solution ionization is practically absent.   The saturated salt solution hardens the blocks since it prevents hydrolysis by mass action.   If the tissue is quite fragile the ribbon may be placed in saturated salt solution instead of distilled water.   Tissue fixed in any fashion may be imbedded in this way, but it is especially valuable for formalin-fixed since shrinkage is prevented.   Lipoidal substances are not removed.

Alcohol Fixation.—If 95 per cent. alcohol or absolute alcohol is used, there is a shrinkage of the tissues during fixation, and it may be imbedded in the same way that Zenker-fixed material is imbedded.   For the preservation in tissue of glycogen so that it may be subsequently stained, pieces of tissue not more than 2 mm. thick are fixed in absolute alcohol.

If the tissue is to be stained for glycogen, it is passed directly from the absolute alcohol to alcohol-ether and to the celloidin. If other stains are to be applied, paraffin, celloidin, or soap sections may be employed.   Tissue after being fixed for twelve hours in absolute alcohol is transferred to 80 per cent. alcohol where it is kept permanently.   Alcohol is more valuable as a hardening agent than as a fixative, and this function it performs when used for dehydration.   For the preservation of many pigments, alcohol is as good as formalin, and perhaps better.

Corrosive-alcohol Fixation.—This consists of 1 part of absolute alcohol added to 2 parts of a saturated aqueous solution of bichlorid of mercury.   Tissue fixed in this solution is thought by some to take a polychrome stain more readily. The tissue is cut not more than 2 mm. thick for fixation and should not remain in the solution for more than one year.   To make paraffin sections, the tissue is passed through the paraffin series.

Müller's Fluid.—This fixative is used mostly for parts of the central nervous system which are left in it from three weeks to a year or more.   Tissue fixed in formalin may be prepared for the Pal-Weigert stain by placing it for a few days in Müller's fluid at 37.5°C.   It is prepared by dissolving 25 gm. potassium bichromate and 10 gm. sodium sulphate in 1 liter of water. Chromaffin cells are brought out by this fixation.

Orth's Fluid.—This fixing solution is especially effective in preserving cytoplasmic structures. It is prepared by adding 10 c.c. of formalin (40 per cent. formaldehyd) to 90 c.c. of Müller's fluid just before the tissue is placed in it. The bits of tissue should not be more than 3 mm. thick and are left in the solution for two days after which they are washed in running water overnight and transferred to 80 per cent. alcohol.

Marchi's Fluid.—To 2 parts of Müller's fluid, add 1 part of 1 per cent. osmic acid. Degenerated nerve fibers are demonstrable after fixation for from four days to a week in this solution kept in the dark.

Flemming's Solution.—To 60 c.c. 1 per cent. chromic acid, add 16 c.c. 2 per cent. osmic acid, and 4 c.c. acetic acid. These solutions must be kept separately and mixed just before the tissue is placed in it. Fix tissue 2 mm. thick for twenty-four hours in the dark; wash in running water overnight, and keep in 80 per cent. alcohol. Imbed in paraffin, cut sections, and stain for five minutes in *anilin water* (distilled water shaken with an excess of anilin and filtered) saturated with safranin o. Dehydrate, and mount in colophonium-chloroform. This method is useful for fat-containing tissue.

Picric Acid.—It is useful in fixing parasitic worms and has been used in fixing embryonic tissues. The material may be placed in a saturated aqueous solution for twenty-four hours, after which it is placed in several changes of 70 per cent. alcohol. Paraffin sections are cut and hematoxylin and eosin may be employed.

Carnoy's Mixture.—Mix equal parts by volume of absolute alcohol, glacial acetic acid, and chloroform with an equal part by weight of bichlorid of mercury. Thin specimens after thirty minutes in this solution are washed with running water and the mercury removed with iodin. It is useful for fixing ova of invertebrates and may be employed where such ova are suspected in tissues.

Pianese's Solution.—To 60 c.c. of 1 per cent. platinum chlorid, add 20 c.c. ¼ per cent. chromic acid, 20 c.c. 2 per cent. osmic acid, and 4 drops of formic acid. Fix 2 mm.

pieces for twenty-four hours in the dark, wash overnight in running water and keep in 80 per cent. alcohol.   It is very useful for the preservation of nuclear division figures and for special stains (page 377) for hyaline substances.

Imbedding in Paraffin.—After remaining overnight or longer in 80 per cent. alcohol, blocks of the Zenker-fixed tissue not more than 2 mm. or 3 mm. may be cut and started through the paraffin series of bottles (Fig. 95).   Blocks from aorta, intestinal wall, or other thin-walled organ or tissue must be cut so that

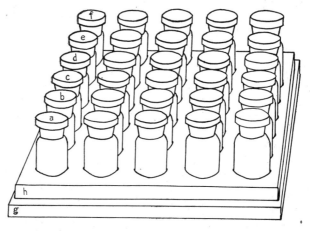

FIG. 95.—Block for paraffin imbedding.   *a*, 95 per cent. alcohol 1; *b*, 95 per cent. alcohol 2; *c*, absolute alcohol 1; *d*, absolute alcohol 2; *e*, chloroform; *f*, chloroform saturated with paraffin; *g*, ¾ in. board on which is nailed *h*, a ¾-in. board in which the 2⅜ in. holes for the bottles are bored; *g*, is 19 in. square and *h* is 18 in. square.   The glass-stoppered bottles (Eimer and Amend) are 4⅝ in. high with stopper in place and 2³⁄₁₆ in. across the bottom.   If tissue is added daily all bottles are refilled at the end of each week.

the technician cannot mount them from the paraffin in such a way that the sections will be cut in the wrong direction.   That is, they must be cut before being dropped into the fixative so that they will be placed in the boats on their flat sides, without the necessity of giving individual directions for each piece of tissue.

Each morning with long forceps the specimen with its tag is moved back one bottle.   Thus, on the seventh day the specimen is removed from the chloroform, saturated with paraffin, and placed in *paraffin* (extra white, with a melting point of 52°C.) melted in the paraffin oven (Fig. 96) which is kept at a temperature below 60°C. The melted paraffin is kept in Stender dishes. The numbered tag is placed beneath the dish that contains the specimen. The specimen is placed in a dish, and after about one hour it is transferred to a second dish. The Zenker-fixed specimens remain in the oven for two hours and even for three hours, as Zenker-fixed material does not shrink while in the oven. The tissue is taken from the second Stender dish

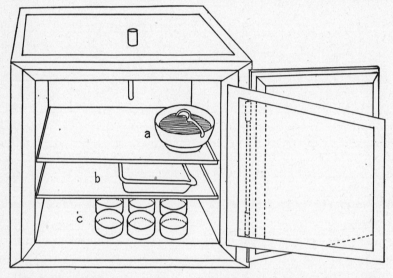

Fig. 96.—Paraffin oven. Upper compartment in which 52°C. paraffin (extra white) is kept in a casserole, *a*. A china-ware ladle is used for transferring the paraffin; *b*, shelf for agate-ware tray in which paper boats (Fig. 97) are placed. *c*, Stender dishes for specimens. A small pair of dressing forceps are kept in the oven for transferring specimens. Regulate at 55°C.

and placed in a *paper boat* (Fig. 97) made for this purpose from ordinary paper. This boat rests on the bottom of an enamel tray, and is filled by means of a small ladle with paraffin from a half-liter casserole. The boat, bearing the tag number on one end, remains in the oven for about fifteen minutes, and is then floated on water until the paraffin completely hardens, when the tissue blocks are carefully cut apart. These blocks with the number tags are placed in a pill-box of pasteboard (Fig. 98) that bears a number and a letter indicating the fixation on one end. The blocks are kept permanently in these boxes.

Imbedding Skin.—Skin, and certain other tissues such as liver or spleen containing large quantities of blood and fixed in Zenker's fluid, cut with difficulty if imbedded in the usual way. To correct this it is better to allow the tissue to remain in the absolute alcohols for two or three hours only, to transfer it to oil of cedar wood (clearing) overnight, to carry through two

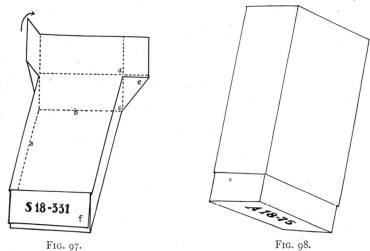

FIG. 97.   FIG. 98.

FIG. 97.—Paper boat for blocking tissue. Take a rectangular piece of medium or heavy weight paper 4 by 6 in. and fold the sides and then to a greater depth the ends at *b*. Make the two adjacent inner sides of the rectangle marked off by the folding coincide at *cd*, turn back on the ends the triangle *e*, crimp all the folded edges and turn back the lip, *f*, on which the number of the specimen is written.

FIG. 98.—Pasteboard box for paraffin blocks. White pill-box measuring 2⅜ by 2¼ by 1¼ in. The number and methods of fixation are written on one end. These boxes are kept permanently.

changes of xylol during twenty minutes and to place it in the paraffin oven a minimum time (thirty minutes).

Cutting Paraffin Sections.—The paraffin blocks whether obtained after fixation in Zenker's fluid, formalin, alcohol, or other fixatives are cut on a rotary microtome (Fig. 99). For the usual work 6-micron sections (3 clicks) are cut; but it may at times be desirable to cut from very dense cellular tissue, such as liver, 4-micron sections (2 clicks). On the micrometer wheel of some microtome models one click is a micron. Before attaching the disks, all excess of paraffin is cut from about the tissue, and the four sides of the surface made exactly parallel. A small drawer in a table should be reserved for paraffin shavings, and the blocks cut apart and trimmed on a sheet of pasteboard tacked to the table directly above this drawer.

As the ribbon comes from the knife it is held with a small pair of fine-pointed forceps, removed from the knife with these

FIG. 99.—Rotary microtome. Obtain at least twelve metal disks with ball attachment to which the paraffin blocks are fastened, so that all the blocks from an autopsy may be attached before cutting is begun. Each click of the micrometer feed represents 2 microns. For routine work 6-micron sections are employed. For certain stains 4-micron sections are required. Obtain at least two Minot microtome knives.

and a needle, and placed in a dish of water at about 45°C. A convenient length of ribbon is from 3 in. to 4 in. The temperature of the laboratory is maintained at from 16° to 18°C. In summer the blocks are removed from ice water and immediately placed in the microtome and sections cut. With a heated scalpel the ribbon is separated at the desired points, these being between the sections so that the individual sections included in the bit of ribbon can be mounted beneath a 22 by 40 mm. cover-glass. The sections are floated on clean *slides* (B. & L. extra white, 3 by 1, medium thickness) on which albumin fixative has been placed by means of a camel's-hair brush, and the excess wiped off with clean laundered unstarched muslin.

For special stains, such as those of Bensley, calculated to bring out *minute detail* very thin sections (2 to 3 microns) must be employed. To cut such sections a small bit of tissue not more than 4 mm. across must be imbedded in the paraffin.

For routine work, it is preferable to use No. 1 cover-glasses, 22 by 40 mm. The length of the ribbon placed on the slide should be the length of the cover-glass and so placed that there is space for the label (24 mm. square, plain, single, narrow black-line body) at the left end of the slide. If No. 1 cover-glasses, 22 mm. square, are used, the ribbon is placed at the center of the slide and usually consists of a single section from the block.

To attach the sections, place them on slides on which there is a very thin coating of albumin fixative, let them dry for a short time, stand on edge in 10-slide staining dishes, and place the dishes in the paraffin oven overnight. Sections from only one block of tissue are floated in the dish at a time. The desired number of sections is placed on slides that bear the number of the tissue scratched on one end by means of a diamond scratch (Fig. 102). Whatever stain is to be used, the paraffin is to be removed with xylol, the xylol removed with absolute alcohol, followed by 95 per cent. alcohol, and the alcohol with water. There should be provided a *set of bottles* containing solutions and stains for histologic work. These bottles should be glass-stoppered and may be 1 liter or 500 c.c. in size, according to the amount of work being done. In order to save solutions, two bottles are provided for 95 per cent. alcohol, one bottle for 95 per cent. alcohol for the removal of iodin from sections, two bottles for absolute alcohol, and two bottles for xylol. The bottles in each pair are labelled 1 and 2; the alcohols and the xylol in the number

2 bottles are kept pure. Sufficient amounts of stains may be kept in 500 c.c. bottles.

If the microtome and knife are good, the three most common errors which make it impossible to obtain a ribbon are imperfect

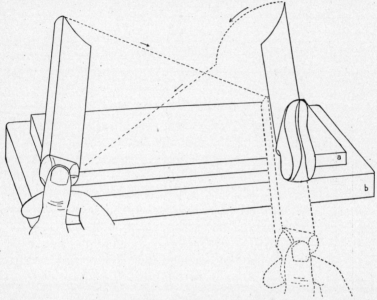

FIG. 100.—Microtome knife hone. The knife, if gross nicks are present, is first placed on a coarse water-stone, *a*, until these are removed and then, on a fine carborundum water-stone. These stones are set in a suitable wooden base, *b*. The knife is drawn across the stone in the directions indicated by the arrows. The knife is strapped like a razor which tends to efface scratches from the bone since the knife is drawn on the strap at right angles to these scratches. Feel the edge of the knife to determine its smoothness. A sharp knife is the first requisite in cutting sections.

FIG. 101.—Leather Strop for microtome knife. Obtained from Charles Emerson, Emerson Place, Charlestown, Mass.

impregnation with paraffin, improper sharpening of the knife (Fig. 100), and too hot or too cold room temperature. If the tissue cut is dense, the knife should be cleansed with a soft cloth between each block and strapped (Fig. 101). If slight

23

wrinkles are present in the section on floating it on the slide, the slide may be slanted at an angle of 45°C. and warmed over a flame until the paraffin melts.

Serial paraffin sections are sections of an entire block cut and mounted in consecutive order. This is desirable in re-constructions of structures, such as an entire embryo. It is not advisable to try to cut the sections thinner than 10 microns.

Dipping the paraffin blocks after they have been trimmed to the correct size in a paraffin which melts at 40°C. may improve the adhesiveness of the sections as they come from the knife. Especial care must be used to make the edges of the block exactly parallel. The microtome knife is set as straight as possible and yet not have the cut surface of the block pressed upon after it drops below the cutting-edge. It may be necessary to set well-worn knives at a considerable angle to clear the block in this way.

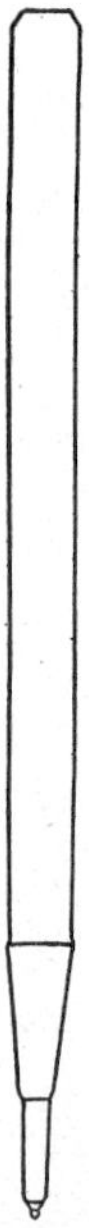

Rapid Paraffin Method.—If apparatus is at hand for only paraffin sections and it becomes necessary to obtain sections within forty-eight to seventy-two hours, this is best done by cutting the blocks as small and thin as possible and passing them hur-riedly through the regular paraffin series.

Sections may be obtained by placing formalin-fixed tissue for three hours in each of the following liquids: 80 per cent. alcohol, 95 per cent. alcohol, acetone 1, acetone 2, benzol or toluol, and melted paraffin in the oven. Sections obtained in this way are inferior to either celloidin sections or frozen sections of formalin-fixed tissue.

FIG. 102. — Diamond scratch. In-expensive chips from diamonds set in metal holders.

Serial celloidin sections are mounted, as soon as they are cut, on slides covered with albumin fixative. The sections may be mounted on glass plates by the molasses method. Again, serial celloidin sections may be fastened to slides by the ether-vapor method, as indicated under stain for tubercle bacilli in tissue (page 370).

Molasses-plate Method for Staining Paraffin or Celloidin Sections in Sheets (Warthin).—The purpose of this method is to stain large numbers of sections at one time while they are kept in the order in which they are removed from the microtome knife. It is, therefore, useful in the staining of serial sections and sections for classes in normal and pathologic histology.

Paraffin ribbons are floated on a warm solution consisting of 10 parts of New Orleans molasses and 90 parts distilled water. Five liters of this solution are made up at one time and preserved by the addition of a crystal of thymol. A perfectly clean and fat-free photographic plate (5 by 7 in.) is slipped into the tray containing the dilute syrup and the ribbons in the proper order drawn upon the plate. The plate is drained, placed for fifteen minutes in the paraffin oven, immersed in xylol (5 minutes), in absolute alcohol (2 minutes), and flooded with thin celloidin (page 332). All the solutions are best kept in trays such as those used for developing photographic plates. The celloidin is dried for two minutes and the plate immersed in warm water to loosen the sheet of celloidin. Stain in the same way that celloidin sections are stained by immersing them in the staining solutions. The sections are cut apart with scissors while in the origanum oil. The sheets are transferred by grasping at two corners with forceps.

If celloidin sections are used the process is the same except that the five-minute bath in xylol to remove the paraffin is omitted. The celloidin sheets may be labeled by writing the label with wax pencil on the dry glass plate.

Albumin Fixative.—To prepare the albumin fixative thoroughly beat up the whites of four eggs with an equal amount of glycerin using an egg-beater, add 1 per cent. sodium salicylate, and let stand for twenty-four hours. Filter through filter paper. The filtrate must be clear. If it is not clear, allow it to stand for several days and filter a second time.

HISTOLOGIC STAINS

It has been mentioned that most of the stains employed for autopsy tissue are used for surgical specimens, but some of the staining methods such as those for frozen sections of fresh tissue or for celloidin sections for routine diagnosis made use of in surgical diagnosis are of little or no service in the examination of autopsy material. For greater convenience of reference the histologic stains that are described are given under this heading. Distilled water is used in making up all stains and throughout the book water refers to distilled water unless tap water is obviously as good.

In a considerable number of the processes of dyeing textile fabrics, an insoluble precipitate of a chemical compound is placed in a cloth in such intimate contact with the fiber that it cannot be washed out. The fabric is then treated with a dye that enters into a definite chemical combination with the insoluble precipitate or *mordant*. This union of dye and mordant is a chemical one. Some histologic dyes are of this character.

Without doubt, some of the dyes *directly* unite chemically with the fixed protoplasm. Thus, de-methylated methylene blue (so-called methylene azur) unites with chromatin, although other nuclear dyes are present in greater concentration. With a majority of the dyes, however, the differential staining of tissue seems not to depend on a chemical union indirect or direct, but on physical properties by virtue of which certain parts of the cells retain the stain longer than other parts during a decolorizing or differentiating process.

Nuclear and Cytoplasmic Stains.—The differentiation of cytoplasm and nucleus is usually the first consideration in tissue sections, and most of the common stains are spoken of as one or the other. Thus, eosin and acid fuchsin are cytoplasmic stains, while basic (neutral) fuchsin and methylene blue are nuclear stains. Since the chromophore group of dyes staining cytoplasm is frequently an acid, they are spoken of as *acid stains*, while the nuclear stains are basic since in a *basic dye* the coloring group is basic and is combined with an indifferent acid. The so-called *neutral stains* of cytology are made by combining basic dyes with acid dyes. The cytoplasmic granules of the three varieties of myeloblastic leukocytes are spoken of as acidophilic, basophilic or neutrophilic according

to their reaction to the components of the stain. Stains used
to bring out plainly a certain structure, as elastic fibrils, are
sometimes spoken of as special *selective stains.*

In *metachromatic stains,* most structures are stained the color
of the aqueous solution, while special structures take that of
the color base. Methyl violet stains cells bluish; but amyloid,
chondromucin, mucin, and the granules of mast cells are colored
red. In this dye the color base (red) is united with chlorin;
and it appears that some base in the substances unites with the
chlorin to free the red color base which is retained in the
structures staining metachromatically.

It will be noted that *Grübler's dyes* are usually specified in
this book. This is because the writer has not, except in a few
cases, tested out others. Certain domestic dyes placed on the
market by the larger supply firms have been found to stain
perfectly and soon the list of these will be complete and their
properties known. Before making any substitution in a
technical method it is required that the practical application
of the proposed substitute be tried. If found satisfactory,
then it is important to learn if the dye as obtained commercially
is uniform from month to month.

Eosin-Methylene Blue Stain (Mallory).—Slides of Zenker-
fixed tissue are removed from the oven and covered with xylol
1 followed by xylol 2, consuming about fifteen minutes
in the two processes. This removes the paraffin. The absolute alcohol 1 and 2 (five minutes) and the 95 per cent.
alcohol 1 and 2 (five minutes) are now poured over the slides
one after the other, using a small funnel to pour the solutions
back into the bottle. It is distinct economy to employ two
bottles (page 352) of each of the solutions, since the second
one remains quite pure and does not have to be discarded after
each series of slides. Cover the sections with water. This is a
general method for removing paraffin from sections. If Zenker's
fluid has been used as a fixative, the mercury is removed in the
manner indicated under Zenker-fixation (page 341). Mercury
is removed from all tissue fixed in fluids containing bichlorid of
mercury, unless the contrary is specified in the technic of the

stains that are to be employed. The eosin-methylene blue
stain is used on Zenker-fixed tissue; and formalin- and alcohol-
fixed tissue cannot be satisfactorily stained with it. Fairly
good results may be obtained if such tissue is "Zenkerized."
It may be applied to the formalin-fixed tissue containing bacteria, but the eosin stain is faint.

The nuclei are usually blue, but may be distinctly purplish.
The cytoplasm of most cells is pinkish; but it may stain a
blue, as is seen in the case of the lymphoblastic cells. Structures, such as hyaline in liver cells (Fig. 103), that are faintly

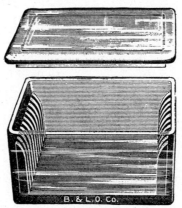

Fig. 104.—Ten-slide staining dish.

visible and readily overlooked with other stains, are brought
out with great distinctness by this stain. This is the best
routine stain for autopsy specimens, but the most perfect
results are obtained on tissue fixed within five minutes after a
surgical removal. Cytoplasmic products, such as fibrils,
may also be brought out very distinctly. Basophilic granules,
such as tigroid or Nissl granules of ganglion cell and the bacillus-
like granules of the cytoplasm of liver cells are well brought
out, staining from a blue to a purple.

To make the stain, water is poured from the staining-dish
(Fig. 104) and the slides covered overnight with a 5 per cent.
aqueous solution of Grübler's yellowish, water-soluble eosin.
On the following morning, the eosin is poured back into the

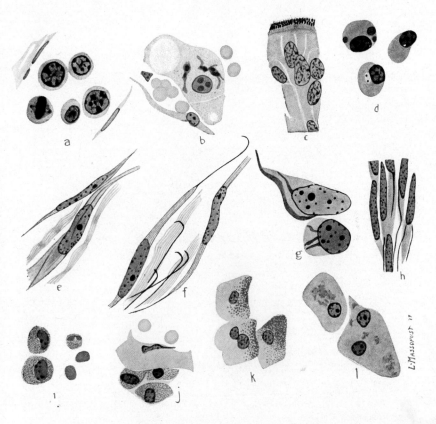

FIG. 103.—(Camera-lucida; oil-immersion) First Row (Eosin-methylene blue stain). *a*, Cells of lymphobastoma showing the character of the cytoplasm of the lymphocytes; *b*, hyalin in liver cells (case of so-called alcoholic cirrhosis); *c*, pertussis bacilli in the cilia of human trachea; *d*, plasma cells note centrosomes in one and hyaline droplets (Russel's bodies) in another. Many differential details of this character cannot be brought out by the hematoxylin stain.

Second Row (phosphotungstic acid-hematoxylin stain). *e*, Ulcer of stomach: fibroblasts in the granulation tissue showing fibroglia fibrils in the cells and collagen fibrils between them; *f*, prostate: two smooth muscle cells showing myoglia fibrils with coarse "hooked" fibrils between them which are formed by fusion of the fine fibrils; *g*, two glia cells that show coarse neuroglia fibrils from a glioma over coccyx; *h*, epithelial cells with fibrils from a hair-matrix carcinoma (so-called rodent ulcer or basal-cell carcinoma).

Third Row (specific stains). *i*, two myelocytes and one neutrophile from spleen of myelogeneous leukemia stained with oxydase stain (Graham); *j*, methyl violet stain showing liver cells with homogeneous amyloid between them and the capillary which is indicated by the endothelial cell and the two red blood corpuscles; *k*, liver cells of a rabbit (Best's stain)—note unilateral position of glycogen; *l*, unstained hemosiderin in liver cells.

bottle, the slide washed in tap water and covered with an aqueous methylene blue solution. The aqueous methylene blue solution is made immediately before it is poured on the slides by adding 20 c.c. of an alkaline methylene blue to 80 c.c. of distilled water. The alkaline methylene blue is quite permanent (two months), and consists of 5 gm. of Grübler's B.X. methylene blue, 5 gm. potassium carbonate, and 500 c.c. of water (Unna). The intense eosin staining may be secured by placing the dish in the paraffin oven for one hour, instead of allowing the slides to stand overnight in the stain at room temperature.

The time during which the slides should be stained in the methylene blue depends largely on the age of the alkaline

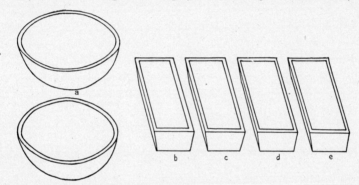

FIG. 105.—Dishes for dehydrating and differentiating eosin-methylene blue sections. *a*, Finger-bowls 4.5 in. across top containing 95 per cent. alcohol to which has been added 1 or 2 drops colophonium-xylol; *b*, glass dish 3¼ by 1⅛ by ⅝ in. containing absolute alcohol 1. These oblong dishes may be obtained from the Bausch and Lomb Optical Co.; *c*, absolute alcohol 2; *d*, xylol 1; *e*, xylol 2.

methylene blue solution. If it is less than one week old, twenty minutes may be sufficient; while if it is one month old, forty minutes may be required. The organ and the time postmortem or postoperative are other factors in determining the length of time for staining with the blue. The time (average thirty minutes) is best determined by removing a slide from the dish and washing it off under the tap. If it is sufficiently stained with the methylene blue, the red does not show macroscopically. After sufficient staining with the methylene blue, this stain is washed out of the dish under the tap and the slides allowed to remain in water for a few minutes until each slide can be differentiated.

The differentiation (Fig. 105) is important. The slide is placed first in a dish of 95 per cent. alcohol to which 1 drop of colophonium-xylol has been added, and lifted up and down with a needle until the first faint pink appears in the preparation, when it is transferred to absolute alcohol contained in an oblong dish. As soon as the first slide has been differentiated, a second one is placed in the dish, and so on until all the dishes (one dish 95 per cent. alcohol; two dishes absolute alcohol; and two dishes xylol) are made to contain a slide. The slides are mounted in colophonium-xylol.

If the slides are too red, it is due usually to insufficient staining in the methylene blue, rather than to too prolonged differentiation.

Phosphotungstic Acid-Hematoxylin Stain (Mallory).— This stain is used on Zenker-fixed material for the demonstration of fibroglia, myoglia, and neuroglia fibrils which are colored from dark blue to black (Fig. 103). It is, therefore, especially valuable for the identification of cells with fibrils. Collagen stains a yellowish brown. Fibrin is blue. Many epithelial structures, such as bile capillaries and the intercellular bridges of prickle cells, are well brought out. Mitotic figures are sharply stained. Centrosomes are distinct. To secure best results, the tissue should be fixed five minutes postoperative. Results obtained on autopsy tissue more than one hour postmortem are not satisfactory. After removal of paraffin, mercury, and iodin, place the slides for ten minutes in ¼ per cent. potassium permanganate. Wash with water, and transfer to 5 per cent. oxalic acid for twenty minutes. Wash, and place overnight in the phosphotungstic acid-hematoxylin solution. This solution is prepared by adding 0.25 gm. hematein-ammonium (Grübler) and 5 gm. phosphotungstic acid (Merck) to 250 c.c. distilled water. The stain is allowed to age for at least one month, or it may be ripened for immediate use by the addition of 10 c.c. of the ¼ per cent. permanganate. For the hematein-ammonium, 0.25 gm. pure hematoxylin crystals may be substituted; but in this case 20 c.c. of the permanganate is added to ripen the solution. Pass the slides directly into 95 per cent. alcohol from the stain, and differentiate for one-half minute or less. Pass quickly through absolute alcohols 1 and 2, xylols 1 and 2, and mount in colophonium-xylol.

Anilin Blue Stain (Mallory).—Perfect results are obtained on tissue fixed five minutes postoperative. This stain is used on Zenker-fixed material for the demonstration of collagen. It is, therefore, especially valuable for the determination of the presence of fibroblasts. Fibroglia, neuroglia, and myoglia fibrils, as well as the nuclei and cytoplasm of cells, stain red (Fig. 103). Certain hyalin substances, such as mucus and amyloid, stain blue; but the wavy character of 'the intensely blue collagen usually makes its differentiation easy. Fibrin stains red, while blood corpuscles stain yellow. This connective tissue stain is applied to perfect paraffin sections and gives much greater detail than *van Gieson's stain.*

After removal of the paraffin, mercury, and iodin, wash and place for twenty minutes in an acid fuchsin solution. The acid fuchsin solution is prepared by adding 2 gm. Grübler's acid fuchsin to 500 c.c. water. Without washing, pass directly for twenty minutes into anilin blue solution. The anilin blue solution is prepared by adding 2.5 gm. Grübler's water-soluble anilin blue and 10 gm. orange G to 500 c.c. 1 per cent. phosphomolybdic acid (Merck). Remove from this stain and differentiate for one-half minute, or less, in 95 per cent. alcohol, and pass hurriedly through the absolute alcohols and xylols to colophonium-xylol.

Elastic Fibril Stain (Verhoeff).—This stain is of value for the morphologic study of tissue which contains many elastic fibrils, such as the walls of blood vessels, mammary gland, or the stroma of tumors. Elastic fibrils are black, the nuclei are dark, while the other structures take more or less of the eosin. In the stain, which is less than one month old, place for fifteen minutes Zenker-fixed celloidin or paraffin sections from which the mercury has not been removed. To prepare the stain, dissolve by heat 1 gm. hematoxylin in 20 c.c. absolute alcohol in a large test-tube, and add 8 c.c. 10 per cent. ferric chlorid and 8 c.c. iodin solution (iodin 2 gm.; potassium iodid 4 gm.; and water 100 c.c.). Remove from the stain, and wash in ½ per cent. ferric chlorid until excessive stain is removed (one minute). Wash and place in 95 per cent. alcohol to remove the iodin (one-half hour). Wash and counterstain with ½ per cent. eosin (one-half minute). Wash and dehydrate in 95 per cent. alcohol (one minute); transfer to origanum oil (five minutes), and mount in colophonium-xylol.

Elastic Fibril Stain (Weigert).—This stain is applicable to tissue fixed by any of the common methods. Elastic fibrils exhibit a dark purple color on a light background. To prepare the stain, dissolve 2 gm. basic fuchsin and 4 gm. resorcin in 200 c.c. water; bring the solution to a boil and add 25 c.c. liquor ferri sesquichlorati. The liquid is boiled and stirred for five minutes, filtered and the precipitate dried. Dissolve the dry precipitate in 200 c.c. boiling 95 per cent. alcohol. Cool, filter, make up to 200 c.c. with 95 per cent. alcohol and add 4 c.c. concentrated hydrochloric acid. To apply the stain, place paraffin sections in the stain for from twenty minutes to one hour; wash with 95 per cent. alcohol until the stain ceases to be given off; dehydrate in absolute alcohol and pass through xylol to colophonium-xylol. Essential oils are not suitable for clearing.

Iron-hematoxylin Stain (Heidenhain).—Cut 4-micron paraffin sections of Zenker-fixed tissue. Stain the sections for five hours in 2 per cent. ferric ammonium sulphate; wash, and place overnight in a hematoxylin solution. The iron solution is a double salt of ammonium and sesquioxide of iron. The crystals must be a clear violet in color. If opaque and yellow they must be rejected. The crystals are kept in a tightly stoppered bottle. To prepare the hematoxylin solution, dissolve 1 gm. hematoxylin in 20 c.c. absolute alcohol by warming, and add 180 c.c. distilled water. It is ripened two weeks before using. Remove from the hematoxylin; wash in water, and then in the 2 per cent. ferric ammonium sulphate for a few minutes at a time, until the slide when washed in water and examined under the microscope in water shows the nuclei well differentiated. All bottles and utensils used in this process should be chemically clean and washed in distilled water before using. Wash in running water for fifteen minutes, and pass through the alcohols and xylols to colophonium-xylol.

Nuclear material is well stained and centrosomes are distinctly brought out.

Staining Soap or Paraffin Sections of Formalin-fixed Tissue with Hematoxylin-eosin.—The tissue is imbedded by the soap method (page 344). Sections may be made by the slow paraffin method but considerable shrinkage occurs. Stain according to the technic given under the staining of celloidin sections (page 334), using the long dishes for slides instead of Stender dishes, until the 95 per cent. alcohol is reached. Transfer from 95 per cent. alcohol to absolute alcohol, and then to xylol rather than to the origanum oil (cretan [Merck]) used for celloidin sections. Mount in colophonium-xylol. By this method the nuclear stain is frequently better than can possibly be obtained by an eosin-methylene blue stain of Zenker-fixed material; but the cytoplasm of many cells, such as lymphocytes, is practically invisible.

Red Nuclear Stain with Lithium Carmin.—A red nuclear stain may be desirable as a contrast to pigment in tissue, to bacteria in the Gram-Weigert stain, to fibrin in Weigert's stain, and for other purposes. For five minutes stain paraffin or celloidin sections of alcohol- or formalin-fixed tissue in lithium carmin. This solution is prepared by dissolving 5 gm. carmin and a crystal of thymol in 100 c.c. of a saturated aqueous solution of lithium carbonate (Orth). Wash hurriedly in water and differentiate for one to two minutes in Czaplewsky solution. Pass through 95 per cent. alcohol to origanum oil, and mount in colophonium-xylol.

An *alum carmin* stains somewhat more sharply but not so heavily. The stain is prepared by adding 2 gm. carmin and 5 gm. potassium alum to 100 c.c. water, boiling for fifteen minutes, cooling, filtering, making up to 100 c.c. and placing in the solution a small crystal of thymol. The stain is applied exactly like the lithium carmin except that the sections are not washed before being placed in the Czaplewsky solution.

Scharlach R. Stain for Fat (Herxheimer).—Place frozen sections of formalin-fixed tissue in 70 per cent. alcohol. Remove from the alcohol and for three minutes place them in a solution saturated with scharlach R. that consists of equal parts of acetone (C. P.) and 70 per cent. alcohol. Transfer the sections for a few seconds to 70 per cent. alcohol, wash in water, and counterstain them with hematoxylin, differentiating in the usual way. The sections are washed in water and mounted in *glycerin jelly*. To prepare the jelly, dissolve 50 gm. gelatin in 250 c.c. distilled water, and add 250 c.c. glycerin and

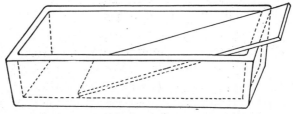

FIG. 106.—Polychrome staining of slides. Dish 3¼ by 1⅛ by ⅝ in. (Obtained from Bausch and Lomb Optical Co.). 10 c.c. of polychrome stain are placed in this dish and mixed with the lower end of the slide while the other end of the slide is drawn up on the end of the dish so that the under preparation side is in contact with the stain. The stain is made by adding 10 drops of polychrome protozoon stain to 10 c.c. 0.003N sodium carbonate.

5 c.c. phenol. To mount sections in glycerin jelly, a 3-oz. Canada balsam bottle, provided with a glass rod and half-filled with jelly, is placed in hot water; and, when melted, a drop of the jelly is placed on the section on a slide and a cover-glass applied.

The saturated solution of scharlach R. in acetone-alcohol should be kept in a 500-c.c. glass-stoppered bottle with an excess of the stain in the bottom of the bottle. To use, filter the saturated solution into a Stender dish provided with a cover.

Neutral fat is colored a bright red instead of the yellow of Sudan. Lipoidal substances (kidney epithelium, cortical cells of the adrenal) may stain from yellow to brown.

Osmium Tetroxid for Fat.—Thin bits of tissue (1 mm.) fixed two days in Flemming's solution are washed overnight in water and placed for a week in 80 per cent. alcohol. Cut paraffin sections; stain with hematoxylin and eosin, and pass through alcohol and chloroform to colophonium-chloroform. Reduction by an unsaturated fatty acid to a lower oxid or to metallic osmium produces a blackening. This is brought about by olein, oleic acid, and the lipoidal substances of myelin.

Frozen sections of fresh- or formalin-fixed tissue may be treated with 1 per cent. osmic acid by drawing the reagent under the cover-glass with filter paper. Osmium tetroxid comes in glass ampules. These are broken in the amount of distilled water required to make a 2 per cent. solution. More dilute solutions are made as required.

Fatty Acid Crystals (Klotz).—Fix thin bits of tissue overnight in a solution made by dissolving 2.5 gm. chrome alum (Merck)

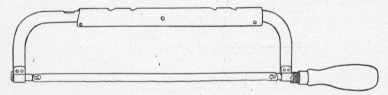

Fig. 107.—Hack-saw (purchased at general hardware stores). It is used for sawing bone into thin lamellæ for fixation and especially for decalcification.

and 5 gm. neutral acetate of copper in 100 c.c. 10 per cent. formalin and adding 5 c.c. acetic acid. The chrome alum (Merck) is first dissolved by boiling it in the formalin and adding the copper salt as the solution cools. If calcified, it may be necessary to saw the material into thin lamellæ with a hack-saw (Fig. 107), so that the acetic acid will remove the lime.

Wash the tissue for one hour in running water, and cut frozen sections. Stain the sections overnight in a ripened saturated solution of hematoxylin in 60 per cent. alcohol. Wash in water and differentiate them until they become brown with Weigert's decolorizer (potassium ferricyanid, 2.5 gm.; borax, 2 gm., and water, 100 c.c.). Wash, counterstain with scharlach R., and mount in glycerin jelly. Fatty acid crystals are

black; neutral fat red.   Cholesterin crystals may be identified
by their shape.

Hemosiderin Reaction (Nishimura).—The iron reaction
is of value to determine the nature of brownish intracellular
or extracellular pigments (Fig. 103).   Place frozen or celloidin
sections of formalin- or alcohol-fixed tissue for one hour in 5 per
cent. ammonium sulphid, and transfer for one hour to equal
parts of 2 per cent. potassium ferrocyanid and 1 per cent.
hydrochloric acid.   Wash in water, and place for a few minutes
in 0.5 per cent. hydrochloric acid.   Wash, and stain for ten
minutes with lithium carmin.   Wash hurriedly in water and

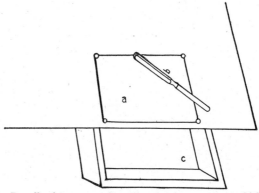

Fig. 108.—Paraffin drawer.   *a*, Pasteboard 8 in. square on which block from
the boats are cut apart with the blunt-point scalpel, *b*, and the paraffin shavings
brushed into the table drawer, *c*.

pass through 95 per cent. alcohol and origanum oil (cretan
[Merck]) to colophonium-xylol.   The hemosiderin granules are
bluish-green; nuclei red.

A section of an entire organ (half of a kidney) may be placed
overnight in the ammonium sulphid solution, for twenty-four
hours in the ferrocyanid-hydrochloric acid solution, and overnight in a 0.5 per cent. hydrochloric acid.   The tissue may be
carried into 80 per cent. glycerin and then into Russian oil
for permanent gross specimens.   A greenish-blue color denotes
hemosiderin.

Small blocks of tissue may be carried through the sulphid
and ferrocyanid solution *en masse* or blocks may be cut from

the surface of whole organs after they have received this treatment. Such blocks may be imbedded in paraffin and sections stained as follows: (1) remove paraffin; (2) 0.5 per cent. hydrochloric acid 1 hour; (3) water; (4) 1 per cent. safranin 15 minutes; (5) water; (6) 95 per cent. alcohol and absolute alcohol to a light pink—about 1 minute; (7) xylol; (8) colophonium-xylol. This method gives the most perfect results.

Reaction for Lead within Cells (McJunkin; Journal of Medical Research, Vol. 27, Page 271). For forty-five minutes place thin paraffin sections of formalin-fixed material in a 10 per cent. solution of potassium hydroxid through which a small stream of hydrogen sulphid has been passed for five minutes. Wash and lightly stain with 0.5 per cent. eosin; pass through the alcohols and xylols to colophonium-xylol. Lead deposits that do not give a reaction for inorganic lead may be demonstrated in this way. The lead appears as minute black granules.

Glycogen Stain (Best).—Rapidly growing tumors, the tissue from cases of diabetes, and inflammatory tissue, are frequently fixed in absolute alcohol for the demonstration of glycogen. The pieces of tissue not more than 2 mm. thick are carried from the absolute alcohol to alcohol-ether and then to the medium celloidin (page 332). The technic is as follows: (1) stain celloidin section with hematoxylin, and differentiate in the usual way; (2) place them for five minutes in the carmin stain. To prepare the carmin stain, to 6 c.c. of a solution consisting of equal parts of methyl alcohol and strong ammonia add 2 c.c. of a carmin solution. To prepare this carmin solution, add 2 gm. carmin, 1 gm. potassium carbonate, and 5 gm. potassium chlorid to 60 c.c. of distilled water, and heat to boiling. Cool, and add 20 c.c. of strong ammonia; (3) remove from the carmin stain, and for ten seconds differentiate in a solution consisting of 80 c.c. absolute alcohol, 40 c.c. methyl alcohol, and 100 c.c. distilled water; pass through 95 per cent. alcohol (one minute) and origanum oil (five minutes) to colophonium-xylol. Do not place in water at any time after staining in the carmin solution. The nuclei are bluish and the glycogen granules carmin red (Fig. 103).

To test frozen sections of *fresh tissue for glycogen*, draw under the cover-glass a solution consisting of equal parts of glycerin and a 1 per cent. Lugol's solution (iodin 1 gm.; potassium iodid 2 gm.; and water 100 c.c.). The glycogen stains a brown that is not made green by concentrated sulphuric acid.

Calcium Reaction.—The calcium of older tissue deposits is chiefly in the form of a carbonate and phosphate with which a soluble silver salt will unite to form silver carbonate and phosphate. These silver salts change over to the black suboxid when exposed to light. Frozen, celloidin, or paraffin sections of formalin-fixed tissue are used. The sections are placed overnight in 2 per cent. silver nitrate, stained with hematoxylin followed by the usual differentiation, dehydrated, and mounted according to the kind of section. After removing from the silver solution, a frozen section of formalin-fixed tissue may be stained for fat by the scharlach R. method. In this case it is mounted in glycerin jelly. This method of staining both lime and fat at the same time is useful in studying lesions of blood vessels.

Gram-Weigert Stain for Gram-positive Bacteria.—This stain is satisfactory for the demonstration in sections of many Gram-positive bacteria. Thin paraffin sections of formalin-fixed tissue are best. Stain with hematoxylin-eosin, staining more heavily than usual with eosin. Place in Gram's staining solution (page 195) for five minutes. Wash, and for one minute apply Gram's iodin. Wash, and differentiate in equal parts of xylol and anilin oil for five minutes or more until properly differentiated.

A stain for fibrin (*Weigert's fibrin stain*) may be obtained by this technic, provided that formalin-fixed sections receive a preparatory treatment with permanganate and oxalic acid as indicated under phosphotungstic acid-hematoxylin stain (page 360). Fibrin stains blue.

Loeffler's Methylene Blue for Gram-negative Bacteria.—The Gram-Weigert method is quite satisfactory for large or medium-sized Gram-positive bacteria in sections. It is more difficult to demonstrate small Gram-negative bacteria. The larger organisms may be clearly brought out in the eosin-methylene blue stain (page 359). Four-micron paraffin sections may be stained overnight in Loeffler's methylene blue, washed in water, differentiated in $\frac{1}{10}$ per cent. acetic acid, hurriedly passed through the absolute alcohols to xylol and mounted in colophonium-xylol.

Polychrome Stain for Bacteria and Protozoa in Tissue.— (McJunkin; Eleventh Report of the Michigan Academy of Science, 1909). This stain serves for the demonstration of Gram-negative bacteria as well as those staining by the Gram method. This method, in common with innumerable other methods for applying polychrome staining to sections of tissue, does not give results comparable to those obtained with smears. The stain used is prepared by adding 1 drop of McJunkin's protozoon stain (page 52) to each cubic centimeter of 0.003 normal sodium carbonate contained in an oblong staining-dish (Fig. 106). The slide with the preparation attached to it is placed in the solution with the preparation side down, and one end allowed to rest on the staining-dish. This is done so as to bring the preparation as near to the surface of the stain as possible. The sections, formalin-fixed and 4-microns thick, remain two hours in the stain in the incubator at 37.5°C. The stain is renewed at the end of the first hour. Some workers prefer to fix the tissue in corrosive-alcohol. Wash in water until the excess of blue is removed and place in 2 per cent. tannin solution for from ten to forty minutes until the sections assume a pinkish tinge. The slide is washed and the excess of water removed from about the sections with a cloth and the sections blotted with soft filter paper. Dip (one second) in absolute alcohol and immediately place in xylol. If dehydration is not complete raise the sections above the xylol and blot two or three times with soft filter paper to complete the dehydration (filter paper-xylol method of dehydration). Mount in colophonium-xylol.

Stain for Treponema Pallidum in the Tissue (Levaditi).— This stain was first employed in demonstrating the treponemata

24

in primary and secondary leutic lesions and in congenital syphilis, but now is of service in showing the presence of the organism in tertiary and so-called parasyphilitic lesions.

Formalin-fixed tissue, cut into thin pieces not to exceed 2 mm. in thickness is placed in distilled water (two changes) for two days. Transfer for five days to 2 per cent. silver nitrate in a glass-stoppered bottle of dark glass. Wash, and place for two days in a bottle containing 2 gm. pyrogallic acid, 5 c.c. formalin, and 100 c.c. distilled water. In the usual way imbed in paraffin; cut sections; remove the paraffin with xylol, and mount in colophonium-xylol. The treponemata have the typical spiral morphology and stain darker than the tissue. Fibrils may occasionally approach this morphology closely, and care must be exercised in basing a diagnosis on too limited a number of the spirochetes. This method is applicable to the other treponemata. It is advisable to remove one bit of tissue from the silver solution about the third day, imbed and examine. If negative the remainder of the tissue may be left in the solution as long as two weeks. A failure to find treponemata is not absolute proof that the tissue is not syphilitic.

Stain for Tubercle Bacilli in the Tissue.—This method has been of great value in showing the distribution of tubercle bacilli in lesions. It is of practical value in certain cases where histologic diagnosis is in doubt, but it must be remembered that a negative examination does not establish a lesion as a non-tuberculous one. The tubercle bacilli must stand out as perfectly defined bright red rods of typical morphology with an absence of red in other structures.

Celloidin Sections.—It is often required to stain for tubercle bacilli in celloidin sections employed for routine surgical diagnosis. A section as thin as can be obtained is floated on a slide and the excess of water is removed from the slide with filter paper. Support the slide on top of a 4- by 11-cm. bottle, and drop on it 95 per cent. alcohol and then absolute alcohol from a dropping-bottle until completely dehydrated. The section is then smoothed out on the slide by pressing firmly with filter paper, and the slide is placed for five minutes in a 4- by 11-cm.

tightly stoppered bottle with 1 cm. of ether in it. Remove, allow to dry for one minute, drop 95 per cent. alcohol on the preparation, and wash with water. Stain for two minutes with hematoxylin (1-5), wash with water and stain for five minutes with carbol-fuchsin (page 196), steaming very gently over a flame. Decolorize with Czaplewsky solution until the section is pink—not more than twenty seconds as over-decolorization must be avoided since the sections are to be dehydrated in alcohol—and then place for one minute in a saturated solution of lithium carbonate. Dehydrate rapidly in 95 per cent. alcohol (thirty seconds), and then in origanum oil (five minutes). Mount in colophonium-xylol.

Paraffin Sections.—Paraffin sections of formalin-, alcohol-, or Zenker-fixed material are stained in this manner, except that the sections are fastened to the slide by placing in the paraffin oven in the usual way. Following the fixation to the slide the paraffin is removed with xylol. To mount, these sections are very hurriedly passed through the alcohols and xylols.

Stain for Leprosy Bacilli in the Tissue (Flexner).—The bacilli are bright red, granular, and present in great numbers within cells, especially endothelial leukocytes. Cut thin paraffin sections of formalin-fixed tissue and for thirty minutes stain with hematoxylin. Decolorize in Czaplewsky solution, and transfer for one minute to a saturated solution of lithium carbonate. Stain in carbol-fuchsin overnight at room temperature. Wash, and for one minute place in an iodin solution consisting of 1 gm. of iodin, 2 gm. potassium iodid and 300 c.c. of water. Wash, blot and differentiate in anilin oil until the bacilli can be seen with the oil-immersion lens. This may require one hour. Pass through xylol to colophonium-xylol.

Safranin for Lipoidal Granules (Babes).—It is useful after fixation in Fleming's fluid. This combination of fixation and staining gives preparations of interest from the standpoint of lipoidal substances in the cytoplasm. To 500 c.c. anilin water add an excess of Grübler's water-soluble safranin o. The *anilin water* is prepared by adding an excess of anilin to distilled water in a half liter bottle, shaking vigorously, and filtering through filter paper. Apply to paraffin sections, staining for two minutes, washing in water, and then passing through the alcohols and xylols to colophonium-xylol. The stain is a heavy one and there must be sufficient differentiation in the 95 per cent. alcohol to remove the dense opaque red from the sections. Nuclei are stained red. A less heavy and more concise nuclear stain is obtained by using a 0.1 per cent. aqueous solution of safranin. Bits of tissue only 2 or 3 mm. across should be blocked.

Mitochondria (Bensley).—The identification of certain cells differentiating from mesenchyma has been made possible by the introduction, especially by Mallory, of stains that bring out the characteristic fibrils of these cells. It is possible that similar advances may be made in the identification of epithelial, endo-thelial, lymphoblastic and other cells, by the employment of a reaction bringing out parts of cytoplasm having a given chemical composition.

Unlike the chromidial granules of the cytoplasm, mitochondria are not chromatin, and they do not stain with de-methylated methylene blue-eosin solutions. Staining reactions show that these granules differ from true lipoidal granules. They are said to be phospholipins (phosphorized lipoids). Lecithin and cholesterin are two common chemical substances that fall in this class of compounds. The granules are soluble in acetic acid, chloroform, and alcohol, but are rendered insoluble in alcohol and chloroform by fixation in a solution containing the chrome salts.

To make the stain, fix bits of fresh (five minutes postoperative) tissue 1 mm. in thickness in a solution freshly prepared by combining 20 c.c. of 2 per cent. osmic acid, 40 c.c. of 2.5 per cent. potassium bichromate, and 0.25 c.c. of acetic acid. Wash for one hour in water, after fixation for twenty-four hours and imbed in paraffin. Treat 2- to 4-micron sections with 0.25 per cent. potassium permanganate (ten minutes) followed by 5 per cent. oxalic acid (20 minutes). Wash in water, and place for five minutes in a stain that has been in the paraffin oven for at least ½ hour and was made by dissolving 20 gm. acid fuchsin

(Grübler) in 100 c.c. anilin water (page 371). Remove from the stain, wash in distilled water, and place for ten seconds in a 1 per cent. methyl green. Carefully remove all excess of water from about the section, blot with soft, fine filter paper, and dehydrate for from one to ten seconds in absolute alcohol. Pass through toluol to colophonium-xylol. If dehydration is not complete after immersion in the absolute alcohol, raise the sections above the toluol and blot with soft filter paper. The mitochondrial granules and filaments are deep red. In the islet cells for pancreas the mitochondria are very fine while in the peripheral portion of the acinar cells they appear as coarse intensely red filaments. The bits of tissue blocked should be only 2 or 3 mm. across if such thin sections are to be cut.

Intra vitam staining of the cytoplasm of certain cells has been secured by the injection of dyes. Among the anilin dyes used are Janus green B (0.02 per cent. in saline), methylene blue, and trypan blue. Carmin (Merck) has been injected intraperitoneally and intravenously as a 1 per cent. solution made by the addition of a minimum amount of alkali. Sections of such tissue have usually been examined by staining frozen sections after fixation in formalin with a stain that contrasts with the intra vitam dye injected. The dye injected is present in certain cells as minute microscopic particles. The writer has employed lampblack in a fine state of suspension for the same purpose (American Journal of Anatomy, 1918; in Press). The lampblack has the advantage over dyes that paraffin sections of perfectly fixed tissue may be made.

Neutral Gentian Islet-cell Stain (Bensley).—In the mitochondria stain of Bensley the cells of the islets of the pancreas with A granules stain a red and those with the B granules a green. With the neutral gentian the granules of the B cells are violet, while the cytoplasm of other cells (A cells and undifferentiated cells) is a yellowish brown and homogeneous. The nuclei of the A cells are more oval and contain less chromatin than the B cells. The peripheral portions of the acinar cells stain heavily while the parts toward the center are light and made up of unstained zymogen granules. Fix in Zenker's fluid without the acetic acid. Do not remove the mercury from the sections. Remove the paraffin with toluol. For twenty-four hours stain 4-micron paraffin sections with a gentian violet-orange G solution in a covered dish. Blot with several layers of soft filter paper without washing, and dehydrate in pure acetone (thirty seconds). Pass through toluol to a solution consisting of 5 c.c. absolute alcohol and 5 c.c. oil of cloves (few seconds), and again place in toluol. Mount in colophonium-xylol.

To make the gentian violet-orange G stain, add 100 c.c. of a filtered 4 per cent. solution of gentian violet to 200 c.c. of a filtered 4 per cent. orange G; filter, and let drain thoroughly, but do not wash the precipitate. Both 4 per cent. solutions are made by heating on a water-bath and stirring with a glass rod. In obtaining the precipitate there must be an excess of orange G. Dry the precipitate overnight at 37.5°C.; powder the dry precipitate; dissolve in 100 c.c. absolute alcohol by shaking, and by placing it in the incubator for twenty-four hours. Of this saturated stock solution, add sufficient of the supernatant stain to 20 per cent. alcohol (about 15 c.c. per 100 c.c. of the 20 per cent. alcohol) to make the color that of a well-ripened alum hematoxylin. Let stand for twenty-four hours, filter, and it is ready for use.

Mast-cell Granule Stain (Mallory).—There is at present some doubt in regard to the origin of the tissue mast-cells and their relations to the basophiles of the blood. Fix the tissue in 95 per cent. alcohol for twenty-four hours. Cut paraffin sections and stain for five minutes in a saturated aqueous solution of thionin. Pass into a 2 per cent. oxalic acid for one-half minute. Wash, and pass through the alcohols and xylols to colophonium-xylol. Nuclei are blue, while the granules of mast-cells are red. This stain was devised for *amebæ*, the nuclei of which are stained red.

Indophenol Stain (Graham)—Neutrophiles and eosinophiles give the so-called oxydase reaction most characteristically (Fig. 103). The mast-cells of the tissue and the basophiles of the blood do not react. Endothelial leukocytes and those endothelial cells which have sufficient cytoplasm for accurate observations have discretely placed granules that may be differentiated from those in the myeloblastic cells. The lymphoblastic cytoplasm does not contain the granules.

Since hydrogen peroxid is added to the alphanaphthol solution to make it immediately active and, since the swollen granules are heavily and permanently stained by treating the preparations with an anilin dye, the method of Graham is better than the other indophenol staining methods devised. To apply this method, remove thin soap sections (page 344) of formalin-fixed tissue attached to slides from the distilled water and stain in dilute (1–5) hematoxylin (page 333) for two minutes; wash them in distilled water, place in a saturated solution of lithium carbonate for five minutes, wash in distilled water for two minutes, and stain for ten minutes in 10 c.c. alphanaphthol solution to which 10 drops 1 per cent. pyronin (Grübler) have been added immediately before placing the sections in it; wash in water ten minutes, differentiate in saturated lithium carbonate for from three to five minutes, and wash in water for two minutes. Dehydrate in 95 per cent. alcohol for thirty seconds and transfer to xylol. To complete the dehydration raise the slide above the xylol two or three times and carefully blot with soft filter paper. Mount in colophonium-xylol. The alphanaphthol solution is prepared by dissolving 1 gm. alphanaphthol (Merck reagent) in 100 c.c. warm 40 per cent. alcohol (made from absolute) and adding 0.2 c.c. 3 per cent. (usual commercial product) hydrogen peroxid. The pyronin solution should contain a small crystal of thymol to prevent the growth of moulds. The hematoxylin should be about two weeks old so that it does not stain diffusely, since a diffuse hematoxylin stain obscures the cytoplasmic granules. (For other details see report by writer in Anatomical Record, Vol. 15.)

Neutrophilic and eosinophilic granules are large, of an intense red color and fill the cytoplasm of the cell. The granules in endothelial leukocytes are smaller and discretely placed; it is only in endothelial cells that have a distinct cytoplasm that the granules appear.

Granules in Lymphoblastic Cells (Schridde).—The identification of the *centrosome* (eosin-methylene blue stain) in a cell is a sufficient basis for saying that a cell is probably not myeloblastic. The centrosome is frequently very conspicuous in lymphoblastic cells, and it may be demonstrated in endothelial cells of blood vessels as well. The limited number (from six to one dozen) of granules lying about the nucleus (paranuclear) of lymphoblastic cells are said by Schridde to be characteristic of them.

Schridde recommends that the tissue (2 or 3 mm. thick) be fixed five minutes postoperative in 10 per cent. formalin and after twenty-four hours transferred to formalin-Müller's fluid (Müller's fluid 90 c.c.; formalin 10 c.c.; distilled water 100 c.c.) and kept in this solution at room temperature for twenty-four hours. Two-micron paraffin sections are cut. In order to cut such thin sections the block that is imbedded must not be more than 3 to 5 mm. across. Remove the paraffin from the sections and place them for thirty minutes in 1 per cent. osmic acid in the dark; wash in distilled water and stain for fifteen minutes in *Altmann's acid fuchsin*. This stain is prepared by dissolving 20 gm. acid fuchsin (Grübler) in 100 c.c. anilin water and filtering. To make the stain the slide is placed in the stain for fifteen minutes in a covered oblong dish (Fig. 106), placed across the rings of a water bath and steamed. The preparation is removed from the stain, carefully blotted with soft filter paper and differentiated in a solution consisting of 10 c.c. 95 per cent. alcohol saturated with picric acid and 70 c.c. 20 per cent. alcohol until the section takes on a bright yellowish light-red color. Pass through 95 per cent. alcohol, absolute alcohol and toluol to colophonium-xylol.

The short bacillus-like granules of the lymphocytes are yellowish; neutrophilic granules brownish red; and eosinophilic granules black red. The cytoplasm and nucleus are a gray, and almost unstained.

This method may be applied to cover-glass *films of blood* as follows: (1) fix in formalin-Müller (1 to 9) one hour; (2) wash and place in 1 per cent. osmic acid in the dark for thirty minutes;

(3) wash and stain in the same way that sections are stained; (4) blot, differentiate, dehydrate, clear and mount in the same way as sections.

Chromaffin Granule Stain.—Fix in Müller's fluid at 37.5°C. for forty-eight hours. Wash overnight; cut paraffin sections, and stain with eosin-methylene blue. The chromaffin granules are brown. The nuclei are not well stained.

Stain for Hyaline Substances (Pianese).—This stain is for tissue containing hyaline substances; special fixation is required. Cut paraffin sections of tissue fixed in Pianese fluid (page 347). Stain for one-half hour in a solution consisting of 0.5 gm. malachite green, 0.1 acid fuchsin, 0.01 gm. martius yellow, and 200 c.c. 20 per cent. alcohol. Pass through absolute alcohol and xylol to colophonium-xylol. Cytoplasm and connective tissue are rose red and nuclei are green. Mucin stains a sky blue, colloid (thyroid) a bright green, and hyaline (sclerosed glomeruli) a brick red.

Mucin Stain.—If tissue is thought to contain mucin at the time of fixation, it is best to shake some of the fresh crushed tissue with a few cubic centimeters of distilled water; filter through filter paper, and on the filtrate stratify 2 per cent. acetic acid. Mucin is precipitated by dilute acetic acid, but pseudomucin is not. To precipitate *pseudomucin*, add 95 per cent. alcohol to some of the same filtrate contained in a second tube. If albumin is present, it is removed by heating before filtration.

It may be desirable to ascertain the exact location of the mucin in the tissue, and in such a case bits of the tissue should be fixed in corrosive-alcohol. For fifteen minutes place paraffin sections without removing the mercury with iodin in 0.5 per cent. thionin. Wash in alcohol; differentiate in oil of cloves, and pass through cedar-oil to colophonium-xylol. Mucin is red, and the remainder of the tissue blue (Hoyer).

Amyloid Stain.—Treat the freshly cut surface of an organ, or microscopic sections of fresh or fixed tissue, with Gram's iodin (water 300 c.c.; potassium iodid 2 gm.; and iodin 1 gm.). Amyloid and glycogen are turned mahogany brown in contrast to the yellowish brown of the surrounding tissue. After treatment with iodin a better differentiation is secured— especially on the cut surface of an organ—by running concentrated sulphuric acid over the part which often changes the brown to a red and then blue. Sections are treated by drawing the iodin under the cover-glass by means of filter paper placed at the opposite side of the cover. Sections of fresh- or formalin-fixed tissue may be stained in 0.5 per cent. *methyl violet,* washed and at once examined in water. The amyloid is pink.

To make permanent mounts of an amyloid stain, unmounted paraffin sections are for ten minutes floated on a 0.5 per cent. solution of methyl violet in the incubator. Cool the solution, and float for ten minutes on 1 per cent. acetic acid. Float on water and then for ten minutes on a 2 per cent. solution of potassium alum. From water float the sections on slides and in the usual way place these in the paraffin oven overnight. With xylol remove the paraffin, and mount in colophonium-xylol (Mayer). The amyloid stains pink with methyl violet. With the anilin blue stain (page 361) the cells are red and the amyloid blue.

Myelin-sheath Stain (Pal-Weigert).—This stain colors the normal myelin sheath a dark blue to black, while the axis cylinders and nerve cells are unstained or are stained yellowish. The blocks of tissue for fixation should not be more than 4 mm. thick. They are cut through the spinal cord, the peripheral nerves, and like structures in such a way that in the sections the fibers will be cut transversely. After this stain, an area of degenerated nerve fibers appears light in color when examined with the low-power lens. With the high-power, such areas show vacuoles corresponding to the degenerated fibers. This differentiation of normal and degenerated nerve tracts makes the stain of great value for the study of tract degenerations, especially in the cord. To secure the best results, the tissue should be fixed as soon after death as possible. After about three hours postmortem, the tissue becomes progressively less favorable for the reaction of the stain.

The technic of the stain is as follows: (1) tissue less than

4 mm. thick is placed in Müller's fluid for four days or longer. A solution consisting of 50 gm. potassium bichromate in 1000 c.c. water may be substituted for Müller's fluid. Less satisfactory results are obtained by an initial fixation in formalin and a secondary fixation for four days in Müller's fluid. Wash the tissue overnight in running water; (2) imbed and cut 20-micron sections. After fixation the tissue may be preserved for some time, if necessary, in 80 per cent. alcohol, though it gradually loses its staining power if kept too long. Old tissue or even celloidin blocks of tissue may be partially rescued by incubating at 37.5°C. for four days in Muller's fluid (Prof. H. C. Tracy); (3) carry the sections through graded alcohol to distilled water and stain them at 37.5°C. for twelve to twenty-four hours in a ripened *Weigert's hematoxylin solution* (1 gm. hematoxylin dissolved in 10 c.c. absolute alcohol and made up to 100 c.c. with distilled water; 1 c.c. saturated lithium carbonate added and the solution boiled). The sections of a deep brown-black color are washed in several changes of tap water which changes them to a blue-black; (4) differentiate in 0.25 per cent. potassium permanganate solution for twenty or thirty seconds—thick sections or overhardened material may take longer; (5) transfer to a decolorizing solution consisting of 0.5 per cent. oxalic acid and 0.5 per cent. acid potassium sulphite freshly prepared. The sections are decolorized for a few seconds until the gray matter becomes a light yellowish brown. The differentiation and decolorization are carried out in small Stender dishes placed over a white surface; (6) transfer sections at once to a large volume of tap water where they are thoroughly washed in order to remove the last trace of acid; (7) dehydrate in 95 per cent. alcohol, clear in origanum oil (Cretan [Merck]), and mount in colophonium-xylol.

Degenerated Myelin-sheath Stain (Marchi).—In distinction to the Weigert method, this stain colors only the degenerated sheaths. For ten days place 4-mm. blocks of formalin-fixed tissue in Müller's fluid (page 346). Change the fluid on the first and third days. The time may be reduced to four days by incubating at 37.5°C. Transfer for ten days to

Marchi's fluid (20 c.c. Müller's fluid and 10 c.c. 1 per cent. osmic acid). Keep in the dark and change solutions on the first and third days. The fluid must be freshly made each time. Wash for one day in distilled water. Cut 20-micron celloidin sections. Dehydrate the sections in alcohol, and then pass through chloroform and mount in colophonium-chloroform. The *colophonium-chloroform* is prepared like colophonium-xylol, substituting chloroform for xylol.

Ganglion Cell Stain (Golgi as modified by Hardesty).— Place bits of the formalin-fixed nervous tissue, not more than 4 mm. thick in Müller's fluid at 37.5°C. for twenty-four hours. Remove the bits of tissue, blot them with filter paper, and agitate them in a silver-nitrate solution (silver nitrate 1.5 gm.; distilled water 200 c.c.; and 1 drop formic acid) until the brown precipitate of silver chromate ceases to come away. Place the tissue in fresh silver solution for from three to six days in the dark. To dehydrate, carry the tissue directly into 95 per cent. alcohol (ten minutes), a second 95 per cent. alcohol (ten minutes), absolute alcohol (fifteen minutes), a second absolute alcohol (fifteen minutes), alcohol-ether (twenty minutes), thin celloidin (twenty minutes), and medium celloidin (twenty minutes). Block, harden in chloroform (fifteen minutes) and transfer to clearing fluid (carbolic acid 50 c.c., oil of cedar wood 50 c.c., bergamot oil 25 c.c.) for thirty minutes to several days. Cut 50-micron sections, keeping the block moistened with the clearing fluid, place sections on the slide, flood with xylol for about five minutes and cover with a thick colophonium-xylol and allow this to harden in a dust-free atmosphere. Do not apply a cover-glass. The stained structures which may be ganglion cells, axones or neuroglia cells—or combinations of these—are colored black in an almost uncolored background. Fetal or embryonic tissue is more satisfactory than adult material.

Nerve Cell and Axis Cylinder Stain (Ranson's modification of Cajal's method).—This stain is especially valuable for the developing central nervous system. Spinal ganglia are well differentiated. Axis cylinders are black except very near the cell where they are brown. The cytoplasm is brown and the nuclei are stained lightly. The technical steps are as follows: (1) fix thin bits of tissue for forty-eight hours in absolute alcohol containing 1 per cent. ammonia; (2) wash five minutes in distilled water; (3) pyridin for twenty-four hours; (4) wash for twenty-four hours in several changes of distilled water; (5) 2 per cent. silver nitrate for forty-eight hours in incubator at 37.5°C.; (6) wash in distilled water; (7) 4 per cent. pyrogallic acid dissolved in 5 per cent. formalin for twenty-four hours; (8) imbed in paraffin, cut 15-micron sections, dissolve out the paraffin with xylol and mount in colophonium-xylol.

Nerve Cell Stain (Held modified by Hardesty).—Pieces of tissue (2 to 4 mm. thick) are fixed in 20 volumes of *Van Gehuchten's fluid* (absolute alcohol 60 c.c.; chloroform 30 c.c.; glacial acetic acid 10 c.c.) for three to twelve hours; transfer to 20 volumes absolute alcohol for two to six hours with two changes; clear in equal parts xylol and cedar oil; imbed in paraffin and cut 6-micron sections. To make the stain, remove the paraffin in the usual way and place for fifteen minutes in 1 per cent. erythrosin (Grübler) in 70 per cent. alcohol; wash in 50 per cent. alcohol three to five minutes; rinse in distilled water and stain for ten minutes in 1 per cent. toluidine blue (Grübler) in distilled water; drain off the stain and carefully differentiate in 0.1 per cent. potassium alum solution until the section assumes a pinkish tinge with traces of blue. Dehydrate in 95 per cent. alcohol for twenty seconds and absolute alcohol for five minutes; pass through xylol and mount in colophonium-xylol.

Nerve cells stain blue. With careful differentiation the internal structures of the cell are well shown; the reticulum is pink, *Nissl's granules*, blue; neurosomes, black-blue. In the developing nervous system, cells in mitosis stain very deeply. Medullated nerves and neuroglia stain pink.

AUTOPSY TECHNIC

It is not usually possible to secure surgical specimens from certain tissue such as the heart, liver, pancreas, brain or cord, although an examination of these organs is required in the study of many disease processes. All the organs may be examined at the autopsy table, the pathologic lesions uncovered in their entirety, and the relationship of the various pathologic changes established. A knowledge of local disease may be obtained by the study of specimens removed at surgical operation, but it is only at autopsy that all pathologic data is brought to light, and the internist and surgeon have placed before them the changes that give rise to the antemortem clinical picture.

Owing to the unquestioned value of autopsies from the scientific and clinical standpoints, better facilities are being provided for this work in connection with hospitals. To per-

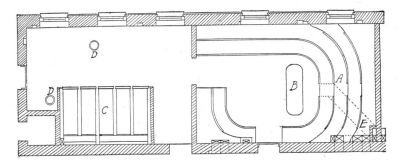

FIG. 109.—Floor elevation of autopsy room. (Drawn from plan received through the courtesy of Dr. F. S. Graves). *A*, Amphitheater seats; *B*, autopsy table; *C*, morgue boxes; *D*, cess-pool; *E*, ventilating shaft.

form an autopsy to the best advantage, it is necessary that the operator be provided with instruments and a suitable table with running water in a room with good light, heat, and ventilation (Fig. 109). It is always preferable to bring a body to a properly equipped autopsy room rather than to make the section at a private home or at an undertaking establishment.

An effort should always be made to hold the postmortem examination as soon after death as possible. Material from autopsies performed within an hour after death is best for microscopic examination. If the body is at once placed in a morgue cooled by an efficient refrigerating system, a period of from three to six hours between the death of the individual and the autopsy does not seriously affect the preservation of the tissue. A morgue in which bodies are kept should adjoin the autopsy room.

The autopsy room is provided with a soap-stone, marble or cement autopsy table equipped with running water. The table is provided with a central waste-water outflow. The water is best supplied from overhead and brought down to the table by a 1-in. rubber hose. One board 3 ft. square on which to place instruments, and another on which to section organs

FIG. 110.—Table to be drawn up against the foot of the autopsy table. *a,* 22-cm. glass dish containing Zenker's fluid; *b,* pint Mason jar with 10 per cent. formalin; *c,* platinum loop and culture media; *d,* scales with metric weights; *e,* Bunsen burner attached overhead; *f,* knife with wooden handle for cauterizing surfaces through which to puncture for cultures. The point of knife may be sharpened for making incisions in the cauterized areas but it is better to use a separate scalpel with sharp point.

are provided. Scales with a full set of weights and with scoop-pans, a dish with Zenker's fluid, and a pint Mason jar containing 10 per cent. formalin are placed on a small table (Fig. 110) which is drawn up against the foot of the autopsy table. A Bunsen burner attached to overhead gas, a knife set in a wooden handle for searing surfaces, a scalpel to be flame-sterilized, a platinum loop, and culture media are also placed on this table. Suitable instruments are important and, although those made

TEMPORARY AUTOPSY SHEET			
Autopsy No.	Hours p.m.	Age:	B.L.
Name:	Date:	Sex:	Color:	Develop:
Nourish:		Rigor mortis:		Lividity:
Edema:			
Brief clinical history:			
Clinical diagnosis:			
External body surfaces:			
Peritoneal cavity:			
Pleural cavities:			
Pericardial cavity:			
Heart: weight:			
Lungs: weight of each:			
Spleen: weight:			
Gastro-intestinal tract:			
Pancreas:			
Liver: weight:			
Kidneys: weight:			
Adrenals:			
Genito-urinary organs:			
Aorta:			
Neck organs:			
Brain: weight:			
Middle ear:			
Naso-pharynx:			
Bone-marrow:			
Spinal cord:			
Anatomical Diagnoses:			

FIG. 111.—Autopsy sheet (8½ by 16 in.) for temporary record.

by Codman and Schurtleff, 120 Boylston St., Boston, Mass. do not form a complete set, they are the best procurable. A printed form-sheet (Fig. 111) is used for taking down the essential data during the autopsy. The common surgical glove may be worn by the operator, but a tight-fitting glove that comes well up on the forearm is more satisfactory. In order to grip slippery organs firmly, thin cotton gloves are worn over the rubber ones. The cotton gloves are inexpensive and are advised as a routine.

The body is placed on its back on the table with a block of wood beneath the neck so as to support the head. The operator stands at the right of the subject.

The data such as the time postmortem, edema, rigor mortis, and the like, are determined and recorded, as indicated on the slip. A brief clinical history and the probable clinical diagnosis are obtained either from a written record supplied by the clinician or from the clinician present at the autopsy. A concise clinical record forms a part of the autopsy protocol. The length of the body is determined by measuring the table on which the body lies.

A wound inflicted during the performance of an autopsy, when a glove is punctured by a sharp fragment of bone, or otherwise, should receive immediate attention, especially if the case is a septic one. The wound must be freely opened up and cauterized with 95 per cent. phenol followed by 95 per cent. alcohol. Once an infection has begun a surgeon should be consulted, and until this is done the part may be kept in a continuous hot bath of sulphonaphthol (2 per cent.).

External Body Surfaces and Extremities.—Besides the determination of development, nourishment, edema, and the like, already noted, a more careful external examination is made. The method of autopsy is determined by the character of the lesions present. In following a procedure that calls special attention to the internal organs there may be a failure to ascertain noteworthy facts about the skin, mucous membranes, and extremities.

The examination should begin with the *scalp* where wounds, bruises, and scars are looked for. External marks of violence require careful observation in cases with medico-legal aspect, but lengthy descriptions are of little use and cannot take the place of expert observation. The mouth is inspected for tumors

25

and inflammatory processes and for abnormal pigmentation. The condition of the teeth is observed.

The *neck* is examined for enlargements in connection with the salivary glands, thyroid gland, and lymph-nodes.   Asymmetry in the thorax is often significant.

The *abdomen* may be distended with gas (usually within the intestines) or with fluid.   Large veins may appear superficially in liver cirrhoses (*caput medusæ*).   Tumor nodules may be found in the abdominal skin, as well as on the skin surface elsewhere. Laparotomy wounds are noted.   The external genitals are examined for discharges and old scars, and the extremities for abnormalities in size and shape.

Skin.—The skin presents a gray color except for the dependent portions that show *postmortem hypostasis*, greenish areas of *putrefactive change* over the abdomen, or *mnmmification* from drying.   An anemia may be inferred if dependent portions are pale.   In pernicious anemia, the skin may be lemon yellow and in jaundice a greenish yellow.   An acute congestion (inflammatory) may not be evident after death.   An *edema* is shown by pitting on pressure.   In *myxedema* the elastic swelling does not pit.   Frequently, cardiac cases show little edema of the face, the part of the body where it is likely to be in evidence in individuals with severe kidney lesions.   Gas (subcutaneous emphysema) may be determined by crepitation, it may escape into the subcutaneous tissue from the lungs, or it may be produced by bacillus aerogenes capsulatus.

Since the blood stream is the most important path for the generalization of disease, both soluble and morphologic disease-producing substances are carried into the skin and visible mucous membranes where they may produce changes.   Carbon monoxid, hydrocyanic acid, and sulphureted hydrogen compounds of hemoglobin are cherry red.   Methemoglobin formed by chlorates and many benzene derivatives is a chocolate color. In *cholemia*, the sclera are greenish yellow.   In *Addison's disease*, the pigmentation is best seen in the axilla, the groin, the lips and the mouth.   In pellagra, the forearms and other skin surfaces receive attention.   Freckles and lentigines are minute to larger foci of brown color due to excessive melanin. In *chloasma* associated with pregnancy the areas are larger. *In vitiligo* there is a congenital absence of pigment in areas, while in *albinism* this deficiency is general. Pigmented and vascular *nevi* are abnormal collections of melanoblasts and blood vessels respectively.

Hemorrhages which appear as *petechiæ*, ecchymoses or hematoma are mechanical, nutritional, toxic, infectious, or intrinsic. They may occur in hemophilia, purpura, scurvy, and the hemorrhagic exanthemata (small-pox, yellow fever, typhus, and scarlatina).

Poisoning with mineral acids (sulphuric, nitric, and hydrochloric acid), organic acids (oxalic, acetic, and carbolic), and alkalies (sodium, potassium, and ammonium hydrates), as well as with certain metallic salts (bichlorid, copper sulphate, silver nitrate, lead acetate, chrome salts) locally is characterized by strong corrosive action. Phosphorous and arsenous acid act less locally, but they produce serious changes after absorption.

Infections, such as anthrax and typhoid, may show characteristic lesions at the site of inoculation, but they soon become generalized; others (tetanus, diphtheria) remain localized; while still others, such as small-pox, yellow fever, malaria, recurrent fever, and the like, show no demonstrable lesion at the point of inoculation.

In focal *inflammatory lesions* of the skin, one distinguishes macules, papules, vesicles, and pustules. *Phlegmon* is an infection—especially with the streptococcus—extending deeply into the subcutaneous submucous or subserous tissues; while *erysipelas* is an infection with a mild streptococcus limited to the corium. Heat, refrigeration, corrosive poisons, and high-voltage currents produce hyperemia, blebs, sloughs, and areas of carbonization. Variola, scarlatina, measles, malignant pustule, furunculosis, acne, favus, herpes tonsurans, and pityriasis versicolor are common inflammatory focal skin lesions. More diffuse lesions are seen in herpes, eczema, pemphigus, lichen planus, and psoriasis. The lesions of secondary syphilis are varied and gumma with ulceration is not common. Tubercu-

losis (lupus vulgaris), leprosy, and actinomycosis are chronic
infections. The mould infections are identified by microscopic
examination of hairs and skin scrapings.

Epidermoid carcinoma and hair-matrix carcinoma (rodent
ulcer) are common primary epithelial tumors.

Mucous Membranes.—It is advisable to examine carefully
the visible mucous membranes before proceeding to section.
About the genital and urinary orifices venereal lesions such as
condyloma acuminata, chancroid or *chancre* are most common,
and scars produced by chancre may be identified. At the various orifices (lower lip, urinary meatus, nipple) cancer appears at
the transition of skin to mucous membrane. Abnormal pigmentation may appear here when not distinct in the skin; the
"*lead line*" is best seen in the mouth near the margin of the gums.
Imperfect development such as hare-lip and cleft-palate are
noted. Herpes in febrile conditions appears on the lips.
Evidence of stomatitis and false membranes in the mouth is
sought. In *noma* the gangrenous condition may extend into
the tissues of the neck. Tertiary syphilis localizes in the tongue;
the hard and soft palate may be involved. An actinomycotic
infection frequently opens into the mouth. The general
condition of the teeth should be recorded. If *pyorrhea alveolaris* is present record it. In all cases that are not perfectly
clear, smears are made and examined microscopically.

Muscles.—In *necrosis* the striations are lost and the fibers
become homogeneous, in the gross appearing yellowish white
(Zenker's degeneration or necrosis). This is met with in the
recti abdominis and large thigh adductors in typhoid fever,
severe sepsis, and the like. In the spinal form of progressive
muscular atrophy, *atrophy* of finger, forearm, and shoulder-
muscles occurs. A myopathic form (primary juvenile progressive muscular atrophy) occurs in children and is hereditary;
a lipomatosis of the muscle accompanies the atrophy of the
fibers and may produce an increase in the size of the part
(pseudohypertrophy). An inflammatory ossification (eques-
trian's bone) may occur. Acute purulent *myositis* follows the
infection of wounds or the extension of an infection from bones

and joints. The gas bacillus grows especially well in the sugar-containing muscle. *Gumma* of muscles is sufficiently common to make any chronic inflammatory process with necrosis of muscle a suspicious one. The *trichinella* is best examined for in the intercostal muscles, where it appears as a minute linear body half the size of a caraway seed by excising, placing on a slide, applying a cover-glass, and adding dilute acetic acid, and examining under the low-power lens.

Lymph-nodes.—Circumscribed collections of lymphoblastic cells (lymph nodules) are found in the spleen, gastro-intestinal mucosa and elsewhere with no definite relationship to lymph-vessels and in the lymph-nodes as invaginations of a definite endothelial lined space (lymph sinuses) which is a part of the system of lymph-vessels. In the lymph-nodes areas of proliferation (germinal centers) appear during early infant life and about these collections of older cells. The centers of these secondary nodules (lymph nodules) appear light in microscopic preparations because both nucleus and cytoplasm are less dense than in the surrounding more mature cells. The older cells, smaller and more dense, are the only ones that normally pass into the endothelial lined lymph- or blood-vessels.

In normal lymph-nodes a few endothelial leukocytes may usually be found in the sinuses and, in *anthracotic nodes* or *hemorrhagic ones*, great numbers of these cells distend the sinuses and pass into the nodules. In young individuals who have congenital weakness of arterial walls and other developmental defects the lymphoid tissue including the thymic tissue may become markedly hyperplastic (status lymphaticus). In acute infections, the regional lymph-nodes may be enlarged from an active congestion or from hyperplasia of the lymphoid tissue, or both.

The usual acute lymphadenitis is toxic (pneumococcus, streptococcus, diphtheria, wound infections). If pyogenic cocci reach the nodes in large numbers a purulent lymphadenitis results. Primary tuberculosis of lymph-glands is seen in early life (scrofula). It is likely to transform the entire gland into a cheesy mass. Rapidly growing *lymphoblastomas* have their origin in the lymph-nodes of the neck, the axilla, the mediastinum or the groin, or in the lymph nodules of the spleen or of the gastro-intestinal tract. Necrosis is common, and glands removed for diagnosis are not infrequently diagnosed as tuberculosis, or chronic inflammation. *Lymphatic leukemia* may or may not exist depending on the growth of the tumor cells in the blood stream. *Hodgkin's disease* is found in the same region. Since in this condition the cellular proliferation is within the gland capsules, the nodes tend to remain separate, while in tuberculosis entire chains of glands are bound together in caseous masses. Secondary epithelial tumors and primary and secondary non-epithelial tumors commonly metastasize in the lymph-glands; and in myelogenous leukemia the tumor cells often proliferate there and cause some enlargement. Tertiary syphilis of lymph-nodes is practically unknown.

Bones.—The changes in the bone-marrow are given in another connection (page 441). Malformations result from defective union of bones (vertebral column and brain-box) or from defective or excessive growth of parts of the skeleton. An important factor in *fractures* is the injury of contiguous soft structures such as nerves, vessels, muscles, brain, cord, bladder, or lungs. Spontaneous fracture always suggests myeloma, or other tumor involving the bone, unless otherwise explained. After extensive crushing of bones *fat embolism* may occur with cerebral or pulmonary symptoms. Of first importance in fractures is the rupture of the skin or mucous membrane surface (compound fracture). In the senile, the marrow cavities are enlarged and lime salts removed (osteoporosis or senile osteomalacia). With absorption of lime salts in puerperal osteomalacia, there is new formation of osteoid tissue and the pelvis often becomes heavy and narrow, due to a bulging forward of the sacral promontory; or the neck of the femur is forced down to a right angle. Necrosis (caries) of the bone is peculiar in that necrotic tissues are removed very slowly, often giving rise to *sequestra* about which the osteoblasts may proliferate to form *involucra*.

Staphylococcus aureus and the tubercle bacillus are the

commonest causes of chronic *osteomyelitis*. Phosphorus causes local periosteal proliferation of the lower jaw followed by necrosis and infection. In adults, the *treponema* produces a diffuse periostitis and gummata; while congenital syphilis of children produces an osteochondritis, shown by an irregular, grayish-yellow zone of granulation tissue at the epiphyseal boundary. *Actinomycosis* may involve the jaw, vertebra or ribs with the production of caries. Osteosarcoma is common, and osteoma rare; exostoses, osteophytes, hyperostoses, and so forth, are not encapsulated and are usually inflammatory. *Rickets* appear during early life (first two years). There is an abnormal proliferation of the chondroblasts, giving rise to enlargements at certain points (rachitic rosary), while the secretion of osseomucin by the osteoblasts is less than normal, resulting in an enlargement of the marrow cavity and a narrowing of the cortical sheath and of the bone trabeculæ. The bones are weakened so that they yield to the body weight and the traction of muscles to produce permanent deformities, among which are rachitic pelvis, pectus carinatum, craniotabes, and kyphosis. The curve of the tibia is often very marked. On sawing through a rib or head of the tibia the epiphyseal line is indistinct due to an irregular admixture of cartilage and osteoid tissue and the part is widened laterally. In *Barlow's disease* (infantile scurvy) there is not only a weakening of the bones but also subperiosteal hemorrhages and fibroses in the marrow cavity. In ostomalacia, as seen in lactating women, the microscopic changes are very similar to those of rickets; but of course the deformities of developmental origin do not result. *Osteitis deformans* (Paget's disease of the bones) consists of a thickening (skull) and enlargement of many bones due to excessive formation of osteoid and fibrous tissue. It occurs in late life.

Joints.—Congenital luxations of the hip and knee occur. The synovial membrane is the only part of the lining of the joint cavity containing blood-vessels, and it extends inward over only the periphery of the cartilages. Injected vessels at the central part of the cartilages are, therefore, certain indications of inflammatory reaction with the formation of new blood-vessels. In tabes and other lesions of the central nervous system atrophy of the large joints may result (neuro-pathic arthropathy). In mild cases of *rheumatic fever*, a non-hemolytic streptococcus may be found; but the organisms appear quickly to die out. The synovial membrane is reddened but it may be impossible to make this out at autopsy, although the cavity is filled with a serous inflammatory exudate. The surrounding tissues show more or less inflammatory edema. Less commonly, the reaction is more marked, with fibrin and neutrophiles present in the exudate. The large joints of the extremities, and sometimes of the vertebræ, are involved. Endocarditis verrucosa is the rule. There is no sharp line between this condition and that produced by the more virulent hemolytic strains of streptococcus that cause a purulent arthritis with an ulcerative endocarditis. The latter process may destroy the cartilage and on healing result in ankylosis; while the joints are usually restored to normal after a single rheumatic attack. Gonococcus and other pyogenic bacteria produce an arthritis that is usually destructive.

Uric acid arthritis is due to the deposition of sodium biurate in cells and in the chondromucin of the cartilages of the small joints of the fingers and toes. At first the synovial membrane is red and thick with a small amount of serous exudate in the joint cavity; but it later becomes fibrous and the joint ankylosed. The severest condition is usually inherited (gout) with deposits (tophi) in the subcutaneous tissue about carti-lages and tendons (ear, tendo Achilles). At autopsy, cases of gout usually show—in addition to the joint changes—a fat heart, sclerosed kidneys, and an amyloid spleen.

In *osteo-arthritis deformans* the chondroblasts of the articular cartilages proliferate, producing irregularities; and at the same time the underlying bone atrophies, while the osteoblasts proliferate in the adjoining periosteum (ossifying periostitis) to produce exostoses about the joint which increase the de-formity. This disease comes on after middle life without acute symptoms and involves the joints of the hand, the hip and shoulder. There is no fibrous or caseous ankylosis of the joint. The exostoses and ecchondroses about the vertebræ may be so extensive that the spinal column assumes a marked rigidity (spondylitis deformans). In *progressive polyarthritis* there are inflammatory symptoms, granulation tissue forms and later extensive fibrous and osseous ankylosis develops. Many joints are involved; the swellings are soft. This form has been called proliferative arthritis deformans by Nichols in distinction to osteo-arthritis deformans which he designates as degenerative. This disease may develop at any age. Joint "mice" are most often found in these conditions.

Joint tuberculosis may begin as a primary infection of the synovial membrane; but the involvement of the cavity is more often secondary to an infection with tubercle bacilli, starting in the large capillaries in the epiphyses of the long bone. The ends of the bones underlying the articular cartilages are involved in the process. It is usually primary in children; while in adults it is secondary to lung and lymph-node tuberculosis. The knee (white swelling), hip-joint (hip-joint disease), and the vertebræ (Pott's disease) are frequently affected. Caseous material often accumulates in large amounts (white abscess or swelling) and may discharge to the surface through a fistula. If this takes place, the diseased tissue becomes secondarily infected with pyogenic organisms. Amyloid disease is not uncommon in severe and prolonged cases.

The *bursæ*, like synovial cavities, are lined with flat cells of mesenchymal origin. *Housemaid's knee* is a common example of hygroma. Occasionally tuberculous bursitis is met with. Acute inflammations may spread through these cavities.

Peritoneal Cavity.—After examining the external body surface, including the visible mucous membranes, the lymph-glands, muscles, bones, and joints, an incision is made down the median line of the body from a point just above the center of the sternum to the symphysis pubis, avoiding the umbilicus. This incision, which is known as the main incision, is carried down to the sternum; but on the abdomen it extends only through the skin and subcutaneous fat. After completing this incision, nick into the peritoneal cavity just below the sternum, and insert two fingers of the left hand and cut down between these fingers to the symphysis. From the peritoneal surface cut through the recti near the lower end of the incision, in order to relax the wall.

Cut the peritoneum and muscles attached to the ribs and the cartilages at the lower border of the thorax, and with long sweeps of the cartilage knife strip back from the thoracic wall the pectoral and other muscles together with the overlying skin. In this operation, cut through the peritoneum close to the lower costal margin. Examine the intercostal muscles for trichinella infection. Examine the mammary gland by cutting into it from the under or muscle surface.

Lesions of the Peritoneum.—The viscera contained in the peritoneal cavity are examined to determine their position, relationship, and any gross lesion appearing on the exposed surfaces. Serous, purulent or chylous fluid is looked for chiefly in the pelvis. Inguinal, femoral, ventral, umbilical, and diaphragmatic are the commonest hernias. Note the size of the spleen and its position if enlarged. The distance of the lower border of the liver below the costal margin and the height of the diaphragm on the two sides in terms of intercostal spaces are recorded. The appendix, the gall-bladder, and the general peritoneal surfaces are examined for evidence of fibrosis, inflammation, or metastatic tumor. Examine *in situ* the organs contained in the pelvis.

In *tuberculous peritonitis* there may be a large amount of serous or serofibrinous exudate; or in the dry form the intestinal loops may be bound firmly together by fibrin and fibrous adhesions. The mesenteric lymph-nodes may be extensively involved and the lymph-vessels may appear as white beaded lines. In typhoid the mesenteric lymph-nodes may reach the size of a hen's egg.

Pleural Cavities.—With the costotome, the ribs are cut through from below upward in the nipple line, converging toward the costo-chondral junction above until the first rib is reached. The first rib should be cut through not at the costochondral junction but outside the midclavicular line. This is done by angling the costotome so as to bring the upper blade beneath the clavicle, when it is pushed through between the clavicle and rib, and the rib cut. With the cartilage knife, cut the soft parts between the ribs. Now pull the lower end of the sternum upward, and with the cartilage knife dissect off the soft tissue from its under surface. The sternoclavicular joint is disarticulated from beneath and the sternum removed. In disarticulating, move the sternum back and forth, to determine accurately where to cut with the knife. Avoid cutting the jugular vein.

Lesions of the Pleura.—A *pneumothorax* consists of a filling of the pleural cavity with air, as a result of rupture of the lung parenchyma by perforating wound, suppuration, tuberculosis, or neoplasm. The lung collapses, and the organs of the opposite side are displaced toward the affected side. Infection is the rule in this condition, and pus may accumulate (pyopneumothorax). *Hemothorax* may follow perforating wounds or fracture of the ribs. Pleuritic transudates (hydrothorax) are usually bilateral; while an exudate resulting from inflammation of the pleura is more often unilateral. Fibrin is almost certain to be deposited on the pleural surfaces when inflammatory exudates fill the cavities. Organization of this fibrin produces thickenings, adhesions, or complete or partial obliteration of the cavities. Tuberculosis and infections with the pyogenic cocci are the most important causes of a pleuritis. Fibrous adhesions may follow any of the infections. Primary tumor (carcinoma) of the pleural mesothelium is uncommon. Secondary cancer is very common, especially in cancer of the breast. Examine the mediastinum for tumors, aneurism, and enlarged thymus.

Pericardial Cavity.—The intercostal space or rib marking the position of the heart apex is noted before the sac is opened. To open the sac, hold with forceps the pericardium at its center, and with scissors cut upward over the great vessels. Maintain the hold with the forceps and continue this incision downward along the right side of the heart.   From the center of the incision again cut downward toward the left to the apex.

If death is very slow, there may be as much as 100 c.c. of pericardial fluid.   If death has not resulted from cardiac paralysis, the left ventricle is often found to be in a state of contraction.

Open the pulmonary artery *in situ* by cutting into it with sharp pointed scissors and opening up toward the lungs, examining for large emboli in the larger branches.   Remove the heart by lifting it upward with the left hand and cutting the vessels from below upward.   Occasionally a patent ductus arteriosus connecting the pulmonary circulation with the aorta may be present.

Lesions of the Pericardium.—*Hydropericardium* is seen in general hydrops in cardiac disease and in nephropathies. *Hematopericardium* results from rupture of aneurism, gunshot wound, and spontaneous rupture of a diseased heart-muscle wall.   Petechial or macular hemorrhages into the pericardium may also take place per diapedesin in the hemorrhagic exanthemata, in hemophilia, and in septic embolism. The pyogenic cocci are the commonest cause of *pericarditis.* The exudate may be purulent or seropurulent but usually much fibrin forms in the fluid.   The contraction of the heart may cause a fibrinous exudate to take on a papillary form, cor villosum.   Obliteration of the cavity (pericarditis obliterans) may follow the organizations of such exudates.   The organization of smaller patches of fibrin gives rise to milk or soldier's spots.   Tuberculosis may take the form of miliary tubercles or a tuberculous inflammation.

Methods of Section.—When the examination has progressed to this point, one of three methods must be chosen for completing the section.   The organs may be removed, beginning with the heart; they may be opened and sectioned *in situ;* or all viscera may be stripped from their attachment posteriorly and removed *en masse.*   The first is the method detailed in this book and the one usually employed in America.   The second method is applicable to organs, when their position and the relationship of parts is very important. The third may be used as a routine; but it is especially valuable when the great vessels, the trachea or esophagus, and the lungs are to receive careful investigation.

Heart.—Weight, 275 gm.; circumference of orifices: tricuspid, 12.5 cm.; pulmonary, 9 cm.; mitral, 10.5 cm.; aortic, 7.5 cm.; and the left ventricular wall 1 cm. thick.

In order to determine the circumference of the orifices measure accurately from cut edge to cut edge, exactly at the ring. In considering a *mean* in weights or measurements, a 20 per cent. variation either way is allowable and this may be exceeded.

Opening the Right Heart (Fig. 112).—To open the heart, the initial position is with the side upward that faces anteriorly as the heart lies in the body. After placing in this position which is readily made out since the right ventricular wall is quite flabby, do not turn the heart in various directions until the cuts designated have been made. With the enterotome, open the right auricle by cutting between the openings of the inferior and superior vena cava. Examine the auricular appendix for thrombi and the septum for a patent foramen ovale.

Now, with one cut of the enterotome open through the tricuspid valve and down the extreme right side of the right ventricle to near its apex. To do this, the heart is held in the left hand in the initial position with apex away from the operator, the short blade pushed down through the tricuspid orifice, and the incision made ½ in. in front of the anterior longitudinal sulcus, in which will be found a descending branch of the left coronary. Reverse the initial position by turning the apex toward the operator. From near the lower end of the first incision push the long blade of the enterotome through the pulmonary orifice, and lay it open with one cut by an incision 1 in. in front of the posterior longitudinal sulcus.

Opening the Left Heart (Fig. 113).—With the enterotome the openings of the pulmonary arteries are joined. Examine the mitral orifice from above. The heart is turned into a second position with the right heart which has been opened posteriorly.   With the apex away from the operator, the short

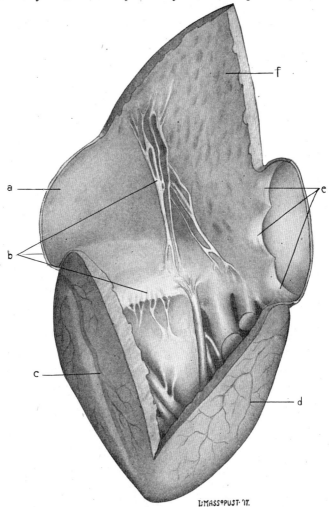

LMASSOPUST '17.

FIG 112.—Opening right side of heart.   Holding the heart in the left hand, with the short blade of the enterotome in the cavity cut down to the apex of the ventricle keeping to the right and ½ in. in front of c, the anterior longitudinal sulcus. a, Right auricle; b, segments of tricuspid valve.   Turn the heart so that the apex is toward the operator and with the long blade in the cavity cut up through the pulmonary valve, e, keeping to the left and 1 in. in front of the posterior longitudinal sulcus, d. f, is the segment of heart muscle pulled upward to expose the parts.

blade is pushed through the orifice and the left ventricle opened along its left side to its apex, keeping 1½ in. in front of the anterior longitudinal sulcus. The short blade of the enterotome is inserted into the cavities, except in opening the aortic and pulmonary orifices. Turn the heart

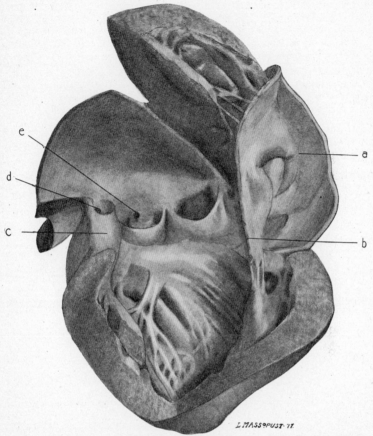

L. MASSOPUST· 77.

FIG. 113.—Opening the left side of the heart. From the left auricle, *a*, push the short blade of the enterotome through the mitral orifice while holding the heart in the left hand with the apex away from the operator and make the incision to the left and 1½ in. in front of the anterior longitudinal sulcus. *b*, is segment of the mitral valve. Reverse the heart so that the apex is toward the operator and from near the lower end of this incision push the long blade through the aortic orifice, *c*, and make the cut to the left and 1 in. in front of the posterior longitudinal sulcus. *d*, Right coronary artery; *e*, left coronary artery.

so that the appex is toward the operator, and from the lower end of the first incision cut up along the ventricular septum 1 in. in front of the posterior longitudinal sulcus where the descending branch of the right coronary may be found, and with one cut lay open the aorta. Avoid cutting through aortic and pulmonary valves and the segments of the mitral valve. Examine the endocardium of the left ventricle and especially that covering the papillary muscles for a tiger-lily appearance which indicates fat. With small, probe-pointed scissors open both right and left coronaries from their orifice in the aorta, examining not only for thrombi but also for places of thickening, and for tortuosities in the vessels.

In opening the heart as indicated, a knowledge of the relative importance and frequency of cardiac lesions is required. The method outlined is a general one and may be departed from in any case where a departure is indicated. Autopsy findings corroborate the clinical diagnosis less often in the case of the heart than in any other organ. It is important to keep in mind all the anatomic and functional possibilities of the organ, as well as the fact that the cardiac cells may be pathologic and yet not show microscopic changes (functional disease).

Changes in the Orifices and Valves.—It may be desirable to make a *hydrostatic test* of the valves before cutting through the orifices, but a careful examination of the orifices and valves after they are laid open usually gives all the information obtained by a doubtful hydrostatic test. The test is more commonly applied to the mitral valve, in which case an initial opening is made with the brain knife into the left ventricle and the cavity filled with water. The water should not flow through the orifice into the left auricle.

After the left auricle has been widely opened, the mitral orifice is examined from above. In case of severe mitral stenosis, there is only a button-hole opening. In the usual case of stenosis and insufficiency, not only is the orifice narrowed, but the segments are shortened, thickened, and distorted, and the columnæ are hypertrophied and blunt. Even in cases of very slight sclerosis such as follows rheumatic fever, the chordæ tendineæ are attached to the very margin of the segments so that perfect approximation of the segments is not possible.

Scleroses about the aortic orifice are equally important. **In** the case of the mitral a slight sclerosis from a benign verrucous *endocarditis* may be followed by an insufficiency; while a high-grade sclerosis from an ulcerated endocarditis in which the necrotic process extends deeply into the walls of the cavity is likely to produce a stenosis, owing to the contraction of the abundant scar tissue about the ring. On the other hand, verrucous granulations of the aortic valves often cement them together to produce some degree of stenosis. If insufficiency of the aortic valves is present, leutic lesions in the arch and elsewhere are searched for. Ulcerative endocarditis is easily recognized; but early or slight verrucous vegetations are mere granules even as small as millet-seed in size. Both aortic and mitral valves may be involved in a toxic endocarditis (arteriosclerosis); the process is extensive elsewhere in the intima of arteries.

Changes in the Cavities.—Cruor, white, and agonal clots are carefully removed with the fingers. Clots may stick to the endocardium, and care should be exercised to ascertain whether some lesion of the endocardium is present at the point where the clot adheres to the wall. Thrombi found in the auricular appendices and between the papillary muscles are attached to the wall; free ball-thrombi occur. Aneurismal dilatations of the cavities are characterized by a local thinning of the wall. A thin area in the wall may mark the site of an infarct. Increase in size of the whole cavity (dilatation) is usually accompanied by a thickening of the wall (hypertrophy).

Changes in the Myocardium.—Tangential cuts into the thickest portion of the left ventricular wall are made. Hypertrophy is usually most marked in the wall of the left ventricle, but in certain pulmonary conditions the musculature of the right heart may be much increased in thickness. Brown atrophy may be seen pathologically in cases of extreme emaciation. A fat degeneration lends a yellowish and greasy appearance to the muscle, which may be diffuse or in bands (tiger-heart). Anemic infarcts are easily recognized and are usually near the apex where they produce a myomalacia that may be followed by an aneurismal dilatation or rupture. The infarct may

26

result from an embolus or it may be produced by a thrombosis of a branch of a coronary artery. In thrombosis the artery shows an atherosclerosis and angina pectoris may have been present. Adipositas cordis is especially characterized by a subepicardial increase in lipoblasts. Infectious lesions are shown by areas of yellowish (necrotic) and reddish (hemorrhagic) blotches intermixed. Aschoff nodules, resulting from mild streptococcic lesions of the arteries, may not be visible in the gross. The healing of malnutritional, infectious or toxic lesions may produce a greater or less sclerosis of the myocardium. Any of the destructive lesions situated in the septum, interfere with the function of the conduction bundles. In cases where such lesions are suspected numerous transverse sections are made through the septum with the brain knife.

Lungs.—Free the lungs by breaking any pleural adhesions that may be present; it may be necessary to use the small cartilage knife to divide strong fibrous adhesions. If the adhesions are very firm, cut the diaphragm off with the base of a lung; or the thoracic organs may be removed *en masse*, placed on a board with the posterior surface up, and the dissection made. Lift the left lung upward by allowing the root to pull through between the first and second finger, and cut through the root from above downward. Right and left lungs are removed in the same way. Open the vein, artery, and bronchus (Fig. 114) to some distance with probe-pointed scissors. Incise the lung with one sweeping cut extending from the pleural surface down to the root, the anterior edge of the lung being held in the left hand with a finger between the lobes. Make the desired number of cross sections.

Changes in the Lungs.—Owing to the extreme vascularity of the lung tissue, malnutritional circulatory lesions are not common and exudation is extensive in the inflammations. Cultural observations are important, but difficult because the few organisms always present are rapidly distributed post-mortem.

Atelectasis.—In the newborn, atelectasis results from a failure after birth of certain parts of the pulmonary tree to fill with air (fetal atelectasis). In the adult, an entire lung or lobe of a lung may become atelectactic from the accumulation of fluid, air, blood, or a tumor mass in the pleural cavity (compression atelectasis). Hydropericardium, kyphosis, or growths in the mediastinal spaces may have the same consequence.

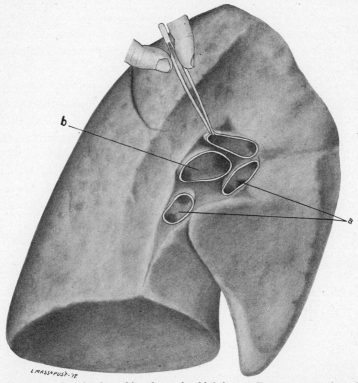

FIG. 114.—Opening bronchi and vessels of left lung. Forceps are on the pulmonary artery which is somewhat larger than the veins; *a*, pulmonary veins; *b*, bronchus. These structures must not be cut too close or the branches shown by the shaded areas in the vessels will be cut through.

Collapse of the air sacs of a small area may be brought about by the obstruction of a bronchus which is followed by the absorption of the air present (obstructive atelectasis). The airless part whether large or small appears dark red and meaty. Induration follows with a disappearance of the alveolar walls or the area becomes pneumonic.

Emphysema.— Focal areas of vesicular emphysema are near the surface, project above the general level, and appear white or of a light color. They result from coughing, obstruction of the larger air passages, glass blowing, loud talking, the effort of playing wind-instruments and so on. Senile emphysema appears to be due to atrophy of the alveolar walls. Rupture of the air-sacs by penetrating wounds, by tearing of the lungs, by fractured ribs, or by rupture of bronchioles in whooping-cough with the escape of air into the connective tissue of the lungs, is interstitial emphysema. Such interstitial emphysema occasionally may appear subcutaneously on the face. With this appearance, infection with the gas bacillus should be suspected.

Circulatory Disturbances.—*Hypostatic congestion* appears in the dependent portions of the lung in prolonged toxic conditions, in which there is present a marked weakness of the heart muscle. It is frequently followed by a *hypostatic pneumonia*. *Chronic passive congestion* follows incompensation of the left heart. The higher grades are seen in mitral stenosis. The color is brownish and the consistency increased. Such an organ is known as a lung of brown induration or a heart-failure lung. The brown color is due to the hemosiderin-containing endothelial leukocytes (so-called heart-failure cells) in the sacs and alveolar walls (Fig. 103). *Hemorrhagic infarcts* appear as irregular raised areas on the pleural surface. The surface areas represent the base of the pyramidal infarcted area. The embolus in the pulmonary artery that has produced the infarct lies toward the root of the lung from the surface area involved. Infarction occurs only in lungs with chronic passive congestion, or from the lodgment of septic emboli.

Pulmonary edema is shown by a great excess of frothy fluid in all parts of the lung, which increases both volume and consistency.

Inflammation.—*Lobular pneumonia* (catarrhal, focal, or bronchopneumonia) is the form usually present in children, and appears as irregular airless areas of a red, or dull whitish color. These areas are often about the size of a cherry and of a rather smooth appearance on section, since fibrin does not fill the alveoli to the extent it does in the lobar type. Such areas may become confluent, giving rise to large areas that contain very little air. Areas of *lobar pneumonia* are rather sharply defined with involvement of lobes or segments of lobes. The involved area is airless, voluminous, sinks in water, and at first is red; but later it becomes more or less grayish. On section the alveoli appear as fine granules. *Pleuritis* is always present in lobar and croupous pneumonia. Chronic *interstitial pneumonia*

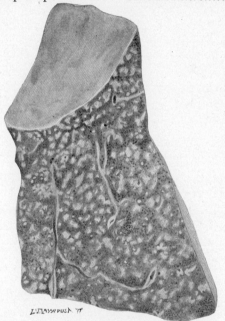

FIG. 115.—Miliary tuberculosis of the lungs.

is a term that has been applied to a fibrosis from a lobar pneumonia that does not resolve, pneumokonioses, tuberculosis, syphilis, and other causes. *Gangrene* follows an infection with putrefactive bacteria from aspirated food particles, rupture of the esophagus, emboli containing putrefactive bacteria, and the like, and is easily recognized by the black foul-smelling, infected area.

Bronchiectatic cavities are carefully probed to determine their connection with the bronchi. The apices of the lungs are minutely examined for old as well as beginning *tuberculosis*, and any suspicious areas are fixed for microscopic examination. From the primary lesions the tubercle bacilli are distributed by way of the blood- and lymph-vessels to form miliary tubercles (Fig. 115), or they are scattered over the mucous membrane surface to form a tuberculous pneumonia. The distribution may be sufficiently diffuse and extensive to produce complete consolidation (caseous pneumonia). Cavities result from the liquefaction of necrotic tissue. In congenital syphilis, the treponemata are diffusely distributed in the alveolar septæ, producing an extensive fibrosis (white pneumonia) and usually

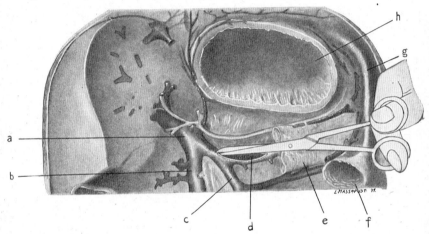

Fig. 116.—Opening the splenic vein, *d*, near the portal, *a*, shown after dissecting away a portion of the pancreas, *e*; *b*, is the superior mesenteric vein; *f*, colon cut across; *g*, spleen; *h*, stomach cut across. In this examination the stomach, colon and pancreas are not incised as shown but are pulled aside and the dissection made.

gummata. Actinomycosis, oidiomycosis, and blastomycosis resemble tuberculosis clinically and in the gross appearance of the lesions.

Metastatic tumor is very common. When suspected, carcinoma arising from the bronchial epithelium must be traced to its origin in a large bronchus (above the third branching).

Spleen.—Weight, 175 gm. Incise the vessels near the hilus and then pull the organ from its position beneath the diaphragm.

Examine the capsular surface for infarcts, fibrous thickenings, inflammations, and tumors. Note the consistency of the organ, place it on the board, and incise in its long diameter. Examine the cut surface for the normal lymph nodules, and for abnormal collections of cells, such as typhoid nodules and tumor metastases. Observe the elevation or depression of the cut surface as regards the capsule, the appearance of the stroma, and the amount of pulp scraped from the surface with a knife. Now make numerous cuts in the short diameter. Examine the splenic and portal veins for thrombosis (Fig. 116).

FIG. 117.—Anemic infarction of the spleen (case of ulcerative endocarditis).

Changes in the Spleen.—In *chronic passive congestion* the volume is increased two or three times, the surface is a dark brown or black color, and the consistency more or less leathery (cyanotic induration). *Banti's disease* (splenic anemia) is a clinical term under which different pathologic lesions have been included by the clinician; but the *splenomegalies* up to one kilo, due to thrombosis of the portal or splenic vein, and those due to a severe cirrhosis of the liver appear to comprise the greater part of these clinical cases. The congestion is more marked than the one of cardiac origin and fibrosis follows the distension of the vessels and the accumulation of hemosiderin-containing leukocytes. Anemic infarcts (Fig. 117) result from the plugging of arteries by emboli. If infected, the emboli produce inflammatory foci or abscesses.

Acute infectious splenic tumor is seen in acute pyogenic infections, or in anthrax, typhoid, pneumonia or scarlet fever; and the increase in size results from the accumulation of the reacting cells in and between the sinuses. The color is dark red, except where the reacting cells form nodules, as in typhoid fever. The consistency is much diminished so that the organ flattens out on the autopsy board, scrapings from the surface are abundant, and the pulp projects above the cut capsule. The spleen is not a parenchymatous organ and the toxic lesions are not very important. In diphtheria, scarlet fever, streptococcus infections and some other toxemias, a necrosis with fibrin formation may take place in the lymph nodules; or, if less strong, foci of endothelial leukocytes may accumulate here. The mildest toxins cause an accumulation of lymphocytes and eosinophiles about the trabeculæ. The toxic lesions are microscopic rather than gross.

Chronic infectious splenic tumor is seen in malaria, kala-azar and possibly in syphilis. In these diseases, there is not only an accumulation of the reacting cells (endothelial leukocytes), but also a fibroblastic proliferation. Splenomegaly is applied to chronic splenic enlargement not due to tumor.

Both primary and secondary *lymphoblastomas* involve the spleen, with great increase in size. In myeloblastoma, the organ reaches its greatest size and may weigh several kilos (splenomyelogenous leukemia). Hodgkin's disease may be primary in the spleen or the spleen may become secondarily involved. Rupture may occur in cases where the spleen is very large.

Atrophy occurs normally in old age and may follow a primary enlargement due to acute processes. *Amyloid* deposits may chiefly involve the lymph nodules (sago spleen), or they may be diffuse (lardaceous spleen). In malaria, hemoglobinemia, pernicious anemia, and other conditions, large amounts of hemosiderin may be present in the spleen where a yellowish coloration is produced. Miliary and conglomerate *tubercles* are common. A perisplenitis giving rise to a condition known as *sugar-coated* spleen results from organization of fibrin on the surface.

Gastro-intestinal Tract.—Cut off the omentum near the transverse colon. Grasp the sigmoid colon and draw it forcibly upward; free it with a knife from its mesocolon downward to the rectum; after pushing all fecal masses upward from the rectum place as low down as convenient a double ligature or

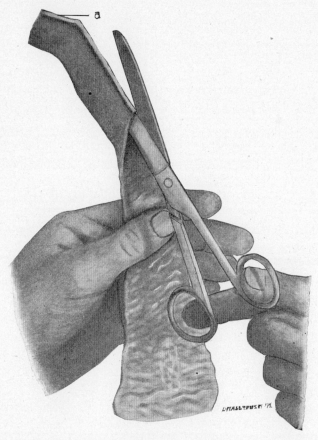

Fig. 118.—The intestines are opened with enterotome in a sink or in a large pan at the sink and are examined as opened. *a*, Attachment of the mesentery.

two clamps on the gut, and cut between the ligatures or the clamps. Free the transverse colon by cutting the lesser omentum which connects it with the stomach. Pull loose from its attachment the ascending colon and cecum; and then, by pulling steadily so as to put the mesentery of the small intestine on the stretch, strip the mesentery from the gut throughout its entire length by cutting it off as near the intestinal wall as possible by using a sawing motion of the brain knife until the duodenum is reached; the lower part of the duodenum is clamped, divided, and the large and small intestine contained in the basin removed to a sink. As the mesentery is separated, run the intestine into a large wash-basin. With the scissors cut off the mesentery as close to its posterior attachment as possible. Note, and remove any retroperitoneal lymph-nodes not included in the mesentery. Hemolymph nodes strikingly red in color may be found in the retroperitoneal region about the celiac axis and elsewhere.

To remove the upper part of the gastro-intestinal tract, separate the stomach from the liver by cutting the hepato-duodenal ligament; note the condition of the portal vein and hepatic artery and probe the common bile duct in both directions. Cut through the diaphragm in the median line, and remove the duodenum, the stomach, and the pancreas by dissecting upward beneath these structures. Clamp the esophagus low down, and cut. The mass of tissue consisting of duodenum, stomach and pancreas, removed by the operation is placed on the autopsy board for section.

The intestines may be opened in a basin, or they may be removed to the sink and opened. With the enterotome, open the colon along one of its longitudinal muscle bands, and the small intestine along the attachment of the mesentery (Fig. 118), examining the entire mucous surface carefully. Open the stomach along the lesser curvature and continue the incision through the duodenum; with small scissors open the ampulla of Vater and dissect up the ducts (Fig. 119).

Changes in the Stomach.—Note gas, mucus, bile, fecal material, and blood contained in the stomach. In cases of suspected poisoning, the contents are placed in a clean Mason jar and sealed.

Postmortem change occurs quickly (one hour after death). This gives the mucosa of infants a transparent gelatinous appearance, while in adults enough blood usually escapes from veins in the submucosa softened by postmortem digestion to produce brown to black linear markings. The lower portion of the esophagus is also often partially digested.

Dilatation of the stomach, with the greater curvature reaching the level of the umbilicus, may be seen in pyloric obstruction from ulcer or carcinoma, as the result of excessive beer-drinking, and in other conditions. In cases of esophageal constriction and certain nervous diseases, a *diminution* in size may be seen. *Hour-glass stomach* follows extensive ulceration near the fundus-pylorus boundary. In gastroptosis a stomach of normal size or a dilated one assumes a low position in the abdomen. A congenital pyloric stenosis due to a great increase in the muscularis in the pyloric region may cause a dilatation in infants.

. *Poisons* may be swallowed accidentally or intentionally. Sulphuric acid turns the mucosa black, nitric acid yellow, while oxalic produces an edematous swelling. Phenol is recognized by its odor. Arsenic, after the lapse of some time, produces inflammatory changes. The alkaloids cause little change. The inflammation that follows corrosive poisons is frequently diphtheritic in character.

Acute gastritis from poisons and infections is shown by hemorrhage, swelling, and ulceration. The lesion of chronic gastritis is at present a questionable one. A polypoid hyperplasia due to leukocytes in the mucosa has been found; or an atrophic condition with a marked thinning of the wall may be present. In chronic passive congestion the wall is thick and tortuous veins may be seen in the submucosa; such veins should be looked for about the opening of the esophagus into the stomach. *Phlegmonous gastritis* is a purulent inflammation of the submucosa.

Peptic (round) *ulcers* occur most often on the lesser curvature and near the pylorus on the posterior wall. Hemorrhages are the rule and perforation may take place. Benign and septic embolism, thrombosis, chemical injury by substances taken with the food, toxic substances from the blood, and mechanical injury are credited with the production of the initial injury leading to ulceration.

Cancer arises near the pylorus (frequently from the wall of a peptic ulcer) and in the cardia. The growth may project into the cavity, polypoid cancer, or it may diffusely infiltrate the entire stomach wall (scirrhous form). In some cases the cancer appears to be an ulcer from the beginning. The cells and stroma may undergo a mucoid change (colloid cancer). Occasionally an epidermoid cancer arises here.

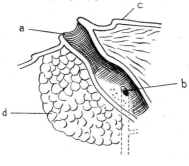
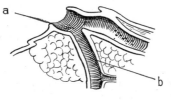
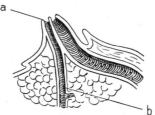

FIG. 119.—Opening the bile and pancreatic ducts (after Corning). *a* Papilla; *b*, pancreatic duct; *c*, duodenum; *d*, pancreas. Flatten the duodenum out on a board and start the dissection with a small pair of probe-pointed scissors from its mucosa.

Pancreas.—Weight, 100 gm. Examination of the ducts is important in all cases of liver and pancreatic disease with indications of obstruction (Fig. 119). To examine the ducts, cut the stomach off above, lay open the duodenum, and place the pancreas on the board with the duodenal mucosa upward. Open up the ampulla with small probe-pointed scissors and, if the main pancreatic duct opens into it, slit it open from its orifice; if the main pancreatic duct opens separately on the papilla, it should be dissected up first. Numerous cross sections are made through the organ. In all cases in which infection may be present sear the surface and make cultures from the organ beneath the sterile surface.

Changes in the Pancreas.—Occasionally accessory pancreatic tissue is found in the wall of the stomach, duodenum, jejunum or Meckel's diverticulum. Postmortem autodigestion is usually present and may be shown by soft whitish areas. The islets are whitish pin-point areas and are more numerous in the tail. In diabetes mellitus islets that appear normal to the naked eye may be changed microscopically (hyaline change). *Fat necrosis* appears as miliary to large yellowish foci with injected peripheries. *Acute pancreatitis* is a widespread inflammation of the pancreas with marked injection, extensive fat necrosis, and usually with liquefaction of the necrotic tissue. *Sclerosis* in the pancreas follows fat necrosis, acute inflammation, and, without doubt, less severe injuries. In hemochromatosis there is a marked increase of fibrous tissue (bronze diabetes). Lipomatosis is common. Retention cysts result from obstruction of the ducts, usually by concretions, and may be large, small, single or multiple. *Primary carcinoma* of the head produces an early and extreme icterus. *Secondary cancer* in the same region is frequent, and for this reason the primary tumor should be carefully located, since the microscopic examination may be of no assistance in a differentiation of the two.

Changes in the Intestines.—The contents of the intestine are fluid and gray in doudenum becoming thicker and yellowish in the lower part of the small intestine and finally formed and brownish in the colon. The contents are found abnormally thin as a result of influences that prevent the absorption of fluid such as abnormal motor activity, which may result from a hypersecretion of mucus and from a transudation of water. Abnormal constituents are described under feces.

An abnormally long appendix (10 in.), congenital stricture or atresia, and Meckel's diverticulum are common *malformations*. Small polyps projecting from the mucosa are of the nature of malformations. The lymph-nodes may show a grayish *pigmentation* that has not been satisfactorily explained; iron-containing pigment and *pseudomelanin* may be deposited in the mucosa.

In chronic passive congestion of hepatic or cardiac origin the intestine is a dark red and tortuous vessels may be visible in the submucosa. *Hemorrhagic infarction* has a varied etiology (thrombosis, embolism, intussusception, volvulus, and strangulation).

Acute enteritis, if severe, is shown by swelling and hemorrhages; but a mild enteritis or one even that is characterized by profound symptoms may not be demonstrable postmortem; or it may appear more or less definitely as a swelling of the lymph nodules (follicular enteritis). It may be produced by poisons such as arsenic and by dysentery, cholera, and other bacteria. Severe bacillary dysentery begins as a necrosis of the projecting epithelial structures and ends in the formation of numerous superficial areas of ulceration. In those conditions such as volvulus, intussusception, and strangulation in which the arterial blood in completely shut off (hemorrhagic infarction), there is rapid necrosis and invasion of the intestinal wall by bacteria. Agonal intussusception, especially in children, is not uncommonly found at autopsy. An involvement of the Peyer's patches (follicular enteritis) is seen in diphtheria, scarlet fever, and severe streptococcus infections. *Typhoid fever* produces a typical swelling, necrosis and ulceration of the lymphoid tissue. *Diphtheritis* is seen in sublimate poisoning, severe constipation, and severe dysentery. Appendicitis and peri-appendicitis are examined for when the peritoneal cavity is first opened. *Tuberculosis* occurs on the mucosa as ulcers, and on the serosa as tubercles and beaded linear markings following the course of the lymph-vessels. Examine the mesenteric lymph-nodes for enlargements, whenever an intestinal lesion is suspected. A chronic enteritis, not clearly defined histologically, may be seen in diseases of the stomach, in chronic alcoholism, and in other conditions.

Round or *peptic ulcers* are limited to the duodenum. Typhoid ulcers are found in the small intestine and colon with the most marked lesion in the last meter of the ileum. They are confined to the lymph structures. Ulcers of tuberculosis and *amebic dysentery* are present in the small intestines and colon; they are not strictly confined to the lymphoid structures but extend transversely around the gut; or are quite irregular in outline.

Syphilitic ulceration and stricture is not uncommon in the rectum. In the late stages of bichlorid poisoning ulcers occur in the small and especially in the large intestine where the poison is eliminated. In uremia, ulcers are similarly produced. Scybalous masses produce ulcers by causing pressure anemia. *Carcinomatous ulcers* occur in the rectum, the cecum, and the duodenum; they may cause constriction of the lumen,

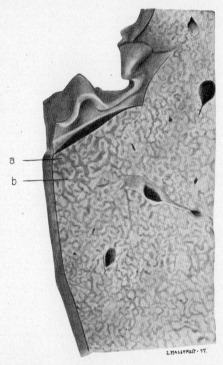

FIG. 120.—Examination of cut surface of the liver. *a*, Corresponds to central portion of lobule while *b* is the periportal connective tissue. Note that parts adjoining central hepatic veins form islands while the portal tracts anastomose.

especially if annular. Abscesses containing yellowish pus and the presence of fistulous tracts about the appendix suggest actinomycosis.

Liver.—Weight, 1800 gm. To remove the liver, make a deep incision transversely through the right and left lobes, place the thumb in this incision, pull upward, and cut through all attachments, first those of the right lobe and then those of the left. After removal of the lungs it is advisable in order to give more space in the abdomen to cut through the diaphragm so that the liver may fall into the thoracic cavity. Examine the capsule for irregularities, and the cut surface to determine the condition of the lobules. The cut surface of a liver has somewhat of a mosaic appearance, and the markings that correspond to the periportal tissue anastomose; while the areas that correspond to the central portions of the lobules do not. That is, parts that in many places are seen to form definite small islands correspond to central portions of lobules (Fig. 120). This is important, because the color of these structures varies greatly, and in different pathologic processes the same structures are of a different color. Make cross incisions at right angles to the first cut. If there is any indication of infection, sear the surface and make a culture.

Changes in the Liver.—It has been remarked that the method of section must be varied according to the indications; thus, if there is evidence of biliary obstruction, the duodenum is opened *in situ* and all structures examined from the ampulla upward, or the entire upper portion of the intestine with pancreas, stomach, and liver may be removed and placed on the board for dissection.

Obstruction of the common or the hepatic duct may be produced by gall-stones, inflammatory lesions of the ducts, compression from without by fibrous adhesions, abscesses, and the like, or by tumors of the ducts or adjoining structures. If closure of the cystic duct takes place, there is a marked enlargement of the gall-bladder; if the hepatic duct is obstructed, bile stasis in the liver follows; while if the blocking takes place in the common duct, dilatation of the gall-bladder and bile stasis are produced. On section of a normal liver, or one with bile stasis, the bile escapes from the bile capillaries nearest the portal tissue, leaving the greatest amount of bile at the center of the lobule. If the composition of the bile is normal, its damming back into the liver produces no change except a slight to moderate necrosis of cells toward the center of the lobule. At autopsy, the gall-bladder is often a bright green due to imbibition of bile; the mucosa undergoes rapid post-mortem *autolysis*. *Cholecystitis* and cholangitis are frequently associated. Edema causing a marked thickening of the gall-bladder wall is frequently present in cholecystitis. Choles-terin *concretions* formed in the gall-bladder and found here and in the ducts are white and irregular. Cholesterin-bilirubin stones are most common and present lamellæ in cross sections. Pure pigment stones are black, very small, and sometimes found in the smaller ducts. *Inflammation* follows infection of the bile in stasis with colon bacillus and other bacteria. The infection may also extend up the ducts in cases in which there is no obstruction. Such an infection may result in *infectious cirrhosis*, since peripheral portions of lobules and entire lobules are destroyed. This variety of cirrhosis is often referred to as biliary cirrhosis and it appears that a majority of the cases diagnosed clinically as *Hanot's cirrhosis* fall in this class. The granulation produced on the surface of the liver is fine and the change spoken of as monolobular in character. Pyogenic organisms may produce empyema of the gall-bladder or ab-scesses in the liver. Cancer of the gall-bladder rapidly in-filtrates the wall and extends into the liver parenchyma.

Chronic passive congestion of the liver results from ob-struction to the venous outflow through the hepatic veins, giving the center of the lobule a deep red appearance. The cells of the periphery frequently contain fat, in which case the center of the lobule is red and the periphery white (nutmeg liver). The central cells do not regenerate if a toxic necrosis occurs and a sclerosis about each central vein results (cyanotic atrophy). Hemorrhage usually accompanies such a necrosis. Fat is normally present in the liver cells. Hemorrhages occur in eclampsia and in central and focal necrosis. In *eclampsia* the irregular hemorrhagic areas do not coincide with the foci of necrosis. Atrophy (so-called brown atrophy) occurs in old age and in emaciation. *Amyloid* deposits cause an enlarge-ment with a rounding of the edges. On section, the organ is pale and glistening, and the consistency is increased.

27

Abscesses frequently follow the lodgment in the liver of infected emboli that come through the portal vein. This happens in cases of appendicitis, amebic dysentery, and less commonly in other inflammatory processes in the peritoneal cavity. Such an infectious process in the liver is called infarction. A red infarct following obstruction of a large branch of the portal vein by an embolus is not common. Pyogenic infections may also reach the liver through the hepatic artery or through the bile ducts. Since *conglomerate tubercles* are not common, caseous masses are always suspicious of gummata.

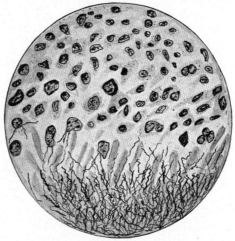

Fig. 121.—Actinomycosis of human liver.   (High power; Gram-Weigert Stain.)

Echinococcus may produce a large cyst with small ones inside (hydatid form) or it may form numerous large ones (multilocular form). *Actinomycosis* (Fig. 121) may be present as a metastatic process, or it may reach the liver from the vertebræ or from the lungs. Secondary carcinomata and metastatic non-epithelial tumors are common. Myelogenous leukemia causes a diffuse liver enlargement.

Scleroses of the liver are common and the severe diffuse forms are spoken of as *cirrhosis*. The causes of the cirrhoses may be mechanical—illustrated by a few cases of extreme carbon deposition and perhaps by *hemochromatosis*—, toxic, or infectious. A liver at autopsy with a granular or nodular surface and a marked increase in consistency (inability to thrust a finger into the parenchyma) is almost always found to be cirrhotic. The liver is smaller than normal unless fat or inflammatory reaction is present to cause an enlargement. Congenital syphilis, and less commonly the acquired infection, may produce an extensive and evenly distributed loss of paren-

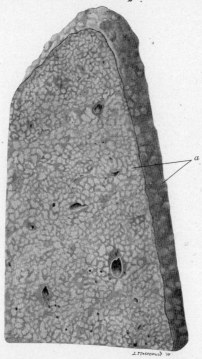

Fig. 122.—Cirrhosis of liver (so-called alcoholic). *a*, Islands of liver cells on the cut and capsular surfaces. Note that many are larger than normal lobules.

chyma with increase of fibrous tissue, giving the surface a granular character (syphilitic cirrhosis). In the acquired form of *syphilitic cirrhosis*, gummata are always present and in the congenital form they are often present. Gross irregularities result from healing of the gummata and the organ may resemble a cluster of grapes (hepar lobatum). *Infectious cirrhosis*, in which there may be a finely granular capsular surface, is caused by a mild infection (colon bacillus) extending through the gall-ducts. *Toxic cirrhosis* follows acute yellow atrophy and the surface is often coarsely nodular. Evidence of a cirrhosis from phosphorus, chloroform, and eclampsia is lacking. The liver in the so-called *alcoholic cirrhosis* (Fig. 122), except when large amounts of fat are present, is granular (hob-nail liver) and the cut surface shows irregular islands of liver cells and not lobules. The etiology of the so-called alcoholic cirrhosis at present is not known (Archives of Internal Medicine, Vol. 19, 1917). In this variety of cirrhosis ascites

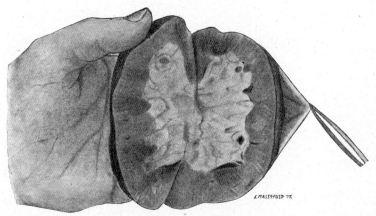

Fig. 123.—Section of kidney. Remove the fat from about kidney, place the organ in left hand with hilum in palm and make a single sweeping cut down to the hilum with the brain knife. Strip capsule with forceps.

is present and the collateral circulation between the portal and the vena cava is often well developed.

Kidneys.—Weight of the two kidneys, 300 gm. Make an incision through the peritoneum and the perinephritic fat along the outer border of the kidney, grasp the organ, and pull it out of its fatty capsule. Cut the ureter several inches below the pelvis. If the pelvis of the kidney or the ureter is involved in any way, the kidney is not disturbed until the ureter has from below been dissected out, opened with probe-pointed scissors, and carefully examined. To section the kidney, place it (Fig. 123) in the palm of the left hand, remove any fat adherent to it, and with one sweep of the brain knife, cut through to the hilus from the convex border. Observe whether or not the parenchyma projects above the cut edge of the capsular surface. With forceps strip the fibrous capsule back on either side. Note the ease with which the capsule strips, and the appearance of the kidney surface beneath it. Note the thickness of the cortex at its narrowest points above the pyramids (4 mm.), the appearance of the glomeruli (minute projecting pin-points of varying color), the straight tubules of the cortex (cortical rays), and the convoluted tubules between these (labyrinth).

Changes in the Kidneys.—*Malformations.*—Persistence of furrows on the surface indicating the fetal lobulation is common. Horseshoe kidney is not uncommon. One kidney may be absent (agenesia); or it may be represented by a rudimentary structure (aplasia). Accurate examination of the ureters is important in these cases. Congenital cysts in medulla and cortex are common in children. The exact relation that these bear to *congenital cystic kidney* is uncertain. Areas of adrenal tissue (cortex) and small masses of fibrous tissue (medulla) may be detected in the gross.

In *pernicious anemia* the kidney is pale with a yellowish to a brown tinge. Chronic passive congestion of the kidney may be shown by a deep cyanosis of the organ at autopsy. *Edema* is almost always inflammatory. For this reason any increase in weight of the kidneys is an important indication of an inflammatory process. Punctate *hemorrhages* are most distinct on the capsular surface of the kidney. *Anemic infarcts* are yellowish wedge-shaped areas with the base of the wedge on the capsular surface. If the infarction is due to a thrombosis, with absorption of the necrotic material the kidney often presents deep scars in a small granular kidney; if due to embolism, the size and shape of the kidney may be normal except for the deep scars. In severe *amyloid* disease, the kidney may be large with a smooth shining surface; or it may be small with a granular surface due to sclerosis.

In *infectious nephritis* the bacteria may first localize in the cortex (hematogenous infection) and then pass through the tubules to the pelvis; or the pelvis may be primarily infected (ascending infections). The way in which bacteria reach the kidney is often a point of controversy. Evidence of infection in the lower tract, marked involvement of the pelvis, variety of organism, and absence of subcapsular foci of infection are points to be considered in determining whether the bacteria reach the kidney through the blood or from the urinary tract below. The term pyelonephritis may be applied when the infection of the pelvis is conspicuous. *Abscess* of the kidney may be hematogenous (cortex usually involved to greatest extent), or the organisms may reach the kidney from the lower urinary tract. In miliary *tuberculosis*, the kidney is involved in conjunction with the other organs. In the other form, one kidney only may be involved. Conglomerate tubercles form and the pelvis is involved, and often extensively so. *Hydronephrosis* results from obstruction of the outflow of urine. In syphilis the kidney is usually not affected.

In *toxic nephritis* the lesion is diffuse; *tubular,* and *intracapillary* or *capsular glomerulonephritis* cannot as a rule be distinguished by the gross examination. Increase in weight and increase in thickness of the cortex points strongly to an acute nephritis. The healing stage of an acute intracapillary glomerulonephritis or the proliferative form of a capsular glomerulonephritis may be prolonged; or the toxin may continue to act over a considerable time. In either case there is produced a chronic process which is associated with a large kidney and with more or less definite urinary findings. Kidneys of this variety have been called *large white kidneys,* and many of these cases are spoken of clinically as *chronic parenchymatous nephritis.* This process produces more or less sclerosis, and, if the individual does not die, the kidney becomes small and granular. An organ that has become secondarily contracted in this way may give rise to the clinical picture called *chronic interstitial nephritis* but the usual, small, granular, sclerotic kidney found at autopsy and diagnosed clinically as chronic interstitial nephritis is an arteriosclerotic process.

Embryonal tumors (so-called sarcoma of the kidney) are not uncommon. Adrenal carcinoma (*hypernephroma*) usually arises in the kidney.

Capsule.—The fat capsule is extensive in sclerosed kidneys. The fibrous capsule is thick and adherent in sclerosis, and when removed leaves a granular surface. In acute enlargements (acute nephritis), the capsule appears thinner than normal.

Adrenals.—Weight, 6 gm. each. The adrenals are removed with the surrounding fat and then dissected free from it. The right one lies close up against the liver. In their removal some care is necessary to avoid tearing them. If any gross change is present, determine its relationship to surrounding structures such as lymph-nodes and sympathetic ganglia. Incise transversely and note the white center (medulla), next to the medulla the brown zone of the cortex (the pigmented reticularis), and the outer yellow part of the cortex (the two outer zones).

Changes in the Adrenals.—Postmortem autolysis, which appears as a liquid mass or cavity at the center of the gland may take place within a few hours. The chrome-reaction is negative unless the gland is fixed very soon after death. Hyperplasia especially of the medulla, has been found in developmental defects of the central nervous system, in status lymphaticus, and in hyperplasia of the genitals. Adrenal cortex (accessory adrenals) is found in the ovary, testis, kidney, broad ligament, and liver. *Necrosis* of the cortex from bacterial toxins (pneumonia, diphtheria) and from certain poisons (phenol, chloroform) occurs and is followed by rapid regeneration. The change may not be recognized in the gross. Pyogenic infections may extend to the adrenals. In diphtheria in children hemorrhage occurs. The etiology of scleroses occasionally found has not been fully determined. Tuberculosis occurs as large caseous nodules, or the entire organ may be represented by a large caseous mass. Both adrenals are usually affected, and the case presents clinically the picture of *Addison's disease.* Occasionally, adrenal carcinoma (hypernephroma) arises from the gland itself. *Neuroblastoma* has its origin in the medulla.   Adenomas appear to be common, but evidence of growth in them is often lacking.   The organs may be extensively involved in amyloid disease.   The infrequency of sclerosis appears to depend on perfect regeneration rather than the absence of toxic processes.

Genito-urinary Organs.—To remove the pelvic organs *en masse*, strip the peritoneum from the pelvic walls, beginning

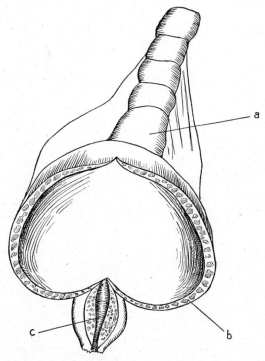

FIG. 124.—Opening bladder and urethra. *a*, Sigmoid colon; *b*, bladder wall pathologically thickened; *c*, prostatic urethra.

in front of the bladder.   Posteriorly separate the fibrous tissue down to the lower end of the rectum which is cut through with the knife.   The fecal matter is forced into the sigmoid before this part of the gut was ligated.   Cut through the urethra in front of the prostate in the male and through the vagina in the female, and remove the pelvic organs *in toto*.   When involved in pathologic processes it is often desirable to examine the structures by opening them before removal.

Place the pelvic organs on the board, open the rectum posteriorly, and wash. Open the bladder (Fig. 124) by cutting up through the urethra and anterior bladder wall. Incise the vagina through the bladder and continue the incision up through the anterior wall of the uterus and then laterally extend it out through the oviducts. Incise the ovaries in the long diameter.

To examine the testicles, cut through the tissues beneath the skin on either side of the root of the penis, and push the testicles up through these incisions. Incise them in the long diameter and with the forceps pick up some parenchyma to determine whether or not the tubules pull out in long threads as they normally do.

Changes in the Genito-urinary Organs.—Male pseudohermaphrodism, phimosis, hypospadias, and epispadias are common developmental defects. Examine the *penis* for hard chancre, chancroid, balanitis, condyloma acuminata, carcinoma, and old scars. Ascertain the presence of pus in the *urethra;* and, if it is indicated, examine the membranous portion of the male urethra for stricture. Stricture may be present in the cavernous portion. Fistulous tracts and false passages may connect with the urethra in cases of stricture and in inflammations about the urethra. In hypertrophy of the *prostate*, the condition of the middle lobe is of greatest importance. The usual histologic picture in prostatic hypertrophy is a combination of chronic inflammation, and glandular hyperplasia and dilatation. Acute inflammation (most often gonorrheal), tuberculosis, and carcinoma are important prostatic lesions. If the origin of metastatic cancer nodules in the liver, bone-marrow, or elsewhere has not been definitely determined, examine every part of the prostate. Cysts may be present in a remnant of the urachus extending from the bladder to the umbilicus. Ecstrophy of the bladder is rare. The urinary *bladder* may be the site of acute inflammation; but the inflammation is more often due to stone, obstruction by hypertrophied prostate, stricture, continuous catheterization in nervous diseases, or tuberculosis, and is therefore chronic. Tuberculosis is common, and usually secondary to renal tuberculosis. The pyogenic bacteria may produce a purulent cystitis; streptococcus may extend deeply and rapidly through the bladder wall to produce a phlegmon. In vesical diphtheritis the mixed infection is very severe and the ulcerated surface blackened. Carcinoma usually grows in the papillary form. Note the bladder contents. The *ureters* may be infected by pyogenic bacteria either from the bladder or the kidneys. Such inflammations, as well as tuberculosis and concretions, may obstruct the ureters and lead to pyonephrosis and hydronephrosis.

The *testicles* are usually hypoplastic if undescended. They always become atrophic in later life, and not uncommonly in earlier life, as the result of mumps. If functional the tubules of the parenchyma string out on teasing. An undescended testicle is usually fibrous and imperfectly developed. Gonorrhea commonly involves the *epididymis*. Tuberculosis likewise involves the epididymis rather than the testicle. Gumma, on the other hand, involves the testicle proper. A diffuse inflammatory process frequently is associated with gummata. A rapidly growing embryoblastoma is the commonest tumor; but mixed tumors of slow growth may occur. Hypernephroma may arise in a testicle. Hydrocele, spermatocele, and varicocele are important affections of the *tunica vaginalis*.

In the female, a minute examination of the external genitals and the mucosa of the *uterus* is made in certain cases in forensic medicine. Examine the opening of the urethra and Bartholin's glands for evidence of gonorrhea, and the vulva and opening of the vagina for chancre and condylomata. Erosions of the *cervix* are often found when prolapse or lacerations are present. In the usual cervicitis there is not only an infiltration with leukocytes but also a cystic dilatation of the cervical glands. Acute *endometritis* results from puerperal infections or from gonorrhea. There are a great variety of rather indefinite conditions that give rise to the so-called chronic hypertrophic endometritis. Tuberculous endometritis is usually secondary to an infection in the tubes. Carcinoma of the body of the uterus usually grows in the glandular form. The cancer arising from the cervix is clinically more malignant than one arising in the fundus; it may be of the glandular or the epidermoid type. *Leiomyoma* which may be submucous, intramural, or subserous, is the commonest tumor and may occasionally infiltrate and give rise to metastases (malignant leiomyoma). Purulent inflammation such as puerperal infection, gonorrhea, and tuberculosis are the important infections of the oviducts. Either gonorrhea or tuberculosis may give rise to extreme enlargements (pyo- or hydrosalpynx). Tubal inflammation frequently extend to the ovaries, forming tubo-ovarian abscesses. In the usual *tubal pregnancy* there is a hemorrhagic mass in the tube but no macroscopic evidence of fetal parts. A slow growing embryoblastoma of the *ovary* (dermoid cyst) is common, while the rapidly growing tumors of this variety may occasionally occur. The papillary *cystadenoma* (often carcinoma) is the commonest tumor. Fibromas and fibrosarcomas are met with. Simple and multilocular cysts from distention of follicles, corpora, and fetal rests are common and should be distinguished from cystic tumors. Such cysts may become infected. Bicornuate uterus, infantile (hypoplastic) uterus and changes in the external genitals associated with female pseudohermaphrodism are the commonest *malformations*.

The approximate duration of pregnancy may be determined from the length of the fetus. The lengths from the second to the tenth month inclusive are as follows: 3 cm.; 7–9 cm.; 10–17 cm.; 18–27 cm.; 28–34 cm.; 35–38 cm.; 39–41 cm.; 42–44 cm.; and 45 to 47 cm. (Mallory and Wright, Pathological Technique).

Aorta.—In the usual technic the aorta is examined as soon as the thoracic, abdominal, and pelvic organs have been completely removed. With the enterotome, open the aorta anteriorly along its entire extent, as it lies in position in front of the vertebral column and continue the incision down the iliacs. If the thoracic and abdominal organs are removed *en* *masse* the aorta and 6 in. of the iliacs should be stripped off with them. At this point examine the inferior vena cava and its branchings, continuing the incision into the femoral.

Changes in the Aorta.—*Arteriosclerosis* (atherosclerosis), as a progressive lesion, usually comes on in the later years of life. In early life, toxic lesions of the blood-vessels may result from the bacterial poisons. Repeated bacterial intoxications, lead, excessive food and drink, and heredity appear to be factors in the causation of arteriosclerosis. The atheromatous areas, irregular in size and shape, are yellowish and raised above the intimal surface. The endothelial lining may be absent (atheromatous ulcers). Calcification is the rule. Syphilis of the aorta is a tertiary lesion produced by localization of the treponemata in the vessel wall. The cellular reaction is similar to that seen in the primary sore, but much less acute. Since the wall is deeply infected, and the fibroblastic proliferation is active, the intima over the foci is translucent, more or less raised and thrown into parallel folds (hickory-bark appearance). In distinction to atheromatous patches syphilis is frequently confined to the arch. Aneurism occurs in high-grade arteriosclerosis and may follow other toxic, mechanical, nutritional, and infectious injuries; but syphilis is the chief cause.

Neck Organs.—Continue the main incision at least 1 in. above the sternum and, if permissible, up to the chin. With the smaller cartilage knife dissect up beneath the skin in front and then behind, keeping close against the vertebræ posteriorly and directly beneath the skin anteriorly. When the tissues have been separated sufficiently, allow the head to drop back over the block and run the brain knife up in front of the larynx until the point appears in the mouth anterior to the tongue. Turn the knife, and with a sawing motion cut back along the ramus of the jaw on either side until the posterior wall of the pharynx is reached, which is divided as high as possible. Now pass the left hand up, pull the tongue strongly downward, cut the remaining attachments on either side, and remove the organs in one mass. Take care to cut outside the tonsils. During the entire operation before the tongue is grasped, traction is made by pulling the esophagus and trachea downward with the left hand.

On the anterior surface, incise each lobe of the thyroid in its longest diameter; examine closely for thymic tissue. Examine the pharynx and incise the tonsils. Now turn the mass over and slit the esophagus down in the median line posteriorly; open into the trachea through this incision (Fig. 125).

Changes in the Neck Organs.—The *tongue* may show cancer on its surface, while gumma is more deeply situated in the muscle. *Epulis* may be found about the gums; a microscopic examination is required to determine the nature of such a growth. Pyogenic cocci and diphtheria bacilli commonly infect the *tonsils*. Primary syphilitic lesions may occur on the tonsils. Lymphoblastoma should be suspected in any chronic glandular enlargement. Phlegmon about the pharynx occurs, and a retro-pharyngeal abscess may form. In liver cirrhosis observe the large veins about the lower end of the esophagus. Cancer as well as

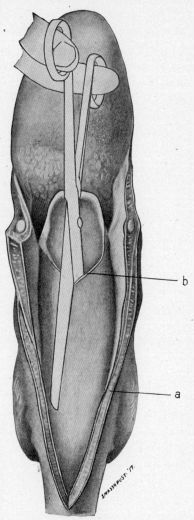

FIG. 125.—Examination of neck organs. *a*, Esophagus opened posteriorly in the median line; *b*, opening the trachea posteriorly in the median line with enterotome.

ulcer occurs in the lower third of the esophagus and, less frequently, in the upper third.

Larynx.—An edema of the larynx involves the epiglottis, and the true and false vocal cords. A diphtheritic membrane covering the false and true vocal cords is easily recognized. Phlegmonous inflammation extends about the false vocal cords and involves the deep tissues of the neck. Tuberculous ulcers occur on the posterior wall between the two cords, and they are usually secondary to a pulmonary tuberculosis, while syphilitic ulcers occur higher up; the syphilitic ulcers are more likely to involve the epiglottis and base of the tongue. Cancer ulcerates and infiltrates about the cartilages. The so-called papilloma projects as a wart-like mass.

Thyroid.—The weight of the thyroid varies from 30 gm. to 60 gm. It is said to be atrophic only when it falls below the minimum. In follicular distention and hyperplasia of the follicles (parenchymatous goiter) it is increased in size but the most pronounced enlargements are seen in cases of follicular distention (colloid goiter). Carcinoma growing in papillary or in solid form may be diagnosed microscopically. Adenomas are encapsulated.

Head.—In the permission given for the performance of an autopsy the head is not infrequently restricted. It is always desirable to section the head, and, if care be exercised in protecting the face from bruises and the hair from being soiled, no visible evidence of the operation appears. The examination extends to all structures within the cranial cavity and may include the naso-pharyngeal and orbital cavities as well as the accessory sinuses.

Removal of Skull-cap.—Insert a sharp-pointed scalpel at the hair margin directly behind the middle of the right ear; and, cutting outward, carry the incision over the vertex of the skull to the same point behind the left ear (Fig. 126). Strip back the anterior and posterior flaps by grasping them with the hands, cutting only when necessary. If cloth-covered gloves are used, the periosteum may be stripped off along with the scalp. Place the hair, if long, beneath the flaps; and wrap a towel about the face and neck to protect the hair from blood. Outline the path to be sawed by cutting through the periosteum and temporal muscles. Anteriorly, this line extends from points immediately above the ears straight around the forehead over the frontal eminences. Posteriorly, two straight lines are carried backward from the two points above the ears to meet at an oblique angle 1 in. in front of the occipital protuberance. The head-holder is clamped on and screwed down

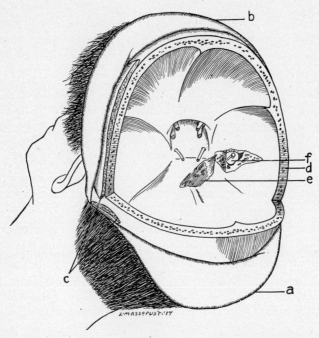

FIG. 126.—Opening the cranial cavity. *a* and *b*, Scalp flaps with hair surface rolled beneath; *c*, cut edges of temporal muscle; *d*, skull-cap removed; *f*, ear-drum and middle ear exposed by splitting off with powerful biting forceps the wedge of bone, *e*.

firmly, with its claws in the temporal region on that part of the skull-cap to be removed. Saw down to and partially through the inner table along the lines marked. To crack through the inner table, drive in the chisel with the hammer. With the chisel inserted in the frontal region, pry off the calvarium. In homicidal cases with injury about the head it is preferable to saw entirely through the bone although the brain substance is marked in places by the saw.

Examination of Skull and Dura and Removal of the Brain.—
Thickening of the skull with sclerosis and ossification of the
diploe are seen in conditions associated with atrophy of the
brain. The skull is abnormally thin in hydrocephalus and in
rickets. In the latter condition, the fontanels fail to close,
or are abnormally large. In later life the outer surface of the
skull bones frequently shows osteophytes to which the periosteum adheres. These result from slight injuries and inflammations. The inner surface may show similar outgrowths, 'but
they are not so dense and are usually red, due to a greater
vascularity.

Inspect the dura, and open the superior longitudinal sinus
with small scissors. With scissors cut through the dura
along the lines sawed, and strip it back over the hemispheres
by cutting the falx cerebri where necessary. Lift up the brain
with the left hand; with the brain knife cut the optic nerves,
other cranial nerves, and the carotids. Draw forward the
temporal lobes and cut the tentorium with the knife. Cut the
cord low down in the canal with a narrow brain knife, and
remove the brain.

In general, it may be said that the dura is thickened if the
convolutions cannot be distinguished through it. Such thickenings follow the chronic hemorrhagic pachymeningitis seen
in syphilis, alcoholism, and arteriosclerosis. Hemorrhages
on the inner surface of the dura are examined. The Pacchionian granules are frequently pulled away with the dura. The
amount of fluid in the space opened by cutting through and
removing the dura is noted.

Section of the Brain.—Examine the vessels at the base,
following the middle cerebral into the fissure of Sylvius. The
condition of the arteries at the base of the brain (circle of Willis)
is noted. If arteriosclerotic, the vessels are tortuous and
present visible thickenings that usually feel hard as a result
of calcification. The stumps of the carotids are examined for
emboli. Small hemorrhages from the arteries, before they
enter the brain substance, may not be detected until the vessels
are completely uncovered.

Place the brain on the board with the base down, Spread the two cerebral hemispheres apart, cut through the corpus callosum on each side (Fig. 127), and extend the incisions into the anterior and posterior cornua, exposing the lateral ventricles and portion of the basal ganglia. With the brain knife make two longitudinal incisions in the direction of these cuts and lateral to the median line, carrying them down through

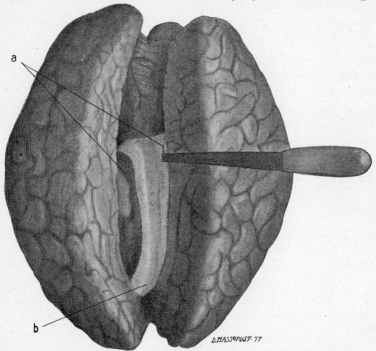

FIG. 127.—Section of cerebrum (primary incisions). *a*, Incisions into the lateral ventricles. Corpus callosum is cut off at *b*, and reflected posteriorly.

the basal ganglia (Fig. 128). Make two incisions outside the first one parallel to them, and two more outside these. The three incisions made on each side in this way in the antero-posterior direction permit the examination of all structures. Cut the corpus callosum in front and reflect it backward. By drawing back the velum interpositum the third ventricle is exposed. The cerebellum is cut through in the median line,

28

and two incisions tangential to the median incisions made through each of the halves (Fig. 129).

If the brain is to be kept for the gross demonstration of lesions and the relationship of parts, a very sharp knife is placed on its side beneath the base of the brain, turned so that the edge comes exactly in the median line, and the cut made

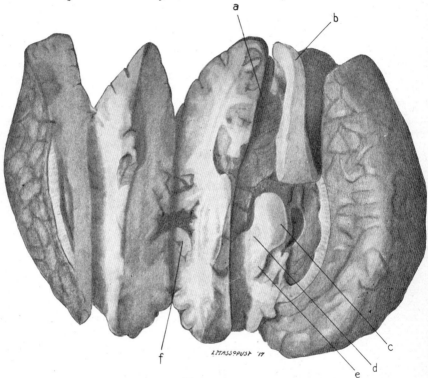

FIG. 128.—Section of the cerebrum (secondary incisions). *a*, Incision made in the line of the opening into the lateral ventricle shown in the previous illustration; *b*, corpus callosum reflected posteriorly; *c*, optic thalamus; *d*, lenticular nucleus; *e*, caudate nucleus; *f*, island of Rheil.

upward accurately in the median line. This method has the advantage over preservation *in toto*, in that many lesions can be seen after this incision and yet the relationship of parts is preserved by subsequent preservation in formalin.

Inner Meninges.—The arcahnoidal granulations are prominent along the superior longitudinal sinus where for their reception there are depressions on the inner surface of the skull. When edema of the brain (so-called wet brain) is present, the pia-arachnoid has a gelatinous transparent appearance and is thickened by the accumulation of fluid. A fibrosis of the pia is shown by an increase opacity, especially in the sulci. The anatomic connection between the meninges and dural endotheliomata may not be demonstrable. In general, *leptomeningitis* is shown by the presence of an exudate, chiefly at the base, that varies in appearance with the etiology. In infections with pyogenic cocci the exudate is diffuse and purulent, while in

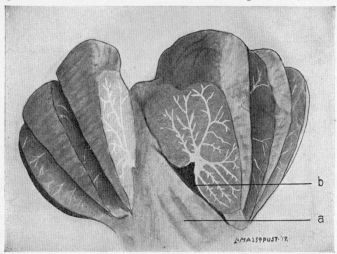

FIG. 129.—Section of the cerebellum by a median and two lateral incisions. *a*, Medulla; *b*, fourth ventricle.

tuberculosis and syphilis there are foci of exudate with few or many endothelial leukocytes. In infantile paralysis, the exudate is not remarkable and the spinal fluid is usually clear.

Examination of the Brain Substance.—In internal hydrocephalus and in conditions associated with atrophy or failure of development of nerve cells, the convolutions are flattened or smaller than normal. Recent hemorrhages (red or black) and old hemorrhages (yellow) may appear on the cortical surface.

On opening the lateral ventricles, excess of fluid and dilatation should be looked for (internal hydrocephalus). A granular ependymitis is shown by a delicate granulation of the lining of the ventricles. Hemorrhages may take place directly into the ventricles, but the blood more often gains entrance to them from the deeper lining nervous tissue. Gliomas with hemorrhagic areas may reach the ventricular surface. Edema of the choroid plexus is shown by an increased volume and by a gelatinous, transparent appearance of this structure. Before making the incision, the cortical surface should be carefully palpated for variations in consistency. Abscesses and areas of softening give a lessened resistance, while tumors and hemorrhages increase the resistance.

On the incised surfaces, search for hemorrhages, areas of softening, and gliomas. Hemorrhage frequently takes place in the last two processes. For this reason it is important to remove a small bit of material from the diseased area, apply a cover-glass, and, with the high-dry or oil-immersion lens of the microscope, examine it in the fresh condition. Granular débris and endothelial leukocytes with much fat (compound granule cells) are found in softening, while in glioma the small round or spindle glioblasts are present. Hemorrhage occurs commonly about the fissure of Sylvius and large ones may occur here without causing death. The blood may come from capillaries and small vessels (anthrax, hemorrhagic exanthemata, hemophilia), or from large vessels.

Apoplectic hemorrhage follows rupture of a large arterial branch and is due to an existing arteriosclerosis, a high blood pressure, or to both. It is the arterial blood pressure that produces the injury to the soft brain tissue. The tissue made necrotic in this way is removed by autolysis and the action of leukocytes, and frequently a cyst results.

Red and white softening follows the closure of vessels by embolism or a thrombosis. Emboli usually come from the valves of the left heart. If a large artery supplying the brain substance is blocked, death follows; while a blocking of one of the large vessels at the base of the brain produces no serious result, owing to the perfect facilities for the immediate establishment of a collateral circulation. Thrombosis usually occurs in sclerosed vessels. In areas of softening as in other processes in the brain and elsewhere, hemorrhage is more or less an accidental happening. If the blood escapes into these areas, a red area of softening results but, if there is little or no blood, the lesion is white. As mentioned, the red ones later become yellow, and cyst formation may take place as the necrotic tissue is removed by autolysis and by the action of leukocytes.

When *atrophy* of the brain substance occurs, the vacated cranial cavity becomes filled with fluid which increases the size of the ventricles and the subdural spaces. The consistency of the brain is increased and the convolutions flattened. The hemispheres are frequently involved to a different degree, making the brain asymmetrical. This is seen in mental diseases, in old age, and in chronic alcoholism.

Secondary degeneration of the cortical motor centers follows destruction of the motor tracts lower down, and gray focal areas (gray degeneration) in the motor region may be visible.

General paresis gives a diffuse sclerosis that may not give gross changes, or there may be a demonstrable increase in consistency.

Purulent encephalitis may or may not be associated with involvement of the meninges by pyogenic bacteria, depending on whether it follows the lodgment of infected emboli or the direct extension of the infectious process into the brain substance from adjoining tissue. *Solitary tubercle* is usually in the cerebellum or the pons while gumma is usually on the cortical surface. Since the syphilitic process occurs most often in connection with the larger vessels of the meninges, it can usually in the gross be distinguished from tubercle.

Glioma is a common tumor of the brain substance. Dural endotheliomas are on the surface. Melanomas arise from the melanoblasts over the cerebellum.

In sectioning the cerebellum as described (page 435) the fourth ventricle is opened. In cases of sudden death, the structures lying in the floor of this ventricle are carefully examined for hemorrhages and other injuries.

After completing the section of the brain, the *pituitary gland* is removed from its bed, fixed *in toto* in Zenker's fluid to be sectioned in its anteroposterior axis. In all cases of inflammation and fracture, and in other conditions where it is indicated examine the venous sinuses at the base of the skull for thrombosis and evidence of infection. With the large bone-forceps grasp the dura covering the basis of the skull, and completely strip from it the bones. The dura may be stripped by grasping it with cloth-covered gloves. After stripping the dura, examine the underlying bone for fractures.

Middle Ear.—With the heavy bone-forceps bite off the roof of the middle ear (petrous portion of the temporal bone). This exposes the tympanic membrane, the bones of the middle ear, the semicircular canals, and the mastoid cells. Otitis media which follows infection with pyogenic bacteria, results in the filling of the middle ear, and frequently of the mastoid cells, with pus. Necrosis of bone is common. Thrombosis of the sinuses and the internal jugular vein, as well as local or general leptomeningitis, may be present. *Cholesteatomata* are looked for.

Nasopharynx (Harke).—Extend the original scalp incision behind the ears downward to the middle of the neck. Dissect the posterior flap downward, uncovering the upper cervical vertebræ. Dissect the anterior flap downward, uncovering the root of the nose and the upper rim of the orbits. Saw down through the base of the skull in the anteroposterior median line, passing slightly to one side through the frontal bone so as to avoid the nasal septum. After the base has been completely separated, cut the ligaments attached about the foramen magnum, and forcibly push the two halves of the skull apart. Examine the sphenoidal and ethmoidal cells, the frontal sinuses, the nasal passages, the antrum of Highmore, and the mucosa of the pharynx for pyogenic inflammations, diphtheritic membrane, gummatous involvement of the bone, chronic inflammation with edema (polyps), and tumors.

Eye.—With small biting forceps, carefully remove the roof of the orbit. Cut through the muscles and conjunctiva, and remove the posterior portion of the eyeball without disturbing the cornea and conjunctiva adjoining it. An edema of the papilla (the point where the optic nerve enters the retina) is spoken of as a *choked disk* or papillitis and is shown by a milk-white appearance of the nerve. In all cases of increased intra-cranial pressure, this is looked for. Localized inflammations or a panophthalmitis may be present. Melanoma, glioma, and neuroblastoma may be primary in the eye. Evidence of exophthalmus may or may not be demonstrable at autopsy.

Spinal Cord.—It is desirable to remove the cord before opening the body cavities anteriorly. Place the body face down with a block under the chest. Protect the face so that it will not be bruised. Make a median line incision extending

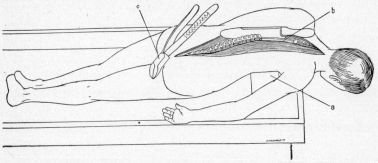

FIG. 130.—Removing the spinal cord. Hang head over end of autopsy table to protect face from bruising. Move wooden block, *a*, under chest to the level at which the transverse laminæ are being sawed. Saw on both sides. Uncover the cord, *b*, by biting off the posterior spinous processes with the strong bone-forceps, *c*. If possible remove the cord before opening the thoracic and abdominal cavities.

the entire length of the spinal column, and strip the soft tissue back on the two sides. Saw through the laminæ and bite off the spinous processes with heavy bone-forceps (Fig. 130). The arches of the cervical vertebræ are divided with the bone-forceps. Cut the spinal nerve roots with a scalpel. Remove the cord with the dura intact. Slit the dura open both pos-teriorly and anteriorly. Make transverse cuts 1 cm. apart.

Examination of the Cord and its Meninges.—When a pachy-meningitis hemorrhagica is found beneath the cerebral dura, the condition is often found to be continued down the cord.

Also in purulent meningitis, the innermeninges of the cord as well as of the brain are frequently affected. No gross lesion may be present in the acute stage of infantile paralysis or there may be injection of vessels and exudate. In cases of a number of years standing with extensive paralysis atrophy may be made out at autopsy. Local hemorrhages from fracture of the vertebræ can be seen through the dura. From a hemorrhage in the left internal capsule with motor and sensory paralysis on the right, atrophy in the left posterior horn may be apparent in the thoracic region. In long standing cases of tabes dorsalis a symmetrical atrophy may be seen posteriorly.

Spina bifida is a common malformation of the lumbosacral region; and depends on the defective closure of the neural canal in this region. The vertebræ are incomplete, and the cord with or without its covering membranes projects through the defect.

Hemorrhages in the cord are necessarily smaller than in the brain, but present a similar appearance. Areas of softening in the cord, unlike those in the brain, do not often result from the closure of arteries; but they are produced by mechanical pressure, tumors, and inflammations. It may be very difficult to detect areas of softening by the color; but when an attempt at removal is made the cord is found abnormally soft. Purulent softening (transverse and diffuse myelitis) follows a localization of pyogenic organisms in the cord. In the early stages of *anterior poliomyelitis*, the vessels of the meninges and cord are injected and this change may be visible at autopsy. The amount of fluid beneath the dura is increased. Areas of multiple sclerosis are grayish red in color like those in the brain, and in cases of this disease such areas are found in both places. It may not be possible at autopsy to make out tract degenerations, such as degeneration of the posterior sensory fibers in *tabes dorsalis*. Tuberculous and syphilitic involvements of the cord are not common. Glioma is more common than other tumors. Cystic cavities extending longitudinally are not uncommon, and although their origin is not the same in all cases the condition is spoken of as *syringomyelia*.

Bone-marrow.—Make a long incision over the middle of

thigh, dissect and push the muscles aside so as to expose the middle third of the femur. Saw into the marrow cavity of the bone with two incisions separated on the surface of the bone by 3 cm. and in the cavity by 1 cm. With the bone-forceps split out this wedge of bone, exposing the marrow.

If the bone-marrow is not hyperplastic, yellow marrow with spicules of bone in it is present in the femur. In this case it is preferable to crush the ends of the ribs with the costotome, place the red marrow obtained on paper, and fix. This is not a good general procedure, for the relation of the cells and stroma is destroyed.

Postmortem changes progress rapidly in the bone-marrow, apparently as the result of autolysis. In infants fat marrow may be found in the long bones in marasmus, Barlow's disease and in cretins. In adults in the atrophy associated with old age, chronic pulmonary tuberculosis, chronic nephritis, inanition, and aplastic anemia the marrow often has a jelly-like appearance. In severe anemias, malaria and hemochromatosis a brownish color may be distinguished.

Hyperplasia of Bone-marrow.—This is a general term that is applied to an increase in red marrow, and especially to the replacement of fat marrow in the diaphyses of long bones with red marrow. The gross appearance of the different varieties of hyperplasia is not distinctive; but microscopically the picture vaires with the cells that are proliferating.

In general, it may be said that the tumors give a marrow less red in color than erythroblastic proliferation. Following extensive losses of red blood corpuscles, the proliferating cell is the *erythroblast;* in *myelogenous leukemia,* it is the myeloblast; in *myeloma,* an unknown cell; while in metastatic tumors, the various tumor cells are the ones that divide. In *lymphoblastoma,* the bone-marrow may be extensively involved; in *status lymphaticus* lymph-nodules may be present in the marrow. Not only in myelogenous leukemia are the myeloblastic cells of the bone-marrow greatly increased, but also in conditions in which great numbers of neutrophiles are migrating into areas of inflammation.

A spontaneous fracture during life or a noticeable frailty of the ribs or other bones at autopsy should call to attention the possible presence of myeloma, in which marrow from various bones is fixed. In *chloroma* the proliferating myeloblasts may take place outside the marrow cavity in connection with the periosteum.

Replacing the Organs and Sewing up the Incisions.—All the organs that are not to be kept, including the brain, are placed in the thoracic-abdominal cavity. Before the organs are replaced, all fluid is thoroughly removed from the cavity by means of a sponge. Likewise fluid and blood are drained from the organs. Sawdust is removed from a barrel with a hand-scoop and sufficient amount of it placed with and over them to absorb all excess of fluid so that none may escape through the incisions; it also supports the sternum, which is now placed in position. Cotton waste may be used for this purpose. Excelsior is not satisfactory. In private residences and embalming establishments it may be possible to get sawdust, in which case paper or cotton or both may be used to fill up the body cavity. Many drying preparations are on the market but are more expensive than sawdust.

With a large cutting needle, threaded with strong wrapping thread, sew up the incision. First tie a knot at the very upper end of the incision and sew up with a continuous suture, holding the thread in the left hand until the next stitch is taken. The wedge-shaped piece of skull is placed in position after a small amount of sawdust has been placed in the cranial cavity, and the cut portions of the temporal muscles are sewed together. Pull the anterior and posterior scalp flaps together, and sew with a continuous suture. If the body is to be shipped, especial care is exercised in replacing the skull-cap. After a head section, ligation of the stumps of the carotids makes possible a more satisfactory injection of the embalming fluid.

Fixation of Autopsy Specimens.—As a routine, all organs are fixed in Zenker's fluid and 10 per cent. formalin. A pint Mason jar is a suitable container for the formalin. The Zenker's fluid (usually 2 liters) is placed in a large flat dish on the table. At the completion of the autopsy this dish is covered, and after twenty-four hours place to wash. After washing overnight, the specimens in the dish are covered with 80 per cent. alcohol.

Blocks for paraffin sections are cut from the thin bits of each of the organs contained in 80 per cent. alcohol in the dish, and placed in a small bottle with the tag attached, which also contains 80 per cent. alcohol. This must be done by the one who performed the autopsy, for it is he who knows the character of the tissues fixed and can select the pieces that will show the lesion best. The number of blocks can almost always be kept below 18. The autopsy number, the number of blocks, and the fixation are indicated on this tag. The bottle may be given to a technician, who runs the tissue through the paraffin series, cuts 6-micron sections and stains them with eosin-methylene blue. When indicated, phosphotungstic acid-hematoxylin, anilin blue, scharlach R, and other stains are made.

The sections are mounted on slides to be covered with 22-mm. by 40-mm. cover-glasses so that several sections may be placed on each slide. The slide bears the autopsy number scratched on it with a diamond scratch. After mounting, plain white labels with narrow black borders are placed on the left ends of the slides, and the autopsy number is written on the upper part of the labels.

For the convenience of the examiner, the slides are placed in a flat tray and the name of the organ written on each slide. The sections showing interesting lesions are checked with one, two, or three checks, according to the importance of the slide, and brief notes may be made on the labels.

The formalin-fixed tissue is used especially for frozen sections to be stained for fat, for a reaction for hemosiderin, for the demonstration of lime, and for Levaditi and bacterial stains. The pint Mason jar containing the formalin-fixed tissue is kept for one year; while the one containing the Zenker-fixed material in 80 per cent. alcohol is kept permanently.

Material on which it may be desirable a glycogen stain is fixed in absolute alcohol. Tissue containing treponemata and protozoa are fixed in corrosive-alcohol. For the preservation of mitochondria, and of other fine cytoplasmic granules, Orth's fluid or the chrome-osmic acid solution of Bensley is employed.

Importance of Proper Fixation of Tissue at Time of Autopsy.— Cutting the tissue from the organs for fixation is extremely important. Usually it is best to fix tissue at the time the organ is examined. From the large organs cut pieces of tissue several centimeters in size; place these firmly on the board, and with a sharp brain knife cut thin slices of tissue not to exceed 3 mm. in thickness. Select the part of the organ or tissue to be fixed; and, in general, cut the slice so that the flat surface will correspond to the paraffin sections that will be cut on the microtome. However, in the case of intestine and other thin-walled organs, a portion of the wall is placed in the fixing fluid, as it is sufficiently thin to fix properly. When possible, include the surfaces of organs and the periphery of lesions. Fix an abundance of any organ that shows a macroscopic lesion, especially if the autopsy is fresh.

If the section at the time of examination is found to be of great value, the amount of tissue fixed and the way in which it is fixed determines the future value of the autopsy. For this reason, all organs are placed in the fixing fluid; and, if indicated, or if the tissue is very fresh, a number of pieces are fixed. If every organ is not fixed at the time of autopsy, the incomplete pathological picture obtained may render a final diagnosis impossible. For example, a local bone lesion may show myeloma on microscopic examination, but no bone-marrow has been fixed; after the autopsy has been done, the clinician reports that the case was diabetes mellitus, but no pancreas has been fixed; or chorion-epithelioma is found in the lung microscopically, but no uterus has been fixed. Needless to say, a knowledge of gross pathology is required for the proper selection of tissue for microscopic study.

Protocol.—The autopsies are given consecutive numbers. For example, A 18.101 is the 101st autopsy made in 1918. This method of numbering is explained under surgical specimens (page 320). The number and fixation are indicated on a merchandise tag which is attached to the wire clamp of the Mason jar. As soon as possible, the operator takes the sheet, which is filled out while the autopsy is being performed, and from this dictates the autopsy protocol to a stenographer. A stenographer may take the dictation during the performance of the autopsy.

The protocol is typewritten on paper measuring 8.5 in. by 13 in. which is plain except for one vertical ruling at the left margin. The protocols for the current year are kept on a file. Those for each year are bound into one or more volumes, depending on the number of autopsies performed.

The bacteriologic findings are added from the bacteriologic card that bears the autopsy number. This card has the record of the cultures and smears made at the time of the autopsy. Routine cultures of the heart's blood are made, and cultures from other organs are made as indicated. The microscopic findings are added to the protocol at the time the histologic sections are examined and at this time changes and additions in the anatomic diagnoses are made.

At the time of the autopsy a card is made out with the name of the patient, age, sex, service and clinical diagnosis. The number of the autopsy is ascertained from these cards. The corrected anatomic diagnoses are added to the cards.

Museum Preparations (Fig. 131).—It may be required to make museum preparations from either autopsy or surgical specimens. In either case the tissue or organ is given a number; for example, M 765 is the 765th museum specimen made in a given laboratory.

Preserved museum specimens however well prepared, cannot take the place of fresh autopsy and surgical material in the demonstration of gross morbid anatomy. On the other hand, it is the only way in which uncommon lesions may be regularly demonstrated for teaching purposes. In valvular lesions of the heart, processes in the brain, and, in general where it is important to define clearly the anatomic relations, the specimens are often placed in round museum jars with clamp-covers in order that they may be readily removed.

Numbering and Recording Museum Specimens.—If the specimen is a surgical one, a gross description is written on the brown slip and from this the museum cards bearing not only the museum number but also the surgical or autopsy number is at once made out.

If it is an autopsy specimen, a brief gross description is taken from the temporary autopsy sheet, and from this the museum card is made out. For tagging the specimens, muslin slips 1 cm. by 4 cm. are kept on a spindle. These tags, which are attached to the specimen, bear the consecutive museum

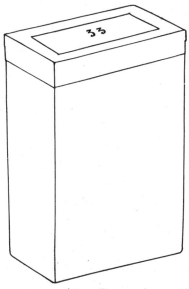

FIG. 131.—Museum preparations. Rectangular museum jar. Most specimens may be mounted in such a way that the essential lesion is brought near to a side of the jar. (Letters and numbers of the desired size may be obtained from the Tablet and Ticket Company, 624 W. Adams St., Chicago.)

numbers; so that the number for a new specimen may be ascertained either from this tag file or from the cards. At the time of making the preparation, the surgical or autopsy number, as the case may be, is also placed on the muslin slip.

Oil Method for Musuem Specimens.—After attaching the numbered muslin slip to the specimen by means of a large cutting needle bearing a coarse thread, the specimen, trimmed and supported in such a way as to show best the lesion present is placed for several days in a large 5- to 10-gallon crock which contains *Kaiserling fixing solution.* Then it is transferred to 80 per cent. alcohol, until the desired color is secured (about one hour), when the specimen is removed to a third jar containing 80 per cent. glycerin, where it remains for from one-half to one hour. Now place it in a fourth jar containing Russian mineral oil. After a week or more in the jar of oil, place it in suitable museum jars filled with oil. The museum numbers are placed on the tops or sides with mucilage letters and numbers (obtained from the Tablet and Ticket Co., 624 West Adams St., Chicago, Ill.). After sticking the numbers on the jars, cover them first with thin celloidin; then dry and apply a varnish consisting of balsam Damar dissolved in xylol. This balsam may be obtained from Bausch and Lomb Optical Co., and is a useful *protection for* all *labels* after they have been coated with celloidin.

Kaiserling's Method for Museum Specimens.—This method, which is one of the oldest, gives excellent results. The specimen properly tagged, trimmed, and supported, is placed for from one to five days, depending on the size of the specimen in a jar containing 15 gm. of potassium nitrate and 30 gm. of potassium acetate to the liter of 20 per cent. formalin. This is the *Kaiserling fixing solution.* Remove the specimen to 80 per cent. alcohol, for about one hour or until the color returns when it is placed in *Kaiserling preserving fluid.* This is prepared by adding 100 gm. of potassium acetate and 200 c.c. of glycerin to 1 liter of water. Crystals of thymol are added to each museum jar to prevent the growth of moulds.

Glycerin Jelly Method for Museum Specimens.—A jelly may be prepared as indicated under scharlach R stain (page 364), and specimens placed in it from the Kaiserling preserving fluid. This method is useful for mounting the half of an eye or other small specimens. Such small specimens may be placed in Stender dishes with the desired surface flat against the bottom, where it is held until the jelly hardens. A thin layer of melted paraffin is then run over the surface. It is often desirable to support the paraffin by covering it with a layer of plaster-of-Paris. The disadvantage of the jelly is the ease with which the blood coloring matter diffuses out into the medium from the specimens.

Mounting Museum Specimens.—Trimming the specimens and mounting them in rectangular jars so that the lesions are shown to the best advantage require considerable care. Gastro-intestinal tract, aorta, bladder, and other thin-walled structures are best mounted on a rectangular glass frame made by bending a glass rod—3 to 5 mm. in diameter depending on the strength required—at the desired points. The specimen is attached to the frame with needle and thread. In using the rectangular jars, the lesion or the most important part of the lesion is placed in contact with the side of the jar. When necessary, it is held firmly in this position by means of pieces of glass rods extending from specimen to the opposite side. Specimens may be cemented in place against the glass surfaces by means of glycerin jelly.

A general rule to follow in preparing museum specimens is to make them as small as possible and yet show the lesion perfectly. It is always easier to shape and trim the specimen after fixation. It is, therefore, advisable to place in the fixing solution the tissue spread out in the way it is to be mounted for one day, and then to remove with gloves and carefully cut to the desired shape and size. Place it in the solution again for one day or more before transferring to the alcohol.

Whichever method is used for preservation, the specimen should be protected from the light as much as possible. It seems that the color is better preserved by the oil method.

Several solutions have been recommended for fixing museum specimens, but none gives a better color than the Kaiserling fixing solution. Some of these are much cheaper than this solution, and one that is satisfactory and inexpensive is a 10 per cent. formalin containing 2 per cent. concentrated ammonia. The solutions following ammonia-formalin fixation are the same as those used after the Kaiserling fixing solution.

Cement for Sealing Museum Jars.—Warm 200 gm. of asphalt (Merck), and dissolve the melted asphalt in 200 c.c. of linseed oil and 400 c.c of turpentine. Warm; and with a small brush apply the cement to the ground surface of the jar, and at once apply the cover. Carefully cement along the line of contact. If the cement is too thick it may be thinned by adding turpentine.

To seal the jars in the case of the oil-specimens it is necessary to use a cement that will not be dissolved by the oil. This is prepared by heating equal parts of beeswax and gum Damar in a basin on a water-bath. Pour the liquid into paper cylinders one-half inch in diameter. The sticks are melted upon the ground glass surface through the agency of a hot scalpel, the cover is applied, and the wax melted again with a small Bunsen flame. This may be used for sealing all museum jars regardless of the method of preservation. It gives a somewhat better effect to the specimen to apply to the edges of the cover one or more coats of "finishing varnish" to which sufficient lampblack has been added to make it a heavy black. This cement is not so easily used but is more satisfactory than the asphalt.

Hand Lotion.—In handling museum specimens avoid getting formalin on the hands. If the hands become roughened a hand lotion may be used. The lotion is prepared by placing 1000 c.c. distilled water, 50 c.c. U.S.P. glycerin, 20 gm. boric acid, 20 gm. (unpowdered) tragacanth (the amount varies with the quality), and 5 gm. sodium benzoate in a bottle and shaking it at intervals during four days. Filter the lotion through a towel on which 1 c.c. oil of geranium has been poured. A good grade of tragacanth should be used.

29

INDEX

Technical methods and formulæ for solutions and stains are indicated by **black-faced** type.

30